IN PARTNERSHIP WITH GOD

IN
PARTNERSHIP
WITH
GOD

Contemporary Jewish Law and Ethics

BYRON L. SHERWIN

SYRACUSE UNIVERSITY PRESS

The paper used in this publication meets the minimum requirements of American National Standard for Information Sciences—Permanence of Paper for Printed Library Materials, ANSI Z39.48-1984. ∞™

Library of Congress Cataloging-in-Publication Data
Sherwin, Byron L.
    In partnership with God : contemporary Jewish law and ethics /
Byron L. Sherwin. — 1st ed.
        p.   cm.
    Includes bibliographical references.
    ISBN 0-8156-2490-5 (alk. paper)
    1. Ethics, Jewish.   2. Judaism—20th century.   I. Title.
BJ1287.S563I5   1990
296.3'85—dc20
                                                    90-35208
                                                    CIP

Manufactured in the United States of America

In Memory of My Teachers
RABBI SEYMOUR SIEGEL
RABBI MOSES ZUCKER

"You shall teach them diligently
unto thy children" (Deut. 6:7):
This refers to your disciples,
for you will find that disciples
are always referred to as children.
—*Midrash Sifre on Deuteronomy, 34*

We have it on tradition that no one is poor except he who lacks knowledge. In the Land of Israel, there is a proverb: He who has this [knowledge], has everything; he who lacks this, what has he? He who has acquired this, what does he lack? He who lacks this, what has he acquired?

—*Talmud, Nedarim* 41a.

BYRON L. SHERWIN is Vice-President for Academic Affairs and David C. Verson Professor of Jewish Philosophy and Mysticism at Spertus College of Judaica, Chicago, Illinois. His publications include *Abraham Joshua Heschel* (1979), *Garden of the Generations: A Genealogical Study* (1981), *Mystical Theology and Social Dissent: The Life and Works of Judah Loew of Prague* (1982), and *The Golem Legend: Origins and Implications* (1985).

CONTENTS

PREFACE

THE APPROACH to Jewish scholarship represented by this volume has three goals. The first is to understand Judaism on its own terms rather than from the perspective of externally imposed and imported categories. The second is both to inform modern Judaism of itself and to apply Jewish learning to the conceptual and practical problems confronting contemporary Judaism. The third is to offer a variety of Jewish scholarship that is a continuation of what came before and that is not an objective "scientific" dissection of the Jewish past. The aim is to perpetuate the ongoing discussion of spiritual, intellectual, and moral problems that constitute Judaism rather than to talk about what Judaism once may have been. The not overly subtle distinction advocated here is between *Jewish* scholarship and scholarship *about* Judaism. The former extends Judaism from the past into the future. The latter may too facilely degenerate into a voyeuristic examination of a tradition whose continuation may or may not be of ultimate concern to the investigator at hand. The approach taken in this volume presumes the vested interest of the scholar in the results of his or her research.

The present endeavor rejects a distinction between the scholar and the object of his or her scholarly work. In this view, the goal of Jewish learning is not simply to advance individual scholarship; the goal is to enhance, perpetuate, and continue Judaism as a vital, dynamic, living entity of which the individual scholar is a part. From this perspective, the scholar is not a spectator but an active protagonist in a drama in which he or she plays a vital role.

In 1905, Solomon Schechter wrote, "It is one of the great tragedies of modern Judaism that it knows itself so little." In 1958, Abraham Joshua Heschel observed, "Judaism today is an unknown religion. The vital issues it raises, the sublime views it discloses, the nobel goals it points to are forgotten. We have failed to learn how much Judaism has to say to the mind, to the soul. . . . Judaism is a source of cognitive insight, a way of thinking, not only an order of living." One may suggest that much of the vast corpus of scholarship produced since 1905 or 1958 has not significantly altered the pertinence of these observations. The program for Jewish scholarship presented in chapter 1 aims at the amelioration of this condition.

The approach to Jewish scholarship that informs this work was primarily inspired by the vision of Jewish scholarship offered by Solomon Schechter and Abraham Joshua Heschel. In their writings, both Schechter and Heschel applied the wisdom of the past to the contemporary issues that confronted them. In his own unique way, each drew from the vast mass of Jewish texts of all past generations to formulate and to re-create an authentic yet novel approach to conceptual, moral, and social problems that he perceived to be of pressing contemporary concern. While the essays that comprise this volume conceptualize and articulate an agenda for contemporary Jewish scholarship that stands outside the mainstream of much of current academic Jewish learning, they further an agenda for American Jewish scholarship similar to that advocated and advanced by Schechter and Heschel.

It would be ungracious of me not to acknowledge the personal support, warm friendship, and gentle encouragement of a number of teachers, colleagues, and friends, each of whom participated in his or her own way in the preparation of this volume. To my master, the late Professor Abraham Joshua Heschel, who guided and nurtured me as a student and later as a novice in Jewish scholarship, I owe a perpetual debt. His demand that the vast resources of the Jewish past be brought to bear on the problems of the present is manifest on almost every page of this work. To my parents for providing me with the awareness that each moment is an opportunity for accomplishment and for self-improvement, I am truly and continuously grateful. My wife Judith, and my son Jason, who allowed me to work unhampered at my desk rather than to spend innumerable hours with them, made the completion of this work possible. To them, my gratitude for their patience and forbearance.

To my friend and colleague, President Howard A. Sulkin of Spertus College of Judaica, Chicago, Illinois, I am grateful for understanding that my scholarly work is not a diversion from my duties as chief academic officer of Spertus College but a necessary component of that position. For the aid and assistance of the staff of the Asher Library of Spertus College, especially that of Kathleen Ladien, Dan Sharon, Robbin Saltzman Katzin, and Yehoshua ben Avraham, I am sincerely thankful. To Rosaline Cohn and the Cohn Scholars Fund, I am grateful for financial support required in preparing this work for publication. To Michael Carasik, I am grateful for helping to prepare the bibliography and for his numerous keen editorial suggestions. My energetic, conscientious, and steadfast secretaries, Sandra Ballard and Pam Spitzner, surely deserve my profound thanks for utilizing

their considerable technical skills in preparing the various drafts of the
typescript of this volume in an expeditious and accurate manner. Their
felicity during the tedium of typing and retyping these pages facilitated the
prompt completion of that arduous project. To them, I am deeply grateful.

To Professor Alan Berger of Syracuse University, I am deeply in-
debted for his support and interest in my work, and I am profoundly grateful for his confidence in my abilities. Without the dedicated perseverance
of the staff of Syracuse University Press, this volume would be diminished
in quality. My particular thanks to Arpena Mesrobian of Syracuse University Press and to copy editor Kathryn Koldehoff.

This volume is dedicated to my revered and beloved teachers, the
late Rabbi Moses Zucker and the late Rabbi Seymour Siegel, both of The
Jewish Theological Seminary of America. Under Professor Zucker's close
tutelage, I came to appreciate not only the intricacies and the subtleties of
rabbinic literature but its aesthetic qualities as well. From Dr. Zucker I
learned that scholarship can be both a labor of love and an art form requiring constant cultivation and development. Demanding as a teacher, en-
dearing as a mentor, and encouraging as a colleague, his presence is severely missed.

Over a period of twenty-six years, until his untimely death in Febru-
ary 1988, Rabbi Seymour Siegel taught, guided, nurtured, and encouraged
my studies. It was he who introduced me to many of the texts and methodologies of study that have preoccupied most of my teaching and scholarship. He initiated me into the study of the complexities of Jewish theology,
the problems of Jewish ethics, the labyrinths of Jewish mysticism, and the
perplexities of Holocaust studies. In many ways, he inspired me and en-
abled me to research and to write this book.

Neither Moses Zucker nor Seymour Siegel was blessed with children.
I hope that I and their other students can in some way perpetuate their
startling erudition, their enviable pedagogical abilities, their ground-break-
ing scholarly work, and their enriched and enriching personalities. The
Talmudic rabbis compare students to children. May we, their students,
their children in learning, carry on the work that they began. May their
memory be a blessing.

Finally, a number of technical points relating to the following pages
bear mention. I have applied a method of transliteration of Hebrew of my
own devising. It eliminates all diacritical marks and endeavors to present
Hebrew terms in a manner that should be familiar to all who read Hebrew.
Further, unless otherwise noted, all citations of the Talmud refer to the
Babylonian Talmud. For those readers who are unable to read Hebrew and
who wish to consult various Hebrew texts quoted, I have tried, where
possible, to note the cited text in a readily available English translation.

To help guide the reader who may be unfamiliar with the names of

many of the Jewish authors cited, especially those from the medieval period, I have tried to offer some form of identification. The title "Rabbi" is
generally restricted below to rabbis who flourished during the Talmudic
period and who are mentioned in the corpus of classical rabbinic (Talmudic
and midrashic) literature. This and other indicators place these sages
largely in the period of late antiquity. I feel that no further identification is
required for purposes of this book, or for reasons of clarity. Scholars of the
medieval period are usually identified by the century and often by the
place in which they lived. For the traditional Jewish scholar used to referring to individual classical—mostly medieval—Jewish authors by the established acronym of their respective names, the acronym is provided where
appropriate. Further aids for the reader are discussed below at the beginning of the bibliography.

Thanksgiving, 1989   BYRON L. SHERWIN
Chicago, Illinois

IN PARTNERSHIP WITH GOD

A Program for Jewish Scholarship

After the Holocaust, Jewish scholarship should be devoted to that which advances Judaism.

—ABRAHAM JOSHUA HESCHEL[1]

IF THE EARLIER SCHOLARS were like angels, then we [later scholars] are like human beings. However, if the earlier scholars were like human beings, then we are like asses."[2] This Talmudic adage articulates the notion of progressive decline, which is assumed as a dogma of Jewish faith by much of classical Jewish literature.[3] From this perspective, the further we move away from the revelation at Mt. Sinai chronologically, the weaker our spiritual and intellectual abilities become. The opposite notion was introduced into Jewish intellectual and religious life by nineteenth-century modern Jewish scholarship (*Wissenschaft des Judentums*) and by early Reform Judaism. In this view, Jewish history and experience (to be understood in Hegelian terms) demonstrate the gradual, inevitable progress of the spiritual and intellectual nature of Judaism and of the Jewish people. From this perspective, the later is always higher. The closer we draw to the future messianic age, the stronger our spiritual and intellectual prowess becomes.[4]

Neither the self-deprecation of the first approach nor the triumphalism of the second is conducive to the creative development of such a vibrant tradition as Judaism. The first perspective leads to the stifling of growth, to the view that "the new is taboo."[5] The second perspective subverts the very notion of tradition by denying its authority and hence its validity as a source of perennial wisdom and truth. This doctrine of "progressive revelation" seems to imply that moderns are in many ways spiritually and intellectually superior to Isaiah, Rabbi Akiva, and Moses Maimonides.

The collision between these two perspectives of inevitable recession and supersession may be cushioned, though not prevented, by evoking the analogy of "a dwarf riding on the shoulders of a giant." Commonly attrib-

1

uted to the seventeenth-century scientist Sir Isaac Newton, this expression seems to have been coined by the twelfth-century French philosopher Bernard of Chartres.[6] By the thirteenth century, this analogy had found its way into Jewish literature. The thirteenth-century Italian halakhist Isaiah di Trani appears to have been responsible for its importation into Jewish writing. In subsequent Jewish literature, this term is frequently found.[7]

The comparison of the cumulative corpus of past tradition to a giant and of the contemporary scholar to a dwarf satisfies the traditional conviction that no single individual—no matter how gifted or learned—can approach the stature of the cumulative wisdom of the tradition. This view protects the tradition from the subversion of the work of earlier authorities by that of later authorities.

Once the dwarf climbs the body of the giant and stands on his shoulders, the dwarf supersedes the giant both in height and in visual perspective. In other words, the view of the later scholar may be accepted as valid without casting aspersions upon the authority or competence of earlier scholars, even while assuming the intrinsic superiority of those earlier scholars.

In his commentary to the Mishnah, the late sixteenth-century talmudist Abraham Azulai discussed the analogy of the dwarf and the giant.

> For the modern is like a dwarf and the ancients are like giants but because the modern is later, he is like a dwarf riding the shoulder of a giant who can see at a distance farther than the giant. And so it is with the modern who may be unable to attain what the ancient had attained, but being later and having had the benefit of the knowledge and great wisdom of the ancients, then, if he himself should discover something new, be it but a trifle, he will certainly with that trifle contribute more wisdom than they; even though his own wisdom would have been nought had he not the benefit of their wisdom.[8]

The doctrine of regressive authority condemns later scholars to the lower and very narrow perspective of a dwarf. The doctrine of progressive authority maintains that the giants of the past were dwarfs compared to the giants of today. The notion of the dwarf riding on the shoulders of a giant claims that the coalescence of the wisdom of the past in the giant makes the stature of the giant necessarily higher and his vista broader than that of the dwarf, who represents only the wisdom of his own generation. However, it also maintains that, by climbing upon the giant's shoulders, the dwarf can exceed that which is attainable by the giant alone.

The regressive view stifles the dwarf's potential. The progressive view pretends that dwarfs are giants. The third view organically links the dwarf to the giant, to the benefit of both. Furthermore, it may well be that the dwarf is not a dwarf at all but only appears to be a dwarf when measured against the enormous stature of the giant. Separated, the giant and the dwarf are destined each to his own individual fate. Together, the giant and the dwarf guarantee both the perpetuation and the development of tradition.

Tradition is a living force that animates and informs the present. Tradition is that which assures the continuity of creativity. Without the dwarf, tradition is like a giant, a relic of bygone days. However, without the giant, there is no viable foundation for future creativity, development, and growth. Without the giant, the dwarf either stands tied close to the ground or is transfixed in midair, waiting to fall into an abyss.

The giant would be unwise to be threatened by what the dwarf might achieve. Indeed, he should be grateful to the dwarf for expanding his purview. The dwarf should be grateful to the giant, for without the giant the vision of the dwarf would remain severely limited. Once perched on the giant's shoulders, the dwarf must overcome the temptation of forgetting that he is not a giant, but a dwarf riding on the shoulders of a giant. It is further incumbent upon the dwarf to know the giant well. What the dwarf will be able to see depends upon the nature of the giant and where the giant will carry him. How should the dwarf relate to the giant who bears him on his shoulders? What should the dwarf search for as he surveys the panorama from his elevated perch? Questions such as these can serve as indicators to help establish an appropriate program for contemporary Jewish scholarship.

It would be tragic if the dwarf, once elevated to the giant's shoulders, was found to suffer from myopia. It would be equally unfortunate if the dwarf discovered that his peripheral vision was severely impaired. Yet, much of contemporary Jewish scholarship seems to suffer from restricted peripheral vision. Scholars seem prone to overspecialization in minute subareas of Jewish studies without surveying the breadth of classical Jewish sources. Some limit their scholarly investigations to specific texts, written in specific lands during specific periods. A paradigmatic feature of modernity, this tendency toward specialization gives license to scholars to know more and more about less and less. Commenting on what he calls the "barbarism" of specialization, the Spanish philosopher José Ortega y Gasset has written the following with specific regard to the modern scientist:

> He is one who, out of all that has to be known in order to be a man of judgment, is only acquainted with one science, and even of the one only knows the small corner in which he is an active investigator. He even proclaims it as a virtue that he takes no cognizance of what lies outside the narrow territory specially cultivated by himself, and gives the name "dilettantism" to any curiosity for the general scheme of knowledge. . . . The specialist "knows" very well his own tiny corner of the universe; he is

radically ignorant of all the rest. . . . We shall have to say that he is a
learned ignoramus.[9]

By analogizing modern Jewish scholarship to modern science, the founders of *Wissenschaft des Judentums* (the science of Judaism) predetermined
the direction toward overspecialization that contemporary Jewish scholarship has taken. By trying to make Jewish scholarship scientific and objective, even "value-free," they placed the giant in the laboratory and did not
climb upon his shoulders. They transformed the giant into a dwarf by de-
grading the exalted status he once had enjoyed. The founders of *Jüdische
Wissenschaft* reduced sacred Jewish literature to belles lettres.[10] The
unique nature and meaning classical Jewish literature held, particularly for
Jews, was now surrendered into the vortex of the "universal human spirit."
The dwarf had climbed off the giant's shoulders and was now preparing to
lock the giant in a laboratory to await vivisection. In this regard, Gershom
Scholem described the program of the *Wissenschaft des Judentums* as "the
liquidation of Judaism as a living organism" and its adherents as "academic
morticians." Scholem's words remind one of Moritz Steinschneider's quip
that modern Jewish scholars "have only one task left: to give the remains of
Judaism a decent burial." Similarly, Zalman Rubashov (Shazar) described
Leopold Zunz's program for the scientific study of Judaism as an agenda
aimed at the "de-Judaization" of Judaism.[11]

While Jewish tradition always emphasized the nexus between thought
and action, theory and practice, modern Jewish scholarship severed that
relationship. For the first time, Jewish learning and Jewish life became
related by chance, rather than by necessity. Whereas in the past the life of
the Jewish scholar fell under the province of the text, now the life of the
text came under the control of the scholar. No longer bearing the dwarf on
his shoulders, the giant was now led about by the dwarf, drawn to places
alien to his nature.

Scientific objectivity rather than the continuity of tradition has become
the primary feature of the new Jewish learning. Consequently, an unprecedented fissure has emerged in the world of Jewish scholarship. For the first
time, the products of Jewish scholarly investigation have become detached
both from the internal dynamic and organic development of Jewish knowledge, and from contemporary Jewish communal concerns and spiritual
needs. Much of contemporary Jewish scholarship seems to have abandoned
its history by casting its destiny with secular academe. How well the giant
will fare in this alien environment remains obscure. Whether the continuity of the tradition of Jewish learning can prevail remains uncertain.

History became the means by which the dwarf would examine and
analyze the giant. Classical Jewish learning perceived the giant as an organism requiring growth and development. Modern Jewish scholarship com-

pares the giant to an archaeological dig and seeks to stratify and identify its layers. Traditional Jewish learning sought a total gestalt, unencumbered by historical considerations: "There is neither earlier nor later in the Torah."[12] Modern Jewish learning has sought to examine each of the giant's cells individually in an elusive search for the essence of the creature. As the leading nineteenth-century Jewish historian Heinrich Graetz put it, "the totality of Judaism is only recognizable through its history; in history the whole essence, the sum of its powers must be made explicit."[13] Nevertheless, minute examination of the parts tends to eclipse the vision of the whole. The historical quest becomes an end in itself. As Leo Baeck observed, "History began to mean more than the content."[14]

The study of the anatomy of the giant became more important than the personality of the giant. For the first time in Jewish experience, Jewish historiography became divorced from Jewish collective memory. Ironically, this new approach to the Jewish past represents a decisive break with the Jewish past.[15] While admirable in itself, the awakening of Jewish historical consciousness has led to the anesthetizing of the Jewish religious consciousness.

Despite its self-proclaimed identification with objective "value-free" universal science, the original agenda of the *Wissenschaft des Judentums* was closely tied to a subjective, particular, value-laden agenda. Early modern Jewish scholarship was to serve as a strategic tool to further the integration of the Jews into the sociopolitical life of the nations in which they resided. *Jüdische Wissenschaft* was not an intellectual parlor game; it was the avant-garde of a particular ideology inextricably related to the crisis of Jewish social and political emancipation and to the struggle to attain it.[16] In a sense, this massive effort to bring about the emancipation of the Jews led to the emancipation of Judaism from its traditional moorings. The giant was surgically transformed—cut down in size with his features re-formed. By casting the history, religion, literature, and institutions of the Jewish people into Western academic categories, the very tradition that these scholars wished to preserve was distorted beyond recognition.

The introduction of the chronological axis into Jewish learning made the enterprise of dating classical Jewish texts into a critical obsession. This approach proves valuable in elucidating the contextual meaning of classical texts and of demonstrating the historical development of the tradition. This endeavor parallels efforts characteristic of scholarship in the humanities and the social sciences. One might even argue that this approach is a modern form of the age-old quest for the *peshat*, the literal and contextual meaning of an examined text.[17] One may suggest that while the *peshat* may be necessary and even desirable, it never can be adequate. It offers an important perspective, but by its very nature, it is one-dimensional. The giant, however, is multidimensional. The text is "a multifaceted mirror which reflects the subject from every side."[18] The last great Jewish mystic, Abraham Isaac Kook, compared the Torah to a mirror in which each succeeding generation observes its own particular reflection. The mirror always remains the same, but the reflections cast into it perpetually change. The task of the dwarf is not to convert the mirror into a window, thereby becoming an impassive voyeur gazing at the past, but to seek his own reflection mirrored in the eyes of the giant. *Wissenschaft des Judentums* smashed the mirror and placed the giant under glass for objective study.

To establish contextual meaning, substantial effort has been invested in discovering a *Grundtext,* an exact primary text for subsequent scholarly investigation. Modern Jewish scholarship has made prodigious contributions in providing reliable readings of primary texts. The danger, however, occurs when finding the correct reading stifles the quest for the text's meaning.

In this regard, it is told that a famous Jewish theologian once received a small package in the mail. The package contained a newly published scholarly work on the Talmud that he had long awaited. Written by a leading Talmudic scholar, this volume already had been heralded by reviewers as a definitive work. The theologian's hands shook with anticipation as he withdrew the book from its wrapping. Feverishly, he turned the pages until he came to a commentary on a passage in the Mishnah that had perplexed him for many years. Anxiously, he began to read the great talmudist's commentary, hoping for a resolution to his perplexity. He read, "The word '*betulah*' ['virgin'] in this passage appears written with the letter '*vov*' in fourteen consulted manuscripts, and without the letter '*vov*' in twelve other manuscripts consulted by this commentator. From this careful investigation one may conclude that whether the correct reading is with or without a '*vov*' is uncertain." The theologian sighed heavily and muttered to himself, "Does the virgin really care whether she has kept or whether she has surrendered her '*vov*'?"

It is also told that, when a certain Lithuanian rabbi was a young scholar, he began a project that would engage him for the remainder of his life. Convinced that Moses Maimonides was a paragon of consistency, he set out to prove that Maimonides never contradicted himself.

The young scholar spent five years studying Maimonides's vast corpus of writings. He diligently recorded the numerous contradictions in Maimonides's work. He then spent the next ten years demonstrating that the contradictions in Maimonides's writings were merely apparent contradictions rather than actual contradictions and that his theory regarding Maimonides's total consistency was both accurate and true. At the conclusion of this decade of scholarly work, he had proven to his satisfaction that all of the apparent inconsistencies in Maimonides's writings were capable of resolution—all but one, which continued to perplex him for many years.

On the day before his death, the scholar resolved the final apparent inconsistency, and he died a happy man, content that he had proven his theory that Maimonides was a model of logical consistency.

When he arrived in heaven, the scholar was informed by one of the angels that he could speak to any one individual in heaven with whom he wished to speak. The scholar, needless to say, asked to speak to Maimonides. When he appeared, Maimonides asked the Lithuanian rabbi why he wished to speak specifically to him. The rabbi told Maimonides about his life's work. Maimonides was curious, and he asked the rabbi to quote the two texts that took him so many years to resolve logically. The scholar proudly quoted the texts from memory. Maimonides thought for a moment and said, "That was no problem at all. The *Grundtext* you used contained a misprint!"

While the thrust of modern Jewish scholarship is largely directed toward discovering the *peshat* of the text, that is, its proper reading and its contextual meaning, a feature of the sources it seeks to examine is their de-emphasis of the ultimate importance of contextual meaning and their denial of the presupposition that a one-dimensional meaning is preferable to a multidimensional exegesis. The *Zohar*, for example, reminds us not to confuse the "outer garb" of the text with its body, soul, or essential meaning.[19] Those who take the text seriously cannot take it only literally.

The chronological axis characteristic of modern Jewish scholarship embodies an assumption that appears incompatible with traditional or classical Jewish scholarship. The latter assumes that the classical texts must be explained and interpreted as if they constituted a single conceptual unit. They are to be treated synchronically rather than diachronically or chronologically. While useful within the parameters of its own program, the chronological axis of modern Jewish scholarship represents an intrusion upon the conceptual presuppositions and the native value system of classical Jewish scholarship.[20] The *peshat* it offers may prove irrelevant (as well as irreverent) from the perspective of traditional Jewish self-understanding. The goal of traditional Jewish learning is not simply to preserve and to transmit but also to generate and to re-create new meaning from the text. From this perspective, one is obliged to receive but also to return what one has received in a new and even altered form. As a midrash observes, "The Holy One gave the Torah to Israel like wheat from which to derive fine flour, or like flax from which to make a garment."[21] To paraphrase a rabbinic proverb, "One who says 'I have only the text,' does not have even the text."[22]

Both the diachronic and the synchronic axes are necessary for a total view of Judaism. The diachronic axis is eminently necessary to understand the context of Jewish texts and institutions. However, the diachronic approach, characteristic of the *Wissenschaft des Judentums* and of much of subsequent Jewish scholarship, is in the final analysis external to Judaism. It is *about* Judaism; it is not Judaism.[23] It is *scholarship about Judaism*, rather than being *Jewish scholarship*. What is advocated here is a program for contemporary *Jewish* scholarship aimed at the perpetuation and the continuous re-creation of Judaism. In this sense, the dwarf desires to help the giant grow so that the vista from his shoulders may be even more elevated than before.

As was already stated, *Jüdische Wissenschaft* tried to embody scientific objectivity and a "value-free" approach to Judaism. In his 1822 essay, "On the Concept of a Science of Judaism," Immanuel Wolf, one of the founders of the *Wissenschaft des Judentums*, described the following as being characteristic of the new Jewish learning, "It treats the object of study in and of itself, for its own sake, and not for any special purpose or definite intention. It begins *without any preconceived opinion* and is not concerned with the final result. Its aim is neither to put its object in a favorable, nor in an unfavorable light, in relation to prevailing views, but to show it as it is. Science is self-sufficient. . . . It therefore needs to serve no other purpose than its own."[24] What is advocated in the present volume is an approach to Jewish scholarship radically different from that proposed by Wolf and implemented by the followers of the *Wissenschaft des Judentums*—past and present. The suggested formulation of a program for contemporary Jewish scholarship would have the features discussed in the following section.

WHAT IS JEWISH ABOUT JEWISH SCHOLARSHIP?

One may not only reject the position that perceives Jewish learning as a scientific endeavor, one may also contend that even in science there is no "immaculate perception," and that to assume such is to perpetuate an "immaculate deception." Texts cannot be read with complete objectivity or conceptual innocence. The reader brings himself or herself to the text, or even into the text. The Hebrew word for "ark" is the same as the Hebrew word for "letter," *teivah*. According to Hasidic sources, like Noah, one must enter the *teivah*.[25] It is not sufficient to gaze at the letter; one must put oneself into it. The goal of *Jewish* scholarship is not simply to *see* the text, "pure and chaste from afar," but to *become* the text. As the sixteenth-century Jewish mystic Judah Loew of Prague observed, the goal of the scholar is not only to study the Torah, but to become the Torah. The ideal Jewish scholar is the Torah incarnate, a literally meant "embodiment" of the text.[26] By becoming the text, the dwarf becomes part of the giant.

Jewish mystics perceived study of the Torah as a vehicle toward establishing a nexus among its author, its text, and its interpreter. Study thereby becomes not only a conduit toward union with God but a means of merging the scholar and the text. The Hasidic master, Moses Hayyim Ephraim of Sudylkow, the grandson of the Ba'al Shem Tov, compared the act of study to the love act: "When a man studies the Torah for its own sake, to keep it and to perform it, then he brings all his limbs close to their source whence they originated and were generated, namely to the Torah . . . and he becomes identical with the Torah in a unification and in a complete union, like the unification of man and woman."[27] Furthermore, the Hasidic sage, Mordecai of Chernobyl, took the scriptural phrase *"ve-zot torat ha-adam"* [literally: "and this is the Torah of man"] (2 Sam. 7:19) to mean that "the man himself becomes the Torah."[28]

The value system of *Jewish* scholarship emerges from the value system of Judaism, which *Jewish* scholarship seeks to study and to advance. The purpose of *Jewish* scholarship is to advance the value system embodied in the Jewish texts and institutions it studies. For *Jewish* scholarship, unlike for Jewish science, Judaism is the subject of study, not an object to study. Therefore, a primary item of the program of *Jewish* scholarship must be the identification of a particularly Jewish way of thinking and of the value system expressed by it. Rather than import foreign categories to Judaism or impose them upon Judaism, one must first discern the authentic endemic categories of Judaism. Seen from this perspective, Jewish scholarship is self-reflective. It is a perpetual exercise in self-examination, self-clarification, and self-understanding.[29] The imposition of an incompatible value system, including a "value-free" system (which is itself a value system in that it places value in the rejection of a priori values), violates the very nature of *Jewish* scholarship.

It may be more appropriate to study Judaism artistically than scientifically. Jewish religion and the cultivation of its moral virtues may be compared to an art. Study of Jewish texts may be compared to the study of artistic works. While it is important to discern the intention and meaning of the artist, that is, while "contextual" interpretation is imperative, the lasting value of a work of art rests in how it is perceived and understood by a long line of subsequent students. Science can examine the physical content of a piece of art, for example, the paint, the wood of a sculpture, but it is incapable of elucidating its continued meaning.

To reduce aesthetics to subjectivity would be a mistake. Like the aesthetic dimension, the religious dimension is objectively present in the world. Like art, it requires a certain sensitivity to be appreciated and to be understood. It is objective and subjective at the same time. One must invest something of oneself to understand great art. One need not be an artist to appreciate great art. However, one must be an artist to be inspired by art to create art. Similarly, in literature, virtually all great writers have been great readers. Literature is a process of reimagination and re-creation.[30] The process of artistic development is often furthered by a series of intentional and unintentional "misreadings."[31] Indeed, unless one can entirely and accurately discern the initial meaning and intention of an author or artist, every reading becomes a misreading. One may view the history of classical Jewish literature as a continuous process of creative misreading of the primary text, the Torah. Indeed, the tradition of *keri* and *ketiv* (write this, but read that) illustrates that one is obliged to misread to elicit the text's proper meaning.[32] Seen from this perspective, contextual reading is important, but not crucial. Viewed in this manner, *Jewish* scholarship is better analogized to artistic rather than to scientific study. The task is to continue the process of creative misreading of the text within the parameters of the value system that teaches us how to relate to the text in the first place. In this way, the continuity of tradition is assured. Through a genuine appreciation of the text, one expands and amplifies its meaning. In authentic study, a dialogue is created between the author and the reader. Through the process of interpretation, the reader becomes a coauthor, a collaborator in the artistic endeavor.[33]

A Torah scroll contains only consonants; it has no vowels. According to Jewish law, a vocalized Torah scroll is invalid for ritual use.[34] It is the reader who provides the vowels, the vocalization of the text. The medieval cabalistic work *Sefer ha-Bahir* compares the consonants to a body and the vowels to a soul.[35] The sixteenth-century halakhist David ibn Zimra noted in a responsum (a legal decision) that "vocalization is like a commentary to the written Torah."[36] By giving vocalization to the text, the reader *animates* and *interprets* the text, giving it life, allowing it to be spoken, to be heard, and to be understood.

According to Moses Maimonides, the Israelites who stood at Mt. Sinai heard "the great voice [of God], but not the articulations of speech." It was Moses who conveyed the Torah "with the articulation of the letters."[37] The unvocalized word of God invites human articulation and vocalization. The task of the scholar is to liberate some of the reservoir of implicit meaning pregnant within the text. The scholar is a midwife whose task is to bring forth new life from the womb of tradition.

According to David ibn Zimra, the Torah may be read according to its "spiritual" meaning and according to its "concrete" meaning. Put another way, the scholar cannot be content with only discovering the text's concrete meaning, its contextual meaning. The scholar is obliged to make audible and explicit the otherwise mute and inaccessible meaning of the text. The scholar's duty is to try to penetrate its inexhaustible meaning. In ibn Zimra's words:

> I found a document written by one of the earlier sages, and I do not know his name. [He taught that one should] know that because the vocalization

is the form and the soul of the letters, the scroll of the Torah is not vocalized. It embodies in all its aspects [literally: "faces"] all of the profound paths. All of these may be expounded in each individual letter: faces within faces, mysteries within mysteries. No limits are known to us. . . . If the scroll had been vocalized, then it would have a limit and a perimeter. . . . It could [then] not have been interpreted except in accordance with the specific vocalization of the word. . . . This is why our sages said, "There are seventy faces to the Torah."[38]

While so much of modern Jewish scholarship has been preoccupied with establishing a correct *Grundtext* as the necessary prerequisite for rooting its *Grundbedeutung* (its original contextual meaning), a number of classical Jewish writers denied that access to an original and accurate *Grundtext* of the most primary of all Jewish texts—the Torah—has been granted to us. In this regard, Levi Yitzhak of Berdichev, the nineteenth-century Hasidic master, taught that between the black letters of the Torah there are white spaces that contain invisible letters that will become known to us in the messianic age. Knowledge of these letters will alter the reading of the text and consequently our understanding of it. Other Jewish mystics taught that the eternal "essential" Torah is never revealed. It remains in its purely spiritual form, an eternal citizen of the divine realm. The form in which we have the Torah is a corrupt, imperfect form. According to the *Sefer Temunah*, for example, the Torah assumes different forms in various aeons. The text we have is not the correct text; it is the version of the text appropriate for our particular age. In our aeon, the Torah is in exile, in an alienated state. A version of this teaching is that the Hebrew alphabet properly consists of twenty-three and not of the twenty-two letters we currently assume it has. The complete actualized text of the Torah embodies this missing letter. When this letter is revealed and each of its proper appearances in the Torah is discerned, the text will be correct, and only then will the proper reading of the text and its meaning be determined.[39] It was apparently the belief that no present text of the Torah is the actual and correct one that led the sixteenth-century sage Judah Loew of Prague to offer a legal ruling—in opposition to most halakhic authorities—that a Torah scroll with a scribal defect may be used in the synagogue. For Judah Loew, the mystic, no Torah scroll contains the absolutely correct primal text.[40]

According to Scripture, the first set of tablets given to Moses was written with "the finger of God." It contained the text in its purely spiritual and essentially correct form. The second set was written by Moses at God's command. This version of the Torah, now in our possession, represents the humanly edited and transmitted version of the originally divine text. When the first set of tablets was broken, "the letters engraved upon it flew heavenward."[41] They have not been returned. With the second set, our set, the process of the humanization of the Torah begins. Once the human process of acceptance, transmission, and "publication" commences, the Torah that we have "is no longer in Heaven" (Deut. 30:12) but falls under the province of the continuous process of human interpretation and even misinterpretation. Once surrendered into human hands and accepted by them, the Torah takes on a life of its own. Prophecy and divine inspiration can no longer write the script of its history. Now, its readers become its coauthors and its interpreters.[42] Its readers become writers who convey its meaning.

The nexus between the book and the "people of the book," between the giver and the recipient of the Torah, establishes the parameters for interpreting the text. On the level of *peshat*, anyone has access to the text; however, participation on the semantic level, license to penetrate and to re-create the deeper meaning of the text, presupposes the commitment of one who has received and has accepted the Torah.[43] As the *Zohar* teaches, only the lover of the Torah will be vouchsafed its most intimate disclosures, meanings, secrets. Only the scholar who is in love and who "makes love" with the Torah is a "true adept in the Torah, a 'master of the house.'"[44] The uncommitted voyeur may grasp the *peshat* but not the essential meaning of the Torah, that is, of Jewish tradition. In this view, *Jewish* scholarship presumes Jewish commitment.

To make love to the Torah it is necessary to disrobe it. In Hebrew, the word "*peshat*" comes from the root "*P-Sh-T*," which also means to "strip" or to "divest." According to some Jewish mystics, the true *peshat* of the text is not its literal, plain, or contextual meaning but its divested, unclad, hidden spiritual meaning.[45] The true meaning of the text must always elude the scholar who identifies the text with its appearance, who seeks the apparent rather than the concealed *peshat*. Only in the act of making love to the Torah, by one committed to it, can its true meaning and nature be discerned.

The *Ethics of the Fathers* states, "Beloved are Israel, for they were given a precious object [the Torah]. A special love was shown them in that they were given a precious object. As it is written (Prov. 4:2): I have given you good doctrine; forsake not My Torah."[46] In his commentary to this passage, the sixteenth-century scholar Samuel of Uceda observed that:

> only to Israel it [the Torah] was given as a gift and not to others. . . . The intention [of the text under discussion] is that to the sages and to [the people of] Israel was given [the license] to interpret [the Torah] and to explain it, and that is evident from the verse: I have given you good doctrine. . . . I gave it to *you* to interpret. . . . I have given this gift to Israel alone. . . . [It is] an inheritance [*morashah*] [through which I (God)] became betrothed [*me'urasah*] to you. No other man can be involved with a woman once she has become betrothed. . . . This may have been the intention of the men of the Great Assembly who established the blessing

of the Torah which reads "who has chosen us from among all peoples and gave us the Torah," meaning that an unconditional gift was given to us to explain and to interpret as we desire. It was given to us alone, and not to any other people.[47]

Elsewhere, Samuel of Uceda noted, "even if a person would live 2000 years, he could not grasp its [the Torah's] totality, for it is without end or limit. . . . One must take delight in knowing about that which one does not yet know."[48] The quest for Torah is itself Torah. As the Hasidic master Mendel of Kotsk said, in the quest for truth, "he who thinks he has finished, is *finished*." The task of Jewish self-understanding is never ending, perpetual. As the words of Judah Loew of Prague remind us, a blessing describes God as "one who *gives* the Torah" (*notein ha-Torah*). As Loew observed, "that is to say, You give the Torah each day." As Loew further reminded us, another blessing praises God for allowing us to be "preoccupied with the words of Torah" (*la-asok be-divrei Torah*).[49] The agenda for *Jewish* scholarship requires learning to be a continuous preoccupation not a hobby. It requires involvement; it assumes commitment.

What is recommended here is that contemporary Jewish scholarship embody the following features:

1. Its purpose should be Jewish self-understanding. As such, it should utilize Jewish categories and should embrace a Jewish value system.

2. It should be a part of, rather than a departure from, classical Jewish scholarship. It should be predicated upon the analogy of a dwarf riding upon the shoulders of a giant.

3. It should perceive its task as the reformulation (not the reformation) of Judaism. It should aim at reimagining and re-creating Judaism for its own age. It should cast a renewed image in the mirror of tradition.

4. The Jewish scholar should be one committed not only to scholarship but to Judaism as well. While availing himself or herself of the findings of historians, philologists, and other scholars, his or her point of departure must be the intersection of the past with the present. While the historian focuses attention upon the past, and while the sociologist may focus attention on the present, the Jewish scholar focuses upon the interaction of the past and the present. Ultimately, the Jewish scholar's problem is a personal one: What in classical Judaism can shape my life as a Jew in the present? How can the traditions of the past be brought to bear on the problems of the present?

5. Neither Jewish scholarship nor Jewish scholars can divorce themselves from Jewish observance or from Jewish life. As a Talmudic text and its midrashic variants put it, "If one studies (Torah) without the intention to observe it, it is better that he had not been born. . . . it would have been

better had he been strangled by the placenta at birth, and had never ventured forth into the world." Quoting this text, the medieval Spanish scholar Jonah Gerondi relates it to the verses in Hosea (8:12)—"The many teachings I [God] wrote for him, have been treated as something alien," and in Jeremiah (8:8c,d)—"Assuredly, for naught has the pen labored, for naught the scribes."[50] Another midrashic text describes the scholar who refuses to apply what he knows to ameliorating social problems within the Jewish community as a destructive individual. "'But the man of separation overthrows it' (Prov. 29:4)—this refers to a sage who knows halakhah, midrash and haggadah, to whom widows and orphans go to plead their cause, but who excuses himself with the plea, 'I am engaged with my studies and have no leisure.' To him God says, 'I regard you as if you have destroyed the world.'"[51]

6. Jewish scholarship should be understood not primarily as the "science of Judaism," but as a Jewish art form. As such, it is an aesthetic as well as a religious and intellectual undertaking. It embraces the objective quest for truth and the subjective search for meaning.

According to Scripture, Bezalel, who built the tabernacle, was the first Jewish artist (Exod. 35:30–35). The Talmud observes that Bezalel "knew how to combine the letters by which the heavens and the earth were created."[52] In other words, artistic creativity derives from the ability to create form and meaning from the otherwise lifeless letters of the text. The vocation of the Jewish scholar is to vocalize the text, to transmute old words into new meanings.

Like the artist who transforms the raw materials of nature into something more than they had been, the Jewish scholar is one who takes the raw materials conveyed through revelation and inherited from tradition and re-creates them. The scholar refuses to allow tradition to become inert. He or she transmits and transports tradition from the past into the present. The scholar's task is to provide tradition with a voice, but that voice must speak in a contemporary idiom.

7. The Jewish scholar should contribute not simply to an understanding about Judaism but to Judaism itself. As the dwarf riding on the giant's shoulders, he or she sees a horizon that the giant does not imagine. It is the scholar's task to guide the giant's movements toward that horizon. It is the vocation of the Jewish scholar to discern where the giant—where Judaism—has come from, where it now is, and to where it must proceed. However, before the dwarf can become a pioneer for the giant, he first must become his heir. To become his heir, he or she must attempt to be at home in all areas of Jewish learning. He or she cannot specialize in a limited area of Jewish scholarship. He or she must know the giant well, from head to toe.

8. Because the materials the Jewish scholar uses are bequeathed by

tradition, what is formulated becomes an organic extension of the past and is therefore authentic. Because the scholar chooses which inherited texts to present, interpret, and express, the work thereby formed is uniquely his or her own.

The tradition is a body of inherited wisdom and experience. The task of the scholar is to give it a soul so that it may transmigrate from the past into the present, to invest the bequest of tradition with extended meaning. The scholar is perpetually confronted with the challenge of liberating the implicit meanings pregnant in sacred texts. By recreating the tradition, the Jewish scholar can become a coauthor of the Torah, a cocreator with God of the tradition.

The evaluation of the validity of the scholar's labors is governed by three criteria: first, authenticity—that the texts used in composing a theological portrait of a specific issue are drawn from the tradition and are interpreted in a manner consistent with the tradition; second, contemporaneity—the scholar's task is to apply old texts to contemporary situations, to give a modern voice to ancient and medieval texts. While there must be continuity with the past, there must also be meaning for the present; and third, communal acceptance—the validity of the artistic work of the scholar is ultimately determined by its ability to communicate a present vision of the past and by the acceptance of that vision by his or her faith community. Ultimately, the Jewish community and not academe determines the disposition of Jewish scholarship.

If the scholar's portrait is not authentic, it is fallacious. If his or her portrayal of a theological or moral issue is not contemporary, it is anachronistic. If the scholar engages in a form of abstract expressionism meaningful only to himself or herself, or if the scholar's faith community cannot identify with what is offered, then his or her work may be authentic and aesthetic, but barren.

Medieval Jewish scholars compared the erudite scholar who has amassed much book learning but who has not grasped its contents to "a donkey carrying books."[53] Erudition is a prerequisite not a destination. Once he or she has collected knowledge, the scholar must be prepared to apply that knowledge to the problems at hand. From the wealth of inherited tradition, the scholar should be able "to derive flour from wheat, a garment from flax."

✜ 2 ✜

Philosophies of Law

Leave it to the People of Israel, for while they are not
prophets, they are the descendants of prophets.

—*Pesahim* 66a

J EWISH THEOLOGY is a palace of faith and conviction grounded in revelation, molded by speculation, and forged by tradition. Engendered by
divine providence and love, carefully crafted by human intuition and
lect, and honed by history and experience, the theological edifice which is
Judaism rests upon three firmly planted pillars: God, Torah, and Israel.
The underlying foundation that supports and that binds together these
three fundamental theological nonnegotiables of Judaism is the commitment to an eternally binding covenant between God and the people of
Israel. At Mt. Sinai, the three foci of Jewish theological concern converge
at one time, in one place. At Mt. Sinai, *God* gives the *Torah* to *Israel*.
Without the covenant, without revelation, Jewish existence is a conclusion
without a premise, a fallacy.[1]

A rabbinic tradition analogizes the theophany at Mt. Sinai to a wedding. According to this tradition, the people of Israel were married to the
Torah at Mt. Sinai.[2] God, the father, gives His daughter, the Torah, as a
bride to the people of Israel.[3] The presence of the Torah in the life of Israel
ensures the perpetual presence of God in the history of Israel. In this regard, the rabbis offered the following parable:

> Once there was a king who had only one daughter, whom another king
> married. When the latter wished to return to his country and take his wife
> with him, the father said, "My daughter whom I have given to you in

This chapter developed from a paper delivered in 1975 at a conference held at the
Jewish Theological Seminary of America. The late Rabbi Jacob Agus, who chaired the conference, encouraged the initial formulation of this essay.

marriage is my only child. My love for her is great. I cannot depart from her. Yet, I cannot ask you not to take her to your realm. It is now her proper home. Permit me this one request. To whatever distant place you take her now to live, always have a chamber ready for me that I may dwell with you and with her, for I can never consider really leaving my daughter." So God said to Israel: "I have given you the Torah from which I cannot really part. I cannot tell you not to receive it in love. Yet, I request only this. Wherever you go with it, make Me a house wherein I may sojourn." As it is written, "Let them make Me a sanctuary so that I may dwell among them" (Exod. 25:8).[4]

As the "daughter" of God, the Torah is both apart from and a part of her parent. In God's giving the Torah to Israel, part of the giver is given with the gift.[5] The Torah is Israel's beloved, Israel's spouse, the touchstone of meaning for Israel's life.[6]

The presence of the Torah binds God to Israel and Israel to God. Through faithfulness to the Torah, the Jew becomes bound to God. Observance of the mitzvoth of the Torah is what binds the Jew to God. As Levi Yitzhak of Berdichev said, "The word *mitzvah* means 'to bind,' which is to say, one who properly performs a *mitzvah* becomes bound to the Creator."[7] Like the word "religion," the word "legal" derives from the Latin root "*ligo*," which means "to be bound." Through law translated into deed, the Jew becomes bonded to God.

Halakhah (Jewish religious law) defines how the Jew goes about performing the mitzvoth of the Torah. The Torah is the soul, the mitzvoth the body, and halakhah the prescription for concrete physical acts for the performance of sacred deeds.[8] Mitzvoth command; halakhah prescribes. The mitzvoth provide a path that leads to God. Halakhah offers the means by which one may proceed down that path. Without the halakhah, the mitzvoth would be blind. Without the mitzvoth, the halakhah would be dumb; halakhah articulates the mitzvoth.

The Torah is a song. The mitzvoth are the words to which it is sung. Halakhah provides the directions for how the song is to be sung. Without the song and without its lyrics, the directions themselves convey no meaning. Without the Torah, without the mitzvoth, halakhah would merely be a collection of empty directives, and performance of the halakhah would be a medley of empty gestures.

To attempt to understand halakhah, one must confront the theological premises that give it life and meaning, direction and purpose. In a sense, halakhah is a form of "applied theology" or of "practical theology"; it is theology in practice. Halakhah articulates the mitzvoth, and the mitzvoth—the commandments—assume a *metzaveh*—one who commands.[9] God is the one who commands, and revelation is the event through which those commands are conveyed. The Torah is the record and the product of the revelatory event. The Torah, the giver of the Torah, and the recipient of the Torah become bound together in a covenant by means of the revelatory event. Consequently, to discuss halakhah without reference to these theological concepts and claims, which it presumes, would be like concluding a discourse that had no beginning.

The starting point for developing a conceptual framework both for understanding and for interpreting halakhah must be a theological one. As the following two sections demonstrate, both a philosophy of halakhah and a process of making halakhic decisions ultimately rest upon specific theologies of revelation. Furthermore, a review of the relevant literature seems to indicate that two distinct theologies of revelation, characteristic of classical Jewish theology, have engendered two distinct philosophies of halakhah and two distinct correlative approaches to the process of halakhic decision making. For reasons that are clarified, one of these approaches is called "the monolithic view," and the other is called "the dialogic view."[10]

THE MONOLITHIC VIEW

The monolithic view is grounded in a particular understanding of the revelatory experience and of its products: Torah and mitzvoth. According to this view, revelation is a monologue of God; the Torah and its commandments are imposed upon passive recipients; there is no human element either in revelation or in the products of revelation.

The classical Talmudic expression of the monolithic view is the following account of the revelation at Mt. Sinai: "The Holy One, blessed be He, overturned the mountain [Mt. Sinai] on them [Israel] like an [inverted] cask and said to them: If you accept the Torah it is well; if not, here shall be your burial place."[11] Thus, revelation and its products—Torah and commandments—are imposed upon the people of Israel. The people have little choice but to accept the commandments of God. There is no dialogue; there is only divine monologue.

In the late Middle Ages, this text was interpreted to mean that God chose Israel for reasons known only to Himself; Israel did not initially freely choose God. The text was interpreted by means of a blunt analogy: God *raped* Israel; the covenant binding God to Israel was forced upon a reluctant people. Israel was coerced into passively accepting the covenant and its laws.[12]

The monolithic view rejects the possibility of all but a passive role for the recipient of revelation. Even the prophet is but a passive vessel in the revelatory experience. Though the voice may be the voice of the prophet, it is really God who is speaking, using the prophet's voice. The prophet is oblivious to his own prophesying. This view, for example, interprets the verse in Psalms, "My mouth shall speak the praise of the Lord" (Ps. 145:21), to mean, "My mouth only produces the words of the *Shekhinah.* . . . One who has reached this stage is a man who is no more than a channel through which the words of the Most High flow."[13] When the prophet prophesies, he is unaware of what he is doing.[14] He is completely passive. God uses the organs of his body, against his will, without his knowledge. In the words of Philo of Alexandria, "Nothing of what he says will be his own, for he that is truly under the control of divine inspiration has no power of apprehension when he speaks. He only serves as a channel for the insistent words of Another's prompting. . . . His organs of speech, mouth and tongue are wholly in the employ of another." Both Philo and the Targum (the Aramaic rendition of Scripture) follow the view that the prophet is but a passive recipient of revelation. He may interpret what he receives to the people;[15] however, he may not supplement the message he has received. He enters into no dialogue with God.[16] In this view, the role of the prophet is compared to the role of a stenographer: God dictates and the prophet records.[17]

This view of revelation maintains that the Torah and its commandments are the dictates of God. As such, they can neither be questioned nor be changed. They are only to be obeyed. The human being worships God, as a servant obeys his or her master, in passive obedience.

In medieval Jewish philosophy, the notion of the immutable nature of the Torah came to be considered a principle of Jewish faith. As He who gave the Torah is immutable and static, that is, perfect, so must the Torah have these qualities. As God is the source of truth, and the Torah is the repository of truth, its commandments must be objectively true and unchanging.[18] As truth is objective and monolithic, so must the commandments be monolithic. There can be but one halakhic option. Truth is either/or; plurality of truth cannot exist. Truth must be exclusive; there can be only one correct answer to each question, specifically to each halakhic question. For many medieval Jewish philosophers, truth and perfection went hand in hand. God is perfect, hence static. The Torah is perfect and true; ergo, it must be static. The Torah represents the divine will; therefore, for the Torah and its commandments to change would imply a change within God, which would entail compromising the perfection of God. God's will—as expressed in the Torah and its commandments and as articulated by halakhah—cannot change, according to this view. For it to do so would imply a lack of divine perfection; to do so would imply that the Torah and its commandments are lacking perfection.

The view that halakhah is objectively true and therefore static apparently led Moses Maimonides and others to attempt to systematize and codify this objective truth. Since halakhah is objectively true and immutable, there can be but a single correct halakhic response to a given halakhic question. Halakhah can only be monolithic; it cannot be pluralistic, since a plurality in halakhic decision would imply a plurality of truths. The attempt made by Maimonides and others to codify Jewish law may be interpreted as an attempt to express the monolithic nature of halakhah in a systematic form. In this view, just as revelation is monolithic, devoid of any human (subjective) element, so must Jewish law—which expresses the concreting of revelation—have this quality. Those who attempt to codify Jewish law consciously defend the notion of law by objective standard rather than admit the presence of a subjective or social element in halakhic decision.

As Maimonides's philosophical magnum opus was meant as a guide for the philosophically perplexed, his legal code, the *Mishneh Torah*, was intended as a guide for the halakhically perplexed. In his philosophical works, Maimonides attempted to remove the impediments and confusions from one seeking philosophical certainty. In the *Mishneh Torah*, Maimonides attempted to remove the confusions from one seeking halakhic truth. He claimed to have extracted the halakhah concerning each issue from the confusing maze of the Talmudic dialectic and from the labyrinth of post-Talmudic halakhic literature. Holding to the monolithic view of the halakhah, Maimonides was unwilling to admit the possibility of a plurality of halakhic options. He claimed to have discovered the singularly valid halakhah. In the introduction to the *Mishneh Torah*, Maimonides wrote:

> I, Moses the son of Maimon the Sefardi, bestirred myself, and relying on the help of God, blessed be He, intently studied all these works, with the view of putting together the results obtained from them in regard to what is forbidden or permitted, clean or unclean, and the other rules of the Torah—all in plain language and terse style, so that thus the entire Oral Law might become systematically known to all, without citing difficulties and solutions or differences of view, one person saying so, and another something else,—but consisting of statements, clear and convincing, and in according with the conclusions drawn from all these compilations and commentaries that have appeared from the time of Moses to the present, so that all the rules shall be accessible to young and old, whether these appertain to the [Pentateuchal] precepts or to the institutions established by the sages and prophets, *so that no other work should be needed for ascertaining any of the laws of Israel*, but that this work might serve as a compendium of the entire Oral Law, including the ordinances, customs and decrees instituted from the days of our teacher Moses till the compilation of the Talmud. Hence, I have entitled this work *Mishneh Torah* [*Second Torah*], for the reason that a person, *who first reads the Written Law and then this compilation, will know from it the whole the Oral Law, without having occasion to consult any other book* [emphasis added].

Just as Maimonides claimed to have reconstructed the certainties of Jewish philosophical speculation in *The Guide of the Perplexed*, so in the

Mishneh Torah did he claim to have reconstructed the halakhic certainties known by former generations. For Maimonides, the "severe vicissitudes" of the "exile" caused both philosophical and halakhic certainty to have been lost. Maimonides, therefore, attempted to recover these lost certainties.[19]

In later attempts at codification, the concept of law by objective standard was reiterated. For example, in the sixteenth century, Joseph Karo consciously attempted to defend the notion of law by objective standard rather than admit the presence of a subjective element in the very code he composed. Though not consistent in practice with the plan he outlined in theory, Karo embraced a methodology that would guarantee automatic, objective decision on a given issue. Karo is, therefore, a representative of the trend that holds halakhah to be autonomous and considers the process of halakhic decision to embody a logic of its own.

As a commentator, Joseph Karo was bold, resourceful, and innovative; as a personality, he was saintly; but as a codifier, he was self-effacing. At least theoretically, Karo followed a methodology in his code that excluded the codifier—namely, himself—from the process of codification. His plan of self-effacement in his own code was not simply an expression of humility, it was part of his attempt to strain legal decision of its subjective element by making it solely dependent upon an objective standard and an objective methodology. For Karo, the objective standard was the consensus of the majority view of three scholars whom Karo considered the authoritative codifiers who preceded him: Isaac Alfasi (Rif), Moses Maimonides (Rambam), and Asher ben Yehiel (Rosh). The objective methodology Karo purported to employ virtually eliminated any subjectivity on the part of the codifier. All the codifier needed to do was find a consensus amongst the triumvirate just noted, or an agreement of any two of them, and that view was *the* Law.[20] Karo assumed that the attempts at codification produced by these three individuals represented the summary and quintessence of all that had gone before.[21] Therefore, while commenting upon the codes, one is free to examine and identify earlier sources; however, in the process of adjudication, the codes are to be considered as having superseded previous views, in that the codes represent the quintessence of all previous traditions and views. As the process of codification progressed, less and less text came to represent more and more of what came before. Whereas Karo's adjudication took into consideration the three great codifiers who preceded him, halakhists who succeeded him had only one code, one view, Karo's view from which to adjudicate. By eliminating options for decision by means of codification and standardization, halakhah became monolithic. One searched for *the* halakhah, now clearly stated in the codes.

As part of his involvement with codification, the sixteenth-century Polish scholar Moses Isserles advocated another criterion, which served to stifle creative thought in halakhic decision making and to obviate change on the basis of any factor, including contemporary social conditions and well-established past precedent. This element served to make the peculiar and particular the standard. Responses to particular problems or specific conditions in specific communities might become frozen as standard and as a precedent for future decisions. This element is Isserles's adaptation of the principle of "following the most recent authorities" (*halakhah ke-batre'ei*).[22] Combined with a general reticence for independent decision in any case, the adoption of this approach together with the process of codification all but eliminated the possibility for the dynamic process of halakhic decision to proceed.

For Moses Isserles, the most recently accepted view became standard. For Joseph Karo, the majority or consensus of three previous authorities automatically determined the law. Legal decisions became the product of an autonomous inner dynamic rather than an expression of law as a developing organism informed by socioeconomic and historical factors. Accepted by individuals in subsequent generations, the approaches of Karo and Isserles, duly codified and frozen, led Jewish law to atrophy. The weight of whole traditions against "the most recent authority" or against a paragraph in the *Shulhan Arukh* did not faze subsequent rabbinical figures. While recognizing that a trend a thousand years in the making may have been overturned by a comparatively recent decision and that the long-standing trend is more representative than the "recent" decision, some modern halakhists hold fast to Isserles's rule and timidly prohibit themselves from overturning past individual authorities, even though that individual had overturned long-standing precedents and even though that precedent may simply represent a response to a particular social or historical situation.

From the notion of *halakhah ke-batre'ei* it is but a small jump to the notion of *gadol ha-dor* or *gadol be-Yisrael*. Once it can be presumed that final authoritative halakhic decision making is vested in the most recent precedent, it is but a minor step to proceed to the idea that halakhic authority may become vested in a single contemporary scholar in whom the entire Torah is virtually embodied. In this view, the *gadol be-Yisrael*, the great halakhic authority, through constant Torah study, acquires a built-in authoritative response to every question and to every situation. This person is presumed to make decisions inspired by God and free of error. He is not necessarily required to justify his views with reasoned argument or with adequate documentation from classical sources. Halakhah, thereby, becomes vested in a person rather than in a process. To be sure, it is difficult to find support in halakhic sources for such an oracular view of the nature of halakhic decision making.[23]

In recent times, these attitudes have come to characterize much of Orthodox Judaism. Grounded in an essentially fundamentalist theology, assuming a monologic theory of revelation, many contemporary spokespersons of Orthodox Judaism assume themselves in particular possession of *the* authentic, "Torah-true" halakhah. The codes, specifically the *Shulhan Arukh*, are considered authoritative. The halakhah is considered divine and objectively true. The power to discern halakhah is by means of consulting the code, and if such consultation is not fruitful, Isserles's standard of *halakhah ke-batre'ei* may be invoked. While these methods theoretically prevail, in actual practice, the specific individual—the *gadol be-Yisrael*—who represents the quintessence of the tradition, who has mastered the methodology for halakhic decision, is consulted. Thus, the prevalent view in Orthodox Judaism today is this first view—the monolithic view—which seeks a single, irrefutable halakhic decision. Orthodoxy represents a continual search in the history of Jewish law for concreting *the* tradition in a central authority.

The monolithic view assumes that truth is regressive; that is, the further we get from the revelation at Mt. Sinai by the passage of time, the further we get from the source of truth. This notion of historically degenerating truth finds its classical expression in the Talmudic citation: "If the earlier scholars were like angels, we are like men; if they were like men, we are like asses."[24] Thus, the authority of a *tanna* is greater than any *amora* simply because he lived at a time period closer to the revelation at Mt. Sinai; the authority of an *amora* is greater than that of the *ga'onim* for the same reason, and so on. In this view, since we are further from the truth than any previous generation, we are less competent at halakhic decision than any previous generation. Therefore, we have to rely upon a book, a code, or a person that represents the quintessence of all that has gone before, and we are unable, therefore, to make any legal innovations. This rejection of the right to legislate or to make innovations is crystallized in the statement of the nineteenth-century halakhist, Moses Schreiber: "*Hadash assur min ha-Torah*," ("the new is taboo").[25]

One may note an implicit inconsistency in this approach. On the one hand, the most recent (or even contemporary) halakhic authority is considered authoritative; on the other hand, truth and halakhic authority are considered historically regressive. To claim that recent or current authorities represent the quintessence of all of that which came before does not really alleviate this contradiction.

In the writings of Samson Raphael Hirsch, considered by many to be the "father of modern orthodoxy," one finds a clear articulation of the monolithic view. For Hirsch, revelation was understood to be the direct communication of the divine will. The role of the people is purely passive. They are merely the recipients of the divine commands, which, according to Hirsch, are as immutable as the laws of nature. As Hirsch considered revelation to be a monologue, he maintained that the products of revelation—Torah and commandments—are devoid of any human element. His fundamentalism was grounded in his view of revelation as a monologue. His view of the static and unchanging nature of halakhah was rooted in an essentially monologic view of revelation and a monolithic view of halakhah.[26]

In more recent years, the monolithic view has been espoused by the leading contemporary orthodox spokesman, Joseph B. Soloveitchik. For Soloveitchik, halakhic truth is objective in its nature. Halakhic truth is a priori. It exists independently of subjective or social concerns or realities. Halakhic truth is like mathematical truth and may be known with mathematical certainty. The function of the halakhist is not to discover but to uncover what is implicit. The halakhist may not legislate, may not develop the law; the halakhist may only elicit the inherent presumed truth of the law. Trained in the proper methodology, the halakhist, of necessity, will elicit the correct conclusion in halakhic decision. In this view, halakhah is an a priori system of categories with an internal logic of its own. These categories may direct human affairs but must not be influenced by them. A particular halakhic decision will be the same whether it is made in response to a specific social or individual human condition or whether it is simply a theoretical exercise. The halakhah, being totally of divine origin, must be objective and autonomous, for only that which is objectively true may be constant and true in an absolute sense. The law proceeds on its own course, unaffected by social or intellectual fashion, unencumbered by any subjective disturbance.[27]

From its earliest to its most recent expression, the monolithic view emphasizes the possibility of only a single halakhic response to each halakhic question. It is grounded in a monologic understanding of revelation. It encourages the need for halakhic certainty through the compilation of codes of law, considered to be both authoritative and binding. It seeks certainty by means of localizing and centralizing halakhic authority in a code of law or in an individual whose views concerning the interpretation of law are considered singularly valid and binding.

THE DIALOGIC VIEW

The dialogic view understands revelation to be a dialogue between God and human beings. It assumes the presence of a human element both in the revelatory event and in the products of revelation—the Torah and its commandments.

The understanding of revelation as a dialogue and of the recipient of revelation as a partner in revelation is deeply rooted in biblical, rabbinic, and post-Talmudic literature. In contrast to the monolithic view of the revelation at Mt. Sinai, which understands the Torah to be imposed upon

Israel, the dialogic view is that Israel freely accepted the Torah with the words "we shall observe and we shall understand" (Exod. 24:3). From this perspective, revelation consists of two components: the giving of the Torah by God (*matan Torah*) and the receiving of the Torah by Israel (*kabbalat ha-Torah*). Without the second component, revelation is meaningless, devoid of impact. It is Israel's willingness to enter into the covenant, to enter into dialogue with God, that is essential to the revelatory event.[28] Revelation consists of a divine initiative and a human response, of God's commandments and of Israel's acceptance of those commandments. In this view, the Torah and its commandments are not imposed upon Israel. Rather, they are offered to Israel. The revelatory event is only complete when the Torah and its commandments are ratified by Israel.

A Talmudic expression of the dialogic view of revelation is the interpretation of the verse in Proverbs (1:8): "Hear, my son, the instruction of thy father, and forsake not the teaching (*torat*) of thy mother," where "father" is said to refer to God, and "mother" is said to refer to the community of Israel (*Knesset Yisrael*).[29] In this view, the Torah is revealed directly by God as well as through the community of Israel. Torah is the product of an ongoing dialogue between God and Israel. Accordingly, the dialogic view perceives the prophet as a "partner in the work of revelation." An example of this perspective is the text, "Rabbi Judah says: . . . the Holy One, blessed be He, said to Moses: Behold, I shall speak to you and you shall answer Me."[30]

The view that revelation is a dialogue between God and man, that there is a human element in the Torah, that the Torah contains the word of God but is not in its totality the word of God, led to a reevaluation of the nature of the Torah in the medieval Jewish mystical tradition. The monolithic view, which in medieval Jewish philosophy embraced the notion of the immutable Torah, was reexamined by the Jewish mystics.

The medieval Jewish mystics claimed that the Torah as it exists in its essential form, in the supernal world of the *sefirot* (divine potencies), is beyond human apprehension. In this world, they claimed, we only know the Torah in the form in which it appears to us. This form, they claimed, necessarily adapts the characteristics of this world, specifically imperfection, change, and flux.

The idea that the Torah and its commandments, as we know them, are not objectively and absolutely true and static is an insight nurtured and developed in the Jewish mystical tradition. According to the *Sefer Temunah*, the form that the Torah takes in this world is conditioned by the nature of the historical aeon that exists at present. Thus, while the essence of the Torah in the supernal realm is static, its form in our world is determined by the conditions of our world.[31] According to the *Zohar*, the Torah adopts a form peculiar to this world to become operative in this world.[32]

According to Judah Loew of Prague, the commandments of the Torah will
prevail for historical and for messianic times but will become obsolete in
the spiritual dimension of the world to come; the commandments are the
matter of which the Torah is the form. They are accidental, while it is
essential. Manifest in this world, the Torah must express itself in terms
alien to its nature. Essentially supernatural, the Torah, as manifest in this
world, must adapt characteristics that reflect the natural world of time, of
history, of space, and of social conditions.[33]

According to the Lurianic mystics, the position of the philosophers—
specifically Maimonides—which held the Torah as we know it to be perfect, immutable, and static, is grounded in an assumption that must be
denied. As noted, the idea of the immutable, static Torah had assumed that
nothing imperfect could emerge from God, who is static and perfect. The
Torah, therefore, it was claimed, must be immutable, static, and perfect
since it came from God. Under the impact of natural catastrophes, historical traumas, and moral evil, the Lurianic mystics rejected this assumption.
The imperfect world, the world saturated with evil, did emerge from the
perfect God for reasons unfathomable to humans. The logical extension of
this view is that the Torah too is imperfect in this world. The Torah is
affected by conditions of this less than perfect world.[34] It must, therefore,
deal with less than perfect human institutions. It must even deal with morally dubious human institutions, such as slavery.

According to Judah Loew of Prague, Moses had to break the first set
of tablets because it represented the essential Torah, which cannot function
in this imperfect world. A second set of tablets, embodying laws operative
in this world, was needed. Imperfect laws are required in an imperfect
world.[35] By their nature, God's laws in the natural, human world must be
imperfect. They cannot be immutable, static, or objectively true. Being
laws in history for human beings, they must inevitably embody a human,
social, and historical element.

The view that the Torah embraces a human as well as a divine element precludes a fundamentalist position. The claim that the Torah, as it
exists in this world, is not static and immutable, allows for the reasoning
that revelation is continuous. From this perspective, change and development of the manifestation of the Torah in this world does not impugn divine perfection and does not imply a change in the divine will that compro-
mises divine perfection. It only asserts that, while the Torah in essence
may be immutable and represents absolute truth, the Torah as it is represented in this world is subject to the changes, developments, and vicissitudes of this world.

According to the dialogic view, the "essential" Torah may reside in
some supernal realm and may exhibit a static state of being; however, as
manifest in this world, it is subject to continuous development and never-

ending interpretation. Already in rabbinic literature the notion that the Torah, being no longer in heaven, is subject to human interpretation, was stressed.[36] This ongoing process of interpretation was understood to be divinely sanctioned and even divinely inspired. The continuous development of the "raw materials" of the revelatory experience was perceived as a fulfillment of a divine mandate and as an expression of the ongoing nature of revelation and of interpretation.

According to a midrash, "The Holy One, blessed be He, gave the Torah to Israel like wheat from which to derive fine flour or like flax to make a garment."[37] In other words, the record of revelation—the sacred texts—are to be refined and developed by human effort. The human element is required to make the Torah whole (shalem). For the monolithic view, the Torah is static, perfect. This view expresses a Greek philosophical notion of perfection. The dialogic view expresses a classical biblical and rabbinic view of perfection. Wholeness, completeness (sheleimut) is perfection. For the dialogic view, it is the continuous interaction of human beings with the Torah that makes the Torah whole, complete, perfect. It is through the continuous development and interpretation of the Torah that an event (Mt. Sinai) meant for all times can speak at any time.

Just as God summons the prophet to be His partner in the ongoing process of revelation, He invites the halakhist to become His partner in the ongoing processes of creation and revelation.[38] According to a midrash, "Not only did all the prophets receive their prophecy from Mt. Sinai, but also each of the sages that arose in every generation received his [wisdom] from Mt. Sinai."[39] Commenting on the verse, "According to the law which they shall teach you, and according to the judgment they shall tell you, you shall do. . . ." (Deut. 17:11), Judah Loew of Prague noted, "All that they [the sages] teach you are permitted to do, do it—for thus God commanded you."[40]

Without the active presence of the human element, the Torah would be mute. God's word would be bereft of a presence in God's world. According to one commentator, the Torah is described as Israel's spouse because it is caused to conceive by the sages of Israel. In this way, the continuous birth and development of tradition are assured.[41]

From the human perspective, truth is relative. For human beings, the truth is that the truth cannot be known, including the truth of the Torah.[42] As the early twentieth-century philosopher Franz Rosenzweig observed, truth is a noun only for God, for man it is but an adjective.

For God, contradictory opposites can be equally true. For human beings, however, a choice between alternatives must be made:

> The masters, the disciples of the wise, sit in manifold assembly and interpret the Torah—some pronouncing things permitted, some pronouncing

the identical things forbidden. Should one ask: How in these circumstances shall I learn Torah, i.e., how shall I learn what is the law?, one
should answer him with the verse—"All is given by one Shepherd" [Ec-
cles. 12:11]—which means, One God gave them, one Leader uttered
them, from the mouth of the Lord of all creation did they come. As it is
written, "God spoke *all* these things" [Exod. 20:1].[43]

Perhaps in the celestial realm, truth is absolute and monolithic. However, in the terrestrial realm, truth is not monolithic but is manifest in a
plurality of modes. The human task is to apply what we can know to what
we should do. The human concern is not with absolute truth but with
applied truth, with operative truth. A "heavenly voice" may inform us that
contradictory views on the identical subject may both be true, may both be
"words of the living God," but the halakhah for a specific issue or in a
specific situation must be one way or the other; it cannot be both ways.
Before truth can be implemented, a decision among options, even among
equally valid options, must be made.[44]

While truth through revelation is provided, human discretion in concrete situations is required.[45] While two equally valid options may be provided, and while they both may be true "words of the living God," only one
can be appropriately applied to a specific situation at a given time and
place. As Rashi (Shlomo Yitzhaki) explained, in such a case, "there is no
falsehood. Each view is true from its own perspective. 'These and these are
the words of the living God.' In other words, at certain times this one
applies, and at other times that one applies, for the change of times and of
conditions determines which option applies to the situation at hand."[46]

Once it leaves the celestial realm and becomes a citizen of the terrestrial realm, the future development of the Torah becomes vested in responsible human hands. The administration and the interpretation of the
revealed word and will of God subsequently fall to human stewardship.
Discerning the meaning of the Torah and explicating the truth of the Torah
become the province of the responsible application of human knowledge
and wisdom. According to a rabbinic text, when Moses requested halakhic
certainty, God responded by indicating that there can be no a priori certainty in halakhic matters. God reminded Moses that the Torah contains
multifaceted meanings and that the application of one or more of those
possible meanings to a specific situation is vested in the majority view of
the sages of each generation.

The words of the Torah are not given as clear-cut decisions. For with
every word which the Holy One, blessed be He, spoke to Moses, He
offered him forty-nine arguments by which a thing may be proven clean,
and forty-nine other arguments by which the same thing may be proven
unclean. When Moses asked: "Master of the Universe, in what way shall

we discern the true law?" God replied: "The majority is to be followed [Exod. 23:2], that is to say, when a majority says it is unclean, it is unclean; when a majority says it is clean, it is clean."[47]

In the commentaries to this text, God is quoted as saying to Moses, "Were I to reveal to you the halakhah, there would be no subsequent interpretation of the Torah. The process of interpretation would be stifled from the outset."[48] As Rabbi Yannai said, "Had the Torah been given in the form of incisive legal decision, we would have no leg upon which to stand,"[49] which means, "the Torah could never be established, for the Torah needs to be interpreted in various ways, all of which are the words of the living God."[50]

In a similar vein, the fifteenth-century Spanish philosopher Joseph Albo observed, "The law of God cannot be perfect so as to be adequate for all times, because the ever new details of human relations, their customs and their acts are too numerous to be embraced in a book. Therefore, Moses was given orally certain general principles, only briefly alluded to in the Torah, by means of which the wise men in every generation may work out the details as they appear."[51] Consequently, the halakhist's task is not to encapsulate the law in codes, not to fossilize the law in immutable a priori categories; the obligation of the halakhist is to ensure the ongoing dynamic development of the law, to cause the "sprouting of branches from roots."[52] In other words, God does not reveal halakhic decisions but halakhic possibilities. The task of the sages of each generation is to discern halakhic decisions for their own generation from among these pluralistic possibilities.

Because the dialogic view assumes the impossibility of knowledge of absolute truth in this world, it can embrace the notion that truth may take a plurality of equally valid forms. Only truths, and not *the* truth, can be vouchsafed to human beings. Consequently, halakhic truth is never a priori, but is always a posteriori. Halakhic truth is evident in a variety of modes. The process of halakhic decision making does not aim at discerning absolute truth but endeavors to posit the product of the dialogue between God's word and God's world, between divine revelation and human intelligence. This product cannot claim to be objectively true. It can only claim to be true within the confines of the human condition and within the parameters of specific historical conditions. As Aryeih Leib Heller, in his nineteenth-century commentary to the *Shulhan Arukh*, pointed out,

> The Torah was not given to the angels. It was given to human beings who possess intelligence. He gave us the Torah in conformity to the ability of the human mind to decide, even though it may not be the truth [objectively speaking], only that it be true according to the conclusions of the human mind. . . . Let truth emerge from the earth [Ps. 85:12], that is, the truth as the sages decide using human intelligence.[53]

For a halakhic decision to be reached, for a choice to be made in a specific situation from equally valid halakhic options, the availability of those options have to be preserved. The process of codification tended to preclude all options but one. Codification tended to prune the tree of halakhah rather than to encourage the sprouting of already-existing or of new branches. The monolithic view, which seeks halakhic certainty, which tries to establish objective halakhic truth, encourages codification. The dialogic view, which assumes equally valid plural modes of halakhah, rejects the claim of the codifiers that halakhah can be expressed in absolute terms in binding and authoritative codes of Jewish law. Advocates of the monolithic view consider codification an urgent desideratum aimed at establishing halakhic certainty. Advocates of the dialogic view consider codification to be a danger to the diversity, the flexibility, and the creativity endemic to the very nature of halakhah and to the nature of the process of halakhic decision making. While the monolithic view aims at arriving at halakhic certainty, by means of codifying Jewish law, the dialogic view strives to keep open the gates of halakhic possibility. The opposition of advocates of the dialogic view to the codification of Jewish law is one characteristic of this endeavor.

CODIFICATION

Those who opposed codification (especially the *Mishneh Torah* and the *Shulhan Arukh*) did so for one or more of the following reasons.[54] First, the codes attempt to establish a single halakhic view as *the* final halakhic position on a given issue. The codes attempt to eliminate the possibility of equally legitimate and defensible halakhic options. They attempt to make halakhah monolithic. Second, the codes either claim or are understood to claim to represent the quintessence of the entire halakhic tradition that preceded them. Their presumption of binding authority is grounded in that claim.

Those who opposed codification rejected the attempt to mold halakhah into an exclusivistic, monolithic structure. They maintained that the codes may claim to be the quintessence of the entire halakhic tradition which preceded them, but in actuality that claim is fallacious. The codes are, therefore, neither authoritative nor binding. Though the codes merely express the predispositions of their respective authors in halakhic matters, they attempt to establish a single halakhist's interpretation as the halakhic norm.

There is not, nor can there be, universal agreement with the author of a given code. This tenet is self-evident, given the existence of equally authoritative precedents on many halakhic issues, and this has also become evident by the proliferation of various codes, each holding views in opposition to those maintained by other codes.

The codes may claim to utilize an objective methodology in arriving at halakhic decisions; but a close examination of the codes and of the responsa written by the authors of the codes clearly demonstrates that the codifiers often departed from their own purported objective methodologies. The codes, therefore, may claim to have removed the subjective concerns of their authors as a factor in halakhic decision, but in actuality they did not do so. Thus, the codes represent the proclivities of their respective authors and should not be considered authoritative or binding.

Opponents of codification, advocating the dialogic view, maintained that, because the codes only represent their individual author's view, they threaten to establish their author's view as the norm, should the codes become accepted as the basis for halakhic decision. This situation might eventually result in having a weak precedent or a minority precedent used by a codifier or the codifier's view unfounded in any precedent becoming a precedent for future decisions. Furthermore, that most of the authors of the codes failed to justify their positions by identifying their sources calls the validity of their views into question. Their approach tends to exacerbate rather than to ameliorate the quality of halakhic decision. Halakhic decision of the codifiers cannot be accepted on faith. The documentation and the reasoning processes underlying their views must be made evident before one can seriously consider their views as being possibly correct.

Opponents of the codes also claimed that in establishing a single halakhic option as the only halakhic option, the codes disregard the importance of local custom as a proper source for halakhic decision. In this expression of the dialogic view, the people have a role in "making" halakhah by means of the development of custom. Codification would eliminate custom as a basis for a number of equally acceptable halakhic options.

Finally, opponents of the codes maintained that the codes could not and should not be considered authoritative for the reasons already stated. The codes are merely an individual author's compilation of his or her views.[55] The codes are simply *guides;* they are not binding. As guides to halakhic decision they may be consulted along with other sources. They only supplement, not supplant nor replace, halakhic decision.

As noted, the second claim leveled against the codifiers is that codification is intrinsically inimical to the halakhic process. By taking a single precedent and elevating it into a norm, the codifiers disregard other equally valid precedents and even reject stronger precedents than the one they may be inclined to accept. Should the codified view become the norm, halakhic judgments other than their own, though firmly rooted in precedent, would become disenfranchised in future halakhic decisions. The historical and social conditions prevalent at the time of the codifier might become the basis for halakhic decision at *all* later times and places. This undesirable result of codification, the opponents of codification maintained, must be contested.[56]

The opponents of codification perceived the codes as a threat to competent yet independent halakhic decision. Once the codes are accepted, they claimed, scholars will become reluctant to oppose them. The halakhic scholar will be replaced by a code, even though the particular scholar may be a more superior halakhist than the author of a specific code. Furthermore, as codification makes the law "popular" and accessible to the masses, laymen will read the codes and make halakhic decisions for themselves based upon the views expressed in the codes. Thus, the authority of local scholars will be undermined. People will consult the codes rather than the scholars, rabbis will rely upon the codes rather upon earlier sources, the masses will be led to err, and the quality of halakhic scholarship among the rabbinate will suffer. A leading advocate of this position was the sixteenth-century Polish halakhist Solomon Luria. In opposition to Moses Isserles, he wrote, "You [Isserles] wonder by what warrant I am empowered to bring certainty into the law. You impugn my authority to disagree with the codifiers. It is knowledge of the law which invests me with the prerogative to take issue with the halakhists and to expose their errors." Elsewhere, Solomon Luria wrote, "I shall acknowledge my error only in the event that you prove my decisions are not founded in the Talmud, or that my line of reasoning is not supported by the early *ga'onim*."[57] In a similar vein in thirteenth-century Spain, Nahmanides (Moses ben Nahman) expressed this view in his glosses to Maimonides's *Sefer Ha-Mitzvot,*

> Notwithstanding my ardent desire to be a disciple of the earlier authorities, to establish and maintain their views, to [adorn myself] by making their [views] a gold chain about my neck and a bracelet upon my hand, I shall not serve them as a "donkey carrying books." I shall explain their methods and appreciate their value, but when their views cannot be comprehended by me, I shall debate before them in all modesty, I shall judge according to what appears best in my eyes . . . for God gives wisdom in all times and in all ages.[58]

By opposing the claim that the codes were authoritative and binding, advocates of the dialogic view allowed for the possibility of a subjective and a social element in halakhic decision. In their view, the composition of the codes made the inclusion of the human element in halakhic decision making so much more important than it had been before codification. The subjective human element was necessary to keep codification from stifling the halakhic process. The presence of the human element in halakhic decision assured the possibility for continuous creative development of halakhah. According to the Hasidic master Israel of Rhyzen, "Why does the Torah have five books while the *Shulhan Arukh* consists of only four books? Where is the missing part of the law?—The missing part is the person. For, without the human element, the halakhah is incomplete."

Because it assumed that the halakhah was neither autonomous nor objectively true in any absolute sense, the dialogic view remained open to halakhic flexibility and diversity. The acceptance of plural modes of halakhic truth made possible and desirable the inclusion of historical, moral, social, and economic factors into the process of halakhic decision making. As a result, the halakhic scholar was permitted and encouraged to apply his learning and experience as well as his best personal judgment in reaching halakhic decisions. Unlike the monolithic view that seeks to eliminate the halakhist and the external conditions characteristic of his time and place from the process of halakhic decision, the dialogic view deems the personal judgment of the halakhist and the historical, social, and economic conditions out of which that judgment came to be crucial and necessary factors in the process of halakhic decision making.[59] A review of the relevant literature demonstrates that an awareness of the need to integrate these factors into the halakhic process has always been characteristic of Jewish legal tradition. With specific reference to the place of custom (*minhag*) and legislation (*takkanot* and *gezerot*) in the history of Jewish legal development, the perennial role of these factors in the halakhic process becomes increasingly clear.

CUSTOM (*MINHAG*)

To accept and to advocate the inclusion of custom into a legal structure is to accept social factors as a basis for law and to enfranchise the people with a role in the initiation and development of law. From the perspective of the monolithic view, this possibility is unacceptable and undesirable, as it threatens to undermine any view of the autonomous nature of halakhah. To admit sociological factors as viable elements in halakhic decision making is also in conflict with the monolithic perspective because it would impose external factors upon the self-contained inner dynamic of halakhic decision making. From the dialogic perspective, however, custom plays a crucial role in the development of halakhah, for it articulates the necessarily dialogical role that the people are encouraged to play both in the revelatory experience and in the development of subsequent tradition. Precisely because the existence of a variety of equally valid customs articulates the notion of plural modes of halakhic truth, the dialogic view embraces and encourages the initiation and the development of customs.

The problem of the relationship between custom and law in Jewish jurisprudence has a long and complicated history.[60] Nevertheless, one may distinguish among three attitudes related to this issue. The first attitude is that custom is inimical to law and that, when law clashes with custom, law always prevails; legal development must proceed oblivious to custom. This, essentially, is the position of the monolithic view. The second attitude is that custom is a variety of law, and as such, it cannot clash with law. This position is held, for different reasons, both by advocates of the monolithic and of the dialogic views. The third attitude is that custom can suspend and replace law in certain circumstances. This, essentially, is the position of the dialogic view.

Advocates of the monolithic view sought to diminish the role of custom and rejected the claim that custom could triumph over law. For example, in one text, the twelfth-century halakhist and grandson of Rashi, Jacob Tam (Rabbenu Tam), chided his colleagues for defending a custom as a replacement for an established law. He wrote, "Even a proper custom does not uproot a law." In this text, he also reminded his reader that the Hebrew letters of the word *"minhag"* (custom) are the same letters that when read backwards spell *"gehinnom"* (hell).[61]

The idea that custom is a variety of law was held by advocates of both the monolithic and the dialogic views. For advocates of the monolithic view, such as Moses Maimonides, only universally accepted, long-standing customs that did not impinge upon established legal precedent seemed to be considered in this regard.[62] Custom, for Maimonides, was a tightly circumscribed element that, in very specific circumstances, may become part of the law, part of Torah. For advocates of the dialogic view, however, custom is law, custom is Torah; *minhag avoteinu, torah hu* (the custom of our forefathers is Torah).[63]

In a number of his responsa, the late thirteenth-century Spanish halakhist Asher ben Yehiel (Rosh) maintained that, in certain circumstances, *minhag okeir et ha-halakhah* (custom uproots the law), even when the law is of scriptural origin or of rabbinic degree (*takkanah*).[64] Similarly, the thirteenth-century German halakhist Meir of Rothenburg (Maharam) is quoted by a later source as having said, "The customs of the community are Torah, even when such customs abrogate *halakhah*."[65] According to the twelfth-century French halakhist Abraham ben David (Rabad) of Posquieres, "The only guiding principle we have is the custom of the people."[66] The claim that "the custom of our forefathers is Torah" heralds back to the earliest forefathers, the biblical patriarchs. A midrash notes, "Rabbi Shimon bar Yohai said: Do not change the customs instituted by our forefathers, the biblical patriarchs."[67]

Rabbi Jonathan found support for the validity of custom in the verse, "Hear, my son, the instruction of thy father, and forsake not the instruction (*torat*) of thy mother" (Prov. 1:8).[68] Because custom derives specifically from one's own forebears, Nahmanides elevated the authority of custom by linking it to the commandment to honor one's parents.[69]

The opinion that custom can supersede or replace law, in certain circumstances, has its roots in a statement found in the Palestinian Talmud: *minhag me'vatteil halakhah* (custom abrogates law).[70] Consideration of the implications of this statement in Talmudic and medieval Jewish literature led to the establishment of certain parameters for the application of this principle. It was generally agreed, for example, that custom could supersede law in commercial matters and in most civil matters but not in the category of law known as "the forbidden and the permitted."[71] Nevertheless, advocates of the monolithic view attempted to restrain the intrusion of custom into all areas of law.

Despite these efforts at constraint, the acceptance of custom as a law-making force in commercial matters opened a door for it to infiltrate and to influence change in other areas, such as laws related to marriage. While marriage laws clearly fell under the category of "the forbidden and the permitted," there were certain commercial and civil documents and transactions connected to marriage, such as the dowry. The interpenetration at these points, between marriage law and commercial law, offered an entrée for custom to move into areas beyond that in which it was originally assigned propriety. From playing a tangential role in these expanded areas of its originally assigned purview, custom began to play a major role in almost all areas of Jewish law. From a limited role in commercial matters related to marriage, custom began to play a central role in introducing major changes with regard to Jewish marriage, for example, the prohibition of polygamy, the prohibition of concubinage, the fusing of the two ceremonies of *erusin* and *kiddushin* into one. In addition, social and economic conditions clearly play a role in these innovations, and in spite of the prohibition against following gentile practices (*hukkat ha-goy*), it is clear that gentile concepts and practices influenced these changes in Jewish law and practice.[72] Moreover, one should note that, without the notion of custom, the Jewish marriage would have no meaning.

A term often used to denote a law that has its origin in custom is the Hebrew word *dat*. In this regard, it is relevant to note that marriages are solemnized "according to the *dat* of Moses and of Israel." In other words, a Jewish marriage comes into being because it is in accordance with the custom of the people of Israel.

Even in the area of criminal law custom played a role. Though the Talmud established the rule that the punishment for defaming the character of another is corporal punishment in the form of whipping (i.e., stripes), this rule was abandoned when local practice had rejected its observance. In such a case, one is obliged "to follow the (local) *takkanah*, and not to follow the talmudic law."[73]

A further principle that was generally accepted regarding custom was that custom may be invoked only to make the observance of the law more stringent but never to justify making it more lenient.[74] There was apparently a fear that if custom could replace any law, the intrusion of custom into law would eventually lead to the progressive abolition of all stringent laws. The fifteenth-century north African halakhist Solomon ben Simeon Duran (Rashbash) wrote, "Were we to abolish laws prohibiting certain things as a result of the [contrary] *minhag*, then one by one all prohibitions would become permitted, and the whole of the Torah set at naught."[75]

Notwithstanding this attempt to restrict the impact of custom, once it was deigned to have a role in legal decision, the dimensions of its influence broadened; the gates of restriction slowly opened. For example, Abraham ben David of Posquieres maintained that, while custom could not override a biblical prohibition, it could override a rabbinic prohibition. This position substantially broadened the power of custom in altering existing law and practice.[76] Once the place of custom in influencing law was established, the entire range of halakhah eventually became its domain.

That popular practice serves as the final arbiter where the law is uncertain is already established by the Talmud: "Whenever the law is uncertain insofar as the court is concerned, and you do not know what one should do [literally: 'the state of the law'], go out and see how the people conduct themselves, and do likewise."[77] However, it is clear that, historically, the role of custom was not limited to arbitrating conflicting legal opinions. Custom emerged as an independent law-creating force, sometimes overriding or supplanting existing legal precedent, sometimes creating law ex nihilo. Particularly in the area of liturgy, the dynamism of legal creativity rooted in custom becomes evident.[78]

Customs initiated by local communities frequently became widely accepted practices; for example, mourner's kaddish, *yahrzeit*, bar mitzvah, and breaking a glass at weddings.[79] Subsequently, rabbinic authorities searched the sources to find "precedents" upon which to "hang" them, and to justify their place in halakhah.[80] If sources were unavailable, a presumption was made that they were once available but are presently obscured. For example, in his discussion of the practice of wearing a certain kind of sleeve on the Sabbath and holidays, the seventeenth-century German rabbi Joseph Yuspa Hahn, in his *Yosif Ometz*, articulated this attitude when he wrote, "All the customs of our ancestors are Torah. What we do not know can be accounted for as being due to the limitation in our own knowledge or the loss of earlier books during the persecutions that befell our leaders of blessed memory."[81]

Once entrenched, custom was difficult to uproot. As Moses Isserles put it, "One must never abolish any custom or scoff at it for it was not fixed without a purpose."[82] Or, as Jacob ben Asher's fourteenth-century code the *Arba'ah Turim* succinctly states, "it is forbidden to alter the customs of our forefathers."[83] Moreover, custom not only stimulated the creation of laws but also reflected the abolition of established laws, as evidenced by the people's custom not to observe them. In other words, by ignoring certain laws, the people, in effect, legislated them out of existence. Those seeking to justify such neglect are wont to quote the Talmudic adage, "Go out and see what people do."[84]

Debate about the place of custom in halakhah and the role of the people in the creation of halakhah extended into the modern period. In modern times, advocates of the monolithic view have taken the position that custom plays no role in halakhah, while advocates of the dialogic view argue for the place of custom in the halakhic process. In the nineteenth century, the leading protagonists on this question were Samson Raphael Hirsch and Zacharias Frankel. The former is generally considered the father of neoorthodoxy, while the latter is considered the ideological father of Conservative Judaism.

Hirsch stressed the direct communication of the divine will. The role of the people is purely passive. They are merely the recipients of the divine will. The source of all Jewish law is God's monologue rather than an interaction between the human and the divine. Hence, custom, which represents the active and dynamic contribution of the people, could not be admitted as a valid source for halakhic decision. Expressing the dialogic view, Frankel claimed that the people play an active role in the birth and development of halakhah. This role is evidenced by the continual development of customs spontaneously created by the people. In Frankel's view, the people have a part to play in the process by which the laws, rooted in custom, become as binding as the word of God.[85]

According to early conservatives, who embraced the dialogic view and who articulated the concept of "Catholic Israel," the law is embodied in the people; it is, therefore, neither progressive nor regressive. It continually develops as the people develop; it reflects the community out of which it emerges, out of the Jewish community, out of "Catholic Israel."[86]

When this idea of "Catholic Israel" was originally formulated, the majority of Jews were observant. It was offered as an alternative to the innovations made by Reform rabbinic synods and to the claim that the Shulhan Arukh was the ultimate halakhic authority. Despite the impact this contention made and the option it offered, the idea of "Catholic Israel" created more problems than it solved. It suggests that law is determined by the majority view among the people. As has been noted many times, this idea of "Catholic Israel" if applied to the biblical period would mean that at the time of the biblical prophet Elijah, when most of the Jews worshipped Baal and only the minority worshipped God, the religion of Israel was in effect Baalism.[87] Thus, while this notion may have served a purpose in the times of Frankel and Solomon Schechter in their opposition to early reform, at a time when "Catholic Israel" was religiously observant, it cannot be expressed with the same kind of force today when most Jews are not religiously observant. One would have to conclude that, if one were to assert this view today, it would follow that observance of the Sabbath and dietary laws, for example, ought to be abandoned simply because the majority of Jews today do not observe these traditions. Thus, Frankel's notion that "Judaism is the religion of the Jews" is one fraught with difficulties.[88]

The redefinition of "Catholic Israel" by Robert Gordis and others in the 1940s and 1950s is also beset with difficulties. These individuals have suggested that "Catholic Israel" does not refer to all Jews, only to the majority of those Jews concerned with Jewish religious tradition and committed to its observance.[89] The problem with this claim is that, if this redefinition (by leading spokespersons for Conservative Judaism) were accepted by the Conservative Jewish movement, it would mean an implicit suggestion for its own dismantling since the majority of observant Jews today are not to be found within the ranks of Conservative Judaism at all but in the ranks of Orthodox Judaism. Thus, if "Catholic Israel" in this definition primarily implies those drawn from the ranks of the orthodox, the conservative movement would become obliged to let orthodoxy decide what Jewish law and practice ought to be. Obviously, Conservative Judaism could not accept this posture, which would entail its dissolution. One may suggest, therefore, that the idea of "Catholic Israel," as Frankel and Schechter employed it and as Gordis reinterpreted it, requires some rethinking. The concept of "*Catholic* Israel" as opposed to "*Reform* (as in 'Protestant') Israel" is no longer relevant. "Catholic Israel," referring to the majority of Jews being observant at present, is no longer accurate. Despite changes in social and historical circumstances, which encouraged the articulation of the notion of "Catholic Israel," having weakened its impact as an idea useful in polemics, certain aspects of the idea may still be profitably employed by conservative theoreticians, especially in the area of Jewish law. Specifically, "Catholic Israel" may be reinterpreted as a concept denoting the social factor in the development of Jewish religious law. While not the single determinant in the halakhic process, "Catholic Israel," so defined, represents *a* major source of halakhic development and legislation.

The dialogic view recognizes that extrahalakhic factors, such as social conditions articulated as customs, could play a central role in halakhic decision making. Similarly, the dialogic view recognizes that economic factors could play a decisive role in altering existing halakhic norms and in establishing new ones. Often, "legal fictions" were employed to maintain the illusion that the requirements of law were being maintained while the actualities of practice were being altered. Examples of legal fictions include the "sale" of *hametz* (leaven) to non-Jews during Passover, the justification of a salaried rabbinate, the collection of interest on borrowed principal, the Jewish use of gentile wine (*stam yeinam*), and the rulings regarding *hefseid merubeh* (substantial financial loss) and *bateil b'shishim* in the context of the dietary laws.[90]

The obligation to consider the economic implications of halakhic decisions, especially in the area of "the forbidden and the permitted," was stated by the thirteenth-century French Talmudic commentator Menahem Meiri. "It is improper for a sage to be excessively pious, seeking overmuch to be stringent and discovering justifications for it. He should rather consider the financial loss [involved]. For the Torah itself took this factor into consideration."[91] Throughout the Middle Ages, halakhic authorities provided justification for practices engendered by changing social, economic, and historical conditions, even in cases in which such practices conflicted with legal precedent of Talmudic or even of biblical origin.[92] Legal casuistry was often utilized to disguise such halakhic alterations.

Changes of climatic conditions also served as a basis for changes in halakhah. For example, Talmudic law established an unequivocal rule requiring one to eat and sleep in the *sukkah* during the Festival of Booths (Sukkot). However, because of often-unfavorable climatic conditions in northern countries, such as in Poland, the custom to eat but not to sleep in the *sukkah* arose and subsequently became a sanctioned practice.[93]

Because of cold weather, people kept a fire burning in their homes during the Sabbath. Occasionally, the fire spread, causing a threat to property. Despite Talmudic prohibitions against extinguishing a fire on the Sabbath where property is endangered, this prohibition was disregarded. The position of the thirteenth-century German Talmudic commentator Mordecai ben Hillel is instructive in this regard. He wrote, "Nowadays, it is the practice in the majority of lands to put out a fire on the Sabbath, but this practice cannot be based upon any precedent. . . . [This practice is prohibited by Talmudic law and] there is no clear permission to allow this."[94]

The role of social, economic, and other factors in modifying or in altering practices required by legal precedent led to their role in establishing new practices, many of which were subsequently translated into law. Only the dialogic view could justify this possibility. Furthermore, the institution of various forms of rabbinic legislation (*takkanot*) also often derived from practices that originated in popular or local customs (especially community *takkanot, takkanot ha-kahal*).[95] Advocates of the dialogic view encouraged and defended these developments as legitimate expressions of social creativity and of historical and socioeconomic influences upon the continuing creation of Jewish law.

HALAKHIC LEGISLATION

Codification aims at making the legal process self-sufficient, autonomous. However, for a legal system to develop throughout the ages, provision for legislation is necessary. In Jewish law, legislation takes the form of *gezerot* and *takkanot*.[96] Such legislation may be perceived as the second area where subjective elements enter into legal decision.

A *gezera* is a restriction added by the sages to safeguard the observance of scriptural law. Such *gezerot* were even considered so important as to override a positive commandment of the Torah. For example, the shofar is not sounded on Rosh Hashanah when it occurs on the Sabbath lest it lead to an infraction of a Sabbath ordinance, despite the fact that blowing the shofar on Rosh Hashanah is established by biblical command.[97]

Because of the difficulties attendant upon annulling past *gezerot*, some medieval halakhists denied themselves the right to make new restrictions of this sort and retroactively restrict the making of *gezerot* to the Talmudic period.[98] One may use this position to defend two suggestions. First, that halakhists today not be concerned with making *gezerot*, that is, with encumbering future generations with additional restrictions. Secondly, if one assumes that the authority to legislate *gezerot* is limited to the Talmudic period, then halakhic decisions of the post-Talmudic period purporting to be *gezerot* would be denied that status. They would remain halakhic options rather than difficult-to-repeal *gezerot*. But what about *gezerot* of the Talmudic period, such as those regulating relationships between Jews and gentiles?

The effective repeal of such *gezerot* by means of the process of legal interpretation and not by simply claiming them "invalid" may be accomplished. The successful medieval attempts to repeal strictures—economic and social—in the area of Jewish-gentile relationships might stand as a model of repeal by means of interpretation. Consciously drawing a distinction between conditions of the rabbinic period and their own age, the medieval scholars redefined "gentiles" to exclude Christians, thereby opening up the possibility for socioeconomic relationships.[99] Hence, through exegetical exercises and by the process of interpretation, social and economic realities can influence the repeal of standing legislation in general and of the *gezerot* of earlier generations in particular. What is suggested is that present and future attempts to repeal standing *gezerot* on the basis of certain social, economic, or moral criteria should be modeled after the manner in which such repeals were effected by medieval scholars, specifically in the area of Jewish-gentile relationships.

The second variety of halakhic legislation relates to *takkanot*. A *takkanah* is a new regulation instituted to cope with a new socioeconomic or historical situation or to improve compliance with existing halakhah. Thus, a *takkanah* may either add new restrictions or remove past restrictions. It may either expand or contract the scope of existing halakhah. The goal of a *takkanah* is stated by the meaning of the term itself—"to set aright." While *gezerot* may be properly said to have ceased with the close of the Talmudic era, most authorities concur that *takkanot* extended from the Talmudic era into and throughout the Middle Ages down to the present. One may distinguish, however, between *takkanot* of the Talmudic era and *takkanot* of subsequent times. A *takkanah* of the Talmudic era in general was universally recognized by all Jewish communities, whereas a *takkanah* of post-Talmudic origin is usually applicable only with regard to a specific constituency.

Probably the best-known post-Talmudic *takkanah* is the one attributed to the late tenth- early eleventh-century rabbinic leader Gershom of Mainz (called Rabbenu Gershom, the Light of the Exile) which banned polygamy among Ashkenazic Jews. It is now generally agreed that monogamy, established as the norm by this *takkanah*, was not an innovation he introduced but an established social practice of European Jewry of his time, which required a basis in legislation. In this case, as well as others, the *takkanah* represents the intrusion of socioeconomic realities into the law. In the case of the ban on polygamy, the custom of the people became the basis for this *takkanah*. In this instance, we have an example of custom serving as the basis for legislation and rabbinic authority ratifying this legislation, which is an example of what was discussed above regarding custom and law. Monogamy became customary. Though rabbinic authority might have stifled custom from becoming law by invoking a veto based upon the idea that monogamy, since it rejects biblical precedent, is *minhag ta'ut* (mistaken custom) or *hukkat ha-goy* (a custom derived from gentile influence)—a certainly accurate claim in this instance—rabbinic authority nevertheless decided to ratify this custom into practice.[100]

Thus a *takkanah* may simply formalize in law that which is already standardized in practice. Rabbinic judgment, albeit a subjective criterion, ultimately determines whether common behavior becomes law. It is suggested that, in its application to specific problems, the *takkanah* be sparingly used. Indeed, even the *takkanah* regarding polygamy could have been avoided and the same aim as that intended by the *takkanah* accomplished by means of standardizing a "monogamy clause" in the *kethubah* (marriage contract) as *genizah* fragments indicate was done in medieval Egypt.[101] One must sparingly use *takkanah* as one must sparingly use the constitutional amendment process in United States law. There is a danger of abuse. There is a danger of social whim becoming standardized through legislation, making enforcement and repeal difficult. The quick pace of changing conditions in contemporary America must be carefully considered before *takkanah* is undertaken in the American Jewish community. One must decide whether the particular social trend is worthy of being translated into law. One must evaluate a potential *takkanah*'s impact upon the rest of the legal system. One must consider how it will be interpreted by members of the lay community. Finally, one ought to be convinced that the social situation occasioning the *takkanah* will be of some considerable duration.

It is suggested that the idea of the post-Talmudic *takkanah* be somewhat reinterpreted along the following lines: whereas post-Talmudic *takkanot* were made for specific geographically cohesive communities,
contemporary *takkanot* may be made for a specific "community" or
constituency not necessarily of the same *geographical* locale but having in
common recognition of an identical source of halakhic authority. Thus, one
might consider members of Conservative synagogues to be members of the
same "community," though not in a geographical sense. *Takkanot* of the
Rabbinical Assembly or of its Law Committee or by its leading halakhic
scholars may be considered a *takkanah* relevant only to the Conservative
Jewish *community*. Secondly, it is suggested that a limit be placed upon
the duration of *takkanot*, for example, seven years. If the *takkanah* takes
root, it will become standardized and need not be reasserted. It will become normative. If the *takkanah* does not take root, it would simply expire.[102] When the halakhist "legislates," when he "makes" a *takkanah*, the
people serve as the final veto power. They decide whether his view will be
accepted into practice. When the people generate "new law," the scholar's
takkanah represents a ratification of "legislation" by the people.[103] In the
former case, the scholar interprets the "written law" to extend the "oral
law." In the second instance, the "oral law" emerges first, retroactively
seeking an anchor in the "written law."[104]

CONCLUSION

One might conclude that the monolithic view, representative of contemporary Orthodox Judaism, is a theologically authentic expression of an historically defensible philosophy of Jewish law.[105] However, as the preceding
discussion demonstrates, the dialogic view, representative of the ideology
of Conservative Judaism, is also a theologically authentic and an historically
defensible philosophy of Jewish law. Though both of these approaches are
theologically authentic and historically defensible, what remains to be determined is which of the two is more conceptually and pragmatically preferable. A number of arguments can be adduced to demonstrate how and
why the dialogic view is the more desirable of the two.

Abraham Isaac Kook compared the Torah to a mirror. While the mirror stays the same, the reflections seen in the mirror constantly change.
Similarly, the text of the Torah remains the same, but how it is perceived
and how it is applied undergo constant change.

According to the dialogic view, the Torah in its supernal essence may
be static and perfect, but as it exists in this world, it takes on characteristics
of this world, such as imperfection and change. The second set of tablets is

all we have; the first set, representing the essential Torah, could not coexist with the terrestrial realm. This second set of tablets, this Torah, is neither perfect nor entirely divine, but is the word of God set down by human hands. In a sense, the monolithic view tries to pretend that the original set of tablets never was shattered, that the Torah in our possession is the supernal, perfect, completely divine word of God, represented by the first set of tablets.

The thrust of historical research conclusively demonstrates that Jewish law is a continually developing, dynamic entity, characterized by constant change, often brought about by changing social, economic, and other factors. These findings accord with the position represented by the dialogic view. The claim of the monolithic view that halakhah is static, autonomous, and monolithic, that it is grounded in a priori truth, that it proceeds oblivious to subjective factors or to socioeconomic conditions and developments cannot be defended, either historically or on the basis of an appeal to halakhic literature itself, as many of the sources noted above clearly demonstrate. Ultimately the monolithic view cannot be verified; it can only be taken on faith. It cannot account for the plurality of halakhic views that have always abounded; nor can it account for the continuing changes in Jewish law occurring even today, even those that are accepted by the Orthodox Jewish community.[106]

In the nineteenth-century, Jewish orthodoxy opposed many alterations then being introduced into Jewish law on the grounds that they were based upon extrahalakhic categories, such as *hukkat ha-goy* (the following of Gentile practice).[107] In this regard, it should be noted that the interpenetration of the Jewish and non-Jewish communities had already stimulated countless changes in Jewish practice in times past, for example, monogamy, which became part and parcel of accepted Jewish practice. Furthermore, for Orthodox Judaism to challenge innovations based on extrahalakhic categories such as *hukkat ha-goy* begs the question. Indeed, the very term "orthodox" is not a Jewish one, and the use of it by Orthodox Judaism could itself be halakhically considered an articulation of *hukkat ha-goy*.[108] That Jewish orthodoxy itself could not function were it to operate consistently within the scope of the monolithic view is evident from many examples that might be presented, but let one example suffice.

Without the acceptance of economic considerations and custom as bases for halakhah, the contemporary rabbinate, including much of the orthodox rabbinate, would not be able to function. The institution of a professional, salaried rabbinate in effect abolishes and supersedes unequivocal, firm precedent to the contrary.[109] Furthermore, the very basis for contemporary halakhic authority, strongly defended by orthodoxy, is rabbinic ordination. However, it is clear historically that the rabbinic ordination of today is not that which was originally instituted in Talmudic times. It is instead based upon a custom with medieval roots. Hence, the very halakhic authority that is used by advocates of the monolithic view—which denies the halakhah-creating prerogative of custom—actually itself derives from custom.[110]

The attempt of the monolithic view to vest halakhic decision in the codes or in the *gedolei ha-dor* cannot be defended. The claim that the authors of the codes and the *gedolei ha-dor* represent objectively true halakhah—devoid of any subjective element—is not conceptually, historically, or psychologically viable. As discussed in this chapter, neither the authors of the codes nor the contemporary *gedolei ha-dor* represent total objectivity. For instance, if the halakhic process is an objective one akin to mathematics, then why does two plus two always equal four, while various halakhists purporting to utilize identical methods and sources conflict with one another?

Neither a code of law nor a *gadol ha-dor* can serve as the final basis for halakhic decision. Careful research into the development of a particular problem in the Jewish legal tradition would have to be undertaken. In the words of Judah Loew of Prague, to adjudicate decisions in Jewish law, not the "signs" (*simanim*) of the codes, but the sources of the totality of halakhic tradition must be consulted.[111] To make decisions in Jewish law, an examination into the development of a specific problem ought to be made. The views on all sides of the question, as it has appeared and reappeared down through the ages, should be identified. Once the plurality of trends on a given subject have been sorted out, these trends are to be examined in relation to the current social mood. If the current social climate and an identifiable trend in the halakhic literature on a given subject agree, despite halakhic norms currently in force, then the past trend may influence a change in current halakhah.

Finally, it would be a mistake to claim, as do many contemporary advocates of the monolithic view within Orthodox Jewry, that the dialogic view—as it has been articulated by the founders of Conservative Judaism—is deviationist or anarchistic. That it is not deviationist, that it is representative of a firmly entrenched position within the history of Jewish theology and law, has been demonstrated in this chapter. That it is not anarchistic is clear from a consideration of a system of checks and balances that is endemic to the philosophy of law represented by the dialogic view. According to this system of checks and balances, the rabbis have the authority to veto specious practices developed by the people. On the other hand, by being unable to abide by decrees of the rabbinic authorities, the people may exercise a veto of their own. In the words of the Talmud, "No decree may be imposed upon the community, unless a majority of the community is able to abide by it."[112]

This interaction between the creativity of the people and the responsibility of the rabbinate allows for innovation and change without anarchy. When the spontaneity of the people embellishes the fabric of halakhah, such creativity is to be encouraged. But when popular practice threatens to alter halakhic essentials, when it promises to change the very nature of halakhah, the rabbinic prerogative of veto should be invoked. As Asher ben Yehiel stated, "one must not alter custom . . . but if a custom is observed in various places, and in observing this custom one commits a sin, one must alter the custom, even if prominent scholars observed it."[113] Furthermore, both in the areas of custom and *takkanah*, certain additional safeguards to protect this system of checks and balances may easily be introduced and implemented.

Before concluding, the exclusion of a consideration of Reform Judaism from the preceding discussion should be explained. To be valid, a theologically authentic and a historically defensible philosophy of Jewish religious law must be drawn from the sources that represent classical Jewish religious thought. Just as Jewish law, to remain authentic, cannot legislate fundamental practices out of existence, Jewish theology cannot arbitrarily dispense with fundamental beliefs. Among the fundamental beliefs of Judaism insofar as Jewish law is concerned, is the assumption that halakhah is binding. By its denial of this claim, Reform Judaism moves itself outside of the boundaries of theologically or historically authentic Judaism.[114] Indeed, it would be difficult, if not impossible, for members of any community to speak meaningfully about a philosophy of law for that community unless the binding quality of that law upon that community is first assumed.

While the monolithic and the dialogic views differ substantially, both are nevertheless defensible within the context of classical Jewish history, theology, and tradition. The same cannot be said of the attitudes toward Jewish law that are representative of Reform Judaism. Historically, one of the distinctions that differentiates among Orthodox, Conservative, and Reform Judaism is the following: Orthodox Judaism holds that both halakhah and the codes are authoritative and binding; Conservative Judaism maintains that while halakhah is binding, the codes are not binding but represent precedents and guides to be used in halakhic decision making; Reform Judaism maintains that neither the codes nor the halakhah are binding.[115]

The monolithic view, which vests halakhic decision making in a central authority, be it a code or a person, requires no system of checks and balances. The dialogic view insists that a system of checks and balances between subjective judgment and objective precedents, between the creative spontaneity of the people and the responsible utilization of authority by the rabbinate, is necessary for dynamic halakhic creativity and for preventing religious anarchy. The dialogic view maintains that "the life of law has not been logic; it has been experience" (Oliver Wendell Holmes). It maintains that law reflects the human condition and must be infused with a human element. However, the dialogic view also realizes that law cannot relinquish its very nature by degenerating into pure subjectivity, by becoming *Gefühlsjurisprudenz* (law by sentiment) as advocates of Reform Judaism seem to suggest.[116]

In the Talmud, there is a case of a scholar who was called "*hakham*," but was not called "rabbi."[117] Discussing this text, the nineteenth-century scholar Joseph Hayyim of Baghdad made this distinction between two forms of halakhic decision making, which relates to the distinction between the monolithic and the dialogic views. In the first form, the halakhist collects all available sources, weighs the pros and cons, and arrives deductively at a rule to be followed. This process, for Joseph Hayyim, exemplified the *hakham* who is not called "rabbi," who is the insufficient halakhist. Such an individual is insufficient as a halakhist because he merely collects and sifts material, thereby arriving at a final ruling; but that ruling is not original, it is that of the authorities on which the *hakham* relies. On the other hand, the complete halakhist, who merits being called "rabbi," collects and sifts past precedents and arrives at a final ruling that brings into play his intellectual skills, individual judgment, and personal creativity as applied to his knowledge of the law.[118]

The monolithic view is admirable in its attempt to formulate a foolproof method for halakhic decision making. Unfortunately, it is an impossible goal to attain. In the final analysis, halakhic decision making, like all legal deliberation, is subject to subjective human judgment and open to human error. For the dialogic view though, it is precisely the opportunity to relate God's word to God's world, the challenge to apply judgment to learning and experience to scholarship, that characterizes the ongoing dialogue that commenced at Mt. Sinai.

🎞 3 🎞

The Nature of Ethics

What is ethics? Not doing in private what one would be
embarassed to do in public.
—YEHIEL BEN YEKUTIEL OF ROME, *Sefer Ma'alot ha-Middot*

WHEN WE ARE PLANNING FOR POSTERITY, we ought to remember
that virtue is not hereditary." Thomas Paine, one of the Founding
Fathers of the United States, made this observation in 1776 in his famous
treatise, *Common Sense*. An identical statement might have been penned
by any one of the authors of any one of the works that comprise classical
Jewish ethical literature.[1] Like Thomas Paine, they knew that moral character is the product of deliberate choice and action and not the result of
genetic roulette.

According to the Talmud, many features of a person's life are determined at the time of conception, but one's moral nature is not among
them. A Talmudic passage observes that there is an angel called "Night"
who oversees the conception of each child. At the moment of conception,
this angel inquires of God about whether the child just conceived will grow
to be weak or strong, poor or rich, and God announces its fate. But, when
the angel asks whether the child will become wicked or virtuous, God remains silent, for only the individual person may determine his or her own
moral character.[2]

In the twelfth century, this view was amplified by Moses Maimonides. "It is impossible for a man to be born endowed by nature from his
very birth with either virtue or vice, just as it is impossible that he should
be born skilled by nature in any particular art."[3] Maimonides insisted that
virtue cannot be acquired by proxy. Each individual is bound "to acquire
virtues that he alone can acquire for himself, as the rabbis . . . say, 'If I am
not for myself, who will be for me?'"[4] Furthermore, the quest for moral

An earlier version of this chapter was published in 1987 as "Occasional Paper No. 4" by
the Dworsky Center for Jewish Studies of the University of Minnesota.

virtue has not been viewed as a terminal course of study and action but as
an endeavor that lasts as long as life endures. Israel Salanter, founder of the
nineteenth-century Musar movement, expressed this view by comparing
the quest for moral virtue to the flight of a bird. Once a bird stops exerting
effort to fly, once a bird stops flapping its wings, it falls. Similarly, Salanter
observed, moral effort requires constant exertion, study, reflection, and
practice.[5]

Maimonides's analogy of the acquisition of moral virtue to the practice of an art is characteristic of the perspective of Jewish ethical literature.
Each individual's life is viewed as a work of art and each person is considered an artist who must determine the nature of that work of art, which is
his or her own life. For Jewish tradition, life is the ultimate art form and
the cultivation of moral virtue is a primary means by which one creates this
art form.

Little Jewish genius was invested throughout the ages in the creation
of great works of art. However, much Jewish genius and effort has been
expended in the attempt to create lives that were works of art. Rather than
concentrate on the creation of *things* of beauty, Jewish tradition focuses on
the creation of *people* of beauty. The particular art form cultivated by the
Jews has not been architecture, painting, or sculpture, but human existence.[6] The Jewish people produced no edifices to rival Notre-Dame, no
paintings like those of Michelangelo or of Raphael. The artistic masterpieces of the Jewish people do not hang in any museum. They appear in no
tourist's guidebook. The great artworks that emerge from Jewish history
are the lives and the teachings of the greatest people it has engendered.
The standard of greatness employed by Jewish tradition to identify these
individuals has not been physical prowess, physical appearance, commercial success, or literary prolificacy. Instead, Jewish tradition evaluates these
individuals by the beauty of the life each created.

An artist viewing a great painting in a museum may stand in awe,
gazing at its beauty. Similarly, as Solomon Schechter observed, "the grand
saintly souls are lovely to look at, just as a great piece of art is."[7] What one
perceives may itself be a source of inspiration. However, the artist who
aspires to create a masterpiece of his or her own, will not rest content with
a dazzled gaze at a masterpiece of the past. Such an artist will proceed to
study the techniques that the master artist applied in the composition of
the work being viewed. The artist might then analyze the painting even
more closely, studying the use of color and shade, the use of line and
shape. Still not content, the artist might compare the work under consideration to other works of the same master artist or of the same historical
period or to other masterpieces from other times and from other places. All
of this study and all of this analysis is undertaken by the aspiring artist with
the hope and with the intention of being able to gain some insight and

some knowledge that he or she may be able to incorporate into his or her own artistic work. The novice artist who desires to create a masterpiece will carefully study the masterpieces of past generations to see what can be learned from them. But, study alone will not suffice. Such study must be supplemented with constant practice. For the beginning artist, talent, skill, study, practice, and persistence are not sufficient in and of themselves. Only in concert, together, can they converge to provide the potential conditions for the emergence of a new, great work of art. Similarly, standing awestruck by the spiritual, intellectual, and moral achievements of the great personalities of the past is not enough for one who wants to shape his or her own life as a work of art. Like the novice artist, such an individual must proceed to study the masterpieces produced in the past to distill from them insight and information that may be incorporated into the creation of one's own work of art, which, in this case, is one's own self. And, as in the case of the artist, the individual concerned with cultivating the art of living cannot be satisfied with a terminal course of study. Rather, he or she must be engaged in continuous study and in perpetual practice of the spiritual and moral virtues.

The classics that comprise Jewish ethical literature are masterpieces that can be perused for inspiration and studied for information by those concerned with the art form of living. The masters who composed these works were maestros in the art of life. Blending personal quests with past wisdom, combining individual experience with collected knowledge, they addressed various aspects of ethical concern. Underlying their works is the fundamental ethical question: How can I best live the life entrusted into my care?[8]

For Jewish ethics, life is too precious and human existence is too precarious not to be treated with the utmost seriousness. Retaining a sense of moral balance is difficult. Virtue is fragile. With each choice, with each action, one walks a tightrope strung over an abyss. Commenting on the verse, "Let your garments be always white; let not oil be lacking on your head" (Eccles. 9:8), a Hasidic master said, "A person should view himself as being dressed in white silken garments with a pitcher of oil balanced on his head, walking a tightrope. A single wrong small step, and he becomes soiled; a single irretrievable slip and he falls into the abyss below."[9]

In its most general sense, ethics concerns the problem of how to live. The works that comprise Jewish ethical literature may be considered "self-help manuals" in the art of living. More specifically, ethics deals with the problem of what kind of behavior is right and what kind of behavior is wrong. What are the right ways of treating ourselves and others? What are the wrong ways of treating ourselves and others? Put another way, the central ethical concern is *how* ought we behave and *how* ought we not behave? However, underlying this basic ethical concern is an even more fundamental problem: *Why* should one strive to be moral? *Why* ought we treat ourselves and others in one manner rather than in another manner? *Why* be concerned with how we treat others?[10]

The masters and the masterpieces of Jewish ethical literature confront such questions as these. The two-issue discussion that follows focuses within more-narrow parameters than the broad boundaries circumscribed by the totality of Jewish ethical tradition and its responses to these questions. The first issue relates to Jewish ethics as a *form* of ethics, specifically as a particular form of theological ethics. Inevitably, some of the responses of Jewish ethical tradition to the questions just posed inform that presentation and analysis. The second issue relates to perspectives *within* Jewish ethics. Like Judaism itself, Jewish ethics is not monolithic; Jewish ethics embraces a variety of perspectives on the nature and goals of the ethical enterprise.

WHAT KIND OF ETHICS IS JEWISH ETHICS?

Jewish ethics is a form of religious or theological ethics. As such, it is to be distinguished from secular ethics. Theological ethics rests upon specific theological assumptions. One such assumption is that ethical guidance ultimately derives from a divine source and is communicated to us in acts of revelation. In other words, theological ethics, in general, and Jewish ethics, in particular, presuppose that morality ultimately has its origins in a source other than ourselves. Secular ethics maintains, on the other hand, that ethics is derived from and is justified by autonomous human origins, such as human reason, human emotion, human intuition, and social mores. Secular ethics rejects the proposition that any guidance from beyond the human or natural realm is either possible or necessary.

Secular ethics denies the validity or the necessity of ethical teachings rooted in revelation, but Jewish ethics generally does not so facilely discount the possibility of justifying ethical behavior on the basis of humanistic criteria. While most of Jewish ethical literature assumes that moral guidance is rooted in an act of divine revelation, it also maintains that moral principles conveyed by revelation may be understood, interpreted, embellished, and applied by utilizing God-given abilities, such as intellect, intuition, experience, and emotion. Furthermore, in the Middle Ages, and possibly even before, Jewish scholars began to assert that moral teachings assumed to be rooted in acts of revelation may also be justified and validated on other grounds, such as rationality. For example, the Ten Commandments, which teach us not to murder, may derive from God's revelation at Mt. Sinai, but the moral prohibition against murder may be also justified on rationalistic or intuitionist grounds. Thus, Jewish ethics presupposes an objective basis for moral behavior by rooting morality in revelation. However, much of Jewish ethical literature also accepts subjective human criteria (rationality, intuition, and emotion) as proper instruments for clarifying and analyzing moral teachings that derive from revelation and tradition.

For many Jewish ethicists and legalists, God has the initial word, but human beings have the last word. Though fallible by nature, their task is to apply divine wisdom—using human intelligence and intuition—to particular human situations. Objective divine revelation and subjective human speculation coalesce to produce guidelines for correct moral behavior. For example, Aryeh Leib Heller put it this way: "The Torah was not given to the angels. It was given to human beings who possess intelligence. He gave us the Torah in conformity with the human mind to decide, even though it may not be the [objective] truth, only that it be true according to the conclusions of the human mind. . . . 'Let truth emerge from the earth' [Psalm 85:12], that is, the truth as the sages decide using human intelligence."[11]

Where Jewish ethics differs from secular ethics is in Jewish ethics' resistance to the claim that ethics can be based upon subjective human criteria *alone*. For most of classical Jewish ethics, humanistic criteria may help to clarify and to reaffirm moral principles conveyed by means of revelation; however, subjective human criteria in the final analysis are unable to provide an adequate foundation upon which moral behavior can be firmly based.[12]

Jewish tradition apparently found the human condition too precarious, human thought and emotion too unreliable, to leave the task of moral guidance to the vicissitudes of the human mind and heart alone. Jewish ethics grants us a vote but not a veto regarding moral principles that derive from revelation and tradition. An examination of a number of the most common varieties of secular ethics may demonstrate why this is so.

What divides various advocates of modern secular ethics is the identity of the criterion for determining what is right and what is wrong. For example, some modern secular philosophers maintain that to act morally is to act rationally.[13] Indeed, for hundreds of years, Western philosophers have claimed a rationalistic basis for moral action. Such a view is in turn predicated on a perception of human beings as rational animals. The difficulty with this view is that there are many interpretations about what rationality might be. An act that may seem rational and hence moral to one person might appear nonrational or irrational to another. Furthermore, the discoveries of modern psychology have offered strong refutation of the Aristotelian portrait of the human being as an essentially rational being. Irrationality has been revealed to be as much a part of human nature as rationality. Finally, rationalistic ethics is always in danger of becoming rationalizing ethics. It may be used to argue that it is never rational to put one's own interest aside for the sake of helping another person. It can be employed to rationalize and hence justify the most heinous of deeds.

Another example of secular ethics is ethics that derives from a sociological approach to morality. In this view, the society in which one lives— the social mores or the state—determines what is right and what is wrong. Morality is decided by the group of which one is a part. The danger of this approach is that, just as an individual may be morally corrupt, so may a group or a nation be morally mistaken. In Nazi Germany, for example, "right" was defined as that which "is useful to the German people." But what is deemed right by the group or by the state may still be wrong. What is defined as useful or beneficial to the group may not be morally justifiable.

Other varieties of secular ethics ground morality in such sources as intuition, individual conscience, or personal sentiment.[14] The approach that locates the basis for morality in personal sentiment is known as the "emotive theory of ethics."[15] From this perspective, one's emotions and one's feelings determine what is good or bad. Morality, according to this theory, would be entirely subjective and would depend upon the varying feelings and emotions of the individual person. Some advocates of emotive theory maintain that, while moral behavior is determined by our likes and our dislikes, such attitudes may be rationally justified. We may be able to explain rationally why we like one thing and dislike another. A problem with the emotive theory of ethics is that human emotions are too volatile and uncertain to provide an adequate basis for establishing a viable ethic. If emotions alone could determine what is right or wrong, a rapist or a murderer might argue that he or she is performing good deeds. To seek a rational basis for our emotions may be an impossible task. However, even if it were possible, one would be left with rationalistic ethics, with all the difficulties that implies.

The intuitionist view of ethics holds that every normal adult person intuits that which is morally good and that which is morally evil. For example, it maintains that "good" cannot be defined but it can be known intuitively. We cannot define "yellow," but we know what yellow is.[16] Similarly, we cannot define that which is morally good, but we can nevertheless recognize it when we see it. One may question the assumption of the intuitionist stance, which claims that we have a fundamental intuition of what is right and what is wrong. Furthermore, the intuitionist position does not adequately address the possibility of one person's intuition contradicting that of another person. In such a case, whose intuition would be morally correct? Nor does the intuitionist posture adequately deal with the possibility that what we identify as moral intuition may simply be a product of cultural conditioning. Finally, can one be trained to exclude self-interest, group pressure, and other extraneous factors in the attempt to intuit honestly that which is good and that which is not good? Intuitionist ethics, emotive ethics, and others mentioned are but a few of the major varieties of modern secular ethics.

By providing both a subjective and an objective basis (revelation and tradition) for ethics, Jewish ethics maintains a kind of system of checks and balances upon the approaches characteristic of secular ethics and the problems they entail. Thus, Jewish ethical literature offers a more complete, more comprehensive, more rounded view of ethical behavior than can be provided by secular ethics alone. While most of secular ethics too easily dismisses the insights and the teachings of theological ethics out of hand, rejecting revelation and religious tradition as invalid foundations upon which to predicate moral behavior, much of Jewish ethical literature encourages the exercise of the individual intellect, intuition, and insight and the incorporation of sources of wisdom imparted from other traditions into the process of moral decision.

Most of the classics of Jewish ethical literature are inclusionary rather than exclusionary. While rooting morality in revelatory acts, many of the authors of classical Jewish ethical literature sought to deepen further, to expand, and to edify their moral quests by looking beyond revelation and tradition. The net result, in many cases, was the expansion and the enrichment of the tradition itself once these imparted insights became incorporated by and assimilated into it.

The basic presuppositions of Jewish ethics are theological. The leitmotivs and the embellishments upon those premises may be drawn from other sources. To understand the nature of Jewish ethics, it is necessary to identify at least some of the theological premises upon which it is based. Among these premises are the assumptions that God exists, that He reveals His will to us in acts of revelation, that He conveys guidance regarding which acts are morally right and which are morally wrong. Also among these assumptions is the claim that human beings are created in the "image of God," and that *because* human beings are in the divine image, they ought to be treated in a certain manner. Consequently, for Jewish ethics, one of the answers to the question, Why should one treat oneself and other human beings in a certain manner, is because human beings are created in God's image. The claim that human beings are created in God's image offers an objective standard for moral behavior.

Rationalistic ethics may prohibit murder because it is not rational for one person to murder another. Emotive ethics may consider murder morally wrong because the emotions dictate that murder is morally wrong. Intuitionist ethics may claim that all normal people intuit that murder is a morally heinous act. But a murderer may be able to justify the action upon rational, emotive, or intuitive grounds. These varieties of secular ethics can provide no objective foundation, no conceptual guarantee, no absolute justification for considering murder morally wrong. By asserting the claim that the human being is created in God's image, Jewish ethics establishes an objective justification, an absolute standard for considering murder morally reprehensible. For Jewish ethics, murder is morally wrong because it contravenes God's revealed will regarding how we ought and ought not behave. For Jewish ethics, *because* the human being is created in God's image, murdering a human being is ipso facto morally wrong. In a rabbinic midrash, one encounters this claim that murder is morally wrong simply because the human being is created in God's image.

A midrash observes that the Ten Commandments were given on two tablets of five commandments each, and that each commandment on each tablet supplements the corresponding commandment on the other tablet. Hence, the first commandment would supplement the sixth, the second would supplement the seventh, and so forth. The first commandment on the first tablet reads, "I am the Lord your God." The first commandment on the second tablet—the sixth commandment—reads, "You shall not murder." The text reads:

> Scripture [thereby] tells us that whosoever spills blood, Scripture imputes it to him as if he has diminished the image of the King [God]. The matter is comparable to a king of flesh and blood who entered a city and erected icons and images and stamped coins [with his image upon them]. After a time, they pushed down the icons, smashed the images and destroyed the coins, and thereby diminished the image of the king. Therefore, whoever spills blood, Scripture imputes it to him as if he had diminished the image of the king, as it is written, "whosoever sheds human blood . . . for in the image of God He made man" [Gen. 9:6].[17]

From this text one can elicit four theological assumptions endemic to Jewish ethics: (1) God exists; (2) the human being is created in God's image; (3) because the human being is created in God's image, certain actions against another person—in this case, murder—are morally wrong; (4) because human beings are created in the image of God, an immoral act against another person is an affront to God, an act against both God's will and His person.

The boundaries of these assumptions were expanded by the Jewish mystics of the sixteenth and seventeenth centuries. These mystics maintained that not only is the human person created in the image of God but that within each person there is an element of divinity, a part of God (*helek elohah mi-ma'al*), a spark of the divine.[18] Therefore, one ought to treat other human beings in a certain manner, not simply because each person is in the divine image, but because God is a part of each person. In this view, how we relate to other persons does not merely *reflect* how we relate to God; how we relate to other persons *is* how we relate to God. Furthermore, Jewish mystical thought maintains that, since all human souls originally stem from Adam's soul, all souls are really part of the same entity. No real distinction can be made between one's neighbor and one's own self. In this view, one must love one's neighbor as oneself *because* one's neighbor *is* oneself. One's relationship to oneself and to others is identical rather than distinct.[19] From this posture, the pervasive secular view, which vests ethical behavior in enlightened rational self-interest, becomes meaningless.

From what has been stated, it should be apparent that Jewish ethics cannot be divorced from Jewish theology. Our attitudes toward and relationships with other humans are inextricably linked to our belief in and relationship with the divine. An example of this is the well-known biblical verse, "You shall love your neighbor as yourself, I am the Lord" (Lev. 19:18). Rabbinic literature interprets this verse, "You shall love your neighbor as yourself *because* I am the Lord, because I have created him [the human being]."[20]

Because Judaism interweaves the relationship between human beings and God, and because Jewish ethics rests upon theological assumptions, it should not be surprising that the relationship between God and humans is considered a primary concern of Jewish ethical literature. Beginning in the sixteenth century, the purview of Jewish ethics is defined as extending to three central areas of concern: the relationship of human beings to God, the relationships of human beings to one another, and the relationship of each individual human being to his or her own self. This view emerges in commentaries to a specific Talmudic text, wherein one reads, "Rabbi Judah said: He who wishes to be pious must fulfill the laws of *Seder Nezikin* [one of six sections of the Mishnah; it deals with tort law]. But Raba said: [He who wishes to be pious must fulfill] the matters [dealt with in tractate] *Avot*. Still others said: [He who wishes to be pious must fulfill] matters [dealt with in tractate] *Berakhot* [which deals with laws of blessings]."[21] Commenting on this text, Samuel Edels (Maharshah), a Polish talmudist of the late sixteenth and early seventeenth centuries, wrote:

> A person can perform three kinds of pious deeds. These are: good [deeds] to Heaven, and good [deeds] to others, and good [deeds] to oneself. As Rabbi Judah said: He who wishes to be pious must fulfill the laws of *Nezikin,* for then one will be able to perform one's deeds so that one will be good to others. And Raba said to fulfill the matters in *Avot,* for then one will be able to perfect one's deeds so that one will be good to oneself in [performing] the moral virtues. Still others said: Fulfill the matters in *Berakhot,* for then one will be able to perfect oneself so that one will be good to Heaven. Each one of these views reflects a single one of these three varieties of good deeds that one can perform.

Edels's commentary to this Talmudic passage was anticipated by the sixteenth-century Jewish mystic Judah Loew of Prague.[22] In his commentary to the Talmud, Loew observed,

> The explanation of this [text] is that human perfection has three independent aspects. A person must be complete within oneself, complete within one's relationship with other people, and one must be complete within one's relationship to one's Creator, i.e., in matters that relate to one's Creator. These three aspects of completion [perfection] include everything. This matter is explained further in "Moses received."

Loew's reference to his further elucidation of this matter in "Moses received" refers to his commentary on the text "Moses received" found in the *Ethics of the Fathers,* in which he wrote,

> One must achieve the good which is one's purpose, thereby justifying one's existence, and when one's existence has been justified, the whole universe has been justified, since all hinges on man. . . . Therefore, a person should endeavor to cultivate good qualities. And what makes a person "good" so that one might say of him: What a fine creature he is? The first requirement is that one must be good in relation to one's own self. . . . The second category of good is that one be good toward the Lord who created man to serve Him and to do His will. The third category is that one be good to others. For a person does not exist by himself. He exists in fellowship with other people. . . . A person is not complete until he is completely pious vis-à-vis these three varieties of [human] perfection: with his Creator, with other people, and with his own self as well. Then he is completely perfect.[23]

Thus, both Edels and Loew divided the moral virtues into three kinds: personal virtues, religious virtues, and social virtues. They portrayed three aspects of moral behavior: the individual's relation to God, the individual's relation to himself or herself, and the individual's relation to others.

In contrast to most classical Western philosophical ethics, and in contrast to most modern secular ethics, Judaism always has considered the relationship between the individual and God to be an essential aspect of ethics. Since ethics deals with human behavior, it must treat the *human* relationship with God. Since Jewish ethics is grounded in a view of the human person as a being created in the divine image, it must treat the relationship of the individual person to the divine source of that image.

Though all of Jewish ethical literature addresses the fundamental questions of how ought one to live, why one ought to live in a certain way, how to create an artful life, how to relate to God, how to relate to oneself, and how to relate to others, the responses offered to these questions varied

from author to author, from land to land, from age to age. Different perspectives—philosophical, mystical, pietistic—represented distinctly different approaches to identical questions. Employment of a variety of literary
styles—biblical exegesis, ethical wills, philosophical treatises, poetry, and
so on—offered stylistic variety in the effort to treat these fundamental
problems. Like Judaism itself, Jewish ethics is not monolithic. Like Judaism itself, Jewish ethics has not been static. Throughout the ages, as Jewish
ethical literature grew and developed, Jewish ethical insight broadened
and deepened. New perspectives were introduced. Contemporary problems meshed with earlier teachings to compose a complex tapestry of moral
insight and ethical elucidation.

PERSPECTIVES WITHIN JEWISH ETHICS

Of the many and varied perspectives that one encounters within the history
and development of Jewish ethical literature and speculation, one may
identify two major approaches: the theocentric and the anthropocentric.
For advocates of the theocentric view, the exclusive purpose of life is service of God, and the goal of life is communion with God. Moral virtues are
perceived as bridges between the human and the divine. By cultivating
and enacting the moral virtues, one serves God's ends, and as a result, one
is brought closer to the divine. In this approach, one does not aspire to
self-fulfillment but to self-abandonment to the will of God. The goal is not
actualization of the self but actualization of the relationship of the self to
God. One practices moral virtue not with the intention of realizing the self
but with the intention only of serving God, of adoring God, and of moving
closer to His presence. In this view, ethics is a means to communion with
God and not an end in itself.

The anthropocentric approach teaches that the purpose of life is individual fulfillment, the perfection of the individual self. Cultivation of the
moral virtues, in this view, is the necessary tool for self-actualization and
self-perfection. One performs virtuous deeds with the primary intention of
improving the self, of propelling the self from a state of incompleteness
toward a goal of self-realization.

Jewish ethical literature also includes a combination of these two approaches. Thus, one may identify a third perspective—the "integrated" approach—which combines features of the theocentric and of the anthropocentric perspectives. In this view, through the cultivation of the moral
virtues, one moves toward the perfection of the individual self; and by so
doing, one becomes a candidate for the final realization of self, which is
attained in communion with God.

An example of the theocentric approach may be found in *The Paths of
the Upright,* one of the most popular works of Jewish ethical literature.
This treatise was composed by the eighteenth-century Italian mystic, poet,
and playwright Moses Hayyim Luzzatto (Ramhal). An example of the anthropocentric approach may be found in the ethical writings of the eleventh-century poet and philosopher Solomon ibn Gabirol. An example of
the combined or "integrated" approach may be found in the ethical writings
of Moses Maimonides.

Before reviewing exemplary representatives of these three perspectives, a number of claims should be stated. First, Jewish ethics is multifaceted and not monolithic. Second, the three examples offered in this
chapter are only examples. Many other Jewish thinkers have presented
similar views, and reference is made to some of them. Third, it would be a
mistake, conceptually and historically, to encounter Jewish ethical literature (or Judaism) with preconceived notions regarding its nature or its
teachings or both. For instance, a popular current understanding of Judaism and of Jewish ethics portrays Judaism and Jewish ethics as universalistic, this-worldly, rationalistic, humanistic, and antiascetic. While one does
encounter these attitudes in Jewish ethical literature, a candid analysis of
Jewish ethics also reveals powerful endemic particularistic, theocentric,
mystical, ascetic, otherworldly views. It would be historically and conceptually dishonest to maintain that this second set of characteristics is peripheral to Judaism or that these characteristics can be explained away as the
products of external influence or that they were only held by individuals at
the fringes of normative Jewish teachings. As Jewish ethical literature unequivocally testifies, these trends are part and parcel of Judaism and of
Jewish ethics. They are at least as normative as other features. The individuals and movements within the history of Judaism who advocate them are
among the most prominent spokespersons for Judaism throughout the ages.
Though some of these views may not be palatable to people today, they
nevertheless are a significant feature of classical Judaism and of classical
Jewish ethics. To survey Jewish ethical literature without reference to
these concepts would be historically inaccurate and conceptually fraudu-
lent.

As already noted, one major approach to Jewish ethics is anthropocentric. In this view, the essential purpose and goal of ethics is human self-
improvement and self-actualization through the inculcation and practice of
moral virtue. While the theocentric approach is often found in the writings
of Jewish pietists and mystics, the anthropocentric posture is common
among Jewish philosophers and rationalists.

Many medieval Jewish philosophers earned their livings practicing
medicine. It is therefore not surprising to find that they drew an analogy between medicine and morality. In this view, morality is a matter of health—

spiritual health. Morality tries to ensure the well-being of the soul just as medicine tries to ensure physical well-being; the goal of ethics is to implant spiritual health into the individual.[24]

Medicine aims at physical health. Morality aspires to spiritual health. Since body and soul are interrelated, how one cares for one's body inevitably affects one's moral behavior. Conversely, how one behaves morally affects one's physical health. Physical excesses in eating or drinking, for example, might injure the body, preventing the individual from practicing the moral virtues. Excessive pride, acquisitiveness, or anger are antithetical to moral virtue and may adversely affect physical health. Both in his philosophical and in his medical writings, Maimonides made observations such as these. For Maimonides, ethics was medicine for the soul. Medicine is to the body what morality is to the soul. Just as the physician must know how the body functions in order to cure it, so must one know one's own soul in order to remedy its maladies. In Maimonides's words:

> The improvement of the moral qualities is brought about by the healing of the soul and its activities. Therefore, just as the physician, who endeavors to cure the human body, must have a perfect knowledge of it in its entirety and in its individual parts, just as he must know what causes sickness so that it may be avoided, and must also be acquainted with the means by which a patient may be cured, so likewise he who tries to cure the soul, wishing to improve the moral qualities, must have a knowledge of the soul in its totality and in its parts, must know how to prevent it from becoming diseased and how to maintain its health.

The anonymous ethical treatise *Sefer ha-Yashar* (*Book of the Righteous*) also draws an analogy between bodily health and medicine and spiritual health and ethics. According to this treatise, the soul, like the body, has visible maladies as well as inner sicknesses. Moral visible sicknesses include sexual immorality, slanderous speech, murder, theft, and others. Inner sicknesses include jealousy, anger, hatred, and so forth. For true moral health, both varieties of illness must be cured. For example, on the matter of anger, the *Book of the Righteous* counsels, "One should not grow angry when one loses a desirable object or if his business matters go awry. If a person conducts himself always in this way, his anger will grow less, and this is a healing for the soul."[25]

In his ethical treatise, *The Improvement of the Moral Qualities*, Solomon ibn Gabirol similarly observed that "just as a scab is a disease of the body, so is anger (or wrath) a disease of the soul." According to ibn Gabirol, just as a physician attempts to engender health and eliminate disease by restoring a harmonious balance among the patient's bodily humors, so does the acquisition of moral virtue require that one's emotions be in a "well-balanced" state. According to him, the inculcation of moral virtue is like the ingestion of properly prescribed medicine for one's ailments.[26]

Morality, in this view, begins with self-understanding. Just as a knowledge of how the body works leads to the wisdom of how to care for it, so do knowledge of the moral virtues of the soul and awareness of the nature of the diseases that might afflict it aid in helping to secure health for the soul.

Ibn Gabirol located the source for the moral virtues in the five senses: sight, hearing, touch, smell, and taste. According to ibn Gabirol, the qualities of the soul are made evident through the five senses. The senses may be developed to control the particular moral virtues that are associated with each of them. For example, he identified the virtues of pride and meekness with the sense of sight. One sees creation in all its greatness and grandeur. From this sight, one is led to the inevitable perception of the insignificance of the individual self when set against the backdrop of the enormity of the world. Such a perception encourages meekness and dispels pride, for pride is the overestimation of the self and its attainments.

Ibn Gabirol's ethical views were essentially secular, humanistic, rationalistic, and universalistic (i.e., they were and are meant for every person, not exclusively for Jews). He articulated a blatantly anthropocentric posture with regard to ethical behavior. His perspective may be contrasted with those who present a theocentric ethical stance.

A basic principle of the Jewish mystical tradition is that life is theocentric, that the purpose of human existence is to fulfill a divine need, to theurgically affect the "inner life" of God. Human fulfillment may be a byproduct of satisfying divinely ordained requirements, but the primary referent of human behavior, in this view, must be God. For the Jewish mystics, a dominant view held that havoc is caused in the upper worlds—the world of the divine (the *sefirot*)—by human sin. God, as it were, is directly affected by human deeds. Sin exacerbates fragmentation and disharmony in God's realm as well as in our own. Virtuous deeds act to repair this fragmentation, to dissolve this disharmony. Therefore, each human deed can accelerate the repair of the world and the unification of the disunified sparks of divinity that inhabit both the upper and lower worlds, or each human action can foster additional disintegration of the divine harmony and unity that existed before creation and that would again prevail in the time of messianic redemption.[27] As the Ba'al Shem Tov put it, "A person should act as if he had a ladder attached to the top of his head, knowing that every move he makes affects that which is above him."[28]

Moses Hayyim Luzzatto was a preeminent Jewish mystic. In his writings, one encounters the theocentric view of life. While advocates of the anthropocentric posture perceived ethics as a means of improving the quality of human life in this world, advocates of the theocentric posture, including Luzzatto, viewed the moral virtues as a means of improving one's relationship with God. In Luzzatto's view, human perfection is not an exercise in self-realization; "true [human] perfection lies only in communion with God. . . . All of man's strivings should be directed toward the Creator, blessed be He. A man should have no other purpose in whatever he does, be it great or small, than to draw nigh to God and to break down all separating walls . . . between himself and his Master, so that he may be drawn to God as iron to a magnet."[29]

The theocentric posture is oriented toward God and the world to come. "The purpose for which man was created," Luzzatto claimed, "is not realized in this world, but in the World to Come. Man's existence in this world is a preparation for his existence in the next world, which is his goal."[30]

While Luzzatto's views are otherworldly, they are not as blatantly ascetic as are those of other advocates of the theocentric posture. In the literature of the *Hasidei Ashkenaz*, the Jewish pietists of medieval Germany, one finds a theocentric position that is both otherworldly and extremely ascetic in orientation.

For the *Hasidei Ashkenaz*, as for Luzzatto, the aim of life was to do the will of God as a means toward ultimate communion with God in the world to come. For the *Hasidei Ashkenaz*, the norm—rather than the goal—should be selfless love of God. Such love can be expressed by doing God's will. While the *Hasidei Ashkenaz* would have agreed with Luzzatto that "only through works, that is through observance of the commandments, can one enter into communion with God," they also believed that God's will extends beyond the commandments. Piety demanded doing more than the law required; it demanded fulfilling God's implicit as well as His explicit will. Eleazar Rokeah, one of the leaders of the *Hasidei Ashkenaz*, expressed these ideas as follows:

> Each person who has the wisdom of God in his heart joyously considers the desire of fulfilling the will of his Creator and of performing His commandments with all his heart. One who loves God is not concerned with the pleasure of this world, and is not desirous of leisure enjoyment with his wife and children. Everything [mundane] is unimportant to him, and nothing matters except performing the will of his Creator, leading others to virtue, sanctifying oneself out of love for Him.[31]

Gershom Scholem characterized the teachings of the *Hasidei Ashkenaz* as "mystical moralism."[32] Virtue for them consisted not merely in following the will of the creator but in resisting the temptation to violate it. Here one finds a common view in Jewish ethical literature—virtue requires the suppression of natural inclinations. The road to virtue is replete with roadblocks and detours. To achieve virtue, these temptations must be overcome. Life is a trial, and each of us is a perpetual defendant.

In the history of Jewish ethics, one encounters two views on the role of our natural inclinations in the pursuit of moral virtue. One view maintains that virtue is natural, that virtue consists of the development and in the refinement of our natural inclinations. A second view argues that to achieve virtue, temptations, trials, and roadblocks to virtue must be overcome, that natural human inclinations need to be conquered and suppressed. Like the eleventh-century Spanish thinker Bahya ibn Pakuda, the *Hasidei Ashkenaz* advocated this second position. Consequently, both Bahya ibn Pakuda and the *Hasidei Ashkenaz* advocated ascetic practices as paths to virtue. For instance, the central work of the *Hasidei Ashkenaz, Sefer Hasidim*, advises that "it is a religious duty for the righteous to fast and inflict pain on themselves on account of possible [divine] retribution incurred by the sins of the wicked."[33] Because this life and this world were viewed as transitory and the next world was viewed as permanent, the *Hasidei Ashkenaz* did not retreat from the possibility that extreme asceticism could bring about death. Their attitude: better death through repentance than life with unrepentant sin. In a responsum by Judah the Pious, author of *Sefer Hasidim*, Judah noted that, if a person inflicts a penance upon himself, such as standing naked in a place infested with bees and "he dies from his suffering, well and good; if he recovers and sins no more, it is also good."[34] Thus, for these pietists, enjoyment of this world was bad because it robbed one of reward in the hereafter. Their attitude was utterly theocentric, blatantly otherworldly, strongly proascetic, and emphatically parochial.

Moses Maimonides's ethical philosophy represents the integrated approach that combines features of the anthropocentric and the theocentric views. For Maimonides, ethics consisted of the inculcation and the cultivation of the moral virtues. However, for Maimonides, moral perfection was but a prelude to the purpose of human existence—communion with God.

In his philosophical magnum opus, *The Guide of the Perplexed*, Maimonides enumerated four stages of human perfection: perfection of possessions, perfection of the body, moral perfection, and intellectual perfection.[35] Following Aristotle, Maimonides maintained that economic security—perfection of possessions—is a necessary prerequisite for attaining the higher degrees of human perfection. According to this view, one cannot expect a person without adequate food, clothing, shelter, and financial security to be preoccupied with higher aspirations. Regarding perfection of possessions, Maimonides observed, "the main design in its acquisition should be to expend it for noble purposes and to expend it for the maintenance of the body and the preservation of life so that its owner may obtain a knowledge of God, insofar as that is vouchsafed unto man."[36]

The second rung on the ladder of human perfection, according to Maimonides, is perfection of the body. Because perfection of the body is a prelude to the higher perfections and to communion with God, Maimonides described the practice of medicine as a preeminently religious activity.[37]

Maimonides described the body as a means toward, and as a tool for, achieving higher goals.[38] However, he also considered the inclinations of the body as potential threats to the moral health of the soul. Maimonides discouraged extreme asceticism because it would weaken the body and thus render it incapable of aspiring to higher aims.[39] Nevertheless, he admonished against indulging the body's inclination toward the passions, particularly toward its passions for food and sex.

Maimonides cautioned proper diet as a means of combating illness and insuring health. In his legal code, the *Mishneh Torah*, Maimonides said, "overeating is like a deadly poison to any constitution and is the principal cause of all disease."[40] Similarly, he required the restriction of sexual activity as a means of achieving bodily perfection. Maimonides's views on sexuality were rather proascetic. In the *Guide*, Maimonides wrote, "One of the intentions of the Torah is purity and sanctification. I mean by this renouncing and avoiding sexual intercourse and causing it to be as infrequent as possible. Consequently, He states clearly that sanctity consists in renouncing sexual intercourse."[41]

Perfection of the body is a necessary prerequisite for moral and intellectual perfection. Maimonides maintained that "the real duty of man is, that in adopting whatever measures he may for his well-being and the preservation of his existence in good health, he should do so with the object of maintaining a perfect condition of the instruments of the soul, which are the limbs of the body, so that his soul may be unhampered, and he may busy himself in acquiring moral and intellectual virtues."[42]

Bodily perfection is a means to an end rather than an end in itself, according to Maimonides. In his legal code, Maimonides wrote, "a man should aim to maintain physical health and vigor so that his soul may be upright, in a condition to know God."[43] Before one can "know God," however, one must first ascend from bodily perfection to the third level of human perfection—moral perfection. Like ibn Gabirol, Maimonides perceived both a healthy body and a healthy soul as a "well-balanced" one. Like Aristotle, Maimonides identified virtue as the mean between extremes. When one's body is infirm, one consults a physician. When one's soul is infirm, when one is morally "unbalanced," one should consult a moral guide, a physician for the soul. Maimonides's legal code states, "What is the corrective for those who are sick in soul? They should go to the wise who are physicians of the soul and they will heal their maladies by instructing them in the dispositions that they should acquire until they are restored to the correct path."[44] As physical health includes the removal of sickness and the infusion of health, so does spiritual health require the removal of vice and the addition of moral virtue. In Maimonides's view, as for Luzzatto and many others, one path to moral virtue is the elimination of bad habits that frustrate virtuous action. Bad habits tend to eliminate volition, which is necessary for the practice of virtue.[45] As Luzzatto observed, "He who has become a slave to habit is no longer his own master, and cannot act differently, even if he should want to do so. His will is held in bondage by certain habits which have become second nature to him."[46]

Once bad habits have been eliminated and the moral virtues have been introduced, Maimonides's writings require these virtues to be perpetually and continuously practiced until they become second nature.[47] Observance of the commandments, according to Maimonides, is especially necessary for the attainment of moral perfection.[48] Now, as Maimonides insisted, one is ready to climb to the highest rung, intellectual perfection. The acquisition of the "intellectual virtues," the attainment of intellectual perfection, was for Maimonides the purpose of human existence. "Through it [intellectual perfection] man is man."[49]

Once one has perfected the part of oneself most like God—the intellect—one is prepared for the climax and for the ultimate purpose of the ascent upon the ladder of perfection—" knowing" God, achieving communion with the divine. For Maimonides, this state of adhesion to God was the absolute expression of human love and worship of God, the acme of human accomplishment, the passport to the world to come, the ultimate purpose of human existence. Thus, Maimonides's integrated approach to ethics placed a high premium on the attainment of human fulfillment in this world. He perceived the anthropocentric posture as a necessary element in the moral quest. Nevertheless, Maimonides ultimately identified the anthropocentric view as being secondary to the theocentric view. The realization and the perfection of the individual self is, in the final analysis, but a prelude to communion with God.

AN ENDNOTE

Far from being an exhaustive discussion of Jewish ethics, this chapter focused upon only three issues crucial to understanding the nature of Jewish ethical literature and tradition. The first issue is a perspective that views life as an art form and ethics as a way of creating and refining that art form. In this view, ethics is not a tangential or compartmentalized facet of life; it is the essential ingredient of an artful, creative, and meaningful human existence. The second area of discussion portrays Jewish ethics as a particular form of ethics (namely, theological ethics), resting upon certain specific assumptions and claims. Finally, the multifaceted nature of Judaism and Jewish ethics is presented through the formulation of three approaches to the nature and goals of Jewish ethics from within Jewish ethical tradition and literature: the theocentric, the anthropocentric, and the integrated.

Because ethics deals with life, it must necessarily be complex. Because Jewish ethics is part of a complicated and rich tradition, it can be neither superficial nor single faceted. Nonetheless, in one medieval Jewish ethical treatise, *Sefer Ma'alot ha-Middot*, an attempt is made to define ethics simply and straightforwardly. "What is ethics? Not doing in private what one would be embarrassed to do in public."[50] Perhaps translated into contemporary terms, this text might read, "Ethical behavior consists of doing only that which one would not be embarrassed to see reported on network television news."

❦ 4 ❦

Health, Healing, and Tradition

Medicine . . . its study and acquisition are preeminently religious activities.

—MOSES MAIMONIDES[1]

There is no wealth like sound health.

—SOLOMON IBN GABIROL[2]

ACCORDING TO HISTORIANS, the first physician whom we can identify by name is Lulu, a Sumerian who lived almost thirty-seven hundred years ago.[3] However, according to Jewish theologians, the first physician whom we can identify by name is God, and the name of the first "licensed" healer is "the healer of God," the angel Raphael.

An ancient Jewish legend relates that God convened the first colloquium on human health and well-being, in heaven on the sixth day of creation. Discussion focused upon an unprecedented problem in bioengineering and in bioethics. At the plenary session, God, the conference's convener, sponsor, and chairperson, posed this problem to His junior colleagues, the angels: "Shall we create human beings in our image and in our likeness?" (Gen. 1:26).

Though the proposed project was eminently doable for God, and though a sizable grant was already in hand, the inquisitive angels wanted to know more about the project. "What will human beings do once they are created? What is the risk factor of creating them?," queried the angels.

After God had described humanity's potential destructiveness and its potential greatness, the angels replied, "What is man that You are mindful of him?" (Ps. 8:5), which in the bureaucratic language of the angels meant,

An earlier version of this chapter was delivered at a conference on medical ethics in honor of the late Professor Paul Ramsey held at the University of Illinois at Chicago in April 1986.

"Drop the project because the potential risks outweigh the potential benefits."

Not yet accustomed to dissent, especially from His nontenured junior colleagues, God pointed one of His divine fingers at them and literally fired them on the spot.

Having destroyed the attendees of the first plenary session, God then created a second set of angels and posed the same question to them. When they offered the identical response as the first group, God destroyed them, too.

A third set of angels was then created. These angels were led by the wise and tactful angel, Labbiel. When the question of creating human beings was posed to these angels, Labbiel responded, "Sovereign of the Universe, do what You wish with Your world. Do what pleases You with Your creation."

God then said to Labbiel, "You have saved your colleagues from destruction. You have healed what your earlier colleagues meant to destroy. Therefore, you will no longer be called 'Labbiel' but 'Raphael,' the 'healer of God.'"

God then appointed Raphael as the Angel of Healing. He gave into Raphael's safekeeping all of the celestial remedies for illness for him to use in the terrestrial world.[4] Thus, Raphael became the first "licensed" medical practitioner, although not the first physician, for the first doctor to "play God" was God Himself.

Self-licensed and self-insured for medical malpractice, God deigned to practice a number of medical specialties. He even performed an operation without a signed consent form from His patient. Scripture informs us that God practiced: anesthesiology, "the Lord God caused a deep sleep to fall upon the man"; orthopedics, "He took one of the ribs"; surgery, He opened and "closed up the flesh"; and plastic surgery, "the Lord God fashioned the rib" (Gen. 2:21–22).

In the beginning, while there were still only few human beings who required medical care, God could tend to them all. But, after humankind began to proliferate, additional staff was required, and so human beings began to practice medicine. But how did this supernal knowledge and wisdom, vouchsafed to God and conveyed to Raphael, come to be under human auspices? Here, again, legend intercedes.

When Adam dwelt in the Garden of Eden, he experienced neither illness nor death. Once expelled from paradise and exposed to the precarious conditions of human existence that would be the destiny of his descendants, Adam became apprehensive, and he asked God for help.

God dispatched the angel Raziel to Adam. In the angel's hand there was a sacred book. The angel opened the book and read it to Adam, and Adam understood its contents and he was pleased, for all wisdom was contained in this book. The book was conveyed by Adam to Enoch. But during the sinful generations that followed, the book was lost.

After the Flood, a variety of illnesses befell Noah's children and grandchildren. So Noah offered sacrifices and entreated God, and God sent Raphael to Noah. Raphael revealed to Noah the wisdom contained in the Book of Raziel, which had been lost, including knowledge of all of the remedies that might be found in nature. Noah recorded all that he was taught about healing in a book, which became the source for all future medical books.

The wise men of various lands, such as India, Egypt and Greece, copied from this book and translated its contents to their respective languages. They subsequently attempted to gain access to the Garden of Eden to secure medicinal materials but perished in the process, and with them perished the medical knowledge they had obtained. For generations, humankind was bereft of medical knowledge, until it was renewed by King Ahashuerus of Persia, the Hebrew physician Asaph, and the Greek physicians Hippocrates and Galen.[5]

According to a different version of this legend, Noah's son Shem was taken to heaven by an angel after the Flood. In heaven, all remedies for all illnesses were revealed to him. Shem recorded these in a book, which he conveyed to Abraham. This book was transmitted from Abraham to Isaac to Jacob, and so on, until it reached King Hezekiah, who hid the book, and the medical insights contained therein had to be rediscovered all over again.[6]

According to these legends and traditions, the art of healing is a gift of grace from God to human beings, a divine trust conveyed into human stewardship. It is, however, a revocable trust, a gift too precious to be bestowed carte blanche. As Paul Ramsey has so aptly put it, "Men ought not to play God before they learn to be men, and after they have learned to be men, they will not play God."[7]

The divine sanction for human beings to heal other human beings is a franchise defined by the limits of a covenant. According to Ramsey, "Men and women are created in covenant, to covenant, and for covenant."[8] The covenant between the physician and patient identified by Ramsey presupposes a covenant between the physician and God.[9] The nature and characteristics of the covenants between God and the physician, between God and the patient, and between the patient and the physician, as perceived by classical Jewish tradition, are delineated in this chapter.

THE BASIS OF THE DIVINE SANCTION TO HEAL

Throughout classical Judaism, discussion of the divine sanction for human beings to preserve the health of, and to cure the illnesses of, other human beings centers around three positions. The first, a present though not a prominent stance, holds that God is not only the ultimate healer but the only healer. In this view, no sanction to heal has been conveyed by God to human beings. The second position, discussed but rejected by Jewish tradition, holds that only human beings heal other human beings, that God plays no role in the art of healing. The third position, widely affirmed within Jewish tradition, considers the practice of medicine to be a virtue and posits a partnership between the divine healer and His human partner and agent, the physician. This stance embodies many nuances and variations.

Though a "minority" view, the position that rejects the sanction to heal is found within classical Jewish sources. That the sanction to heal had to be exegetically established and legally justified demonstrates by inference that it was not presumed a priori.[10] Indeed, as late as the nineteenth century, no less a Jewish thinker than Nahman of Brazlav could question the efficacy of medical practice. Nahman is quoted as having said that, since the Angel of Death is too busy to kill everyone himself, he, therefore, appoints messengers called "physicians" all over the world to take care of some of the killing for him.[11] Nahman's view is similar to that expressed in a poem that was often quoted in medieval Jewish literature.

> Fate has said unto the
> fool—become a doctor
> For thou canst slay thy
> patients, and from their
> death canst prosper
> Thou shalt have more advantage
> than the Angel of Death,
> For he killeth men but
> attaineth no wealth.[12]

Two theological premises underlie the position that denies human beings a role in the practice of healing. The first is a variation on the theme of divine retribution, and the second is a variation of the notion of divine providence. From this perspective, the doctrine of divine retribution, that is, the claim that God rewards virtue and punishes sin, understands illness to be a divinely afflicted punishment for human sin.[13] In this view, only God who afflicts may be the healer who cures. The verse "For I the Lord am your healer" (Exod. 15:26) is taken to mean that God is not only a healer but that God is the only healer. Furthermore, this stance maintains that human medical intervention must be construed as an attempt to contravene God's will as a challenge to the sovereignty of divine providence.[14]

The second position claims that the practice of medicine is an exclusively human concern, that the physician cures through his or her own skill alone. This approach is rejected outright by classical Jewish sources.

Various medieval commentators on the Talmudic passages that report King Hezekiah's suppression of the Book of Remedies explain that Hezekiah hid the book because people were relying solely upon the book for their healing, thereby disenfranchising God from His role as the healer of human maladies. A similar perspective is reflected in the biblical book of Chronicles: "In the thirty-ninth year of his reign [King] Asa suffered from an acute foot ailment, but ill as he was he did not turn to the Lord, but [only] to physicians. And Asa slept with his fathers, dying in the forty-first year of his reign" (2 Chron. 16:12–14). It is in this spirit that the medieval commentators interpret the Talmud's enigmatic statement, "the best doctors are destined for hell."[15] Rashi interprets this statement as a censure of the physician's tendency to disavow his or her reliance upon God, his or her partner, in the process of healing.

Commenting both on this passage and on the passage that relates Hezekiah's suppression of the Book of Remedies, Judah Loew of Prague explained that medical practice, though sanctioned, must also be sanctified. It must embody elements of the natural and the supernatural, it must articulate the human application of the divine power to heal. The physician who is solely a naturalist, who denies the spiritual dimension, is deficient and is therefore destined for the realm of deficiency and negation: hell. Further, the physician who treats only the body and not the soul wallows in the physical world, denies human nature as a composite of the spiritual and the material, and is therefore denied entrance into the spiritual realm and is assigned instead to its opposite: to hell.[16]

The third and dominant position in Judaism affirms the sanction to heal. In opposition to the first position, which relegates healing to a divine monopoly, this stance maintains that healing is not a usurpation of God's prerogative but an expression of *imitatio Dei*. In opposition to the second position, which excludes God from the curative process, this position considers the physician to be a partner and a colleague of God in the act and in the art of healing. In this view, no physician is a sole practitioner. Every physician practices with a senior partner—God. Medical practice articulates a covenantal relationship between God and the physician.

While ancient Judaism had priests who were physicians, medieval Judaism considered the physician to be a priest, a servant of God, a vicar of God. In this view, God is the ultimate physician, and the human physician serves as His agent. In sixteenth-century Poland, Moses Matt wrote, "The patient must trust in God, and must realize that everything is dependent upon His will. He must continuously pray that God will help the physician so that the physician will not err in his treatment and so that he will be cured by the physician, for the physician is an agent of God."[17]

In many of the "Physician's Prayers" that derive from medieval Jewish literature this theme is expressed. For example, the medieval Jewish philosopher, poet, and physician Judah ha-Levi wrote:

Not upon my power of
healing I rely
Only for Thine healing
do I watch.[18]

In his "Physician's Prayer," the seventeenth-century preacher and physician Jacob Zahalon wrote, "Thou art the physician, not me. I am but clay in the Potter's hand, in the hand of the Creator of all things, and as the instrument through which You cure Your creatures."[19]

The covenantal relationship between God and the physician is the premise of which the covenantal relationship between the physician and the patient is the corollary. In the words of Abraham Joshua Heschel,

> The doctor enters a covenant with the patient; he penetrates his life, affecting his mode of living, often deciding his fate. The doctor's role is one of royal authority, while the patient's mood is one of anxiety and helplessness. The patient is literally a sufferer, while the doctor is the incarnation of his hope. The patient must not be defined as a client who contracts a physician for services; he is a human being entrusted to the care of a physician. The physician is the trustee holding the patient's health in trust. In return, the patient's earnest is reliance, commitment . . . [God's] chief commandment is, "Choose life" (Deut. 30:19). The doctor is God's partner in the struggle between life and death. . . . Medicine is prayer in the form of a deed. . . . The body is a sanctuary, the doctor is a priest. . . . The act of healing is the highest form of *imitatio Dei*.[20]

In his commentary to the Talmudic passage "the best of physicians are destined for hell," Samuel Edels interpreted it to mean that the physician who considers himself the best of physicians is destined to reside in hell as a punishment for two interrelated sins: pride and murder. Edels explained that the haughty physician will mistakenly rely on his own prowess in complex life-threatening situations rather than adequately study the case and consult fellow physicians. Such an arrogant physician is likely to mistreat the patient, which would endanger the life of the patient. The death of the patient would then be the result of negligence, and the physician would be guilty of homicide. From this perspective, the practice of medicine is spiritual brinkmanship. Both the life of the patient and the soul of the physician are constantly at risk.

Related to the view that the physician is a catalyst for divine healing is the view that the physician is one whose task is not to effect a cure but to help Nature effect a cure. God creates Nature as the physician's tools, to be employed in the art of healing. The wise physician knows how to utilize these tools. In the words of the medieval Jewish physician and philosopher Isaac Israeli, "the physician does not bring about the cure, but prepares the way for Nature; for Nature is the actual healer."[21]

In classical Jewish sources, the sanction to heal is affirmed by means of four primary methods: (1) through exegetical analysis of Scripture; (2) through reasoned analysis; (3) through legal analysis; (4) through reflection upon the claim that there exists a divine-human partnership in "the work of creation."[22]

The locus classicus in rabbinic literature for the sanction of medical practice is a Talmudic commentary on the scriptural verses "When men quarrel and one strikes the other with stone or fist, and he does not die but has to take to his bed—if he then gets up and walks outdoors upon his staff, the assailant shall go unpunished, except that he must pay for his idleness and his healing" (Exod. 21:18–19). From the obligation of the assailant to pay the medical costs of his victim, the sanction to heal is inferred. The school of Rabbi Ishmael inferred from the term "his healing" (literally: "and to heal he shall heal") that "permission [reshut] was granted [by God] to the physician to heal."[23]

A second exegetical tradition curiously relates the obligation upon the physician to treat the sick to the biblical injunction requiring the return of lost property to its owner (Deut. 22:2). The Talmud extends the obligation to rescue one's property to a further obligation to rescue one's fellow person from danger.[24] Maimonides further extended this biblical injunction to the obligation to render medical care.[25]

Nahmanides, himself a physician, related the sanction to heal to the generic verse, "You should love your neighbor as yourself" (Lev. 19:18).[26] However, he also tied the sanction to heal to the verse "Do not stand [idly] by the blood of your brother" (Lev. 19:16), which is invoked by the Talmud to require one to aid an imperiled individual, in this case, an individual imperiled by illness.[27]

As noted previously, the Talmud rests the sanction to heal on a verse in Exodus (21:19) that deals with the law of torts, that is, with an affliction brought about through a human agent. This led a number of the medieval Jewish commentators to distinguish between humanly afflicted and divinely afflicted illnesses. Some commentators asserted that the sanction to heal that is implicit in Exodus (21:19) applies only to humanly afflicted illnesses, lest one conclude that "God afflicts and human beings cure."[28] Further, some concluded that, since "internal illnesses" are likely to be divinely engendered, the sanction to heal does not include the practice of "internal medicine."[29] This position, however, is effectively refuted by subsequent commentaries on a number of grounds, not least of which is that the Talmudic rabbis themselves practiced "internal medicine," which, it is presumed, they would not have done, were such practice proscribed.[30]

Nahmanides, in his *Commentary to the Torah* (Lev. 26:11), drew a bizarre distinction between the physician's obligation to heal and upon the patient's obligation to seek medical care. Nahmanides words affirm the obligation of the physician to heal but deny the correlative obligation of the patient to seek a medical cure, since there is no specific scriptural sanction in that regard. Nevertheless, the logical weakness of his argument is rebutted by subsequent commentators who have pointed out that without an affirmation of the patient's right to be healed, the scripturally sanctioned obligation of the physician to heal would be meaningless.[31]

After rejecting Nahmanides's position, the eighteenth-century commentator Hayyim Joseph David Azulai affirmed that "nowadays one must not rely on miracles, and the afflicted individual is duty bound to conduct himself in accordance with the natural order by calling on a physician to heal him. In fact, to depart from the general practice by claiming greater merit than the many saints [of past] generations who were themselves cured by physicians is almost sinful on account of the implied arrogance and the reliance upon miracles when life is threatened. . . . Hence, one should adopt the ways of all people and be healed by physicians."[32]

Moses Maimonides, the greatest medieval Jewish philosopher and physician, considered the sanction to heal to be logically self-evident. In the *Mishneh Torah*, Maimonides categorically stated the obligation to heal without recourse to any proof text, a phenomenon that surprised some subsequent commentators.[33]

Echoing a statement found in Maimonides's medical writings, Jacob Zahalon wrote that, just as it is unreasonable for an individual to argue that belief in divine providence should lead one to deny oneself food, so it is equally unreasonable for one to argue that belief in divine providence should lead one to deny oneself medical care. As Zahalon wrote, "It is not viable for a healthy person who has a desire to eat, to say that if life has been decreed for me by God I shall live without food, and if death has been decreed, I shall die, because such a person would be guilty of suicide. . . . Similarly, the sick person who refuses to avail himself of medical care because he believes God has either already decreed life or death, is also guilty of suicide."[34]

A similar argument, grounded in the assumption that God provides the raw materials for human beings to develop their own sustenance, that human existence coexists with God, is expressed in the following text:

> It occurred that Rabbi Ishmael and Rabbi Akiva were strolling in the streets of Jerusalem accompanied by another person. They were met by a sick person. He said to them, "My masters, tell me by what means I may be cured." They told him, "Do thus and so until you are cured." He asked them, "And who afflicted me?" They replied, "The Holy One, blessed is He." [The sick person] responded, "You have entered into a matter which does not pertain to you. [God] has afflicted and you seek to cure! Are you not transgressing His will?"

Then Rabbi Ishmael and Rabbi Akiva asked him, "What is your oc-
cupation?" He answered, "I am a tiller of the soil and here is the sickle in
my hand." They asked him, "Who created the vineyard?" He answered,
"The Holy One, blessed be He." Rabbi Akiva and Rabbi Ishmael said to
him, "And you enter into a matter which does not pertain to you! [God]
created [the vineyard] and you cut His fruits from it." He said to them,
"Do you not see the sickle in my hand? If I did not plow, sow, fertilize and
weed nothing would sprout." They said to him, "Foolish man! Have you
never in your life heard that it is written, 'As for man, his days are as
grass; as grass of the field, so he flourishes' [Ps. 103:15]. Just as if one does
not weed, fertilize and plow, the trees will not produce [fruit] and if fruit
is produced but is not watered or fertilized it will not live but die, so with
regard to the body. Drugs and medicaments are the fertilizer and the
physician is the tiller of the soil."[35]

Thus, despite the assumption that illness may be an affliction from God as
punishment for sin, Jewish tradition did not accept any human condition as
irredeemable. It was assumed that, though God may send illness, He nevertheless desires a cure, that the practice of medicine should be viewed as
an act of virtue and not as an act of presumption aimed at the subversion of
God's will. As David ben Samuel ha-Levi noted in his commentary to the
legal code, *Shulhan Arukh,* true healing comes only from God. Nevertheless, God has given His human creatures the sanction and the ability to
heal. God's supernatural healing and human beings' natural healing are not
mutually exclusive, they are mutually inclusive.[36] When divine healing
is not forthcoming, even when the patient is presumed to be suffering from
a divinely afflicted malady, human medical intervention is not only permitted but appropriate.[37]

Scripture describes Moses's sister, Miriam, as having been afflicted
with leprosy by God as punishment for the sin of slander (Num. 12:8-11).
Commenting on this text, a midrash states, "When Moses saw what befell
his sister . . . Moses said: 'Master of the Universe, already long ago You
granted me the power to heal. If you will heal her, it is well, but if not, I
will heal her.'"[38]

THE NATURE OF THE SANCTION TO HEAL

The very existence of a scriptural sanction to heal was taken by the medieval Jewish commentators as an indication that healing cannot be considered an enterprise aimed at subverting God's design.[39] Nonetheless, the
nature of, and the boundaries governing, the sanction to heal were debated
and discussed, particularly by the medieval sources. As in any covenant,

the covenants between God and the physician and between the physician and the patient are defined by certain limitations, which are open to various interpretations.

The Talmudic text states that "permission" is granted to the physician to heal. The use of the term "permission" provoked a debate among the medievals about whether the sanction to heal is a "permission," wherein it is optional, or whether it is an unqualified "obligation" (mitzvah), an unequivocal "covenantal imperative."

Most sources agree that the "permission" to heal constitutes an obligation upon the physician to heal. This position is linked to the assumption that saving life, that rescuing an imperiled person, is an obligation by which one is scripturally enjoined. As the legal code *Arba'ah Turim* puts it, "The Torah gave permission to the physician to heal; moreover, it is a religious obligation, and it is included in the obligation to save life."[40]

This obligation to save life (*pikuah nefesh*) is virtually unequivocal in Judaism. Hence, relating healing to the obligation to save life made healing an indisputable obligation. Indeed, Jewish law went so far as to set aside other religious obligations, such as Sabbath observance, when life is threatened. In this regard, the Talmud observes that the commandments of the Torah were given to "live by" (Lev. 18:5) but not to die because of.[41] While some commentators enjoined the physician from treating internal ailments, the codes of Jewish law reject that position on the grounds that, since one is enjoined to protect life, since all internal ailments might be life threatening, all internal ailments should be treated. Additionally, Jewish law insists that almost any religious obligation, for example, Sabbath observance, can be suspended to treat an individual suffering from an internal ailment.[42]

The codes also condemn a physician who refuses to render care in a life-threatening situation as a potential murderer. Not only is a physician who refuses care condemned, so is a physician who renders less than the best possible available medical care. "No one should occupy himself with medicine unless he is expert and no one in the environs is better than he (and he is licensed); otherwise, he is shedding blood."[43]

Along similar lines, the sixteenth-century chronicler and physician Solomon ibn Verga explained the Talmudic phrase "the best of physicians is destined for hell" to mean that the physician should picture hell as being open to receive him for neglecting a patient in his care.[44]

According to Jewish law, a person whose actions bring about the death of another, even accidentally, is liable for manslaughter. In this regard, the Talmud and the medieval codes observe that one reason a specific sanction to heal is afforded the physician is to free him or her from liability for manslaughter in cases of medical practice or even in cases of medical malpractice where criminal negligence is absent.[45]

Since the physician's obligation to heal is considered a religious injunction, the question of whether the physician is entitled to be paid for his or her services is discussed in Jewish religious literature. While some sources deny the physician's right to be compensated for his or her services, most of the sources accept the propriety of paying the physician for medical care.[46] Indeed, the Talmud itself observes that "a physician who charges nothing is worth nothing."[47]

Though the patient was obliged to pay the physician for medical care, the physician was admonished against being motivated by a pecuniary interest in the rendering of medical care. Many of the commentators on the Talmudic statement "the best of physicians are destined for hell" observe that this phrase refers to the physician who places economic concerns before medical concerns.[48] In addition to cautioning the physician who puts his or her economic gain before a patient's welfare, Jewish law restricted the collection of fees to those patients who could afford them. The physician is permitted to charge those who can pay but is obliged to treat gratis those who cannot pay for medical care.[49]

According to Jewish tradition, the primary tasks of the physician are not pathology and curing those persons already sick, they are pedagogy and preventive medicine. In this regard, the medieval pietist text *Sefer Hasidim* describes the wise physician as one who instructs patients on how to prevent illness.[50]

As a pedagogue, the physician is encouraged not only to teach his or her patient how to preserve health but to serve as a "role model" for the patient. As the medieval Jewish physician and scholar Judah ibn Tibbon wrote to his son, also a physician, "There is no more disgraceful object than a sick physician." He then quoted Ben Mishle (Samuel the Prince) who said: "How shall he heal the malady who himself suffers from its pain."[51]

The Jewish medievals understood the physician to have two primary tasks: "to maintain health if it be present, and to restore it if it be absent."[52] Of these two tasks, preservation of health was considered paramount. In the words of Isaac Israeli, "The need of the physician is twofold, preserving health and curing disease; and the demand for the former is greater than for the latter; for it is better for man that he avoid becoming ill than that he become ill and be cured."[53]

That medicine is not restricted to the treatment of illness but extended to the preservation of health is related to Maimonides's observation that a physician should know a patient both in health and in sickness. For Maimonides, the physician who was aware of the patient's healthy state was better equipped to diagnose a patient when the patient became ill.[54] In this vein, Zahalon advised the physician to instruct a patient who has recovered from an illness on how to conduct himself so that the illness would not return.[55] Maimonides observed that only fools believe that medical care relates to times of illness but does not relate to the preservation of health.[56]

Maimonides further recommended that, since the scope of medical knowledge is so vast, it is best to rely upon the advice of one's colleagues in difficult cases. For this reason, Maimonides advocated group medical practice, so that a pool of knowledge, drawn from various specialists, could be utilized both in treatment and in diagnosis.[57]

PATIENT: HEAL THYSELF

In the New Testament, Jesus refers to a proverb that was apparently popular in his day, "Physician, heal thyself" (Luke 4:23). Rabbinic and medieval Jewish tradition might have coined a correlative proverb, "Patient, heal thyself." The latter proverb would articulate the view that the patient (and not the physician) is primarily responsible for his or her own health and that the initiation of required medical care is primarily the responsibility of the patient.

As noted, Talmudic sources relate the sanction to heal to the discussion in Exodus (21:19) of an individual wounded by another and in need of medical care. Discussing this verse, the eighteenth-century biblical commentator Hayyim ibn Attar stated that the injunction of this verse with regard to medical care primarily falls neither upon the physician nor upon the assailant but upon the injured victim. According to ibn Attar, the victim of an assault is *required* to seek medical attention. Thus, while the decision to render medical treatment may not be obligatory upon the physician according to some interpreters of Jewish law, the obligation to seek medical treatment, particularly in life-threatening situations, would be upon the patient.[58]

Reliance on God for healing is considered necessary but not sufficient. One commentator on the *Shulhan Arukh* code observed that relying exclusively on God for healing is imprudent and, therefore, morally undesirable. Further, such a person would be guilty of intentionally inflicting self-injury, which is prohibited by Jewish law. One who refuses to seek medical care is compared to an individual who deliberately walks through fire with the expectation that reliance upon God would provide protection from injury.[59]

There is a long-standing view that illness may be a divine punishment for sin. This view holds that incorrect actions, freely performed, may lead to illness and even to death. Put another way, this doctrine may be interpreted to mean that one may suffer illness because of one's physical and moral vices, that one's misdeeds directed against oneself may lead to illness. Consequently, responsibility for preventing illness and for engendering health rests primarily with the patient and only secondarily with the physician. A midrashic text puts it this way: "Rabbi Aha said: It depends upon a person himself that diseases should not come upon him. What is the proof? For, said Rabbi Aha, Scripture states, 'The Lord will keep away [from you] all sickness' [Deut. 7:15]; this means it is from you [i.e., dependent upon you] that disease should not come upon you."[60] The patient's primary responsibility for the preservation of his or her own health is related by Jewish law to two legal prohibitions, which are exegetically derived from the verse in Deuteronomy (4:9), "But take utmost care and watch yourselves scrupulously." These two prohibitions are (1) not to take any action that might endanger one's own life,[61] (2) to remove any obstacle considered dangerous to one's life.[62] Both of these laws rest upon a theological assumption that affirms life to be a gift of God, a trust, which each person maintains as a steward and trustee of God. In the words of the Talmud, "Let Him who gave me my life take it away, but no one should injure oneself."[63] Thus, the concern with health is, in the final analysis, a preoccupation with how one cares for the life God entrusts to him or to her.

The preservation of health is an act of worship, an expression of divine service. In the words of the thirteenth-century philosopher Shem Tov ben Joseph ibn Falaquera, "a person must care for his body, like an artisan for his tools. For the body is the instrument through which one serves one's Creator."[64] This notion is further illustrated by the following midrashic text, which does not perceive cleanliness as next to godliness but describes cleanliness as an act of divine worship:

"A kindly man benefits himself; a cruel man makes trouble for himself" [Prov. 11:17], applies to Hillel the Elder. Once, when he concluded his studies with his disciples, he walked along with them. His disciples asked him: "Master, where are you going?" He answered: "To perform a religious duty." "Which religious duty is it?," they asked. He replied: "To wash in the bath-house." Said they: "Is that a religious duty?" He responded: "Yes, it is. If the statues of kings which are erected in theatres and circuses are scoured and washed by the person who is appointed to care for them, and who thereby obtains his maintenance through them— even more, he is exalted in the company of the great of the Kingdom— how much more should I, who have been created in the [divine] image and likeness; as it is written, 'For in the image of God made He man' [Gen. 9:6]."[65]

In his *Treatise on Asthma*, Maimonides listed six "obligatory regulations" that one should attempt to observe in order to preserve one's health. These obligations are (1) clean air to breathe, (2) proper diet, (3) regulation of emotion, (4) moderate bodily exercise, (5) proper sleep, and (6) proper excretion.[66]

Regarding clean air, Maimonides observed that "the concern for clean air is the foremost rule in preserving the health of one's body and soul."[67]

For Maimonides, proper diet was a religious obligation, since "improper diet is like a fatal poison. It is the basis for all illness." Maimonides particularly cautioned against the hazards to health that derive from overeating. For Maimonides, gluttony was a moral illness that inevitably resulted in physical illness.[68] Elsewhere Maimonides observed, "I have seen gluttons who throw their food and poke it back into their mouths like ruminating beasts. This is one of the biggest causes of disease."[69] Still elsewhere, Maimonides advised that it is a general rule of the preservation of health, and a specific rule with regard to proper diet, that "if a person took as good care of himself as he does of his animals, he would be saved from many illnesses."[70] Relating earlier Greek, Arabic, and Jewish sources, the twelfth-century poet and physician Joseph ben Meir Zabara observed:

> Galen was asked: What is the greatest cure? Moderation in food and drink. And a certain sage has said: Who diminishes his eating will lengthen the time of his eating and will abide in health. . . . And our sages of blessed memory have said: Diminish your eating and you will diminish your disease. . . . And when Galen was asked: Why do you stint on your food?, he replied: My purpose is to eat to live; the purpose of others is to live to eat. . . . He that fills his belly each day undermines his health.[71]

It is noteworthy that Zabara's words caution against eating beef. In this regard he quoted Hippocrates, "Guard yourself from eating beef and make not your stomach a graveyard for cattle."[72] For Zabara, a restrained diet led not only to physical well-being but to moral health as well. Restraint in diet, in his view, is an expression of the virtue of elevating reason over unbridled desire, prudence over gluttony, temperance over overindulgence.[73]

For regulating the emotions, most of the Jewish medievals advocated the "golden mean."[74] Of special concern were the dangerous potentialities posed by worry and depression. In this regard, the medieval philosopher and physician Joseph ibn Aknin quoted an earlier proverb, "Sickness is the prison of the body, and worry is the prison of the mind."[75]

In his discussion of the beneficial effects of exercise, Maimonides observed that physical exercise should relate to "exercise of the soul," that physical exercise should lead one to the development of an emotional and psychological state of happiness, joy, and contentment.[76] Physical exercise is considered an essential element in the health regimen of any individual. The *Mishneh Torah* says: "If one leads a sedentary life and does not take exercise, neglects the calls of nature, or is constipated—even if he eats wholesome food and takes care of himself with medical rules—he will, throughout his life, be subject to aches and pains, and his strength will fail him."[77] In his *Treatise on Asthma*, Maimonides claimed that "inactivity is as big an evil where preservation of health is aimed at as moderate exercise is a great boon to it."[78] Similarly, ibn Falaquera observed, "the exercising of the body is a bulwark against disease, and a source of strength for the limbs. . . . An overdose of exercise, however, is harmful."[79]

The normal functioning of the urinary tract and of the bowels was considered an expression of divine grace and a condition that one should strive to maintain. After attending to nature's call, a blessing is to be recited: "Blessed are You, O Lord our God, King of the Universe, who has formed human beings in wisdom, and created in him many orifices and ducts. It is revealed and known before the Throne of Glory, that if one of these be opened, or one of those closed, that it would be impossible to exist and to stand before You. Blessed are You, God, who heals all flesh and does wonders."[80] Further, the rabbis recommend leisure in the bathroom. The Talmud observes, "He who prolongs his stay in the privy, prolongs his days and years."[81]

Maimonides words link proper excretory functioning to a happy and healthy life. In the *Mishneh Torah,* he insisted that "one should not neglect the call of nature, but should respond immediately." He further observed that, "It is a leading principle of medicine that if there is constipation or if the bowels move with difficulty, grave disorders result."[82] Maimonides summed up a number of the features of his health regimen with these words:

> A great principle of hygiene, as physicians say, is as follows: As long as a person takes active exercise, works hard, does not overeat, and keeps his bowels open, he will be free from disease and will increase in vigor. . . . Whoever lives in accordance with the directions I have set forth has my assurance that he will not be sick until he grows old and dies; he will not be in need of a physician . . . unless his constitution be congenitally defective or he has acquired bad habits . . . or if the world should be visited by pestilence and drought.[83]

Maimonides's concern with the deleterious effects of bad habits is sprinkled throughout his works.[84] For Maimonides and other medieval Jewish philosophers and pietists, bad habits pose a serious threat to one's moral health as well as to one's physical well-being. In their view, bad habits are morally dangerous because they undermine the very premise upon which ethics rests: the availability of moral volition. Rather than the person having the habit, the habit has the person, restricting moral choice, inviting spiritual illness. In this regard, Moses Hayyim Luzzatto observed, "He who has thus become a slave to habit is no longer his own master, and cannot act differently, even if he should want to do so. He is held in bondage by certain habits which have become second nature to him."[85]

HEALTH AS WHOLENESS

As discussed, the preservation of health is a primary desideratum, according to Jewish tradition, both for the physician and for the patient. But, what is "health" as understood by Jewish tradition?

The concept of holistic health, understood by some to be a contemporary innovation, is actually very old. Even in English, the term "holistic health" is an etymological redundancy, since the word "health" has its roots in the Old English "hal" and the Old High German "heil," meaning "whole." Similarly, medieval Jewish literature uses the term "shelemut," which derives from the word "shalem," meaning "whole." Thus, health relates to the preservation of wholeness when present and to its restoration when absent.[86] A second term used in Hebrew to denote health is "bari" which derives from the verb "to create." Thus, health is not a static state, but a dynamic one; it is continuous regeneration, "re-creation" in a literal sense.

Medieval Jewish writers such as Maimonides echoed Plato's observation that, "The cure of many diseases is unknown to the physicians . . . because they are ignorant of the whole [body and soul] which ought to be studied also; for the part can never be well, unless the whole is well. For all good and evil, whether in the body or in human nature, originates . . . in the soul, and overflows from thence . . . and therefore, if the head and body are to be well, you must begin by curing the soul; that is the first thing."[87]

In Plato's view, virtue is endemic to the health of the soul, and as such, one must go beyond medicine to find the best means of attaining the end of medicine, which is health. Plato's claim that health is dependent upon and related to virtue reverberates throughout medieval Jewish literature. From this perspective, medical ethics is not restricted to or focused upon the nature of ethical behavior in the practice of medicine. It is not restricted to a consideration of the moral implications of such issues as abortion, euthanasia, bioengineering, or experimentation on human subjects. Its scope is immeasurably larger. From this perspective, the primary concern of medical ethics is health; and ethics itself, the concern with how one ought to live, is at the root of health. Just as the part cannot be complete without the whole, so can medical ethics not be whole unless it relates to ethics per se, ethics here being understood as the health of the soul. Indeed, this is precisely Maimonides's understanding of the nature of ethics. For Maimonides, the virtuous soul was the healthy soul; the healing of the soul related to the inculcation of moral virtue.

> The improvement of the moral qualities is brought about by the healing of the soul and its activities. Therefore, just as the physician, who endeavors to cure the human body, must have a perfect knowledge of it in its entirety and its individual parts, just as he must know what causes sickness that it may be avoided, and must also be acquainted with the means by which a patient may be cured, so likewise, he who tries to cure the soul, wishing to improve the moral qualities, must have a knowledge of the soul in its totality and its parts, must know how to prevent it from becoming diseased, and how to maintain its health.[88]

It is not coincidental that Maimonides's younger contemporary, Joseph ibn Aknin, entitled his ethical treatise *Hygiene of the Soul*.[89] Neither is it surprising that Maimonides's immediate predecessor in the history of Jewish philosophy, Abraham ibn Daud, entitled his discussion of ethics "On the Healing of the Soul."[90]

For the Jewish medievals, virtue constituted the health of the soul. Just as doctors of the body are required for instruction regarding the maintenance of physical health, ethicists are necessary as "doctors of the soul" to provide instruction vis-à-vis moral health.[91]

In his *Medical Aphorisms* Maimonides stated, "It is a well-known assertion of philosophers that the soul can be healthy or diseased, just as the body is either healthy or diseased. These illnesses of the soul and their health which are alluded to by philosophers undoubtedly refer to the opinions and morals of people. Therefore, I consider untrue opinions and bad morals, with all their different varieties, as types of human illness."[92]

The analogy between physical and spiritual health, the health of the body and the health of the soul, maintaining health and maintaining virtue, preventing illness and dispelling vice, leads back to the notion that places primary responsibility for health upon the individual person rather than upon the physician or upon society at large. Just as each individual is responsible for his or her spiritual health, for his or her moral well-being, so is one primarily responsible for one's own physical well-being, for one's own bodily health.[93]

The verse in Deuteronomy (4:9), "But take utmost care and watch yourselves [or your souls] scrupulously" (Hebrew: *me'od*; literally "very much") has been taken to mean that each individual must take primary responsibility for his or her own health. However, as the medieval commentaries explain, health is not restricted to physical well-being but is also extended to spiritual and psychological well-being. Indeed, one commentator maintained that since the emphatic "*me'od*" is used in relationship to the care of one's soul in this verse, the obligation to maintain physical health is secondary to the obligation to maintain spiritual health.[94]

For the Jewish medievals, health of the body was a necessary but insufficient characteristic of a healthy person. For example, as ibn Falaquera observed, echoing earlier medieval traditions, "What profit has one in his bodily health, if one's soul is ill? . . . The malady of the soul is more serious than the malady of the body."[95] Similarly, for Maimonides, bodily health was not an end in itself but a means to the attainment of higher human ends. Physical health is but a foundation upon which one may then begin to build a life of moral and intellectual virtue. As Maimonides wrote, "The real duty of man is, that in adopting whatever measures he may for his well-being and the preservation of his existence in good health, he should do so with the object of maintaining a perfect condition of the instruments of the soul, which are the limbs of the body, so that his soul may be unhampered, and he may busy himself in acquiring the moral and mental virtues."[96]

Nahman of Brazlav opposed treating illness on a purely physical basis. In Hasidic thought, illness is viewed as the outward manifestation of an inner spiritual disturbance. To treat the body alone might remove the symptoms but not their cause. For Nahman, treating the corporeal aspect of a patient without attending to his or her spiritual dimension would inevitably prove faulty. According to Nahman, the true healer cannot be a mechanic. The true healer must be a person of spiritual depth to aspire to be a complete healer. Nahman described physicians who neglect the spiritual dimension either of their own selves or of their patients as a new variety of "sorcerer," trying to manipulate natural forces without recourse to the spiritual.[97]

Understanding health as being both physical and spiritual rejects the conception of health as being limited to an absence of physical illness or to the presence of physical well-being alone. Not only the healthy body but the healthy person is the goal, according to Jewish tradition.

As health, in this view, focuses upon the whole person, medical treatment is understood to be treatment of the person who suffers from a disease and not merely the treatment of the disease which afflicts the person. As Maimonides noted, quoting the Greek physicians, "the physician should not treat the disease but the patient who is suffering from it."[98]

In Jewish tradition, the maintenance and the preservation of health requires careful attention to psychological and spiritual conditions, as well as to physiological factors. In treatment of illness, consideration of psychological factors is also demanded. As noted earlier in this chapter, medical intervention is required by Jewish law as an act of saving life or as an act of alleviating a threat to life (*pikuah nefesh*). This concern with preserving life is extended to physiological and to psychological disturbances. The Talmud, for instance, requires a threat to mental equilibrium (*teiruf da'at*) to be treated as a threat to one's physiological equilibrium, as a threat to life.[99] This principle is applied by subsequent Jewish legal opinion to such issues as contraception and abortion. In a 1913 responsum, Mordecai Winkler stated, "Mental health risk has been definitely equated to physical health risk [in Jewish law]. A woman who is in danger of losing her mental health unless a pregnancy is interrupted would qualify accordingly."[100]

From these sources it should be evident that medieval Jewish literature posits a teleological understanding of the nature of health. The purpose of bodily health is to prepare the foundation for moral and spiritual health, whereby the human being may realize the qualities essential to being human. Thus, the concern with health is, in the final analysis, a concern with how one lives the life divinely entrusted into one's care. Ultimately, health is a matter of life and death. As Zabara recorded, "When the brother of a certain man died, they asked, 'What occasioned his death?' 'His life,' was the reply."[101]

5

A View of Euthanasia

Scripture says: "You should love your neighbor as yourself" [Lev. 19:18]; therefore, choose an easy death for him.[1]

THE "MIRACLES" OF MODERN MEDICINE have engendered the complexities of modern medical ethics. Advances in medical technology have exacerbated moral decision making in medical settings. One of the most compelling issues confronting contemporary bioethics is euthanasia. The word "euthanasia" derives from the Greek and means a "good death."

Modern philosophers often distinguish between two kinds of euthanasia: active and passive. Active euthanasia refers to an action that causes or accelerates death. Passive euthanasia refers to the withdrawal of life support. In addition, a distinction is also often made between "voluntary" and "involuntary" euthanasia. In voluntary euthanasia, the individual whose life is in question takes an action that brings his or her own life to an end. In involuntary euthanasia, an action to end the patient's life is taken without his or her explicit consent to end his or her life. Thus, euthanasia may take a variety of forms: active-voluntary, passive-voluntary, active-involuntary, and passive-involuntary.

An example of active-voluntary euthanasia would be where the patient wills to end his or her own life and actively implements this decision. For instance, if a person with terminal cancer makes a conscious decision to die by swallowing an overdose of painkilling medicine that, besides alleviating pain, may also accelerate death, this would be a case of active-voluntary euthanasia.

Passive-voluntary euthanasia would be where the patient chooses to remove the means that are prolonging his or her life, without which he or

This chapter was originally published in 1987 in the *Journal of Aging and Judaism*, vol. 2, no. 1.

she *might* otherwise die. For example, if a patient who may not be able to breathe normally removes a respirator or an intravenous unit (IV), which then brings about his or her death, this would be an example of passive-voluntary euthanasia.

Active-involuntary euthanasia would be when a party *other than the patient* takes deliberate action to accelerate the patient's death. Passive-involuntary euthanasia would be when a party other than the patient removes certain life-support systems without the patient's knowledge or consent—for example, if a patient has a flat electroencephalogram (EEG) and is in an irreversible coma but the heart and lungs are operating because of mechanical assistance, then "pulling the plug" would be an example of passive-involuntary euthanasia.

To be sure, the distinction among these four forms of euthanasia is helpful, but it is also often hazy. For instance, is "pulling the plug" passive or active euthanasia; does it remove an action, for example, is it the introduction of "heroic measures," or is it an action aimed at accelerating death?

Before looking at some of the responses Jewish sources offer to the complex and multifaceted problem of euthanasia, it might be helpful to try to identify further some of the questions and situations these sources might address.

VOLUNTARY EUTHANASIA—May a Patient Choose to Take an Action That Would End His or Her Own Life?

Under this general question many more specific questions may be subsumed: Does one have a right to die as well as a right to live? To whom does one's life belong—to oneself, to society, to God? What obligation does one have to preserve one's life? To what extent does this obligation extend?

One who decides to end one's life may do so in a variety of ways. Is killing oneself always suicide? Is suicide justifiable? Would active-voluntary euthanasia (e.g., through self-injection) *or* passive-voluntary euthanasia (e.g., through cessation of administering certain drugs) be any more or less morally problematic than the other?

Would asking someone else to end one's life be voluntary or involuntary euthanasia? Would the person who does the asking or the person who actually performs the action be morally responsible for an act of euthanasia? Is euthanasia murder?

How might the motives of a person who undertakes an act of voluntary euthanasia be considered in evaluating the morality or the immorality of the action? Suppose a person decides upon voluntary euthanasia to alleviate his or her own pain and suffering; could "pain and suffering" include psychological anguish? What if a patient or a family member of a patient chooses voluntary euthanasia to alleviate the psychological or financial burden or both to his or her family?

INVOLUNTARY EUTHANASIA—May a Party Other than the Patient Choose to Take Action That Would Result in the Ending of the Patient's Life?

In many cases the patient is in no condition, physically or mentally, to make a decision as far as euthanasia is concerned—for example, the patient may be drugged or in a coma. In such a case, it might fall to someone other than the patient—such as a relative—to make a decision about whether to take action that would or might result in the patient's death. Or a patient might decide to take an action of active or passive euthanasia on his or her own. In such a case, the means employed and the motives that lead to this action would have to be morally evaluated. Would a moral distinction be made between active and passive euthanasia in such a case? Would "pulling the plug" be comparable to giving the patient a lethal dose of painkiller? Would deliberately injecting a lethal dose of painkiller be distinguished morally from doing so accidentally? Would shooting the patient to end his or her misery be murder? (Would it be murder if the patient pleaded that it be done?) Would practicing euthanasia on a relative or a friend be murder if the primary motive, rather than mercy, is hatred for the patient? If the family of the patient—either individually or collectively—authorizes medical personnel to practice euthanasia on the patient, would the family members be morally liable for the action since the doctor or nurse would be acting as their agent, or would the medical personnel themselves be morally liable for the action since they actually performed the act itself?

In some hospitals, it is standard procedure for physicians to practice euthanasia without consulting the patient or the patient's family. Some reasons for this include (1) the patient may not be conscious, or the patient may already be "medically dead" and unable to make such a decision;[2] (2) the physician might not want to burden the patient's family with having to make such an extraordinary decision about their loved one; (3) the physician may have to consider the needs of other patients and the availability of personnel and machinery (e.g., heart-lung machines) to treat other patients, who might have a better chance of survival. Physicians treating severely ill or terminal patients have to ask themselves many questions, such as should treatment be rendered, or should the patient be allowed to die naturally without initiating treatment? For example, an elderly patient suffers heart failure. The heart is so weak that resuscitation would only prolong the process of death. Should a do-not-resuscitate (DNR) order be maintained, or should the patient be put on a heart-lung machine? Should the cardiorespiratory functions simply be allowed to cease naturally? Once treatment has been initiated but irreparable life-threatening damage (e.g., brain damage) has been inflicted, should treatment be discontinued that would or might directly lead to the patient's death? Should artificial hydration or nutrition be removed once it had been introduced? Should active or passive euthanasia be practiced on a terminal patient? At what point? Should the physician use his or her best medical judgment as the basis for practicing euthanasia in any or all circumstances? Should the physician practice euthanasia at the request of the patient's family if it is in agreement with the physician's own medical judgment? If it does not so concur? Should the physician take into account local legal options (e.g., stipulations of a "living will"), hospital policies, (e.g., a DNR directive), his or her religion's teachings, his or her physician's oath in practicing euthanasia? Should a physician or a nurse practice euthanasia simply because it is ordered by a higher medical authority, or should the moral judgment always be his or her own, independent from that of others? How does Jewish tradition deal with euthanasia?

Though as a rule Judaism condemns murder and suicide, there are exceptions to the rule. For example, martyrdom—killing oneself or others, or allowing oneself and others to be killed—for "the sanctification of God's Name" is not considered murder or suicide by Talmudic and subsequent Jewish tradition.[3] Killing in self-defense and other forms of "justified homicide" have been sanctioned as "necessary evils" by rabbinic tradition.[4] Neither were all examples of manslaughter considered murder; rabbinic tradition required conditions such as premeditation and malicious intent before defining an act as murder.[5]

Since martyrdom is one of the exceptions to suicide and murder, it is interesting that post-Talmudic Jewish sources found a precedent for euthanasia in a Talmudic text that discusses martyrdom:

It was said that within but few days Rabbi Jose ben Kisma died and all the great men of Rome went to his burial and made a great lamentation for him. On their return, they found Rabbi Hanina ben Teradion sitting and occupying himself with the Torah, publicly gathering assemblies, and keeping a scroll of the Torah in his bosom. Straightaway they took hold of him, wrapt him in the scroll of the Torah, placed bundles of branches around him and set them on fire. They then brought tufts of wool, which they had soaked in water, and placed them over his heart, so that he should not expire quickly. His daughter exclaimed, "Father, that I should see you in this state!" He replied, "If it were I alone being burnt it would have been a thing hard to bear; but now I am burning together with the scroll of the Torah, He who will have regard for the plight of the Torah will also have regard for my plight." His disciples called out, "Rabbi, what seest thou?" He answered them, "The parchments are being burnt but the letters are soaring high." "Open then thy mouth" [said they] "so that the fire enter into thee." He replied: "Let Him who gave me [my soul] take it away, but no one should injure oneself." The executioner then said to him, "Rabbi, if I raise the flame and take away the tufts of wool from over thy heart, will thou cause me to enter into the life to come?" "Yes," he replied. "Then swear unto me" [he urged]. He swore unto him. He thereupon raised the flame and removed the tufts of wool from over his heart, and his soul departed speedily. The executioner then jumped and threw himself into the fire. And a *bath kol* [a heavenly voice] exclaimed: "Rabbi Hanina ben Teradion and the executioner have been assigned to the World to Come." When Rabbi heard it he wept and said: "One may acquire eternal life in a single hour, another after many years."[6]

This Talmudic text was interpreted by later authorities as having established the following principles:

1. Martyrdom is not to be considered self-murder or suicide.
2. An individual's life belongs not to himself or herself but to God.
3. Active-voluntary euthanasia is prohibited, but passive-voluntary euthanasia *may* be permitted. When the rabbi is encouraged to open his mouth so that the fire may enter and end his agony (i.e., active-voluntary euthanasia), he refuses. But, when the executioner offers to remove the soaked tufts of wool artificially prolonging his life (i.e., a life-support system), the rabbi gives him permission (i.e., passive-voluntary euthanasia).

As discussed later in this chapter, the views on euthanasia that are drawn from this Talmudic text are reiterated in subsequent Jewish literature.

ACTIVE EUTHANASIA IS PROHIBITED

The *Sefer Hasidim*, states: "If a person is suffering from extreme pain and he says to another: 'You see that I shall not live [long]; [therefore,] kill me because I cannot bear the pain,' one is forbidden to touch him [the terminal patient]." The text continues and proscribes the terminal patient from taking his or her own life. "If a person is suffering great pain and he knows that he will not live [long], he cannot kill himself. And this principle we learn from Rabbi Hanina ben Teradion who refused to open his mouth [to allow the fire to enter and take his life]."[7]

In one of the "minor tractates" of the Talmud, we read:

A dying man [*goses*] is regarded as a living entity in respect to all matters in the world. Whosoever touches or moves him is a murderer [if by so doing his death is accelerated]. Rabbi Meir used to say: He may be compared to a lamp which is dripping [going out]; should one touch it, one extinguishes it. Similarly, whoever closes the eyes of a dying man [thereby accelerating his death] is considered as if he had taken his life.[8]

This prohibition against practicing active euthanasia is reiterated by the medieval codes of Jewish law. It extends to the patient, the attending physician, the family and friends of the patient, and to all other individuals.[9] In his legal code, the *Mishneh Torah*, Maimonides wrote:

One who is in a dying condition is regarded as a living person in all respects. . . . He who touches him [thereby accelerating his death] is guilty of shedding blood. To what may he [the dying person] be compared? To a flickering flame, which is extinguished as soon as one touches it. Whoever closes the eyes of a dying person while the soul is about to depart is shedding blood. One should wait a while; perhaps he is just in a swoon.[10]

The fourteenth-century code of Jacob ben Asher is called the *Arba'ah Turim*. In many ways, it served as the model for Joseph Karo's sixteenth-century code, the *Shulhan Arukh*. Echoing earlier texts, Jacob ben Asher wrote: "A dying man is to be considered a living person in all respects . . . [therefore] anyone who hastens the exiting of the person's soul is a shedder of blood."[11] The *Shulhan Arukh* reads, "A patient on his deathbed is considered a living person in every respect . . . and it is forbidden to cause him to die quickly . . . and whosoever closes his eyes with the onset of death is regarded as shedding blood."[12]

The nineteenth-century *Kitzur Shulhan Arukh* by Solomon Ganzfried embellishes a bit on the earlier sources: "Even if one has been dying for a long time, which causes agony to the patient and his family, it is still forbidden to accelerate his death."[13]

The premises upon which classical Jewish views regarding active euthanasia are based include the following

1. An individual's life is not his or her own "property" but God's, and therefore God has the final disposition over it. In other words, each person serves as God's steward for the life given into his or her care. As Hanina ben Teradion put it, "Let Him who gave me my soul take it away."[14]

2. Jewish law does not dwell on the issue of quality of life. Rather, Jewish law maintains that each moment of life is inherently valuable in and of itself, independent of its quality. Life being sacred—each moment of life being intrinsically valuable—every effort must be made to preserve each moment of life, even to the moment of death. For example, according to Jewish law, "even if they find a person crushed [under a fallen building] so that he can live only for a short time, they must continue to dig," and if this

has occurred on the Sabbath, one is *required* to violate the Sabbath even if it means granting the victim only "momentary life."[15]

3. An individual is prohibited from inflicting self-injury, particulary the ultimate self-injury—suicide, which is generally defined as self-homicide.[16]

4. Since "there is no agency for wrongful acts," and since murder is a wrongful act, one cannot act as the agent of a person who desires death and bring about or accelerate that person's death, even at that person's explicit request.[17] In this regard, the physician is explicitly enjoined from employing medical intervention for the intention of accelerating death.[18]

PASSIVE EUTHANASIA MAY BE PERMITTED

As noted, the Talmudic case of Hanina ben Teradion is used by some post-Talmudic sources as a precedent for the permissibility of passive euthanasia. The rabbi permitted the tufts of wool which were "artificially" sustaining his life to be removed. This would seem to permit both voluntary and involuntary passive euthanasia, either on the part of the patient (voluntary) or on the part of another party (voluntary or involuntary), such as a physician. To be sure, Jewish law would not permit the removal of all life-support mechanisms. For example, it generally would not permit withholding insulin from a diabetic.[19] The text of the story of Hanina ben Teradion clearly relates to an individual who has no chance of survival in any case.

In many of the same sources noted above proscribing active euthanasia, one finds material that permits passive euthanasia. The *Sefer Hasidim* observes, "One may not [artificially] prolong the act of dying. If, for example, someone is dying and nearby a woodcutter insists on chopping wood, thereby disturbing the dying person so that he cannot die, we remove the woodcutter from the vicinity of the dying person. Also, one must not place salt in the mouth of a dying person in order to prevent death from overtaking him."[20] This view is adapted and is quoted almost verbatim in subsequent codes of Jewish law. In his gloss to the *Shulhan Arukh*, Moses Isserles observed, "It is forbidden to cause one's death to be accelerated, even in the case of one who has been terminally ill for a long time . . . *however*, if there is some factor which is preventing the exit of the soul such as a nearby woodchopper or salt placed under his tongue—and these things are impeding his death—it is permissible to remove them because in so doing one actively does nothing but remove an obstacle [preventing his natural death]."[21] Again, echoing the *Sefer Hasidim*, the *Shulhan Arukh* states, "One must not scream at the moment at which the soul [of another] departs, lest the soul return and the person suffer great pain. That is to say, it is not simply permitted to remove an obstacle to one's [natural] death, but one cannot lengthen the pain and suffering of the patient."[22]

In this regard, Isserles interpreted the view of the *Sefer Hasidim* as meaning that "it is certain that for one to do anything that stifles the [natural] process of dying [of a dying person] is forbidden."[23] Similarly, the sixteenth-century Italian rabbi Joshua Boaz referred to the *Sefer Hasidim* as being the basis of his own view, "it is permissible to remove any obstacle preventing [death] because so doing is not an action in and of itself."[24] Furthermore, in a seventeenth-century responsum by Jacob ben Samuel, the author takes the controversial view that any medical or pharmacological intervention that impedes the natural process of dying should not be introduced.[25]

Commenting on the phrase in Ecclesiastes (3:2), "There is a time to die," the *Sefer Hasidim* observes that Ecclesiastes does *not* also state that "there is a time to live." The reason for this, according to the *Sefer Hasidim*, is that, when the "time to die" arrives, it is not the time to extend life. Consequently, the *Sefer Hasidim* prohibits efforts to resuscitate a terminal patient on the grounds that extending the process of dying by resuscitation would cause the patient continued unnecessary anguish and pain.[26] This text might serve as the basis for justifying a DNR order for terminal patients whose condition has reached the point of death and whose resuscitation through heroic measures would only prolong their death and extend their agony. Just as some sources consider active euthanasia to be a presumption of God's authority over life and death, the *Sefer Hasidim* insists that extending the process of dying, when the terminal patient is in severe pain, is also a presumption of God's authority over life and death and a presumptive rejection of the scriptural view that "there is a time to die."

It should be noted, though, that the specific removal of natural hydration and food from a terminal patient to hasten death is specifically proscribed, probably because such withdrawal is considered cruel.[27] According to a text in the *Sefer Hasidim*, however, the removal of food and water are required in two kinds of cases. One is in the case in which nutrition or hydration would harm the patient. The second is in the case of a terminal patient where death is imminent. Such a patient must be made comfortable, for example, by keeping his or her lips and mouth moist, but such a patient must not be fed, lest the process of dying be prolonged and painful agony be unduly lengthened.[28]

From the literature reviewed to this point, it would appear that the Jewish view of euthanasia is that active euthanasia is prohibited, but passive euthanasia may be permissible and even desirable; for while classical Jewish sources place great value on saving and prolonging human life, they put no premium on needlessly prolonging the act of dying.[29] However, the sources seem uncompromising in the view that active euthanasia, under any circumstances, is a form of suicide or murder and is therefore prohibited. Indeed, a number of contemporary Jewish scholars, after reviewing the relevant sources, have come to this conclusion. For example, Immanuel Jakobovits, in his significant work *Jewish Medical Ethics*, summarizes the Jewish position on euthanasia as follows:

> It is clear, then, even when the patient is already known to be on his deathbed and close to the end, any form of *active euthanasia* is strictly prohibited. In fact, it is condemned as plain murder. In purely legal terms, this is borne out by the ruling that anyone who kills a dying person is liable to the death penalty as a common murderer. At the same time, Jewish law sanctions, and perhaps even demands, the withdrawal of any factor—whether extraneous to the patient himself or not—which may artificially delay his demise in the final phase.[30]

Despite this apparent consensus on the matter, a number of contemporary scholars have attempted to discover and to formulate a basis for active euthanasia under certain circumstances. This reevaluation of the sources has been prompted by certain contemporary medical and pharmacological developments and by the present proliferation of terminal cancer cases brought about by the lengthening of the average human life span.

ACTIVE EUTHANASIA RECONSIDERED

There seems to be unanimity of opinion in Judaism that life is intrinsically precious, even "momentary life." This assumption makes moot any discussion regarding life versus the quality of life. This claim also serves as a foundation for the condemnation of murder and suicide, of killing and self-killing. However, as noted above, exceptions to the prohibition against killing and self-killing were condoned by classical Jewish tradition, such as in cases of martyrdom and "justifiable homicide." These exceptions to the rule lead one to conclude that the value of life itself is not *always* considered absolute. The permissibility, even the desirability, of martyrdom assumes that there are occasions where life itself may be set aside because the preservation of life is not always an absolute moral imperative.

While it is true that the dominant view of Jewish tradition is that life itself is of intrinsic value, there exists an alternative view that relates both to cases of martyrdom and to cases of pain and anguish. For example, one Talmudic text maintains that a life of unbearable pain, a life coming to an inevitable and an excruciating end, is not a life worth continuing, that such a life is like having no life at all.

A Talmudic passage describes an individual who is overcome with a severe physical affliction as one "whose life is no life."[31] Similarly, a nineteenth-century commentary on the Mishnah observes that "great pain is worse than death." And while "a dying person [*goses*] is like a living person in all respects," the Mishnah in effect "devalued" the monetary worth of a dying person who wished to vow the equivalent of his monetary worth as a donation to the sanctuary.[32] The Mishnah reads, "One at the point of death [*goses*] . . . cannot have his worth vowed, nor be subject to valuation." On this text, the Talmud comments, "It is quite right that one at the point of death cannot have his worth vowed, because he has no monetary value; nor can he be made the subject of a valuation because he is not fit to be made subject of a valuation.[33] Thus, the imperative "Choose life" (Deut. 30:19) is not as absolute as is often assumed.

A further examination of classical Jewish sources related to martyrdom reveals that life in and of itself was not always considered of ultimate value. Such an examination also reveals precedents for taking one's own life and allowing oneself to be killed rather than to endure the physical torture that was frequently a martyr's fate. In such cases, taking one's own life was often not considered suicide. What proves intriguing is the pertinence and the applicability that instances in which martyrs chose death to physical suffering, chose to accelerate their own death rather than to withstand physical agony, may have to the problem of euthanasia, in general, and to the problem of active euthanasia, in particular.[34]

Talmudic literature records many instances of martyrdom. One, noted above, was the case of Rabbi Hanina ben Teradion. Another text describes how four hundred Jewish children drowned themselves at sea to avoid submitting to rape at the hands of Romans. In a medieval commentary to the tale of the children, a reference is made to the case of Hanina ben Teradion. The two cases taken together are interpreted by Jacob Tam as meaning that, to avoid sufferings certain to result in death, it is permitted to take one's own life, and in such an instance it is required (not necessarily prohibited) to injure oneself by choosing death.[35]

While suicide is proscribed by Jewish law, the prohibition against suicide was clearly set aside in the aforementioned cases of martyrdom. In other sources, suicide was redefined so that killing oneself was not always defined as suicide.[36] One such source is a controversial nineteenth-century responsum by Saul Berlin.

Berlin's responsum maintains that an individual who takes his or her own life because of mental or physical pain and anguish is not to be considered a suicide. According to Berlin, the earlier halakhic regulations prohibiting suicide were primarily intended for cases where the act resulted from a pessimistic view of life. However, Berlin asserted, a person who takes his or her own life to avoid continued pain and anguish is not to be considered a suicide.[37]

The controversial and unprecedented nature of Berlin's responsum and the possibly tenuous analogy between cases of martyrdom and cases of euthanasia, while suggestive, still do not adequately defend an option for active euthanasia within Jewish tradition. Consequently, it is necessary to look further.

In a late midrash on Proverbs, the text tells us,

> It happened that a woman who had aged considerably appeared before Rabbi Yose ben Halafta. She said: "Rabbi, I am much too old, life has become a burden for me. I can no longer taste food or drink, and I wish to die." Rabbi Yose answered her: "To what do you ascribe your longevity?" She answered that it was her habit to pray in the synagogue every morning, and despite occasional more pressing needs she never had missed a service. Rabbi Yose advised her to refrain from attending services for three consecutive days. She heeded his advice and on the third day she took ill and died.[38]

This text may be interpreted as a reinforcement of the view that passive euthanasia is permitted by Jewish law under certain conditions. The woman's withholding of her prayers removed the cause of the extension of her life. Similarly, the removal of life-support systems from a patient to whom—like this woman—life has become a burden, would be permissible.[39] Nevertheless, it may be argued that this case underscores the inability always to make a clear-cut distinction between passive and active euthanasia. Her discontinuance of her prayers or a physician's or nurse's "pulling the plug" may be considered a deliberate action aimed at precipitating an accelerated death. Once the line between passive and active euthanasia becomes so blurred, one may attempt to cross the line with care and with caution. For if the woman's withholding of her prayers is a sanctioned action deliberately designed to accelerate her own death, then other actions designed to hasten the death of those to whom life has become an unbearable burden might also be eligible for the sanction of Jewish tradition.

The underlying assumption of this midrashic text is the efficacy of prayer in attaining particular results. Here, the woman effected those results (her own death) by withholding prayer.[40] But, what about a case in which one actively prays for death to avoid enduring pain and suffering? The woman's withholding of her prayers caused her *own* death, but what about a case in which prayer is aimed at bringing about the death of another? It would seem to reason that if the rabbis permitted one actively to pray for one's own death and even for the death of another, rather than have one endure pain and suffering, then a basis of an argument could be made for a rabbinic precedent as far as both voluntary and involuntary active euthanasia are concerned. In the Talmud one finds such a precedent.

On the day that Rabbi Judah was dying, the rabbis decreed a public fast
and offered prayers for heavenly mercy [so that he would not die]. . . .
Rabbi Judah's handmaid ascended to the roof and prayed: "The immortals
[the angels] desire him [to join them] and the mortals desire him [to remain with them]; may it be the will [of God] that the mortals may over-
power the immortals [i.e., that he would not die]." When, however, she
saw how often he resorted to the privy, painfully removing and replacing
his *tefillin* [in terrible agony], she prayed: "May it be the will [of God] that
the immortals may over-power the mortals." The rabbis meanwhile continued their prayers for heavenly mercy. She took a jar and threw it down
from the roof to the ground. [For a moment,] they stopped praying, and
the soul of Rabbi Judah departed.[41]

Some interpret this text to mean that the death of Rabbi Judah was
caused by the rabbis' cessation of their prayers when they were startled by
the noise of the shattering jar. Others interpret this text to mean that his
death was caused by the handmaiden's active prayer aimed at bringing
about Rabbi Judah's death in order to alleviate his substantial suffering. It
is in this latter sense that the text was interpreted by the fourteenth-century
Talmudic commentator, Rabbenu Nissim (Ran). "Sometimes one must request mercy on behalf of the ill so that he might die, as in the case of a
patient who is terminal and who is in great pain."[42]

The question of whether one may pray for the death of a patient in
pain is discussed in a lengthy responsum by the nineteenth-century Turk-
ish rabbi Hayyim Palaggi. In this case, a woman has been suffering for
many years with a degenerative terminal disease. She has been afforded
the best available medical treatment. Her family has provided constant and
loving care. Hope for a remission has been abandoned by the patient, by
the family, and by the attending physicians. Her condition progressively
has deteriorated. Her pain has become constant and unbearable. Her illness has left her an invalid. She has prayed to God to die, preferring death
to life as a liberation from pain. She has asked her family to pray for her
death, but they have refused. Palaggi has been asked whether there are
any grounds for prohibiting prayers that she might find rest in death.

In a long and complicated argument, the details of which need not be
restated here, Palaggi ruled that, while family members may not pray for
her death, others may do so. In the course of reaching this conclusion,
Palaggi quoted a number of earlier sources, including the previously cited
statement of Rabbenu Nissim. Thus, Palaggi reaffirmed the earlier view
that active prayer for the death of a terminal patient in pain, whose life has
become a self-burden, is both permissible and even desirable. It is noteworthy that Palaggi did not even question the woman's right to pray for
death on her own behalf.

Among Palaggi's reasons for refusing the patient's family permission to pray for her death was the possibility of their actions being motivated by less than honorable motives. Palaggi specifically considered the possibility of the patient's spouse wishing her death so as to remarry someone already in mind. Palaggi also reflected on the possibility that the members of the patient's family may have desired her death—consciously or subconsciously—to free themselves from the burden of her care and support. This insightful psychological observation should be considered in cases of involuntary euthanasia, where the patient's family is confronted with the decision—even at the patient's request—to bring about the patient's accelerated death either by active or by passive euthanasia. As Palaggi noted, consideration for the patient is the only consideration. The financial or psychological condition of family members must not be the determining factor in such discussions. The establishment of ethics committees in many hospitals has helped to relieve patients' families of the anguish of such decisions and of the future guilt that may be precipitated by the realization that a decision to accelerate death might have been because of conscious or subconscious ulterior motives. As Palaggi noted, "strangers" cannot be held under suspicion of ulterior motives.

What is also significant about Palaggi's responsum is the manner in which he dealt with the endemic conflict of principles embodied in any examination of euthanasia from a Jewish perspective. These conflicting principles are preserving life and relieving agony. Palaggi attempted to obviate this apparently unresolvable conflict by reframing the question. According to Palaggi the question is, to what point is one morally obligated to continue life? By stating the question in this manner, Palaggi found a loophole in the categorical imperative to continue preserving life. He was therefore able to conclude that, in certain instances, such as the one at hand, it is both permissible and even desirable to take positive action that will liberate a terminal patient from agony by accelerating his or her death.

To be sure, Palaggi did not explicitly advocate active euthanasia in the sense of performing concrete medical or other intervention other than prayer to accelerate the death of a terminal patient in agony. Nevertheless, Palaggi established the viability of an attitude that would recommend active euthanasia in particular instances. And, while it was not his intention to do so, his view might be extended a step further to serve as the basis for advocating active euthanasia in cases similar to that of the woman described in his responsum.[43]

A further basis for a possible justification for active euthanasia from classical Jewish sources may be posited by combining related precedent with a form of argument characteristic of Jewish legal discourse. The precedent is the Talmudic text in which the term "euthanasia"—an easy, good, or quick death—occurs (Hebrew: *mitah yafah*). The form of argument is a fortiori (Hebrew: *kal va-homer*; literally: "the light and the weighty"). An example of this form of inference would be, "Here is a teetotaler who does not touch cider; he will certainly refuse whiskey." The acceptability of applying this form of argument is stated in the Talmud.[44]

The term *mitah yafah* is used in the course of Talmudic discussion concerning the execution of criminals convicted of capital offenses. In one text, the verse "You should love your neighbor as yourself" (Lev. 19:18) is interpreted to mean that the criminal is to be given a *mitah yafah;* the pain usually inflicted by the various types of death sentences is to be reduced both in time and in degree by administering a painkilling drug.[45] At this point, one may argue either from one comparable case to another or from the "weighty" to the "light" case.

1. The terminal patient is compared by the Talmud to a criminal condemned to death in that his or her case is hopeless.[46] From this equation one might argue that the terminal patient ought to be given at least the same consideration as a criminal about to be executed for having committed a capital offense.

2. One may also argue that if a criminal, guilty of having committed a capital offense, is shown such consideration, how much more should be shown the terminal patient, innocent of any capital offense?

3. One may extend these lines of argument to a further consideration of how cases of martyrdom, that is, cases of "justified" self-homicide, might be extended to cases of active euthanasia. As noted earlier in this chapter, some sources maintain that it is permissible in cases of martyrdom to allow oneself to be killed quickly or to take one's own life rather than to endure prolonged suffering and anguish.[47] One may maintain that, if such cases of martyrdom are not to be considered suicide or self-homicide, so cases in which an individual suffering agony takes his or her own life are similarly not to be condemned as suicide, and that certain cases of accelerating one's own death, to be free of excruciating pain, may be justifiable.

4. Jewish law forbids self-harm. Jewish law further prohibits an individual from intentionally placing himself or herself in a harmful or a potentially harmful or dangerous situation. Yet, even though Jewish legal authorities recognize the potentially hazardous nature of various types of medical, pharmacological, and surgical intervention, they nevertheless sanction such intervention. Therefore, the rule against potential danger may be set aside where such treatment is concerned. Consideration of the following halakhic precedents in this regard leads to further conclusions regarding possible justification of various forms of active euthanasia within the framework of Jewish law.

According to some halakhic authorities, when conventional therapies have been exhausted, experimental therapy may be introduced by a competent physician. This approach is sanctioned even if death were to result from such experimental therapy, especially where a terminal patient is involved. As long as even the most remote possibility of remission exists, hazardous therapy, even life-threatening therapy, may be employed. Using such therapy, though it is known in advance that it might immediately end the patient's life, would be a form of active euthanasia that would not be proscribed by Jewish law.

The prohibition against placing oneself in danger is also set aside when a medical or surgical procedure potentially endangers the life of a patient whose life is not clearly endangered by his or her medical condition. Specifically, if the purpose of the procedure is to reduce or eliminate substantial pain, such a procedure is permitted, despite its potential threat to the life of the patient.[48] From this perspective, as from that of Palaggi, the imperative to reduce or to eliminate pain is given precedence over the obligation to sustain life at all costs. One may extend this argument to a conclusion that would sanction the administering of painkilling drugs or procedures, even if it is known in advance that the patient might die as a result of such action. Hence, active euthanasia employed with the specific primary intention of alleviating unbearable pain would be an acceptable moral option, even if, in the act of alleviating pain, the death of the patient resulted.

In this case, as in those previously discussed, an a fortiori argument can be made: if administering a painkilling drug or undertaking a pain-alleviating procedure that may accelerate the patient's death can be done in cases in which death is not imminent, then it should be permissible to administer a painkilling drug or a painkilling procedure that may accelerate the patient's death in cases in which death is certainly imminent. From this basis, one may argue that, if there is a choice between prolonging the process of dying, where death seems imminent and certain, and taking action that will alleviate pain but that will also accelerate the process of death, where death is imminent and certain, then the latter option is both morally viable and legally permissible.

Not only may one make a case for active euthanasia in Jewish law, one may also argue that in certain circumstances the killer is not to be considered a murderer. To consider an act as murder, according to Jewish law, two of the conditions that must be satisfied are premeditation and malice (see Exod. 21:14). Rabbinic literature specifically exonerates a physician who kills his patient, even if he acted with willfulness, when malice is not also present. Though the medieval codes link premeditation with malice, there is no logical or psychological reason to do so. The rabbinic precedent may stand on its own.[49] Thus, under certain circumstances, according to this minority view, the physician may be legally (but not necessarily morally) blameless for practicing active euthanasia.

One specific case in which active euthanasia by patient, agent, or physician may be more justifiable than others, according to some of the literature, would be that in which the patient is afflicted with a terminal disease, such as cancer.

Talmudic law distinguishes between *goses*, that is, one terminally ill, and *tereifah* (literally, torn), that is, one terminally ill, for instance, as the result of irreparable organic damage. Apparently, in the former case, recovery is at least theoretically possible, whereas in the latter case, recovery is altogether impossible. One who kills a *goses* is considered a murderer by the Talmud and the codes. But one who kills a *tereifah* is not guilty of murder.[50]

Though the majority view found in classical and contemporary Jewish literature condemns active euthanasia, this chapter's discussion and the sources noted herein indicate the viability and the defensibility of a minority view supporting voluntary euthanasia when the primary motive is to alleviate pain and suffering. Indeed, a number of contemporary rabbinic decisions and views affirm this position. For example, David Shohet, writing in *Conservative Judaism* as early as 1952, came to this conclusion after a review of the classical Jewish sources on the matter. His article states that an adequate defense can be made to "support the contention that to bring a merciful end to intolerable suffering to a patient who has no longer any hope of recovery and his death is imminent, is an act which may be considered lawful and ethical in Jewish law."[51]

CONCLUSION

Continued developments in medical technology, increased life expectancy, and the rapid "graying" of the American people all point to an inevitable collision of events that have made, and will continue to make, the problem of euthanasia evermore severe in the foreseeable future. For the American Jewish community, with its median age already substantially higher than that of the American population as a whole, the problem of euthanasia is of particular and immediate pertinence.

It is only reasonable for Jewish patients, families, medical professionals, social workers, clergy, and those involved with the Jewish hospice movement to look to Jewish tradition—particularly to Jewish law and bioethics—for direction and for guidance in dealing with life's challenges and crises, especially those that come at life's end, such as the process of dying and the problem of euthanasia.

Jewish sources have developed a variety of concrete attitudes and views regarding the attempt to resolve the inevitable conflict between a commitment to valuing life and a commitment to mitigating pain and suffering during the process of dying. What emerges from a consideration of a vast number of classical sources is that Jewish tradition puts a high premium on extending life, but it recognizes that prolonging the process of painful death is not necessarily desirable. Therefore, it endorses passive euthanasia in most cases where death is imminent and inevitable and where the process of dying is accompanied by considerable and unbearable suffering and anguish. This attitude, as noted above, also relates to the introduction of heroic measures. In some instances, when death is near and certain and where considerable pain will ensue, heroic measures, or resuscitation, are not encouraged and, according to some authorities, are proscribed.

The preceding discussion outlines the dominant view in Jewish sources prohibiting active euthanasia of any kind. However, in view of contemporary realities, I have felt it necessary to defend a position within the framework of classical Jewish sources that would justify active euthanasia in at least certain circumstances. I believe that patients, families of patients, physicians, health care workers, and social service professionals, who deal with the death and dying of individuals, whose last days are overwhelmed with unbearable agony, should be able to advocate and to practice active euthanasia without feeling that they are criminals, without being burdened with great guilt for actions that they sincerely consider merciful, without feeling that they have transgressed divine and human laws, and without feeling that they have rejected the teachings of Jewish tradition. To be sure, Judaism instructs us to "choose life" (Deut. 30:19), but Judaism also recognizes that "there is a time to die" (Eccles. 3:2). In each case in which the problem of euthanasia presents itself, each person involved must decide which verse applies and how the fulfillment of that verse may best be implemented.

6

The Ethics of Giving and Receiving

> Once Samson of Shepetivka went to see Ezekiel Landau, the great sage and chief rabbi of Prague, to discuss matters of scholarship. The two rabbis never had met before. Samson of Shepetivka approached Ezekiel Landau in disguise, dressed as a beggar, asking for alms. Landau, who was a very busy man, treated his colleague—whom he thought to be an unlettered beggar—very rudely, whereupon Samson said, "How can you, a sage and a religious leader, treat a poor person in this fashion? You should rise at my presence, and you should respond to my needs, for God's presence stands at my side. As it is written: God stands at the right hand of the needy to save him from those who would condemn him" (—Ps. 109:31).

COLLECTING AND DISPERSING CHARITABLE FUNDS, sustaining and operating a plethora of philanthropic institutions and agencies, and striving to satisfy seemingly endless needs with substantial though clearly finite resources are central preoccupations of contemporary American Jewry.[1] Giving charity is probably the single commandment of the Torah most popularly and pervasively observed—intentionally or unintentionally—by American Jews. The largess of American Jewry supports a wide variety of Jewish and non-Jewish institutions and causes.

The centrality of *zedakah* to Jewish life and thought is hardly a modern phenomenon.[2] Throughout the ages, from biblical times onward, *zedakah* has been an ongoing primary concern of Jewish life and of Jewish religious thought. The Talmud quotes Rabbi Assi's statement, "*Zedakah* is as important as all the other commandments put together."[3] Maimonides described *zedakah* as an essential feature of Jewish communal life when he wrote, "We never have seen nor heard of a Jewish community that does not have a *zedakah* fund."[4] Because *zedakah* has played, and continues to play, such a pivotal role in Jewish life, it is both informative and relevant to survey the attitudes and views of classical Jewish literature regarding *zedakah*. A host of scattered references to *zedakah* are sprinkled throughout classical Jewish religious literature. As Nahmanides observed, "we need not provide specific references to the statements of the sages regarding *zedakah*, for the entire Talmud and all works of *haggadah* are replete with them . . . as if they are innumerable."[5] While various medieval treatises of Jewish law and ethics contain chapters and short discussions of *zedakah*, surprisingly only one work in classical Jewish religious literature is devoted exclusively to this topic. As Solomon Schechter observed, "We have only one book entirely devoted to the study of philanthropy, *Me'il Zedakah* by Elijah Cohen."[6]

THE PREMISES OF *ZEDAKAH*

A few hours before his death on 20 November 1915, Solomon Schechter, "the father of Conservative Judaism in America," delivered his last lecture. The subject was *zedakah*. At the time of his death, Schechter was working on a comprehensive study of *zedakah*, for Schechter was convinced that American Jewish philanthropy—already a substantial enterprise in his day—had to be examined and understood from "a Jewish point of view." In his lecture, Schechter identified the claim, "all wealth belongs to God," as the first and primary underlying principle and premise of *zedakah*. He observed that "the idea that God is the sole owner of everything we possess is current not only in the poetic portions, the Haggadah of the Bible so to speak, or the homiletical interpretations of the rabbis, but also forms a basis for many a civil and religious law."[7]

The corollary of the claim that all wealth belongs to God is the description of human beings as the stewards, guardians, or trustees of God's possessions. It is a human responsibility to manage properly the wealth God has entrusted to our care. Properly giving *zedakah* represents a way of fulfilling that responsibility. Failing in that task is tantamount to stealing from God and from the deserving recipients of *zedakah*, according to some rabbinic and medieval sources. Schechter correctly identified these ideas of divine ownership of all property and human stewardship of God's property as being introduced by the Bible, amplified by the Talmudic rabbis, and developed further by medieval Jewish ethical sources.

Scriptural verses, such as the following, attest to the biblical view that God is the owner and the proprietor of the world and of everything contained therein.

The earth is the Lord's and the fullness thereof (Ps. 24:1).

Mine is the gold and the silver, says the Lord of hosts (Hag. 2:8).

Riches and honor are Yours to dispense; You have dominion over all. . . .
All is from You, and it is Your gift that we have given to You (1 Chron.
29:12, 14).

Verses such as these are cited in the Talmudic and medieval sources
to reinforce and to expand the notion that *what we own, we owe*. For
example, the *Ethics of the Fathers* observes, "Give Him of His own, for
both you and whatever is yours are His, as David said [1 Chron. 29:14]: 'All
is from You, and it is Your gift that we have given You.'"[8] Along similar
lines, the medieval ethical treatise *Sefer Ma'alot ha-Middot* says,

> Come and see how beloved of God are those who give *zedakah*. For, even
> though they give nothing of their own but of that which is God's, as it is
> written, "Mine is the gold and the silver, says the Lord" [Hag. 2:8], and it
> is also said, "all is from You, and it is Your gift that we have given You" [1
> Chron. 29:14], nevertheless, the Holy One, blessed be He, accounts it to
> you as if you have given of your own [property].[9]

The corollary to the concept of divine ownership, the notion of human stewardship, is also affirmed in rabbinic literature and amplified in
medieval ethical literature. For example, a midrash quotes God as saying,
"Honor the Lord from whatever substance He has bestowed upon you. You
are only My steward."[10] According to the *Sefer Hasidim*, a wealthy individual who does not help support the poor is to be considered a thief. "God
says to him [the wealthy person]: I have supplied you with abundant
wealth so that you may give to the needy to the extent of your means. Yet,
you did not give. I [God] shall punish you as if you have robbed those
people and as if you have denied having in your possession something that
I entrusted to you. The wealth I put into your hand for distribution to the
poor, you appropriated for yourself."[11] A final example of a classical Jewish
text that describes charity as the fulfillment of human stewardship and
trusteeship for God's possessions is from *Torat Moshe*, a commentary to
the Pentateuch by the sixteenth-century cabalist Moses Alsheikh. A verse
in Exodus (22:24) reads, "If you lend money to my people, to the poor who
is in your power, do not act toward him as a creditor: exact no interest from
him." Commenting on this verse, Alsheikh used the word "*epitropos*" to
characterize the loaner.[12] This Talmudic term, which derives from the
Greek, denotes a court-appointed guardian or trustee. According to Alsheikh, by giving *zedakah* in the form of an interest-free loan to the poor,

one is simply administering funds for social welfare entrusted into one's hands by the owner of the funds, namely, God.[13]

If divine ownership of all property and human stewardship of that property is the first premise of *zedakah*, then the pressing and omnipresent neediness of the poor is the second premise upon which *zedakah* rests. By the biblical era, the fact that "there will never cease to be needy ones in your land" was already recognized. The appropriate response to the needs of the poor was immediately identified as the giving of *zedakah:* this "is why I command you: open your hand to the poor and needy kinsman in your land" (Deut. 15:11).

In various places throughout the *Me'il Zedakah*, the author persistently advocated the cause of the poor. *Zedakah*, he insisted, is necessary because the needs of the poor are real and because the entitlement of the poor to aid is justified. Indeed, he observed, without the presence of the poor, the rich would be unable to fulfill the mitzvah of *zedakah;* in other words, the rich need the poor as much as the poor need the rich. In advocating the cause of the needy, the *Me'il Zedakah* defends the perpetual requirements of the poor against the endless disparagements of the uncharitable. For example, the *Me'il Zedakah* rejects the view that poverty is a state that people bring upon themselves either by their own indolence or as a divine punishment for sin.

Abraham Lincoln's view that God must have loved the poor since he made so many of them is similar to views found in the *Me'il Zedakah* and in earlier Jewish literature. God's love of the poor and His identification with them neutralizes the view of the poor as having been rejected and punished by God. Abraham Cronbach summarized the view of the *Me'il Zedakah:* "To the contention that the poor are devoid of decency, the answer is that the poor are devoid of iniquity."[14]

The proposition that poverty is not a result of sin but a catalyst for virtue is epitomized by this midrashic statement:

The Holy One, in casting about among all the most desirable conditions in the world, found no condition more beneficial for Israel than poverty, for through poverty they come to fear the Lord. If they have no bread to eat, no clothes to wear, no oil for anointing, then they seek the Lord of mercy and find Him. Thus it is through poverty that they come to fear the Lord. For they who act out of love come to it only through poverty. They who bestow many kinds of charity come to it only through poverty. And those who fear Heaven come to it only through poverty, as is said, "He raises up the poor out of the dust" [1 Sam. 2:8].[15]

According to this midrash, not only are the poor virtuous but poverty itself may be perceived as a virtue. That poverty is a virtue that precipitates communion with God is not a dominant motif in Jewish literature;

however, neither is it a theme unknown to Jewish literature. Two of the most important works in Jewish mystical-ethical literature, the *Sefer Hasidim* and the *Zohar*, exalt poverty as a religious virtue.

According to the *Zohar*, the poor are not alienated from God because of their sins. Instead, they are endeared to God because of their impoverished state. The *Zohar* teaches that

> the prayers of the poor are received by God ahead of all other prayers. "Happy is he who is considerate of the poor" (Ps. 41:2). . . . How great is the reward that the poor merit of the Lord . . . for they are closest to God. . . . The poor man is closer to God than anyone else . . . for God abides in these broken vessels, as it is written, "I dwell on high, amid holiness, but also with the contrite and humble in spirit" (Isa. 57:15). . . . Therefore we have been taught that he who reviles the indigent scoffs at the Divinity. . . . Happy is he who encounters a poor man, for this poor man is a gift sent to him by God.[16]

Were poverty a divine punishment, then *zedakah* would not be the fulfillment of a religious imperative but an intervention in God's execution of justice.[17] While *zedakah* is invariably portrayed as a virtue, poverty is rarely so portrayed. For most Jewish sources, poverty is not a divine punishment but a personal calamity. According to one Talmudic source, poverty deprives a person of one's senses; poverty can make one mad. Another Talmudic source compares poverty with death, and a third source observes that "poverty in one's home is worse than fifty plagues."[18] A midrashic text summarizes this apprehension of poverty as a disaster. "There is nothing in the world more grievous than poverty—the most terrible of all sufferings. . . . Our teachers have said: If all troubles were assembled on one side and poverty on the other, poverty would outweigh them all."[19]

The catastrophe of poverty was understood to pose a physical and a psychological danger to the poor; it was also seen as a moral danger. Driven by destitution, the indigent person might become prone to immoral acts, such as robbery, the *Me'il Zedakah* observes. For precisely this reason, the nineteenth-century Hasidic master Aaron of Karlin taught that "one must have a greater fear of a poor person than of a sword." Thus, poverty, like wealth, has its temptations. *Zedakah* is a way not only of physically and fiscally helping the needy but a way of aiding him or her morally as well.

INFINITE NEEDS AND FINITE RESOURCES

Throughout history, the needs of the indigent always have surpassed the resources of potential and actual benefactors. The realization that the needs

of the poor seem virtually infinite and eternal leads many a potential donor
to the conclusion that any philanthropic effort is ultimately futile. The *Me'il
Zedakah* argues against this conclusion. Because the impossible cannot be
realized is no reason for being dissuaded from achieving the possible. The
enormity of the need cannot serve as a justification for not seeking to assuage it. In considering the incongruity between resources and needs, the
literature on *zedakah* discusses assigning priorities to the needs while not
losing sight of the individuality of the requirements of the needy. Even
during the Talmudic period, our sources were aware that needs varied both
in kind and in degree. The multiple levels of giving *zedakah* outlined by
Maimonides, as well as by others, paralleled a recognition that needs also
existed on a series of levels. Just as there were levels and degrees of aid, so
were there levels and degrees of need. It is noteworthy, and perhaps not
coincidental, that Maimonides identified eight levels of *zedakah*, while a
midrash notes that biblical Hebrew has eight words to denote the poor.[20]

The literature on *zedakah* relentlessly observes that need cannot be
quantified on the basis of objective criteria. An individual's needs cannot
be determined through calculating the objective minimum that any person
might require to be sustained. The sources refuse to objectify another person's need; each person is perceived as an individual with subjective, individ-
ualistic, idiosyncratic needs. The sources refuse to categorize the welfare
client. The demands of his or her personality, past experience, self-respect,
and personal dignity are never overlooked. The goal in Jewish social welfare—not always attainable, though never forgotten—is to provide the individual that which is "sufficient for *his* need" (Deut. 15:8). That the individual need of the client is of paramount concern is expressed in the
following Talmudic text. Commenting on the verse, "Rather, you must
open your hand and lend him sufficient for whatever he needs" (Deut.
15:8), the Talmud says, "'For whatever he needs'" [Deut. 15:8] [includes]
even a horse to ride and a slave to run before him. It is related about Hillel
the Elder that he bought for a certain poor man who was of a good family a
horse to ride upon and a slave to run before him. On one occasion he could
not find a slave to run before him, so he himself ran before him for three
miles."[21] Maimonides interpreted this text to mean that the poor man mentioned in the text was not simply of a good family but was once rich.

Since poverty is more psychologically debilitating for a person who
has lost his or her wealth than it is to a person who has never had wealth,
the needs of this individual are greater. To ensure the dignity of this person, more than the gift of a dole is required. Maimonides's demand that
the personal experience and economic history of the individual must be
considered when giving him *zedakah*, is Talmudic in origin. "It has been
taught that if a person [who was rich] has become poor and requires public
assistance, if he had been used to vessels of gold, they give him vessels of
silver; if of silver, they give him vessels of copper; if copper, they give him

vessels of glass. Rabbi Mena said: They give him vessels of silver or glass only for his personal use. How about that teaching which said that if a man had been used to wear clothes of fine wool, they give him clothes of fine wool? Again, these are only for his personal use."[22] The attitude articulated by this text represents the Talmudic rabbis' intense awareness of the fragility of economic life and the vulnerability of the wealthy to its fluctuations. Consequently, rabbinic views on *zedakah* incorporate this awareness. In the words of a midrash, "There is an ever rotating wheel in this world, and he who is rich today may not be so tomorrow."[23]

TREATING THE WELFARE RECIPIENT

Zedakah is both person centered and need centered. The gift must be appropriate to the person and to that person's particular present need. On the verse, "Open your hand to your brother" (Deut. 15:11), a rabbinic midrash comments, "To one for whom bread is suitable, give bread; for one who needs dough, give dough; for one who requires money, give money; for one who needs to be fed, feed him."[24] This approach of the Talmudic rabbis, later codified in medieval legal codes, is that *zedakah* is a response to a specific individual situation and need; it is not a solution to an abstract social problem.[25] To help guarantee the dignity of the poor, efforts were made to guarantee the anonymity both of the donor and of the recipient of *zedakah*. Especially in cases in which the rich had lost their possessions, joining the ranks of the poor, anonymity was desired. For example, "Just as there was a 'vestry of secret givers' in the Temple, so there was one in every city, for the sake of noble people, who had come down in life, so that they may be helped in secret."[26]

According to a Talmudic tale, Mar Ukba had a poor man in his neighborhood. So as not to embarrass this poor man, Mar Ukba used to throw four coins into his house under his door every day. One day the poor man decided to discover the identity of his benefactor. When Mar Ukba saw that the man was watching as he approached the house, Mar Ukba ran away and hid in a furnace from which the fire had been just swept out. When Mar Ukba's extreme measures to escape being known were questioned, the Talmud explained them by quoting the well-known rabbinic adage: Better to throw oneself in a fiery furnace than publicly to shame one's neighbor.[27] Elsewhere the Talmud states, "A person who gives *zedakah* in secret is greater than Moses, our teacher."[28]

According to Maimonides's eight levels of charity, giving anonymously to a poor person who does not know the identity of his benefactor is the next to highest kind of *zedakah*. It protects the dignity of the recipient and expresses the altruism of the benefactor. However, according to Maimonides and many other sources, the highest form of *zedakah* is not a gift but a loan. By giving a loan or by entering into partnership with the needy person his or her dignity is preserved by allowing him or her to maintain at least a facade of self-sufficiency. In such cases, to be sure, there is no requirement or even an expectation that the loan be repaid. Nor is any interest attached to the loan. The goal of this form of *zedakah* is to preserve the dignity of the needy and to help extricate him or her from being needy, to allow him or her to attain economic self-sufficiency.

Once again, in the case of giving *zedakah* as a loan, one finds a special sensitivity toward the needs of the previously wealthy. For example, a Talmudic text recounts that Rabbi Jonah examined how to fulfill the mitzvah of *zedakah*. "What did Rabbi Jonah do? When he saw a previously wealthy poor person he would say: I have heard that you have inherited some wealth. Take this loan now and you will repay me. After he took it, he [Rabbi Jonah] would say: It is a gift for you."[29]

The view that a loan is better than a gift has firm Talmudic precedent: "He who lends [money to the poor] is greater than he who gives a charitable gift; and he who forms a partnership [with the poor] is greater than all."[30] On this text, Rashi commented that a loan is better than a gift because a poor person, who might be ashamed to accept a gift, would readily agree to a loan. Also, a donor might be willing to make a loan of a greater sum than he might be willing to make a gift. A second text succinctly states, "One who gives *zedakah*, many blessings come upon him; superior to him is one who lends his funds [to the poor]; superior to all is one [who forms a partnership with the poor] on terms of half the profits [for each] or on terms of sharing what remains."[31] According to a number of sources, lending is superior to giving because loans are common between the rich as well as the poor, while *zedakah* is for the poor alone. A gift demeans by the very fact that the recipient is on a level subordinate to that of the donor, but in the case of a loan, both parties are deemed equal.

The aim of giving loans to the poor was to help them to exchange dependency for self-sufficiency. Just as rabbinic sources were concerned about the need to rescue the poor from indigency, so are they preoccupied with the need to prevent one from sliding into poverty. *Zedakah* was not only to be therapeutic but preventive as well. Commenting on the phrase in Leviticus (25:35), "then you shall uphold him," Rashi warned, "Do not let him come down until he falls [completely] for then it will be difficult to raise him. Rather, uphold him at the time that his means [begin to] fail. To what is this comparable? To a burden that rests on a donkey. While it is still on the donkey one [person can] hold it and set it back in place, but if it fell to the ground even five people cannot set it back in its place."[32]

To make sure that communal funds were distributed to the truly needy, means to investigate the authenticity of need were developed and employed. Funds were always too sparse to expend on "deceivers." In addition, as the *Me'il Zedakah* observes, the presence of "cheats" was often used as an excuse not to contribute by recalcitrant potential donors. According to Maimonides, if a person asks for food, that is, for the fulfillment of an immediate need, such a person's need is not to be investigated. The need may be too pressing to endure an inquiry. However, if a person asks for other types of aid, such as clothing, the need is not immediate and life threatening; therefore, an investigation into the grounds for the request is warranted.[33] Regarding imposters, the Mishnah teaches, "He that does not need to take yet takes shall not depart from this world before he falls in need of his fellows. . . . And if a man is not lame or dumb or blind or halting, yet he makes himself like unto one of them, he shall not die in old age until he becomes like one of them, as it is written [Prov. 11:27], 'He that searches after mischief, it shall come upon him.'"[34] Furthermore, as Maimonides noted, community officials would investigate the claims of potential clients seeking communal welfare to remove imposters from community welfare roles.

Besides admonishing and seeking to unmask imposters, Maimonides dealt with the case of the truly needy person who hesitates or refuses to accept aid. In such a case, Maimonides counseled that aid should be given as a gift or as a loan. Maimonides's source seems to be this Talmudic statement: "Our rabbis taught: If a person has no means and does not wish to be maintained [out of the poor funds] he should be granted [the sum he requires] as a loan and it can be presented to him as a gift; so [says] Rabbi Meir. The sages however said that it is given to him as a gift and then it is granted to him as a loan."[35]

According to Maimonides, who relied on Talmudic sources, the deceiver is accursed. The indigent individual who is too proud to accept help needed for survival is self-destructive. The truly needy, however, is entitled to receive what is needed. Nevertheless, every effort must be made before one begins to receive public aid. "One should always restrain himself and submit to privation rather than be dependent upon other people or cast himself upon public charity."[36]

The constant disparity between available funds and ever-present need required setting priorities in the dispensing of aid. For Maimonides, charity begins at home. The first priority is the support of one's own family. While one is required to help the indigent, one is forbidden to join them in the process. Maimonides writes, "A poor man who is one's relative has priority over all others, the poor of one's own household have priority over the other poor of his city, and the poor of his city have priority over the poor of another city."[37] Similarly, in his fourteenth-century ethical treatise *Menorat ha-Ma'or*, Isaac Aboab insists that a person's first obligation is self-support, then support of one's parents, support of one's children, and only then is one obliged to render support for the needy.[38]

Safeguards were established to prevent the enthusiastic donor from becoming generous to the extent of self-impoverishment. For this reason, restrictions upon the percentage of one's possessions one was able to contribute was limited to 20 percent by rabbinic decree.[39] Safeguards were established to protect the overzealous from joining the ranks of the impoverished and thereby becoming themselves public charges. About the Hasidic master Levi Yitzhak of Berdichev, it is told that, after he would collect his salary, he would begin to walk home to deposit it with his wife for household expenses. On the way, he would inevitably meet people in need. Giving each individual a portion of his salary, he would arrive home empty-handed. Eventually, his wife was so desperate for funds that she brought suit against him for failing to support his wife and his children. The judge found Levi Yitzhak guilty and ordered that the salary be paid directly to her. Being the rabbi of the town, Levi Yitzhak was not only the defendant in the case but the judge as well.

In meeting the needs of others, priorities were established. As already noted, one is obliged to care for one's own family before one is required to take care of another's family. Immediate needs, such as hunger, were to supersede other less-pressing needs. A woman's needs were to take precedent over those of a man because she was considered more vulnerable to harm or to abuse. The needs of orphans were given priority because they had no family; no one else but the community could care for them.[40]

Communal funds aided the indigent and others. Brides were provided with dowries, newlyweds with furnishings. The dead were buried, the sick cared for and attended. Interest-free loans were made. Newly arrived immigrants were cared for until they could plant roots of their own. In the rabbinic period and throughout the Middle Ages, Jews were held for ransom by kings, pirates, and other extortionists. Therefore, ransoming of captives—especially, women and children—became a priority of communal *zedakah* funds.[41]

All of the needs for which communal funds were expended would have been left unattended if observance of the mitzvah of *zedakah* had been neglected. Dispensing of funds assumed the giving of funds. It is imperative, therefore, to examine how the giving of *zedakah* was envisaged by our sources, beginning with the Bible.

THE ETHICS OF GIVING

It would be a linguistic and conceptual mistake to equate *zedakah* with charity or with philanthropy. "*Zedakah*" derives from a Hebrew root that denotes "justice" and "righteousness." Thus, "*zedakah*" denotes contributing to help the needy because it is just to do so, because it is right to do so, because it is a duty to do so. "Charity" and "philanthropy" derive from Latin and Greek roots that denote altruistic love of others. These terms—rooted in Christian theological attitudes—express the view that one should help one another because one loves the other. From this perspective, social welfare flows from altruistic benevolence rather than from legal requirements and social obligations.[42]

Jewish tradition considers the fate of the indigent too precarious to be left to spontaneous expressions of love or of altruisim. The poor, the sick, the disabled, the disadvantaged might not prove to be especially lovable. Prospective donors might not be moved by spontaneous generosity to assuage the situation of the unfortunate. Therefore, Jewish tradition, from the Bible onward, considers *zedakah* to be a legal duty, a social responsibility, a repayment of a debt to God. Giving *zedakah* is the fulfillment of a commandment rather than an act of optional benevolence. Indeed, the anonymous medieval ethical treatise *Orhot Zaddikim* discourages impulsive giving and encourages regular habitual giving.

> Our sages of blessed memory said further: The quality of generosity depends upon habit, for a person cannot be considered generous unless that person gives of his own free will at all times, at all hours, according to his ability. A person who gives a thousand gold pieces to a worthy person at one time is not as generous as one who gives a thousand gold pieces on a thousand different occasions, each to a worthy cause. For the person who gave a thousand gold pieces at one time had a sudden impulse to be generous, but after that the desire left him.[43]

Biblical tradition could not rest content with a general or vague admonition to "open your hand to the poor and needy" (Deut. 15:14). Rather, Scripture established specific laws of *zedakah*. Those who had were obliged to give; those who were in need were entitled to take. The law defined the parameters of giving. *Zedakah* was more a tax, a legal obligation, than an act of capricious kindness. The biblical laws of *zedakah* translated justice and righteousness from abstract categories to concrete legal requirements.

The biblical laws of *zedakah* assume and address an agricultural society. These laws establish a number of specific ways of aiding the needy. According to one biblical injunction, the products of the corners of each field should not be collected by the owner of the field but should be left for the needy. Neither the products of a field nor of a vineyard should be completely collected; something should be left for the poor (Lev. 19:9–10, 23:22). On each seventh year, the land is to be left fallow. Whatever the land produces during that year may be claimed by the needy (Exod. 23:10–

11). According to the Talmud, this institution of a sabbatical year is to remind us that the earth ultimately belongs to God, that God owns what we possess.[44]

That which was not reaped when a field was harvested went to the needy (Deut. 24:19). A tithe of all one's net yield was to be given to the needy (Deut. 26:12). On festivals special contributions were to be made so that the needy could also rejoice at those times (Deut. 16:9–14). Each fiftieth year, on the Jubilee, all real estate holdings were to be returned to their original owners (Lev. 25:9–15). In this way, the impoverished could be restored economically. Interest could not be charged of one in need (Lev. 25:35–37, Exod. 22:24). Discussing this prohibition against charging interest, the commentaries observe that the Hebrew word "*neshekh*" (interest) is related to the word "*neshikhah*" (a bite). As Rashi put it, "*Neshekh* means interest since it is like the bite (*neshikhah*) of a snake which bites making a small wound on one's foot which he does not feel, but suddenly it blows up as far as his head. So with interest—one does not feel it and it is not at first noticeable until the interest increases and causes one to lose much money."[45]

The biblical characterization of a just society was one where the needy were cared for, where the vulnerable were protected. The unjust society, the society deserving of destruction, such as Sodom and Gomorrah, is one that neglects the indigent. For example, the prophet Ezekiel observed (Ezek. 16:49), "Only this was the sin of your sister Sodom: arrogance! She and her daughters had plenty of bread and untroubled tranquillity; yet she did not support the poor and the needy."

The legal obligation of *zedakah*, established by the Bible, was developed by the Talmudic rabbis and was codified in the medieval legal codes. Through this process of development, an attempt was made to relate the laws of *zedakah* to a society that was primarily commercial rather than primarily agricultural, to an urban as well as to an agrarian society. Despite these adaptations of biblical agricultural statutes to later socioeconomic situations, the understanding of *zedakah* as a legal duty and as a religious imperative remained constant. According to Maimonides, one who gave *zedakah* fulfilled a positive commandment. One who did not give *zedakah* violated a negative commandment.[46] Furthermore, Maimonides insisted, "It is our duty to be more careful in the performance of the commandment of almsgiving than in that of any other positive commandment."[47]

Despite the emphasis upon *zedakah* as an unequivocal religious, social, and legal obligation, it would be a mistake to conclude that the idea of philanthropy and benevolence is absent from Judaism. Though some authors claim that the Jewish conception of *zedakah* is lacking in that it emphasizes law to the neglect of love, such a claim can hardly be substantiated by the Jewish sources themselves. Jewish religious literature seeks instead

to strike a balance between law and love, between obligation and generosity. *Zedakah* represents a minimal requirement, but more is hoped for,
more is expected.

Zedakah is a necessary but insufficient expression of concern for the
well-being of others. *Zedakah* is complemented by *gemilut hasadim*, acts of
loving-kindness. *Zedakah* is what is required by law. *Gemilut hasadim* is an
expression of love and of profound concern for others. According to Rashi,
zedakah denotes the act of giving, while *gemilut hasadim* refers to the noble intentions infused within the act.[48] According to Judah Loew of Prague,
the difference between the virtue of giving *zedakah* and the virtue of doing
gemilut hasadim is that *zedakah* is determined by the needs of the recipient, but *gemilut hasadim* flows from the goodness of the benefactor. In
zedakah, the recipient benefits only from the benefactor's money. In *gemilut hasadim*, the recipient enjoys the good nature of the benefactor.[49] Judah
Loew offered this distinction as a commentary to the following Talmudic
statement: "Our rabbis taught: In three respects is *gemilut hasadim* superior to *zedakah*. *Zedakah* can be done only with one's money, but *gemilut
hasadim* can be done with one's person and with one's money. *Zedakah* can
be given to the poor alone, but *gemilut hasadim* can be given to the rich as
well as to the poor. *Zedakah* can be given only to the living while *gemilut
hasadim* can be done both to the living and to the dead."[50]

Zedakah is justice in action. *Gemilut hasadim* is mercy and love in
action. "What is *gemilut hasadim*?," *Sefer Ma'alot ha-Middot* asks. "That
one will be merciful to all creatures, as the Creator, may He be blessed, is
merciful and full of compassion." In practicing *zedakah*, one fulfills social
obligations. By practicing *gemilut hasadim*, one expresses *imitatio Dei*, that
which we have in common with God. Through *gemilut hasadim* one articulates one's having been created in the image of the divine.[51]

Giving *zedakah* fulfills legal requirements; *gemilut hasadim* transcends legal demands. In his philosophical work, *The Guide of the Perplexed*, Maimonides discussed this distinction between *zedakah* and *hesed*
(the root of "*hasadim*"). According to Maimonides, *zedakah* refers to giving
one one's just due, while *hesed* refers to absolute beneficence. *Zedakah*
means granting something to someone who has a right of entitlement.
Hesed is the practice of benevolence toward one who has no claim upon
what he or she receives.[52]

Among the actions identified as acts of loving-kindness, as expressions
of *gemilut hasadim*, are visiting the sick, burying the dead, comforting the
mourner, caring for animals, hospitality to strangers, and giving *zedakah*
without ulterior motives. While the Talmud put restrictions upon how
much *zedakah* one might give, acts of loving-kindness were assigned no
such restrictions.[53]

Acts characterized as *gemilut hasadim* are considered expressions of loving-kindness because they may be done selflessly, without thoughts of recompense from the recipient. For example, when Jacob is dying, he asks Joseph to treat him with "kindness (*hesed*) and with truth (*emet*)." On this verse (Gen. 47:29), Rashi commented, "The kindness that is shown to the dead is a true kindness (*hesed shel emet*), for [in such a case] one does not expect the payment of recompense [from the recipient]."[54]

In *Menorat ha-Ma'or*, Isaac Aboab wrote that "*zedakah* given self-lessly for the sake of Heaven, graciously and compassionately, is called *gemilut hasadim*." Thus Aboab identified *gemilut hasadim* as an exalted variety of *zedakah*. Aboab refused to assign *zedakah* to one realm and *gemilut hasadim* to another. Instead, Aboab perceived a certain fluidity between dutiful actions and benevolent actions. For Aboab, as well as for others, actions that may benefit others embrace a wide spectrum from self-serving or reluctant giving of *zedakah* to perfectly selfless acts of loving-kindness.[55] This notion of "gradations of benevolence" underlies Maimonides's well-known eight levels of *zedakah*.[56]

The majority of the sources agree (for exceptions, see below) that even the self-serving donor, even the stingy donor, even the recalcitrant donor fulfills the mitzvah of *zedakah* though his intentions may be far from honorable or benevolent. The primary goal is that the needy be cared for. Nevertheless, virtually all sources also agree that what is hoped for is that "the donor of *zedakah* will give for the sake of Heaven; that is, selflessly, that his intention in giving will not be public acclaim or acknowledgment."[57]

The *Sefer Hasidim* cautioned against giving *zedakah* for self-aggrandizement, for public acclaim, for fear of public censure for not giving. According to Rashi, giving *zedakah* to the poor only when they reach dire destitution is an example of a good deed that is really bad, of a good deed badly done.[58] The hesitant or the recalcitrant donor is to be condemned and not to be emulated. Along similar lines, a midrash describes different types of donors, comparing them to different kinds of nuts.

Rabbi Levi said: There are three kinds of nuts: *Perek* nuts whose shell is soft, those whose shell is moderately hard, and those whose shell is very hard. The soft-shelled nut bursts open of itself; the moderately hard-shelled nuts crack open when struck; and the hard-shelled nut is too hard to be cracked, so that when you strike it with a stone you shatter it, and then you do not get good of it. So, too, the people of Israel: There are those among them who do good of their own accord—these are the soft-hearted; there are those among them who, when you ask them to give to charity, will give at once—these are the moderately soft-hearted; and there are those among them whom, no matter how hard you press them, nothing good ever comes. Nevertheless, Rabbi Levi went on to say, among the people of Israel, even the door which will not open to give charity will open wide to give when [illness presses and] the physician comes.[59]

Rabbi Levi's final remark, that even one who initially refuses to give will eventually give when sickness strikes, reflects a view found in biblical rabbinic and medieval sources. According to a well-established tradition, giving *zedakah* offers the promise of reward as well as protection from sickness, death, and harm. Despite their attempt to encourage benevolence and generosity, the sources felt obliged to appeal to more base human motives to stimulate the giving of *zedakah*. In their view, selflessness was a goal to which few could or would aspire. Therefore, given the predilections of human nature, it became popular to appeal for *zedakah* by invoking the promise of reward, the assurance of protection, and the fear of punishment for failing to contribute to *zedakah*. Thus, especially in Talmudic and in medieval sources, giving *zedakah* was portrayed as bestowing prophylactic if not magical protection upon the donor. For example, the following Talmudic statements portray giving charity as a way of fending off calamity, as a way of bringing redemption, as a way of guaranteeing well-being:

> Rabbi Isaac also said, He who gives a small coin to a poor man obtains six blessings. . . . Rabbi Joshua ben Levi said, He who does charity habitually will have sons wise, wealthy and versed in *aggadah*. . . . Rabbi Judah says: Great is charity in that it brings the redemption nearer. . . . Death is stronger than all [strong things in the world], but charity saves from death. . . . Why this double mention of *zedakah* [in Prov. 10:2, 11:4]? One [mention refers to] delivery from an unnatural death, and one [mention refers to] delivery from the punishments of purgatory (*gehinnom*).[60]

Similarly, the High Holiday liturgy continuously reminds one that *zedakah* is one way to "avert the evil decree." According to some sources, giving charity has the power to prevent harm in this world and in the next, to ensure well-being in this world and in the next, and even to guarantee the resurrection of the dead. An entire chapter of the midrash *Pirke de Rabbi Eliezer* offers examples of how giving charity made possible (and therefore will continue to make possible) the resurrection of the dead.[61]

The Talmud compares a poor person, a blind person, a diseased person, and a childless person with a dead person.[62] As noted, giving *zedakah* was viewed as a way of delivering one from death. Post-Talmudic sources, such as the *Me'il Zedakah*, combined these two views and concluded that *zedakah* cannot only deliver one from death but also from situations that are comparable with death. In a similar vein, the *Midrash on Psalms* understands the verse "Blessed is he that considers the poor; the Lord will deliver him in time of trouble" (Ps. 41:1) to mean that God will deliver one who "is considerate and gives money to the poor." [63]

The aforementioned tension between the always-present requirements of the needy and the desired virtue of the donor pervades the literature regarding *zedakah*. According to some traditions, the act of *zedakah* is essential; the motivation of the donor is secondary. The donor whose primary intention is the expectation of reward, protection from harm, social approval, or personal aggrandizement is still adjudged as having fulfilled the mitzvah of *zedakah*, even though helping the needy might not have been the central motivation behind his or her gift. Even a stingy, recalcitrant, resentful donor was considered to have fulfilled the mitzvah of giving *zedakah*. What was paramount was that the indigent be served. On the other hand, some traditions refused to consider recalcitrant or self-serving giving as fulfilling the mitzvah of giving *zedakah*. For these sources, *zedakah* given with improper intentions perverts the very aim of the entire institution of *zedakah*—the establishment of a just society.

Such texts as the *Me'il Zedakah* railed against those who gave *zedakah* to attain divinely conferred or socially bestowed rewards. This treatise warned that those who used *zedakah* as a tool to attain social approval or social status will ultimately become destitute, that giving *zedakah* for self-glorification is a religious abomination rather than a religious virtue. *Orhot Zaddikim* even claimed, "he who gives *zedakah* to the poor grudgingly loses the merit of the deed, even though he gives much; it is better that he give only one coin with a pleasing countenance." This text echoes an earlier rabbinic statement, "If one gives his fellow all the good gifts in the world with a downcast face, Scripture accounts it to him as though he had given him naught."[64]

Besides the tension between the actions and the intentions of the donor, the literature regarding *zedakah* articulates a further tension between the obligation of the donor to give and the ability of the donor to give. On the one hand, *zedakah* was viewed as an obligatory tax with defined minimal and maximal amounts. On the other hand, *zedakah* was perceived as a gift, an expression of generosity, limited only by the beneficence of the donor.

Biblical law established and rabbinic law developed the view that everyone was obliged to donate, even the poor.[65] The medieval codes express the inevitable tension between the needs of the prospective recipients and the abilities and generosity of the prospective donors. The codes therefore establish that 10 percent ought to be considered the average donation. Less brands one an evil person. One-third of a shekel is defined as the minimal donation. One-fifth of one's income is established by the Talmud as the ceiling on donations to *zedakah*.[66] The ceiling of one-fifth was instituted because the rabbis apparently felt that individuals might otherwise impoverish themselves, thereby becoming clients of social welfare through over-exuberant or impulsive giving. This quantification circumscribes the limits of *zedakah*. Unlike *gemilut hasadim*, *zedakah* is defined within precise perimeters. However, those who saw no clear distinction between *zedakah* and *gemilut hasadim*, those who considered a gift surpassing 20 percent to be well within the grasp of the wealthy, and those who perceived the condition of the indigent to be too precarious to be dependent upon strictures on giving, refused to be bound by these limitations.

The endeavor of Maimonides and others to identify levels of *zedakah* may be an attempt to diffuse these tensions presented by the literature on *zedakah*. Rather than present opposing views as contradictions, Maimonides placed these diffuse and often-conflicting opinions as points on a spectrum. On one side is the altruistic donor who preserves the individuality and the dignity of the person in need. On the other side is the self-serving or reluctant donor who must be cajoled into giving. A spectrum of attitudes and motivations links these two extremes. The mitzvah of *zedakah* covers a wide field, from selflessness to niggardliness, from minimal legal obligation to extreme selfless generosity, from self-serving intention to saintly service of others.

In the Gospel of Mark (10:25), Jesus is quoted as saying, "It is easier for a camel to go through the eye of a needle than for a rich man to enter the Kingdom of God." However, the Talmud says, "In accordance with the camel is its burden."[67] For Jewish tradition, the wealthy have an opportunity not granted to others. Heaven can be theirs—not by surrendering their wealth but by using it as faithful stewards for the sake of God.

Judaism's teachings regarding *zedakah* articulate its views of the ethics of giving and of receiving. Throughout the ages, the perennial problem has been that needs always outstrip available resources and the will of those with resources to depart from them. In this regard, it is told that the Hasidic master Naftali of Ropshitz once prayed to God that the wealthy be willing to give and that the needy be willing to receive. After he had so prayed, he was asked if his prayer had been answered. The master responded that it had been half answered.

"Does this mean," asked the questioner, "that the wealthy will give and the needy will receive half of what is required?"

The master thought for a moment and said, "I asked God for two things: that the wealthy should give what is required and that the needy should accept it. My prayer was half answered because I was assured that the needy are ready to accept what may be given. Whether the wealthy are willing to give what is needed, I still do not know."[68]

⚜ 7 ⚜

Repentance in Judaism

Great is repentance, for it brings healing to the world.
—*Yoma* 86a

ACCORDING TO A TALMUDIC LEGEND, when Moses ascended to heaven to receive the Torah, the angels protested to God. The Torah is too sublime a work for God to surrender it to flesh and blood, they maintained. The Torah, they asserted, should remain in heaven, with them. God then commanded Moses to rebut the angels, and Moses did so handily.

The Torah deals with human behavior, Moses reminded the angels. The laws of the Torah are relevant to human beings because they have free will and because they are imperfect creatures. These same laws of the Torah are not pertinent to angels who have no inclination toward sin and who are incapable of moral volition. Since angels cannot choose to steal or to murder, commandments forbidding those actions are irrelevant to them but not to humans, who do steal and who do murder. Because human creatures possess moral volition, they require the option of obeying or violating the laws set down to guide but not to compel moral behavior.[1]

According to Judah Loew of Prague, moral volition is the single particular trait that elevates the human creature over animals, and over angels as well.[2] Maimonides also perceived the ability to make moral choices as being an essential feature of human existence. Without moral choice, human beings would not truly be human. Even God does not coerce human beings into acting in a particular manner. Maimonides wrote,

> Free will is bestowed on every human being. If one desires to turn toward the good way and be righteous, he has the power to do so. If one wishes to turn toward the evil way and be wicked, he is at liberty to do so. And so it is written in the Torah, "Behold, the man has become as one of us, to

An earlier version of this essay was presented in the Solomon Goldman Lecture Series at Spertus College of Judaica in 1986.

119

know good and evil" [Gen. 3:22]—which means that the human species
has become unique in the world—there being no other species like it in
the following respect; namely, that a person, of himself and by the exercise of intelligence and reason, knows what is good and what is evil, and
there is none who can prevent him from doing that which is good or that
which is evil. . . . This doctrine [of free will] is an important principle, the
pillar of the Torah and the commandments, as it says "See, I set before
you this day life and good, and death and evil" [Deut. 30:15]. . . . This
means that the power is in your hands and whatever a person desires to do
among the things that human beings do, he can do, whether they are good
or evil. . . . The Creator neither puts compulsion on human beings nor
decrees that they do good or evil, but it is all left to their discretion.[3]

According to Maimonides, were humans creatures of moral necessity
rather than beings with moral choice, the Torah would be unnecessary,
moral guidance would be superfluous, moral responsibility would be irrelevant. "If God had decreed that a person should be either righteous or
wicked, or if there were some force inherent in his nature which irresisti-
bly drew him to a particular course . . . [if] his destiny had been decreed,
or his innate constitution inevitably drew him to that from which he could
not set himself free, what purpose would there be for the whole of the
Torah?"[4]; Free will is like the gift of a precious double-edged sword. With
choice comes error. The ability to choose becomes meaningless unless it
includes the possibility of choosing incorrectly. Without freedom, the
movement toward moral perfection becomes impossible.

When Alexander Pope wrote that "to err is human," he echoed a
sentiment of biblical origin: "There is no person who does not sin" (1 Kings
8:46; 2 Chron. 6:36). This observation is both realistic and optimistic. Because human beings are imperfect by nature, they err. But, because humans possess moral will, human error can be surmounted. As the Bible has
God say to Cain, "Sin couches at the door . . . yet you can be its master"
(Gen. 4:7).

The biblical view is that, though sin is real, it can be subdued. Rec-
tification is possible. According to a rabbinic legend, "when Cain went
forth [after killing Abel], Adam met him and asked: What happened at your
trial [for killing Abel]? Cain answered: I repented and was pardoned.
When Adam heard this, he slapped himself on the face, and said to Cain:
So great is the power of repentance, and I did not know it!"[5]

As Maimonides stated, were an individual to believe that there were
no remedy for sin, "he would persist in his error and sometimes perhaps
disobey even more because of the fact that no stratagem remains at his
disposal. If, however, he believes in repentance, he can correct himself
and return to a better and more perfect state than the one he was in before
he sinned."[6]

How to repent of sin has been a constant preoccupation of Jewish religious literature.[7] Jewish tradition felt compelled to do more than prescribe certain actions and proscribe others, encourage moral virtue and dissuade moral vice. To be complete, Jewish religious literature, in general, and Jewish ethical literature, in particular, had to treat the inevitable issues of moral error and of moral rehabilitation.

A reflection of this ongoing concern with sin and repentance is a prayer recited three times daily by observant Jews (in the *Amidah*):

> Our Father, forgive us
> for we have sinned.
> Our King, pardon us,
> for we have transgressed.
> For You forgive and pardon.

The corollary of "to err is human" is "to forgive divine."[8] The biblical assurance is that, while sin is always possible, repentance and reconciliation are always available. Were sin not a persistent reality, repentance would not be an urgent necessity.

THE NATURE OF SIN

Though biblical Hebrew uses about twenty words to denote "sin," three of these terms are prominent: "*heit,*" "*pesha,*" "*avon.*"[9] "*Heit*" denotes missing the mark, failing in one's duty, committing an offensive action. "*Pesha*" denotes a breach in the sense of a breach of a covenant or of a breach of a relationship. "*Pesha*" also can refer to an act of rebellion, particularly against God. "*Avon*" denotes crookedness, a figurative way of referring to transgression and the guilt incurred by it. Though postbiblical Jewish literature does not always sustain the distinctions among these varieties of sin, it does perpetuate the various meanings that these different terms denote. Furthermore, various views regarding the nature of repentance are predicated upon these different views of the nature of sin. For example, once sin is understood as an act causing a breach in a relationship, repentance is perceived as a process that aims at healing that breach. Once sin is viewed as an act of alienation, repentance is perceived as an act of reconciliation. If sin means departure, *teshuvah*—repentance—means return. While sin causes a breach, a wound, repentance effects a cure, a healing.[10]

A constant motif in Jewish literature compares sin to sickness and repentance to healing. For example, in his "Sermon for *Rosh Hashana*," the thirteenth-century scholar Bahya ben Asher wrote, "Repentance is a cure, as it is written, 'Return and be healed' [Isa. 6:10]. It is a cure because sin is the sickness of the soul. Just as the physical body is subject to health and sickness, so is the soul. The health of the body is indicated by its good deeds, and its sickness by its sins. Just as a physical sickness is cured by its antithesis, so is the sick, sinful soul restored to health by its antithesis."[11]

For Bahya ben Asher and other thinkers, sin is a moral malady that afflicts the soul, robbing one of spiritual health in the same way that a physical ailment deprives one of physical health. However, whereas some bodily illnesses are incurable, the restoration of spiritual health is perpetually possible and is readily available through repentance. In this regard, Joseph Albo wrote, "It is like the case of a person who is suffering from a serious illness which is regarded as incurable. Then a physician comes and says to the patient: I will tell you of a drug which will cure you of your illness. The patient thinks that since it can cure what is regarded as an incurable disease, the drug must be very costly, and extremely difficult to obtain. But the physician says: Do not think there is any difficulty in obtaining this drug."[12]

According to Albo, a substantial impediment to the restoration of spiritual health through repentance is the individual's failure to recognize the existence of his or her malady. Awareness of illness is the first step toward a cure. Without such an awareness, the malady can only worsen. "If a person does not recognize or know that he has sinned, he will never regret doing the thing he does, nor repent, as a sick person cannot be cured as long as he does not know or feel that he is sick, for he will never seek a cure. So if one does not know he has sinned, he never will repent."[13] Once an individual is aware of his or her malady, it can only be expected that a cure will be sought. For sin, there is but one cure—repentance. As Bahya ibn Pakuda stated, one "must have firm knowledge that repentance is the only cure for his malady, the path to recovery from his bad deed and evil act, through which he may correct his error and rectify his misdeed."[14]

In Bahya ibn Pakuda's work, as in much of the literature regarding sin and repentance, considerable discussion is devoted to factors that inhibit repentance and thereby prevent spiritual well-being.[15] One, already noted, is a lack of awareness of spiritual illness. A second is habit. As Bahya ibn Pakuda related, "Another thing which makes repentance difficult is that habit makes wrongdoing almost necessary to a person, like the natural actions from which it is almost impossible for one to abstain.[16]

Habit undercuts the process of repentance because it deprives the individual of moral volition, which is the underlying premise that makes rehabilitation possible. Regarding habit, Moses Hayyim Luzzatto observed,

"He who has thus become a slave to habit is no longer his own master, and cannot act differently, even should he want to. His will is held in bondage by certain habits which have become second nature with him."[17]

Just as harmful physical habits must be broken before bodily health can be attained, so deleterious moral habits must be eliminated before spiritual well-being can be achieved. Intellectual resolve to liberate oneself from improper actions is a necessary but not a sufficient step in the process of repentance. Subsequent actions must prove to be correlative with intellectual resolutions.

REPENTANCE: THE PROCESS OF SPIRITUAL REHABILITATION

For much of medieval Jewish literature, intellectual resolve is the first step of a three-step process of repentance. According to Joseph Albo, "the elements of repentance by which a person may be cleansed of his iniquities and purified of his sin before God are correction of *thought, speech* and *action*."[18] In his encyclopedic mystical-ethical treatise *Shnei Luhot ha-Brit*, Isaiah Horowitz observed that, since sins are committed by thought, by speech, and by action, repentance must also embrace these three elements.[19] Albo defined intellectual resolve or "correction of thought" as feeling regret on account of one's sins. "Correction of speech" signifies that one should confess one's sins. "Correction of action" means that one must not repeat one's sinful actions.

Regret, remorse, and intellectual recognition of one's sins constitutes the first necessary step on the road to moral recovery and to spiritual rehabilitation. According to the sixteenth-century sage Moses di Trani, this intellectual factor in repentance is the most important of the three elements. In his *Beit Elohim*, di Trani stated, "The essence of repentance is regret over the past and departure from sin in the future. Without both of these elements, repentance cannot be complete. . . . Therefore, the essence of repentance is intellectual in two ways: that one have thoughts of remorse and that one intellectually resolve to depart from the sin one has committed."[20] For di Trani the essentials of repentance were remorse and resolve: remorse over what happened and resolve not to repeat it. Remorse without resolve is invalid because it indicates that the remorse is insincere. Resolve without remorse is invalid because a motivation other than contrition might underlie that resolve. It may be that the opportunity to recommit a specific act does not become available, or it may be that the sinner no longer finds the specific sin attractive.

Without the intellectual awareness that one has acted incorrectly, the process of repentance is thwarted at the outset. One cannot resolve to avoid repeating a mistake unless one first recognizes that an error has been committed. As Bahya ibn Pakuda observed, "a man's undertaking never to repeat his sins is a sign of his knowledge that what he has done is wrong."[21] Similarly, as noted above, Albo's work points out that, just as a person who is unaware of his illness will not seek a cure, so one who remains unaware of the specific nature of his sin will not seek repentance. According to Albo, a major obstacle to such awareness is the human tendency to blame others for their own mistakes. Albo calls this tendency "self-excuse." As an example, Albo refers to Adam, who tried to excuse himself for his sin by blaming Eve for his own transgression. But for Albo, "self-excuse" provides no alibi, "for man was given reason so that he should always watch his conduct and not sin."[22]

While self-excuse is one of many motives that may inhibit repentance, there are a variety of motives that may initiate repentance. One such motive might be fear of divine punishment, fear of alienation from one's better nature or from one's fellow or from God. Another motive, already discussed, may be the desire for spiritual well-being.

Awareness of the reality of one's own mortality can also serve as a powerful stimulant for self-examination and for repentance. The Talmudic rabbis perceived the recognition of human finitude not as a cause for fatalistic morbidity but as an opportunity for self-improvement. Realizing the transient nature of one's own existence can lead to an avoidance of sin and to a desire for repentance. For instance, in the *Ethics of the Fathers* we read, "Akavya ben Mahalalel said: Meditate on three things and you will be spared from the power of sin: Consider whence you came, where you are going, and before whom you are destined to give an accounting. Whence you came—from a putrid drop of semen. Where you are going—to a place of dust and maggots. Before whom you are destined to give an accounting—before the King of Kings, the Holy One, praised be He."[23]

Because life is so fragile, so precarious, repentance must not be deferred. "Rabbi Eliezer said: Repent one day before your death. His disciples asked him: Master, does a person know the day of his death? To this question, he responded: Even more so then; let a person repent today, for tomorrow he might die, and all his days will have been spent in repentance."[24] In a similar vein, a midrash comments on the verse in Psalms (144:4), "One's days are like a passing shadow." "What kind of shadow? If life is like a shadow cast by a wall it endures. . . . Rabbi Huna in the name of Rabbi Aha explained: Life is like a bird which flies past, and its shadow flies past with it. Samuel said: Life is like the shadow of a bee which has no substance at all."[25] Jonah Gerondi in his treatise *Shaarey Teshuvah* discussed this midrash in a chapter entitled, "To teach the ways by which one may awaken himself to return to God."[26]

In his discussion of the contemplation of death as a catalyst for repentance, Isaiah Horowitz also quoted this midrash. Horowitz then referred to an observation made by Samuel of Uceda in his commentary to the *Ethics of the Fathers*. Commenting on Hillel's often-quoted phrase, "If not now, when?" Samuel of Uceda wrote, "The text does not say 'If not *today*, when?' in order to inform us that even today itself is in doubt regarding whether one will survive or not, for at every instant one potentially can die. Therefore, since all one has is the present moment, the text reads, 'If not *now*, when?'"[27] Samuel of Uceda then referred back to Jonah Gerondi's work where he commented, "'If not now, when?' i.e., I cannot afford to delay for one or two days my exertions on behalf of the perfection of my soul. . . . When perfection of the soul is delayed, the evil inclination grows stronger . . . and self-improvement becomes difficult thereafter. . . . It may be that one's days will not be prolonged and that one will die before one has rendered his portion of repentance."[28]

Underlying much of the discussion in rabbinic and medieval sources regarding repentance as a response to the fear of death is the assumption of a life after death, where one's deeds will be examined and judged. While the performance of virtuous deeds and doing repentance are understood to be beneficial in their own right, they are also viewed as instruments to accrue reward and to avoid divine punishment in the world to come. From this perspective, fear of death is linked to fear of God, fear of divine punishment, and fear of possible obliteration in the world to come.[29] Along these lines, Bahya ibn Pakuda interpreted the Talmudic statement, "Repent one day before your death," as an admonition to prepare for the next life in this life by accumulating good deeds and by repenting bad deeds in the here and now. In Bahya's words, "Are we not obliged to fear for ourselves . . . and consider the matter of our provisions for the next world before there is need of it, even one day before?" Among the conditions of remorse that Bahya listed is "fear of God's speedy punishment." Among the conditions of one's "undertaking never to repeat one's sins" is "imagining your death while the Lord is angry with you for your former failure to fulfill your obligations toward Him."[30]

While fear is an accepted and an often-effective motive for repentance, many sources consider love to be the preferable motivation for repentance.[31] According to Isaiah Horowitz, repentance out of fear is always tainted by self-interest. "One should not repent out of fear, namely, out of fear of punishment, for then one repents for one's own sake. Rather, one should repent out of love for the Creator and for sake of his Name."[32] For one who truly loves God, the alienation from God caused by sin, like the separation of any lover from his or her beloved, becomes unbearable. Reconciliation becomes not merely desirable but crucial.

Repentance out of love flows from a desire for return, for healing a rupture of relationship rather than from a hope of reward or from a fear of punishment. The more intense the love, the more significant the relationship, the greater the yearning for reconciliation. In this regard, the sixteenth-century mystic Elijah di Vidas commented, "Sin causes the alienation of the love between an individual and God, as it is written, 'Your sins have separated you from your God' [Isa. 59:2]. Therefore, since a lover does not wish his beloved to become estranged from him, the one who is obliged to the other should confess his faults to his beloved, saying to her: Truly, I have sinned against you, but do not leave me because of my offense."[33] Similarly, Maimonides described repentance as a means of reconciliation between the individual and God: "Great is repentance for it brings one near to the divine. . . . Last night a certain individual was separated from God, as it says: 'Your iniquities have separated you from your God' (Isa.: 59:2). . . . Today, the same person [having repented] becomes closely attached to the divine."[34]

To effect complete reconciliation, the return must be mutual. Therefore, repentance requires both a human initiative and a divine response. The corollary of human contrition is divine grace (*hesed*).[35] A midrash observes, "Consider the parable of a prince who was far away from his father—a hundred days journey away. His friends said to him: Return to your father. He replied: I cannot; I have not the strength. Thereupon his father sent word to him saying: Come back as far as you are able, and I will go the rest of the way to meet you. So the Holy One says to Israel: 'Return to Me, and I shall return to you' [Mal. 3:7]."[36]

The medieval Jewish mystics maintained that God has not only a desire for, but an interest in, human repentance. According to the cabalists, sin harms the soul of the sinner, and it also injures God Himself. In the words of the *Zohar*, "Whosoever transgresses the laws of the Torah causes damage above, as it were, causes damage below, damages himself, and damages all worlds."[37] In this view, repentance repairs the damage one's sin causes to one's own self, and it restores God from the harm done against Him. For the Jewish mystics, therefore, repentance is *for God's sake*, as well as for our own. It fulfills a divine and a human need.[38] "Repentance," says the *Zohar*, "repairs all. It repairs what is above and below. It repairs damage to oneself and to all worlds."[39] Repentance unifies God's Name, fragmented by human sin. Repentance must be done "for the sake of My Name" (Isa. 48:9), "for My Name's sake" (Ezek. 20:44).[40]

As already stated, remorse and resolve represent the first of three steps in the process of repentance. The motivations for this first step have been discussed. Confession is the second step. From an intellectual awareness of one's misdeeds and out of a resolve not to repeat them, the penitent moves toward a specification of his or her faults by making a verbal declaration. Confession translates intellectual assent into verbal commitment. To Maimonides, "It is necessary that one make oral confession and utter the resolutions one has made in one's mind" (literally: "in one's heart").[41]

Confession constitutes a concrete act of renouncing one's misdeeds. It serves as a transition between the intellectually abstract and the concrete changes in behavior that must follow to make repentance complete and to validate the sincerity of the penitent's resolve.[42] Maimonides identified confession as a religious obligation. Summarizing the vast biblical and rabbinic literature regarding confession that preceded him and adding some embellishments of his own, Maimonides wrote,

> With regard to all the precepts of the Torah, affirmative or negative, if a person transgressed any one of them, either willfully or in error, and repents and turns away from his sin, he is duty bound to confess before God, blessed be He, as it is written, "When a man or a woman shall commit any sin people commit, to do a trespass against the Lord, and that person be guilty, then they shall confess their sin which they have done" [Num. 5:6–7]; this means confess in words, and this confession is an affirmative commandment. How does one confess? The penitent says: "I beseech you, O Lord, I have sinned, I have acted perversely, I have transgressed before you, and I have done such and such, and I repent and am ashamed of my deeds, and I never shall do this again." This constitutes the essence of the confession. The fuller and more detailed the confession one makes, the more praiseworthy he is.[43]

Confession of sin became both a public and a private activity. The prayerbook contains public confessionals, recited during communal prayer (such as those recited on the Day of Atonement), and private confessionals (such as the deathbed confessional).[44] Regarding private confession, Isaiah Horowitz recorded that his father would make private confession of his sins three times daily. "And every night before he would retire he would list the deeds he performed that day. Then, he would sit alone and contemplate them. He would scrutinize the actions he performed not only that day but all the days of his life up until that point."[45] A similar custom was practiced by Levi Yitzhak of Berdichev. Each night before he went to bed, he would recount all the improper deeds he did during that day. He would list them on a sheet of paper, and then he would read them aloud, saying, "Today Levi Yitzhak did such and such. Tomorrow, Levi Yitzhak will not do such and such." As he would recite the list, again and again, Levi Yitzhak would become overwhelmed with remorse and contrition, so much so that he would begin to cry. Only when his tears had wiped the paper clean of ink would Levi Yitzhak retire for the night. In his discussion of private confessional prayers, Horowitz noted the custom of a particular sage to pray that he not be allowed to become angry because "the sin in which all other sins are subsumed is the sin of anger," for anger "is the cause of all sins."

One of the texts upon which Maimonides and others based standard formulae for confession was the Talmudic citation, "Our rabbis taught: How does one make confession? [One says:] I have done wrong [*aviti*], I have transgressed [*pashati*], I have sinned [*hatati*]."[46] The Talmudic discussion that follows this citation refers to the distinction among the three previously mentioned varieties of sin: *heit, avon, pesha*. Confession therefore must be made for each of these types of sin. This is why the three varieties of sin are mentioned in the confessional: *Aviti* refers to *avon, pashati* refers to *pesha*, and *hatati* refers to *heit*. The Talmud distinguishes among these three by defining *heit* as an unwitting offense, *avon* as a deliberate misdeed, and *pesha* as an act of rebellion.

Pesha denotes an act of human rebellion against divine sovereignty. In this view, sin represents an act of treason against the Kingdom of Heaven and against the authority of God as sovereign of the universe. From this perspective, repentance entails a reacceptance of God's kingship, a reaffirmation of the laws of His kingdom, a reinstatement of the individual as a citizen of the kingdom of God.[47]

Sin as rebellion means that the individual sets himself or herself up as a moral sovereign, recognizing neither God nor objective moral law as providing viable standards for human behavior. *Pesha* infers an individual's refusal to be accountable to any standards of morality other than those that he or she arbitrarily establishes. Actions become self-serving rather than being aimed at serving God or at helping others. Repentance means a restoration of one's relationship with a source beyond the self, a reaffirmation of the binding quality of God's law upon human affairs.

The third and final step in the process of repentance is what Albo termed "correction of action." Unless one's intellectual remorse and resolve are translated into concrete action, one's repentance is incomplete and ineffectual. Unless one's verbal confessions result in enacted commitment, one's confession becomes a lie; it is not an expression of sincere remorse. "Correction of action" requires the avoidance of past sins and the performance of deeds of virtue. In this regard, Maimonides summed up Talmudic teachings. "What is complete repentance? When an opportunity presents itself for repeating an offense once committed, and the offender, while able to commit the offense, nevertheless refrains from doing so, not out of fear or failure of vigor, but because he is truly repentant."[48]

Jonah Gerondi, who compared sin to an illness from which one ought to be cured, commented, "His soul is sick because of those [sinful] deeds, and one who begins to recover from an illness must guard against a relapse."[49] Other sources observe that, like the process of healing physical illness, the process of recovering from a moral malady is not immediate but requires time and effort.

The two steps that constitute "correction of action" are "depart from evil, and do good" (Ps. 34:15). *Orhot Zaddikim* lists abandonment of sin and reversing one's deeds as being among the essentials of repentance.[50]

When discussing "reversing one's deeds," this text cites a midrash, "If you have committed bundles of transgressions, counteract them by performing corresponding bundles of sacred deeds."[51] Similarly, in *The Meditation of the Sad Soul*, Abraham bar Hiyya said, "The definition of repentance is the regret of a man for his evil deeds and sins, the implication being that after he has committed the transgression, he repents and firmly observes the commandment he has transgressed."[52]

If performed out of fear of punishment, such deeds may not bring about atonement, as they may be intended as a means of bribing God by offering good deeds in exchange for divine forgiveness. Only if performed out of love and out of a sincere desire for moral rehabilitation do virtuous deeds surely expiate past misdeeds.[53] To effect complete repentance, sincerity of deed, sincerity of thought, and sincerity of speech are all required. Repentance absolves the misdeeds of the past and initiates the virtues of the future. *Teshuvah* is a process of return, rehabilitation, and renewal.

A sin is an action that alienates an individual from himself or herself and from God. *Teshuvah* denotes return to one's own self and to God. But, because a sin against God may also be an offense against one's fellow, repentance was not deemed truly complete unless reconciliation also was made with the injured party.[54] Furthermore, in seeking God's forgiveness, one is obliged to forgive those who have trespassed against him or her.[55] In so doing, the individual imitates the ways of God, granting forgiveness and practicing mercy. Like God, the individual desires and achieves reconciliation. Thereby, theology and ethics become intertwined. What characterizes God's dealings with us becomes a feature of our relationship with one another.

According to a midrash, after David sinned, he entreated God, "Master of the World, you are a great God and my sins are also great. It is only becoming for a great God that He should forgive great sins."[56] By forgiving those who have sinned against him or her, the human person can share in that divine greatness. By seeking the forgiveness of God and of others, the divine image each person bears, though disfigured by sin, may be restored.

Without sin, repentance would not be possible, but without repentance true virtue would not be attainable. It is precisely for this reason that the repentant sinner is exalted even above the purest saint.[57]

Parent-Child Relations in Jewish Tradition

A parent's love is for his child; his child's love is for his own children.

—*Sotah* 49a

T**HE GREAT FIGURES** of the Bible were great in many ways but not as parents. They succeeded in many things but not in parenting. The first parents, Adam and Eve, raised two boys in the best of all possible environments, and we know what one did to the other. Noah's relationship with his sons left much to be desired. Abraham, the father of the three Western faiths, was a terrible father. He expelled one of his sons from his home, and he almost killed the other as a sacrifice to God. Isaac and Rebecca played favorites between their sons and tore their family apart. Jacob doted obsessively on Joseph, making his other children jealous. He let his oldest son seduce his concubine without saying a word until he was on his deathbed. He responded passively to the rape of his daughter, Dinah. Jacob, who wrestled with God, refused to confront the troublesome behavior of his children. Abraham, who argued with God to save the evil cities of Sodom and Gomorrah, refused to confront his jealous wife, Sarah, when she asked him to banish his son, Ishmael, from his family. Moses is remembered for his greatness as a liberator, a prophet, a leader, and a lawgiver but not as an effective father. King David, the eventual father of the Messiah, had irreconcilable differences with Absalom, his son. The parents of the Jewish people, biblical role models, who are revered for so many things, were failures as parents. Thus, one cannot look to the lives of the great figures of Scripture for insights in how to parent. However, one can find such insights in postbiblical Jewish literature, in the writings of the Talmudic rabbis and the medieval philosophers, moralists, mystics, and legalists. As a preface to an investigation of these sources, one may first

An earlier version of this essay was presented in the Solomon Goldman Lecture Series at Spertus College of Judaica in 1987.

consider a legal case that came before a rabbinical court hundreds of years ago.

Once it happened that a man died and left a will. In the will he specified, "My son will inherit all I own, but only when he starts to act like a fool." The rabbinical court met, and it could not discern the meaning of this unusual condition. Not knowing how to adjudicate the case, the members of the court went to the home of Rabbi Joshua ben Korha to see if he could unravel the problem.

When they arrived at the home of the great sage, Joshua ben Korha, they found him playing "horsie" with his young son. The scholar was crawling on his hands and knees. A reed was sticking out of his mouth, and his young child was pulling him by rope across the room while the scholar was neighing like a horse. Seeing this, the members of the court returned to the academy.

The next day when Rabbi Joshua came to the academy, they asked his opinion on the case before them. Rabbi Joshua began to laugh. Said he to them, "Did you not see how I was playing with my son? Did I not look like a fool? The clause in the will simply means that the son will inherit everything only when he becomes a parent. When a person has children, it is not unusual to act like a fool when it comes to them."[1]

Plato defined love as a form of madness.[2] Certainly, the irrational love of a parent for a child may appear to others as a form of foolishness, as a form of madness, although it is simply a form of unabashed love. This story reflects the Yiddish proverb, *"meshuggah fun kinder,"* which may have one of two meanings: one is crazy when it comes to one's children, or one's children make one crazy. Indeed, both may be equally true.

Compared to the vast volume of classical Jewish literature that deals with the relationship of children to their parents, the quantity of sources that treat the relationship of parents to their children is scant indeed. One modern scholar has suggested that this lack is because the unrestrained affection that historically has characterized the Jewish parent's relationship with his or her children is an emotion too elusive to be encapsulated in Jewish religious literature.[3] However, as enticing as this explanation might be, it cannot adequately be defended. Jewish religious literature left no human relationship unexamined, even the most intimate ones.

Postbiblical Jewish religious literature is grounded in Hebrew Scripture. Because the relationship of children to their parents is discussed numerous times in Scripture, it can only be expected that this relationship would preoccupy postbiblical literature to a considerable degree. The relationship, particularly the legal duties, of parents toward their children is hardly discussed in Hebrew Scripture. Consequently, little discussion of this relationship is found in postbiblical Jewish literature. For example, the fifth commandment of the Ten Commandments relates to the obligations of children toward their parents, while none of the Ten Commandments deals with the relationship of parents toward their children. The greater attention paid in this chapter to child-parent relations than to parent-child relations reflects this imbalance in the classical sources.

WHY HONOR PARENTS?

The fifth commandment obliges a child to honor his or her parents. Of the Ten Commandments, a reason for observance is provided only here. No rationale is offered for the other nine commandments. No reason is given, for example, for why one should not murder or steal or covet. According to the text, one should honor one's parents "[so] that you may long endure on the land which the Lord your God is giving you" (Exod. 20:12, Deut. 5:16). In other words, longevity is the promised reward for observing this commandment, while a curtailed life is the threatened punishment for its violation.[4]

Some of the medieval Jewish biblical commentators took the promise of reward at face value. To the biblical assurance of longevity, they added the promises of prosperity and of spiritual rewards in the world to come.[5] Other commentators perceived the promise of reward either as being an inadequate motivation or as being too mercenary a basis for observance, so they offered alternative and supplementary reasons and motivations for why a child ought to honor his or her parents.

Unlike many of the other commandments of the Torah, honoring parents has not been an activity limited to Jews. It has always been widely practiced in many cultures, Eastern and Western. Such diverse figures as Plato and Confucius taught that a child should honor his or her parents. Because honoring parents was perceived as a universal human trait, some Jewish thinkers maintained that the inclination of a child to honor his or her parents is a feature of human nature, that it is natural for a child to honor his or her parents.[6] In this view, the primary reason for honoring one's parents is not the promise of reward or the fear of punishment. One honors one's parents because it is natural to do so. A hint that the Talmudic rabbis also considered honoring parents a universal moral trait may be detected in rabbinic accounts of Gentiles, who went to extremes in honoring their parents, and in rabbinic texts that predicate a gentile appreciation of Judaism upon the Jewish emphasis of filial responsibility.[7]

That Jews have no monopoly on the virtue of honoring parents is also found in a responsum by Benjamin Ze'ev ben Matityahu who flourished in sixteenth-century Turkey. This responsum was written to answer the question of why a blessing accompanies the performance of virtually every commandment, while no blessing is prescribed with regard to honoring parents. The answer is that "one only recites a blessing when performing deeds that distinguish us from non-Jews, i.e., in those deeds that non-Jews do not perform at all. However, with regard to those deeds that even non-Jews occasionally perform, we recite no blessing, because in performing them, we are not more holy than are they, since they observe them as do we. An example of this is honoring one's parents."[8]

The twelfth-century biblical commentator Abraham ibn Ezra expanded upon the notion that honoring parents is an innate human quality, when he addressed the issue of why honoring parents is both a feature of human nature and of rational human behavior. According to ibn Ezra, it is both natural and rational for an individual to express gratitude toward those who have been generous toward him or her. Foremost among those deserving of gratitude are one's parents. Honoring one's parents is but a natural and a rational reciprocation on the part of a child for the benefits he or she has received from his or her parents. Acts of generosity by the parent toward the child evoke acts of honor and gratitude by the child toward the parent. As ibn Ezra wrote, "From rational examination [it is clear that] God implanted in the human mind the obligation for each individual to benefit one who has benefited him. Therefore, a child who comes into existence, who is cared for and supported by his parents, [feels] obliged to honor them all his life."[9] Hence, ibn Ezra identified human nature and human rationality as the basis for the commandment to honor one's parents. It seems that ibn Ezra affirmed the popular medieval view that the human being is essentially a rational being. Therefore, to act humanly and morally, one must act rationally. For ibn Ezra, one should honor one's parents because it is both natural and rational to do so. Furthermore, according to ibn Ezra, it is rational to honor one's parents because it is rational for one to be grateful toward those who have benefited him or her.

The approach that roots filial duty in filial gratitude for parental generosity appears in numerous sources. An example is the anonymously written thirteenth-century ethical-legal treatise, *Sefer ha-Hinukh*, traditionally ascribed to Aaron ha-Levi of Barcelona. Here we read,

At the root of this commandment [to honor parents] is the notion that it is proper for an individual to acknowledge and to treat with loving-kindness another person who has treated him with goodness, and he should not be a scoundrel, an ingrate who turns a cold shoulder [to him]—for this is an evil quality, utterly vile before God and humankind. It is for a person to realize that his parents are the cause of his being in the world; hence, it is truly proper for him to give them every honor and every benefit that he can, since they brought him into the world and then labored through many troubles over him when he was young.[10]

By attempting to discover a humanistic basis for the obligation to honor one's parents, ibn Ezra and others tried to fortify and to justify on the basis of humanistic criteria that which was believed to have been conveyed through an act of divine revelation. By so doing, they attempted to root ethical behavior both in a human and in a divine source. They maintained that what has been granted by means of revelation may be further justified by means of human intellect and human intuition. This approach, however, was not universally accepted by Jewish scholars. Some felt that it is adequate to ground ethical behavior in revealed commandments, that the attempt to seek additional justifications or motivations for moral action is superfluous and potentially dangerous. From this perspective, human nature and rationality is too precarious a foundation upon which to predicate ethical action. Furthermore, in this view, to base religious behavior upon secular humanistic premises is counterproductive and a contradiction in terms. The position that the exclusively viable foundation for Jewish ethics in general, and for filial duty in particular, is divine revelation and the will to fulfill divine commands is affirmed by Don Isaac Abravanel in his commentary on the Bible.

> God wanted to explain to you that it is improper to base these worthwhile virtues and qualities upon the human intellect. Rather they should be observed because it was commanded by God to follow them, so that one might cleave to Him and achieve fulfillment and to goodness. Their observance cannot be justified from any other perspective, such as rational legal ethics. . . . even though human reason establishes that a man will revere his parents from his youth, your motivation in revering your parents and in observing the commandments should be because I [God] commanded you regarding it. For this reason the text states: "I am the Lord your God," i.e., that your motivation derives from His commandment rather than from another motivation.[11]

Abravanel's view seems rooted in a Talmudic text. As noted, the Talmud acknowledged that Gentiles also honor their parents. However, after recounting a Talmudic episode of how a non-Jew named Dama, son of Nethinah, honored his father, the text concludes, "He who is commanded and fulfills [the command] is greater than he who fulfills it though not commanded."[12]

The view that one should honor one's parents because it is natural to do so is attacked on grounds different from those of Abravanel. The approach taken by Ibn Ezra assumes that that which is natural is that which is moral. However, an alternate philosophy of ethics perceives the moral task as the suppression of one's natural instincts. From this perspective, the goal of ethics is to subdue natural instincts, such as the tendencies toward violence, promiscuity, excessive acquisitiveness, gluttony, and so forth.

Some sources observe that it is precisely because it is sometimes unnatural for an individual to want to care for his or her parents, especially if they are very elderly, ill, or senile, that makes a requirement to honor and to care for one's parents necessary. In this view, if honoring and caring for parents were instinctual, then to command filial duty would be superfluous and unnecessary.[13]

Just as there are those who deny the existence of a natural proclivity on the part of children to honor their parents, so there are those who deny the assumption that it is rational for children to honor their parents in reciprocity for parental generosity. The expectation for filial gratitude assumes that the recipient is grateful to his or her benefactor. When gratitude is absent, the rationale of gratitude as a basis for honoring parents collapses. For example, there are those like Jeremiah (20:14–18) and Job (3:11–12) who perceive life itself as an imposed burden rather than as a gift. Even those who consider life to be good are not obliged to accept their existence as a product of parental generosity. While many parents have children out of love, such is not always the case.

According to some medieval sources, if gratitude toward parents is relevant, it is because of the effort the parent expends in raising a child and not because of their engendering the child. Conceiving the child might simply be the result of lust or personal pleasure, whereas the efforts expended in nurturing and in teaching a child require constant care and deliberation. In this regard, the fourteenth-century scholar Israel ibn Al-Nakawa wrote, "A person should honor his parents more for the moral instruction they gave him than for their having brought him into this world. For in bringing him into this world, their own pleasure was their motive."[14] A more extreme view than that of ibn Al-Nakawa is posited by Bahya ibn Pakuda. Bahya claims that parental generosity cannot be assumed, that a parent's care for his or her children is but an extension of his or her own self-interest. A child's expression of gratitude is therefore without foundation. Bahya wrote,

> It is clear that the parent's intention is to benefit himself through the child, for the child is part of the parent, who places great hopes in him. Remark how he gives preference to the child in food, drink, and clothing, how he guards him against all misfortunes and finds all the pain and trouble involved in safeguarding his peace a trifle, so strong is mercy and compassion toward his children impressed on a parent's nature. Nevertheless, both the Torah and reason oblige the children to obey, honor, and fear their parents.[15]

A final objection to the attempt to ground filial devotion upon humanistic criteria is the view that the commandment to honor one's parents is not an end in itself but a means to higher ends. In this view, ethical behavior toward one's parents serves as a conduit to the worship of God, the divine parent; the ethical is a prolegomenon to the theological. Honoring one's parents is a first step toward the recognition that one is not self-caused, that one is responsible to others than one's own self. Even the gratitude one might seek to express toward one's parents is only preparation for expressing gratitude to God. For example, after stating that the root of the commandment to honor parents rests in "the notion that it is fitting for a person to acknowledge with loving-kindness the persons who treated him with goodness . . . [and who] are the cause of his being in the world," the *Sefer ha-Hinukh,* quoted above, proceeds to state:

> When one sets this quality firmly in his character, a person will rise from this to recognize the goodness of God, blessed be He, who is the primary cause of his existence and the existence of all his forebears, back to Adam, the first person. And [he will realize] that God brought him into this world, provided for his needs his entire life, brought him to his proper estate with all his limbs whole, and gave him a cognitive and intelligent spirit—and, if not for this spirit, he would be "like a horse, like a mule, without understanding" [Ps. 32:9]. Then let him reckon in his mind how very right it is for him to take care about serving and worshipping Him, be He blessed.

The biblical text describes the Ten Commandments as having been written on two tablets of five commandments each. According to a subsequent tradition, the first five commandments, inscribed on the first tablet, deal with human obligations toward God, while the second set of five commandments treats interpersonal relations. It would then seem that the fifth commandment, which deals with honoring parents—the last commandment on the first tablet—appears misplaced. Nahmanides, Abravanel, and others attempted to resolve this apparent difficulty by maintaining that, because honoring parents is a first step to honoring God, it properly belongs on the first tablet. In this view, giving honor to a human parent serves as a prelude to and as a preparation for bestowing honor toward God, the ultimate parent.[16]

The *Zohar* derives the honor of parents from the honor due God. Following the Talmud, the *Zohar* describes God as providing a person with his or her soul, while one's parents provide a person with his or her body. Because the soul is the most essential part of the person, God is considered the primary parent and, consequently, the parent first deserving reverence and respect.[17] The *Zohar* states, "As one must honor and revere God for the soul that he infused within us, so one must honor and revere one's parents for the body they provided, for one's parents are partners with God and they provide the body. As they are partners in the act of one's creation, so they should be partners in the receipt of reverence and of honor."[18]

By acknowledging God as the primary parent and as the ultimate source of one's existence, by acknowledging one's own parents as the most direct source of one's own being, one is led to the inescapable conclusion that no one is the source of his or her own being. From this perspective, filial duty derives from an awareness of that which transcends us, of that from which our very existence and our personal identity derive. This view maintains that one should honor one's parents because this commandment evokes the awareness that each of us is a creature of God, the creator; a child of parents; a member of a family; and an heir to a tradition. Theologically, this means that honoring parents entails honoring the divine parent. Sociologically, this means that honoring parents indicates an awareness of one's membership in a family unit that both includes and transcends the self. Historically, this means that, by honoring one's parents, one thereby commits oneself to the perpetuation of the moral values of one's forebears and to the tradition that they have conveyed.

The sociopolitical implications of filial duty were discussed by Maimonides and Gersonides (Levi ben Gershon). According to Maimonides, the family unit was the foundation upon which society rested. In fact, Maimonides considered the "government of the household" to be a branch of political science. Following Plato, Maimonides observed that, when the family structure is weak, society inevitably becomes destabilized.[19]

Gersonides considered the family the basic political unit upon which larger political entities, such as cities and states, were based. When the parent-child relationship functions properly, the larger society can function better. When the family serves as a conduit for moral values, the larger society is strengthened, the society's future becomes more assured. In his commentary on the Torah, Gersonides wrote, "Through this [commandment of honoring one's parents] proper family government can be established. This represents the beginning of how proper state government is attained; a consensus among its citizens will occur, and the young will accept moral instruction from their elders."[20]

Besides stressing the political implications of honoring parents, the fourteenth-century Gersonides, like the fifteenth-century Joseph Albo and the sixteenth-century Don Isaac Abravanel, emphasized its meaning for history and tradition. For Gersonides, Albo, and Abravanel, the family functioned as the conduit through which tradition was conveyed from ancestors to descendants, from the past to the future. In their view, the very existence of Judaism itself was vested in the willingness of children to accept and to convey the moral and the religious values of their forebears. Honoring parents is thereby a means to an end that transcends both the individual family and the individual self, namely, the perpetuation of Jewish life, thought, and tradition. According to Albo and Abravanel, the historical implication of the observance or the lack of observance of the com-

mandment to honor one's parents impinges upon the very continuation of
Judaism as a living tradition.[21]

HOW TO HONOR PARENTS

Scripture, which establishes the concept of filial duty in Jewish tradition, is
not very forthcoming about *how* that duty ought to be performed. The fifth
of the Ten Commandments requires a child to honor his or her parents,
but it does not delineate the nature of honor, or the kinds of actions it
might entail. Similarly, a verse in Leviticus (19:3) requires a child to "fear"
or to "revere" his or her parent, but it does not inform us about the implications or requirements of this command. While Scripture demands specific attitudes, it does not adequately delineate the actions that are to articulate those attitudes. That task falls to postbiblical Jewish tradition.[22]

The tradition is reluctant to specify and to quantify filial obligation. It
prefers to expect unlimited filial devotion rather than to legislate specific
minimally required duties. Ideally, the honor and devotion due one's parents are "beyond measure."[23] In this regard, the following stories are typical:

> Rabbi Tarfon had a mother. When she wished to mount into bed, he
> would bend down to let her ascend [by stepping on him, and when she
> wished to descend, she would do so by stepping on him]. He went to the
> academy and boasted of his observance of filial piety. [Whereupon] his
> colleagues said to him: You have not yet even reached half the honor [due
> her].[24]
>
> Rabbi Tarfon's mother once went walking in the courtyard one Sab-
> bath day, when her shoe tore and came off. Rabbi Tarfon came and placed
> his hands under her feet, and she walked in this manner until she reached
> her couch. Once, Rabbi Tarfon became ill and his colleagues came to visit
> him. His mother said to them: Pray for my son for he does me excessive
> honor. They said to her: What does he do for you? She told them what
> had happened. They responded: Were he to do that a thousand times, he
> has not yet bestowed even half the honor [due you] that is required by the
> Torah.[25]

In a similar vein, Maimonides, in his discussion of the duties owed by a
child to a parent, observed that "the obligations a child owes his parents
are too numerous to list, and a discussion of them would be overly long."[26]

Despite the inclination of the Talmudic and medieval sages to consider filial duty as having an infinite scope, those who translated sentiment
into statute were obliged to focus upon clearly defined acts of obligation.
Maimonides, who in his commentary to the Mishnah described filial obligations as being innumerable, nevertheless provided specific circumscribed

duties in his legal code, the *Mishneh Torah*. By so doing, Maimonides and others gave notice that one who enacts all of the specifically required duties of filial obligation is deemed as having partially satisfied an obligation of infinite demands.[27]

The Bible requires that a child honor and revere his or her parent. The Talmud proceeds to describe what constitutes honor and reverence. "Our rabbis taught: What is 'reverence' and what is 'honor'? 'Reverence' means that one must neither stand in his [parent's] place nor sit in his place, nor contradict his words, nor tip the scales against him [in a scholarly dispute]. 'Honor' means that he [the child] must give him [the parent] food and drink, clothe and cover him, lead him in and out."[28] Furthermore, these sources maintain that a child is obliged to honor and revere both parents equally and that the obligation to honor parents falls equally on a son and on a daughter.[29]

Underlying the specific duties imposed upon the child is the expectation not only of their performance but of their performance in a certain manner. Attitude as well as action is demanded. For example, the Talmud records a case of a person who was deemed reprehensible not because he failed to fulfill his obligations toward his father but because of the attitude that accompanied his actions. "A man once fed his father on pheasants [which were very expensive]. When his father asked him how he could afford them, he answered: What business is it of yours old man, grind [chew] and eat. . . . A man once fed his father fatted hens. Once the father asked: Son, where did you get these hens? The son answered: Old man, eat and be quiet; just as dogs eat and are quiet."[30]

Honor and reverence relate to attitudes as much as to deeds. The aim of the deed is to articulate the attitude. When the attitude is absent, the deed is crippled. Doing the right thing from the wrong motivation can be counterproductive. If honoring one's parents requires one to help ensure the parent's sense of dignity and of self-worth, if it aims at showing the parents that children are concerned with their well-being, then the attitudinal requirement becomes as important as the obligation of deed.

For some of the sources, the attitudinal requirements incumbent upon the child must include love to be complete. According to Rashi, for example, love is the particular motivation behind a child's desire to support his or her parent financially. The medieval mystical-ethical treatise *Sefer Hareidim* perceives love of parents to be a natural outgrowth of a child's gratitude for his or her parents' generosity toward him or her. This text insists that a child honor his or her parents by manifesting a "powerful love as they have loved him." In this passage, *Sefer Hareidim* quotes the *Zohar*, which says, "one ought to do all for his parents and love them more than himself, and everything he possesses ought to be considered as nought in his zeal to do their will."[31]

The Talmud and the medieval legal codes require a child to honor a parent throughout that parent's life and afterwards as well. Specifically, the child is obliged to mourn his or her parents and to speak of them with honor and respect after they have died.[32] Some sources depict the honor one can pay one's parents after death as being superior to that which can be rendered while they are still alive. These sources maintain that, as long as the parent is alive, there exists a possibility that filial duty may be practiced for less than noble motives; however, after death, honor and homage paid one's parents can flow only from sincere filial devotion and from an authentic desire to serve God. For example, "One who honors his parents after death is as if he honored them in their lifetime, since one who honors them while they are alive may do so from fear or for the sake of an inheritance, but he who honors them after their death does so for the sake of Heaven only."[33]

Having established a number of specific deeds required of a child regarding his or her parent, Talmudic and medieval sources hasten to clarify further the implications of those obligations. For example, after establishing that a child must support his or her parents financially, the Talmud immediately asks whether the funds for support should be drawn from the assets of the parent or of the child. While the sources are unanimous in demanding that a child make a gift of self, of personal services, they are divided about whether a child should give of his or her substance as well. This division of view led to a number of possibilities.[34]

Some maintained that the commandment of honoring parents unequivocally entails the obligation of the child to support his or her parent financially. A number of advocates of this view placed this obligation even upon children who could not afford parental support.[35] Others claimed that no such obligation exists, especially if the child is devoid of resources.[36] A third position argued that, since "charity begins at home," the child is so obligated, especially if the child is prosperous and the parent is not prosperous.[37] This third view claims that a child who is *able* to help his or her parent must do so and indeed may be compelled by the court to do so, whereas a child who is financially unable to render financial support to his or her parent is not obliged to do so. In one version of this view, a child is obliged to donate to his or her parent at least an amount equal to that which he or she is obliged to give to charity, that is, a percentage of income, usually between 10 and 20 percent. This approach takes into account both the need of the parent for support and the ability of the child to render that support. The child must give, but despite the child's resources, the child is not compelled to give more than he or she can afford or more than he or she is obliged to give to the needy in general.

Just as a child was required to perform certain deeds for his or her parent, so was the child obliged to restrain from doing certain things to his or her parent. For example, a child was enjoined from injuring his or her parent either through deeds or through words. Biblical law even required the death penalty for wounding or cursing a parent (e.g., Exod. 21:15, Lev. 20:9; see Deut. 27:16). This punishment, though it appears not to have been enforced in the postbiblical era, is nevertheless reiterated by rabbinic and medieval literature.[38] The underlying principle here is that a child is obliged to take pains not to distress his or her parent either physically or emotionally. A child must try to provide his or her parents with happiness and with joy. "A wise man makes his father happy. A fool of a man humiliates his mother [Prov. 15:20]."

According to one commentator, a reason why one should not injure one's parents is because in so doing one injures oneself. Since one's parents are one's own "flesh and blood," since one's soul is "bound up" with that of one's parents, to cause injury to them is to cause injury to oneself. In this view, harming one's parents is a form of masochism.[39]

The Talmudic and medieval sources are keenly aware of the profound psychological strain that may be placed upon a child attempting to fulfill his or her filial responsibilities. Caring for one's parents, for example, may stretch the limits of a child's psychological endurance, especially if the parent becomes senile. In such a case, the child is not freed from filial duty. However, the child is encouraged to arrange for professional care of the parent.[40] In addition, the behavior of an overbearing parent might psychologically inhibit the child from rendering honor and reverence and might actually encourage the child to reject filial piety altogether. Consequently, the parent is enjoined from becoming too demanding. As the essential issue is the child's moral and religious development and not the imposition of parental authority, a parent may forgo honor due, especially when it contributes to the child's personal development. Maimonides set down the law as follows: "Although children are commanded to go to the above mentioned lengths [in honoring parents], the father is forbidden to impose too heavy a yoke upon them, to be too exacting with them in matters pertaining to his honor, lest he cause them to stumble. He should forgive them and shut his eyes, for a father has the right to forgo the honor due him."[41]

The *Sefer Hasidim* cautions parents not to be so overbearing as to "enrage the child so that he has no option but to rebel against them." This text also observes that, since even the most attentive child is unable to fulfill the obligations of filial piety completely, the parents would be well advised to relinquish the honor due them, even if the child is not informed that such honor has been waived.[42] The aim of allowing the parent to "waive honor" is to prevent parental inflexibility from engendering the moral degeneration of the child. But, while the parent is encouraged to be flexible when dealing with the child, the parent is simultaneously discouraged from thereby inviting the child's physical or psychological abuse upon that parent.[43]

WHEN TO HONOR PARENTS

There are occasions when filial responsibility may temporarily be put aside in the name of a higher duty or for the purpose of fulfilling a more immediate obligation. One such occasion is when filial duty conflicts with the responsibility one owes to one's own wife and children. In this regard, the Talmud quotes a popular contemporary proverb, "A father's love is for his children; the children's love is for their own children."[44]

While marriage does not free one from filial duty, it does serve to supplant filial love with the love of one's mate. Nahmanides wrote, "[Scripture] states that the female is the bone of the bone and the flesh of the flesh of the male. . . . His desire is for her to be with him always, as it was implanted in human nature, beginning with Adam for all subsequent generations, for males to cleave to their wives, to leave their parents, and to see themselves as one flesh with their wives. . . . Here [we see that] a man leaves the nearness of his parents and his relatives, and sees that his wife is closer to him than are they."[45] Nahmanides's statement echoes a midrash. "Until a man marries his love centers in his parents. But, when he marries, his love is bestowed upon his wife. . . . Does a man then leave his parents regarding the obligation to honor them? Rather, his soul cleaves to the soul of his wife."[46]

In certain cases, not only could the love of parents be supplanted by love of one's spouse but the obligation of filial duty could be supplanted as well. For example, while the Talmud holds men and women equally obligated to their parents, it also makes provision for an exception— especially in the case of the wife—when filial duty might bring tension into the marriage.[47] In an interesting responsum, the thirteenth-century Spanish scholar Solomon ibn Adret (Rashba) deals with the case of a woman who lives with her husband and her in-laws. There is constant tension between the woman and her mother-in-law, which, in turn, creates marital strife between the woman and her husband. Solomon ibn Adret is asked to give a ruling about whether the woman has a right to demand that she and her husband leave the domicile of her in-laws. He responded, "A woman can certainly tell her husband, 'I refuse to live with people who pain me,'" for if her husband may not pain her, she certainly need not live among others who pain her and occasion quarrels between herself and her husband."[48] It is to be hoped that marriage can create a new family without causing tensions with one's parents. However, if the formation of the new family does precipitate conflict, one may limit, but not deny, one's filial responsibilities.

WHO ARE ONE'S PARENTS?

In the biblical texts requiring one to honor and revere one's parents, it is not clear whether "parents" refers only to one's biological parents or to others as well. The postbiblical sources address the issue of who may be included in the category of "parent."

The respect shown by Moses to Jethro, his father-in-law, and the honor shown by David to Saul, his father-in-law, served as the biblical basis for the later requirement of extending filial respect to one's in-laws.[49] According to the *Sefer Hareidim*, "The reason why a person must honor one's in-laws is because a husband and a wife are considered as one person, and the parents of one are considered the parents of the other."[50] Nevertheless, as discussed, a number of authorities restrict the honor due both parents and in-laws when it causes marital tensions between husband and wife.

The honor due parents was also extended to stepparents and even to an older brother.[51] If a younger brother was distinguished as a scholar, honor was extended to him as well.[52] Though a number of sources state that "one's grandchildren are as one's children" and that a man loves his grandchildren more than his children, there is a surprising reticence in extending the honor due parents to one's grandparents.[53] In fact, some authorities (e.g., Maimonides) ignore the question, while others reject the existence of such an obligation.[54] Some maintain that filial responsibility does indeed extend to grandparents, but they say that one should be cautious and not express greater honor toward one's grandparents than toward one's parents.[55]

JEWISH PARENTING

There are few biblical verses that relate to the obligations of a parent toward a child. The Talmud, however, provides the following list: "A father is obliged to circumcise his son, to redeem him [if he is a firstborn; see Num.

18:15], to teach him Torah, to have him wed, and to teach him a craft. Some say, to teach him to swim too. Rabbi Judah said: He who does not teach his son a craft . . . is as though he taught him to steal."[56] According to a variant reading of this text, a father is also obliged to teach his son practical citizenship (*yishuv medinah*).[57]

The parent's obligation to circumcise a son, to redeem him, and to teach him Torah relates to the parent's duty to ensure the perpetuation of traditions and to have the son initiated into the Jewish community. In so doing, the son's history mates with his destiny. Teaching the child the Torah aims not only at helping to continue tradition, it attempts to result in an intellectually, morally, and spiritually developed person. The parent's obligation to have a child wed, to teach him a craft, and to teach him practical citizenship relates to the parent's duty to permit the child to become an independent citizen of society. A crucial step toward a child's independence is his or her becoming independent from the parent. Marriage is considered an important step in a person's independence from his or her parent. With marriage, the child's primary relationship and source of identity is as a spouse rather than as a child. With marriage, a new person, a new family, a new sociopolitical unit is established. By obliging a parent to see that his or her child is married, the Talmud prods the parent to recognize and to guarantee the independence of the child.

For a child to be independent, the child must be economically self-sustaining. Teaching a child a way to earn a living is deemed part of a child's moral instruction. As Rabbi Judah candidly observed, "He who does not teach his son a craft may be regarded . . . as if he is teaching him to steal." On this statement Rashi commented, "Because the child has been taught no trade, he will be bereft of sustenance, and will then steal from others." The parent must provide a means to help ensure a child's independent fiscal survival. A parent must also guide a child toward independent physical survival. It is for this reason that one Talmudic opinion requires a parent to teach a child how to swim. "What is the reason [why a parent should teach his child how to swim]?," the Talmud asks. "[Because] his life may depend on it," the text answers.[58] Finally, the parent is obliged to teach the child "practical citizenship," so that the child may function as an upright and productive member of society. The role of the parent as teacher encompasses not only the intellectual and the religious spheres of existence but also its social and the political dimensions.

The Talmudic insistence that a parent is obliged to convey to the child a way of life as well as a way of earning a living may underlie the Talmudic view regarding parental obligations to support their children financially. Perhaps because children were apprenticed to a master craftsman or were betrothed early in life, the Talmud—astonishing though it may sound today—had few requirements regarding the obligations of a parent to support a child financially. Financial support was more a social expectation than a legal requirement. Apparently, the central parental duty is deemed by Jewish tradition pedagogic and not financial. The obligation of parents to support their children financially is nowhere explicitly stated in the Bible. That the Talmud records a debate on the question of whether a parent is obliged to provide monetary support demonstrates that "child support" was far from assumed by ancient Jewish law.

Talmudic law and subsequent codes of Jewish law assume no legal obligation upon a mother to support her children, even if she is financially capable of providing such support.[59] According to one Talmudic opinion, neither is a father legally bound to support his own children financially. Though this opinion is ultimately rejected, that it is considered demonstrates a hesitancy on the part of the Talmudic rabbis to demand that a father support his children financially.

The final view that emerges from the Talmudic debate about whether a father is obliged to support his children financially is that such an obligation exists—but only until the child reaches the age of six![60] In the *Mishneh Torah*, Maimonides circumscribed and further limited this obligation. Maimonides maintained that the obligation of paternal child support must only be consonant with the child's needs and not with the father's wealth. Thus, even if the father is wealthy, his obligation extends only toward meeting the minimal needs of his children. He is under no obligation to support his children at a level corresponding to his resources. From the age of six until the age of puberty, the father's obligation is more moral than legal. He can be socially embarrassed into supporting his children as "charity cases," but he cannot be otherwise compelled by the courts to support them. This position, with roots in the Talmud, codified by Maimonides, is reiterated in Joseph Karo's *Shulhan Arukh*.

> A man is obliged to support his sons and his daughters until they are six years of age. . . . From then until their age of majority he *may* support them, as the scholars have decreed. If he refuses, he may be held up to scorn and ridicule and abuse. However, if he still refuses, it may be publicly announced: So and so is cruel in not wishing to support his children. He is subordinate to an unclean bird who [even] feeds its young. But he cannot be [legally] compelled to support them. . . . If he has the means to support them, he can be [legally] compelled, against his will, to give "charity" for their support [from the age of six] until they reach the age of majority.[61]

On this passage, the commentaries clearly state that, even if the father—like the mother—has the means to support his children, he—like her—is under no legal obligation to do so. Although Karo's code finds no legal basis for compelling a father to support his children after the age of six, Karo does posit a legal obligation upon a father who is unable to teach his own son after the age of six, to engage and to pay a suitable teacher.[62] This requirement demonstrates the centrality of one's own child's education within the parental endeavor, according to classical Jewish law and literature. It is presumed that the father will support the child financially during the tenure of the child's schooling.

THE PARENT AS PEDAGOGUE

The course of study that the parent is to teach the child is a course in the art of living as an individual in a society. The goals are to guide the child from ignorance to wisdom, from moral neutrality to virtue, from dependence to independence, from infancy to maturity. The parent must prepare the child to function as a self-sufficient adult in an interdependent society. In the Torah itself, the study of the words of the Torah is described as the central parental activity. The passage in Deuteronomy that entered the liturgy as part of the Shema requires parents to teach the words of the Torah diligently and constantly to their children (Deut. 6:4–9, 11:13–21). Through Torah study, the parent transmits to his or her child that which has been transmitted to him or her: a tradition, a history, a way of mastering the art of living, an anchor, an identity. Maimonides interpreted the biblical statement—"And you shall teach them to your children" (Deut. 11:19)—as having established a legal requirement upon a father to teach Torah to his children.[63]

Though the obligation to teach the Torah to one's children is explicitly stated in Scripture, the specific obligation of a parent to guide his or her child in the cultivation of moral virtue is established explicitly neither by the Bible nor by the Talmud. The parent's moral instruction of the child is considered subsumed under the general obligation of the parent to teach the child to study and to practice the Torah. Throughout biblical, rabbinic, and apocryphal literature, the implicit duty of a parent to direct his or her child's moral development is stated. For example, the statement in Proverbs (1:8), "My son, heed the instruction (*musar*) of your father; forsake not the teaching (*torat*) of your mother," was later interpreted as a clear obligation of a parent to offer, and of a child to accept, moral guidance. The apocryphal Book of Tobit clearly records a father's moral teachings to his son: "My boy, beware of any immorality," Tobit tells his son (Tob. 4:12). A father is expected to "guide his sons and his daughters in a straight path," counsels the Talmud.[64] Elsewhere, the Talmud warns that "a father should be careful to draw his son away from falsehood."[65]

According to Proverbs (1:8), a child exhibits wisdom when he or she gives joy to a parent by accepting that parent's moral instruction. By practicing the values conveyed by one's parents, the child thereby honors his or her parents. By internalizing the values of one's parents, the child guarantees that something of his or her parents will be perpetuated after their deaths, that the traditions conveyed to the child by the parents will survive.[66] The quality of "parenting" is demonstrated through the activities of one's child. "The Zhitomer rebbe was once walking along with his son when they came upon a drunken man and his drunken son, both stumbling into the gutter. 'I envy that man,' said the rabbi to his son. 'He has accomplished his goal of having a son like himself. I do not yet know whether you will be like me. I can only hope that the drunkard is not more successful with his son than I am with you.'"

One is obliged to honor one's parent even if the parent acts foolishly (e.g., if the parent throws a purse of money into the sea) and even if the parent humiliates the child in public.[67] However, if the parent is "wicked," if the parent rejects the very moral and religious principles that he or she is supposed to convey to the child, there is a question of whether the child is bound to honor such a parent. On this issue the sources are divided.

According to one view, the obligation upon a child is unrelated to the nature of a parent. As Maimonides stated, "Even if one's parent is an evil person, a habitual transgressor, it is the duty of the child to honor and to revere the parent."[68] An alternate view relates that as long a one's parent is "wicked," one is not obliged to honor or to revere that parent. However, if a parent repents of his or her faults, the obligation is immediately reinstated.[69] A comparatively extreme position on this problem is taken by the twelfth-century rabbi Eliezer of Metz. He wrote, "If one's parent is wicked, even by failing to observe a single commandment written in the Torah, one is free from honoring or from revering such a parent."[70]

Israel ibn Al-Nakawa echoed the view of Eliezer of Metz. According to ibn Al-Nakawa, the honor and the reverence of a child for a parent depends upon how well that parent teaches the child, especially in terms of the personal example set. In this view, the obligation upon the child is indeed related to the nature and to the behavior of the parent. It is here, in medieval Jewish ethical literature, that the obligations of the parent to instruct the child in morals becomes most explicit as ibn Al-Nakawa wrote, "As the parent is obliged to teach the child ethics, to set the child on the right path, to guide the child in the performance of the commandments and of virtuous deeds, so is the child obliged to heed the parent, to accept the parent's words, and to obey the parent's commands, even regarding secular matters."

According to ibn Al-Nakawa, the focal point of the parent-child relationship is the intellectual, moral, and spiritual development of the child. The parent who guides and who nurtures this development is worthy of honor and of reverence. The parent who neglects or who frustrates this development becomes unworthy of attention, honor, or reverence. He continued, "If the parent is a sinner, and his intention is to mislead the child and to prevent his child from doing the will of the Creator—for example, if the parent teaches the child to rob or to steal or to murder, or something similar, or even to transgress a single religious precept—then the child is obliged to reject the commands of his parent, to rebel against the parent's dicta and to refuse [to obey] the parent's words."[71]

This text points to a number of fundamental concepts related to Jewish views of the nature of parenting and to the duties of a parent toward a child. First and foremost is the claim that pedagogy is the essence of parenting. The primary task of the parent is to teach the child. The primary duty of the child is to learn. Second is the claim that both parent and child are bound by certain identical obligations to God, to tradition, to morality, to law, and to society. The task of the parent is to make the child aware of these obligations through instruction as well as through personal example. As the parent who fails in his or her own moral or religious obligations thereby denies the basis upon which the obligation to honor parents rests, he or she thereby forfeits the right to demand filial devotion on the part of his or her children. If the parent rejects the commandments, the parent cannot then reasonably expect the child to obey the commandments in general, or the commandment to honor parents in particular. If filial duty is not an end in itself but a means to higher ends, such as revering God, accepting tradition, serving society, or becoming a moral person, then the neglectful parent undermines the foundation of the obligation to honor parents and consequently becomes undeserving of such honor.

Underlying ibn Al-Nakawa's position are two assumptions. The first is that the obligation of a child toward a parent is contingent upon whether the parent fulfills the central parental obligation toward the child: moral and religious instruction. The second is that filial duty is not an absolute duty. It is subordinate to the duty to the divine, incumbent both upon the child and the parent. When there is a clash between one's duties to one's parent and one's obligations to God, the obligation to fulfill the divine will take precedent. For example, a midrash states, "'You shall each revere his father and mother, and keep My Sabbaths: I the Lord am your God' [Lev. 19:3]. . . . One might think that one is obliged to obey one's parents even if they asked one to transgress a commandment of the Torah. Therefore, Scripture says 'and keep My Sabbaths,' i.e., all of you [parents and children] are obliged to honor Me."[72]

The child is obliged to ignore the parent when the parent asks the child to transgress God's commandments; the child is also obliged to set aside the honor of the parent if another commandment must be performed. If the child can have another perform the competing obligation, the child must do so and attend to the will of the parent.[73] However, if it is the commandment of studying the Torah that competes with the obligation to honor one's parents, study takes precedence.[74]

From a psychological perspective, a number of sources indicate that the parent who neglects the moral instruction of the child will eventually resent his or her own child if the child who is devoid of moral instruction becomes a scoundrel. Similarly, the child deprived of parental guidance will inevitably come to resent the parent for the parent's neglect of his or her moral and intellectual development. Such a child may—with justification—be unable to honor or to revere a parent who has failed to convey moral instruction either pedagogically or by personal example.[75] It thus emerges that proper parental pedagogy is in the best interests of the child, is a fundamental parental obligation, and is also in the self-interest of the parent and in the best interest of a mutually beneficial parent-child relationship.

Part of the art of parenting is knowing when to be tender and when to be firm, when to be insistent and when to be flexible. It was precisely for this reason that the Talmudic and medieval sources offered parents the option of "*mehilah*" (forgoing their honor and their parental authority).[76] Since the essential issue in honoring parents and in rearing children is the moral and spiritual development of the child and not the imposition of parental authority over the child, the parent is cautioned not to spark the child's rebellion by being overbearing or unnecessarily authoritarian. Parental inflexibility must not be permitted to become a catalyst for the moral degeneration of the child. A further concern is that an oppressively dictatorial parent might cause such anguish in the child that the child will become unduly distraught, even to the point of committing suicide.[77] On the other hand, the parent is warned not to become so flexible as to induce moral anarchy from the child. While the parent is occasionally encouraged to temper authority over the child, the parent is also cautioned against inviting the child's physical or psychological abuse. The parent is encouraged to find a middle ground—determined by the particular disposition of the child—between being apathetic and being unduly domineering in his or her relationship with the child.

The goal of parental instruction is the development of the child within the framework of a moral and religious tradition. The child thereby becomes a link between the past and the future. Nevertheless, the child's moral instruction is also crucial to the child's ability to function as an informed moral agent in society. As Gersonides observed, when the parent-child relationship functions properly, when the family serves as a conduit for moral values, society as a whole is enriched and improved. In this view, the moral instruction conveyed by parents to their children has implications not only for the individual child, not only for the perpetuation of tradition, but also for the society of which he or she is a part.

❧ 9 ❧

Bar Mitzvah, Bat Mitzvah

If I had the power, I would abolish the Bar Mitzvah
ceremony in this country.

—MOSES FEINSTEIN[1]

T HE PLACE BAR MITZVAH HAS ASSUMED in the social and religious life of
the Jewish community in the United States is unparalleled in Jewish
history.[2] Already in 1887, a commentator on American Jewish life described bar mitzvah as "the most important religious occasion amongst our
Jewish brethren."[3] However, associated with its popularity have been the
abuses of its observance. These abuses have brought the very legitimacy of
the celebration of bar mitzvah and bat mitzvah into question. Feinstein's
attack assumes that to have no celebration is better than to have a distorted
one. Indeed, a particular ceremony related to a child's becoming bar mitzvah or bat mitzvah is optional rather than required. The ceremony merely
provides a vehicle for the public acknowledgment of a status that is automatically conferred when a child reaches the age of religious majority.

Contrary to popular misconceptions, a child need not have a bar mitzvah or bat mitzvah to be Jewish. One's status as a Jew is granted either by
birth or by religious conversion. A rabbi does not "bar or bat mitzvah" a
child. The term is a noun, not a verb. It represents a status defined by
Jewish religious law. It is not a status given by another person. Unlike
Catholic confirmation, this status is defined by religious law and is not
granted by the clergy.

Supporting his opposition to the bar mitzvah ceremony, Feinstein
wrote, "It is well known that it has brought no one closer to study or observance." Similarly, in an interesting case in which a child's trust fund had
been petitioned for monies to finance a lavish bar mitzvah party, a New
York County Supreme Court judge wrote in his decision, "It [bar mitzvah]

An earlier version of this chapter was published in *Judaism*, vol. 22, no. 1, in 1973.

was never meant to be an excuse for pleasures or showing off. The spiritual values which the ceremony symbolizes may not be thrust into second place by ostentation and expensive banquets."[4]

Observations regarding the vulgarization of the bar mitzvah ceremony range from satire to condemnation. Feinstein's remark about the bar mitzvah ceremony's not bringing anyone closer to observance or to study is reiterated by the old quip, "The Ten Lost Tribes were not lost, they only became bar mitzvah." The severe attrition rate of religious-school attendance after bar mitzvah offers statistical support for this view.[5] The satirical descriptions of bar mitzvah celebrations ranging from the garish to the grotesque by North American novelists, such as Mordecai Richler, may simply be amplified reportage.[6] By 1891, during the height of Jewish immigration to the United States, bar mitzvah had already become a subject of satire.

A Talmudic passage claims that, before a child is born, it knows the entire Torah, all of the teachings of Judaism. But, just before a child is born, an angel taps the child under the nose, causing it to forget everything it has learned.[7] Gerson Rosensweig, the author of the satirical *Tractate America*, published in 1891, stated that in America, the angel waits until after bar mitzvah. The angel then strikes the boy, causing him to forget everything he has learned about Judaism.[8]

Attacks upon the bar mitzvah ceremony and celebration are not limited to North America. Writing in 1810 about the bar mitzvah ceremony (which he called "confirmation") in Germany, Maimon Frankel observed, "In the Jewish religion we presently find amongst many honored ceremonies some which can hardly pass the test of common sense. These not only miss their purpose, but are frequently harmful to it. Among these latter, we count the meaningless ceremonial at confirmation time. . . . most certainly a harmful impression must result when such a theatrical act happens to an entirely unprepared youth."[9] At the beginning of the twentieth century in Germany, the Jewish philosopher Franz Rosenzweig lamented that "the moment of the Bar Mitzvah has unfortunately lost most of its meaning in the last decades."[10] In sixteenth-century Poland, garish receptions were condemned by the Talmudic commentator, Solomon Luria, as "occasions for wild levity, just for the purpose of stuffing the gullet."[11]

Despite its widespread practice, scholarly literature regarding the nature, history, and development of the bar mitzvah and bat mitzvah is surprisingly sparse.[12] There are a number of anthropological studies that compare bar mitzvah to tribal "coming of age" ordeals. What these studies indicate is that there is a lack of physical ordeal and an absence of physical mutilation attached to the process of "coming of age" in Jewish tradition. In addition, there are Freudian analyses of bar mitzvah that applaud the occasion as "an institutionalized experience, tending toward the resolution of ambivalent feelings derived from Oedipus conflict."[13] But, what does classical Jewish literature understand bar mitzvah and bat mitzvah to be? That is the question that will be the focus of the remainder of this chapter.

DEFINING THE TERM

Since its inclusion in *Webster's Dictionary of the English Language,* the need to translate "bar mitzvah" into English has been eliminated. One should note, however, that *Webster's* perpetuates the literal translation of "bar mitzvah" as "son of the (divine) law." Thousands of greeting cards annually perpetuate the translation "son of the commandments." However, the term "bar mitzvah" has a different meaning altogether.

The Talmud notes that an agent of a man who is not a slave is "as himself" because he is a *"bar mitzvah,"* "subject to scriptural command."[14] Furthermore, a phrase in Exodus (21:12) reads, "he who smites a man that he dies." On this phrase, a Talmudic commentary notes, "I might have thought the verse applies to the slaying of a man since *ish d'var mitzvah"* (a man is bound by law).[15] As these texts indicate, the term denotes class membership among those bound to observe the law.

That the Hebrew equivalent (*"ben"*) of the Aramaic word *"bar"* can denote class membership and should not be translated as "son of" is evident from a consideration of Hebrew terms such as *"ben-Yisrael"* (an Israelite), *"ben-bayit"* (a member of a household), *"ben-Adam"* (human being, not son-of-man), *"b'nei bakar"* (cattle). Similarly, it may be suggested that "bar mitzvah" denotes full membership in the community of mitzvah (one who is bound by and subject to divine command).[16]

THE ORIGIN OF BAR MITZVAH

For more than a century, it has generally been assumed that bar mitzvah is a comparatively late development in Jewish life, dating from not before the fifteenth century.[17] However, a careful study of the issue demonstrates that both the term "bar mitzvah" and the practice of a rite of initiation into Jewish religious majority date from a time preceding the fifteenth century.

The earliest use of the term "bar mitzvah" in its current sense appears to be a text in *Midrash Tanhuma.* The passage reads, "Can even minors don *tefillin?* We are taught, 'You shall observe' [Exod. 13:10], i.e., everyone who learns to observe can [learn to] do. This eliminates minors because they are not bound to observe. But, if a minor is *'bar mitzvah'* [i.e., obliged to observe] and *'bar de'ah'* [i.e., knowledgeable], he is obligated [to don *tefillin*]."[18]

A number of commentators found this text problematic.[19] It would seem contradictory to describe a minor as bar mitzvah. While logically valid, this observation overlooks the Talmudic view that religious majority may be established in a variety of ways, only one of which was attaining the age of majority (thirteen years and one day for a male).[20]

As discussed in more detail in this chapter, there were three ways in which one could attain the status of religious majority.[21] One was by reaching the age of religious majority. Another way was by proving the manifestation of certain physical or intellectual signs of maturity by means of physical or intellectual examination. A third view maintains that one was not granted religious majority until one had reached the appropriate age *and* had manifested the necessary physical and intellectual signs of maturity. Relating this third position to the text under examination, one may maintain that the text can refer either to one who had reached the age of majority but who is considered a minor by virtue of not having manifested the appropriate physical and intellectual signs of maturity, or to one who had manifested the necessary signs but who had not yet reached the appropriate age. Furthermore, even if one discounts the *Midrash Tanhuma* text, there is still another source, predating the fifteenth century, that clearly uses the term "bar mitzvah" in the current sense; namely, a responsum of the thirteenth-century scholar Asher ben Yehiel.[22] Not only the term "bar mitzvah," but a ceremony akin to that currently practiced is attributed to a period before the fifteenth century.

A central event in the bar mitzvah ceremony is calling the child to the Torah. A fourteenth-century writer reported that by the eighth century, Yehudai Gaon had observed the following custom: "At the first occasion when his son was called up to the Torah, the Gaon, Rabbi Yehudai, rose to his feet in the synagogue and recited this blessing [i.e., 'Blessed be He who has freed me from responsibility for this one']."[23]

Another ceremony is mentioned in a "minor" tractate of the Talmud, *Soferim:* "At the age of thirteen, the boy was taken round and presented to every elder to be blessed and to pray for him that he might be worthy to study the Torah and to engage in good deeds."[24]

The Talmud, Rashi, and the medieval codes of law designate thirteen years and one day as the age of majority for a male.[25] One may conclude that, while the exact origin of the bar mitzvah ceremony is indeterminable, it is clear that thirteen had been established as the age of male majority and that some ceremony related to the attainment of male majority had been established well in advance of the fifteenth century. As has been the case with many Jewish religious practices and institutions, bar mitzvah was a spontaneous, creative development, probably rooted in popular practice. Once established as being usual and customary, it only required subsequent legal justification and codification.[26] Once the practice took root, "precedents" for it were found in earlier texts. The development of bar mitzvah served as a pretext to locate its "implicit" origin in texts from earlier periods.

CRITERIA FOR MAJORITY

As noted, one may identify three approaches, found in classical Jewish literature, to the issue of how religious majority may be established. First, the manifestation of clearly discernible physical or intellectual "signs" is sufficient cause to establish majority.[27] Second, the attainment of a specific age is the single determinant for establishing religious majority. Third, *both* the manifestation of signs *and* the attainment of the appropriate age are the necessary prerequisites for establishing religious majority. Clearly, the last approach is the most stringent.

According to Jewish law, the emergence of two hairs is the physical sign that establishes maturity. (There is even a debate about whether these two hairs are facial or pubic.)[28] The presence of a minimum growth of two strands of hair seems to be considered indicative of other factors relating to physical maturity. In other words, their emergence is an effect of the onset of puberty and not an essential characteristic of puberty. Their emergence is a sign that indicates the onset of the procreative ability.[29]

It would appear that the emergence of the physical signs of puberty and the presumption of the procreative ability was the earliest manner of establishing religious majority. The enforcement of the age requirement as an additional criterion of majority seems to have been optional. Later, when the signs were observed to coincide with a given age, the requirements for majority became the demonstration of the physical signs *and* the attainment of the requisite age.[30] Even later, age alone became the necessary and sufficient condition for establishing majority. A presumption was established, independent of physical evidence, that the signs had become manifest by a specific age, which is thirteen years and one day for a male.[31] In this regard, it is noteworthy that the late medieval sources assume that children in ancient times could indeed be presumed to have exhibited signs at an earlier age than in their own times. For example, Solomon Luria stated that in his own time "most boys becoming bar mitzvah have not attained the signs of physical maturity."[32] Furthermore, in his supercommentary to the Talmud, Meir Schiff observed that "in former generations a child not yet eight would require a [physical] examination [to substantiate puberty] but after eight such examination was not required because he was no longer considered a minor. In later generations, no examination was needed after a boy became thirteen [since age was accepted as a presumption of maturity]."[33]

One of the justifications for exempting minors from obeying various commandments, particularly "positive" ones, was because minors were presumed to "lack understanding" (Hebrew: *"lav b'nei de'ah ninhu"*).[34] They were presumed incapable of intellectual discernment upon which moral choice is predicated. Devoid of the intellectual ability to make an informed moral decision, minors were not considered viable or responsible moral agents. For example, a verse in Exodus (21:14) reads, "When a man schemes against another and kills him treacherously, you may take him from My very altar to be put to death." The reflections on this verse found in various halakhic midrashim exempt a minor from such punishment on the assumption that premeditation represents a level of intellectual sophistication attainable by a "man," but not by a minor.[35]

Eligibility for the assumption of duties and obligations by one who neither had reached the age of majority nor had exhibited the signs of puberty was, in some cases, granted to minors who had demonstrated an exceptional degree of intellectual development. For example, according to the Talmud and the codes, a child over seven years of age who knows whom he addresses when saying grace may be counted in a quorum for saying grace.[36] According to some of the codes, a child who knows how to care for tefillin may don them.[37] A minor who can read from the Torah may be called to the Torah.[38]

In a discussion of when one's vows become binding, the Talmud establishes age as the necessary and sufficient requirement. Before a male is thirteen years and one day old, he is examined to see if he knows to whom he vows when he vows.[39] If he passes this intellectual test before he is thirteen, his vows are nevertheless invalid. However, if he fails after he is thirteen, his vows are nonetheless binding, the assumption being that the necessary and sufficient condition for majority is age alone.[40] This notion rejects the view of other sources that accept intellectual precocity as being adequate. It further rejects the view that requires both the attainment of the prerequisite age and the manifestation of the appropriate signs to establish majority. This position presumes majority on the basis of the attainment of age *alone*, even when the physical and intellectual "signs" are absent. This view, known as "Rava's presumption," was codified by Moses Isserles and has emerged with time as the standard opinion.[41] The celebration of bar mitzvah at the age of thirteen, even when the "signs" of maturity are not evident, which is accepted as the standard view in most cases, is based upon Isserles's codification of Rava's presumption found in the Talmudic discussion regarding when vows become binding.[42]

A mature human being is presumed by classical Jewish sources to have both the *yetzer ha-tov* (inclination toward good) and the *yetzer ha-ra* (inclination toward evil).[43] The onset of puberty was interpreted by some sources as being synonymous with the infusion of the *yetzer ha-ra*, often identified with the sexual drive and the procreative ability. However, the dominant view in the classical sources asserts that a child is born with the *yetzer ha-ra* and acquires the *yetzer ha-tov* at the age of thirteen, thereby making the individual capable of moral choice and discernment.[44]

PRECEDENTS

Once the age for male majority was established at thirteen, and once the bar mitzvah ceremony had taken on certain distinguishing features, precedents were sought to "justify" it in the name of antiquity. These "precedents" were assumed to be implicit within various texts of the biblical narrative and elsewhere.

According to a midrash, at the age of thirteen, Abraham rejected idolatry and affirmed his faith in God.[45] In other words, when Abraham became bar mitzvah, Judaism was born. According to the Talmud, at the age of thirteen, Bezalel fashioned the Tabernacle.[46] However, two occasions are most often mentioned as precedents for setting the age of male majority at thirteen. They are Simeon and Levi's war against Shechem and the maturity of Jacob and Esau.

"The two sons of Jacob, Simeon and Levi, took each *man* his sword" (Gen. 34:25). "Rabbi Simeon ben Eleazar said: They were thirteen years old [at that time and each is therefore called a man]."[47] This text indicates that already in rabbinic times there was a tradition that "*ish*" (man) refers to one who had attained the age of thirteen. In post-Talmudic literature, this text served as precedent for establishing the legal age of male majority at thirteen. It is so utilized, for example, by a variety of medieval halakhists.[48] A second midrashic text reads:

> "And the boys grew" [*va yigdalu ha-na'arim;* the boys became *gedolim;* they achieved majority, Gen. 25:27]. Rabbi Phineas said: "They [Jacob and Esau] were like a myrtle and a wild rose bush growing side by side; when they attained maturity one yielded its fragrance and the other its thorns. So for thirteen years both went to school and came home from school. After this age, one [Jacob] went to the house of study and the other [Esau] went to idolatrous shrines." Rabbi Eleazar ben Simeon said: "A man is responsible for his son until the age of thirteen; thereafter he must say: 'Blessed is He who has freed me of the responsibility for this boy.'"[49]

Some of the implications of this blessing are discussed later in this chapter. Suffice it here to note that the present text also indicates that in Talmudic times thirteen was considered the age of majority; it is when one becomes a *gadol*. In post-Talmudic times, this text served as a precedent for establishing the age of *gadluth* (majority) at thirteen.[50]

Support for establishing majority at thirteen was further sought in exegesis and analogy. Some sources derive the standard from a verse in Isaiah (43:21): "This people which I created for Myself, that they may tell My praise." The numerical value of "*zu*" (this) is thirteen. Only at thirteen does one reach one's majority and consequently become obligated "to tell My praise." Some sources claim that, just as it is established that God has attributes of mercy, which number thirteen, and that there are thirteen rules of exegesis, so is the standard for male majority set at thirteen.[51]

STATUTE

According to an old rabbinic tradition, all measurements related to the observance of the commandments were "laws [orally] given to Moses [by God] at Sinai."[52] Attainment of majority by the male at the age of thirteen years was considered by the medievals to have been among these measurements revealed by God to Moses during the Sinaitic revelation.[53] According to this view, any standard (including the standard for male majority) need not be determined by logic or by exegesis because it had already been established in the initial revelation of the Torah.[54]

The otherwise enigmatic passage in the *Ethics of the Fathers*, "thirteen years for the performance of the commandments," was taken by many to establish the statutory nature of fixing male majority at thirteen.[55] The *Zohar* also considered the age requirement a fixed standard by means of which a child's majority may be determined. The *Zohar* and the fifteenth-century halakhist Simon ben Zemah Duran compare a child under thirteen to an *orlah* (a tree on which the fruit is not mature enough for sacred use [see Lev. 19:23]). To paraphrase the *Zohar*, when a boy becomes thirteen, he is said to emerge from his years of *orlah* [immaturity] and is liberated from the sphere of the unclean spirit [*orlah*] to which he had been assigned.[56]

LEVELS OF MATURITY

Contrary to popular belief, reaching the age of thirteen grants a male only partial and not full majority. According to halakhic and extrahalakhic sources, one is not completely responsible for one's deeds until the age of twenty. Twenty is the age of majority according to the Bible. It is when social as well as individual responsibility is assumed. Only he who has reached that age is required to serve in the army (Num. 1:3, 26:4), to be counted in the census (Exod. 38:26 and Num. 1, 3:18, 26:4), and to pay taxes (Exod. 30:14).

According to rabbinic tradition, one becomes liable for one's deeds to the "Earthly Court" at thirteen, but only at twenty does one become liable for one's deeds to the "Heavenly Court." As a midrash puts it, "The Heavenly Court as a rule inflicts penalties only on sinners who are twenty years old and upward, and the terrestrial court does so only on those who are thirteen years old or more."[57]

There is a biblical precedent for the notion that only those twenty years or older may be candidates for divine punishment, which is usually identified with *kareth* (extirpation). The Bible reports that only those over twenty years of age were held liable for the "sin of the spies" and were not permitted to enter the Promised Land (Num. 14:29, 32:11).[58]

The *Zohar* most explicitly distinguishes between these two stages of attaining majority: thirteen and twenty. It considers each stage to signify a spiritual metamorphosis. A new person is born; a new soul is bestowed. New vistas for spiritual and intellectual development open.[59]

> We must now explain who is he who is called "son" to the Holy One Blessed be He. Come and see. A boy who has reached the age of thirteen becomes a son of the Community of Israel until he is twenty. When he is twenty, if he is worthy, he becomes a son of the Holy One, one of those of whom it is written, "Sons are you to the Lord your God" [Deut. 14:1]. Thus when David had reached his thirteenth year it was said concerning him: The Lord said unto me: "My son art thou and today I have begotten thee" [Ps. 2:7]. What does this mean? It signifies that up till that time he was not in the state of sonship, and the supernal soul did not rest upon him because he was in the years of impurity [*orlah*]. But as soon as he reached the age when he became, being worthy, a son of the Community of Israel, he was, as it were, begotten anew: Today *I* have begotten you—I, and not the "other side" as hereto: I alone. And when Solomon was twenty, what do we read concerning him? "I was a son of my father" [Prov. 4:3], "father" referring to the Heavenly Father.[60]

On a less metaphysical level, there are adequate precedents to establish the view that, in terms of certain commercial and religious activities, twenty and not thirteen was considered the age of majority. In commercial law, for example, only a son over twenty years of age was permitted to dispose of his deceased father's real estate, the presumption being that until that age he is too apt to be naïve in commercial matters where land (as opposed to movable goods) is concerned.[61]

In ritual law, for example, there is a tradition that one who leads the congregation in prayer must be at least twenty years of age.[62] While it was assumed that a priest became eligible to serve when he displayed the signs of physical maturity, it appears that in practice a priest did not begin to serve until twenty. No less an authority than Rabbi Judah the Exilarch set the age for a priest's or a levite's eligibility for temple service at twenty, basing his view upon a verse in Ezra (3:8), "The Levites, from twenty years and upward [were] to have the oversight of the work of the house of the Lord."[63]

Shlomo Goren makes an interesting and insightful distinction between the two stages of majority. The first stage, he claims, is characterized by requiring individual responsibility, that is, one becomes responsible for one's own deeds. The second stage is characterized by the imposition of and assumption of social or national responsibility, for example, the army, temple service. The sin of the spies was a social sin, a failure to execute a public trust and, therefore, only those over twenty were punished. *Kareth* is physical and metaphysical ostracism from society for one's failure to attend to one's social responsibilities.[64] One who suffers *kareth* is detached from the society he or she failed; it means being "cut off from amongst his kin" (Lev. 17:10), "from his people" (Lev. 18:29).[65]

Goren's point is well taken, and the relevance of his distinction for contemporary Israeli and American society is clear.[66] Between thirteen and twenty a great deal occurs in the life of a young person. He or she becomes socially alert and intellectually keen. His or her broadening social conscience encourages him or her to define the role he or she wishes to play in society.

Finally, it is curious that while the age of initial majority is different for males and females, the age of complete majority is identical: twenty years. This age may reflect the rabbinic and medieval view that twenty represents the acme of human physical development. For example, Adam and Eve are described at their creation as having had the bodies of twenty-year-old people.[67]

A PROBLEMATIC BLESSING

Of all of the practices and ceremonies usually associated with bar mitzvah, only one is particular to it; namely, the blessing recited by the father. The origin of this blessing is found in a midrash noted above. "Rabbi Eleazar ben Simeon said: A man is responsible for his son until the age of thirteen; thereafter, he must say, 'Blessed be He who has freed me of responsibility for this one' [his son]."[68]

Other accoutrements usually identified with bar mitzvah are not necessarily tied to a male's attaining this status. For example, while a male usually begins to don tefillin regularly beginning with bar mitzvah, and while tefillin often are identified with bar mitzvah, males may begin donning tefillin well in advance of their thirteenth birthday. Some authorities maintain that a male is forbidden to don tefillin before his bar mitzvah; others permit him to don tefillin a few months prior to his bar mitzvah to become accustomed to this practice; still other authorities hold that, as soon as a child can properly care for his tefillin, he may don them. Some authorities permit a learned youth of twelve to don tefillin.[69] Among certain North African communities, it is standard to begin wearing tefillin at the age of twelve.[70]

A second example relates to calling the male to the Torah. While in many communities it has become customary to call a child to the Torah for the first time on the occasion of his bar mitzvah, this practice is not universally accepted. In various Sephardic communities it is not uncommon to call a minor to the Torah. Indeed, as noted, the Talmud establishes the precedent for calling a minor to the Torah.[71]

In eastern Europe the common practice was to call the male to the Torah at the occasion on which the Torah was read immediately after his thirteenth birthday (usually on a Monday or a Thursday). Some followed the practice of calling the child to read the *haftarah* on the Sabbath before his thirteenth birthday because a minor is permitted to recite the *haftarah*.[72] The practice of the male being called for the *haftarah* has become common practice today, particularly in North America. However, since the *haftarah* may be recited by a minor, this practice is not unique to the bar mitzvah.

The bar mitzvah party was incorporated into the earlier concept of the *se'udat mitzvah*. Furthermore, the learned address to be delivered at the bar mitzvah party became customary precisely because it was a *se'udat mitzvah* at which such an address was a major feature.[73] Consequently, the bar mitzvah party as it was originally conceived, that is, as an opportunity for a *se'udat mitzvah*, is not necessarily unique to this occasion. A *se'udat mitzvah* could be celebrated in any case. Furthermore, it is doubtful whether the majority of bar mitzvah parties held in contemporary North America, which are largely devoid of religious content and are not usually highlighted by a learned address by the bar mitzvah himself or by his father, would qualify as fulfilling the requirements or of having the features of a *se'udat mitzvah*. Thus, as previously stated, the single feature of the celebration of bar mitzvah, unique unto itself, is the recitation of the blessing by the father, "Blessed be He who has freed me of responsibility for this one." This blessing is itself problematic.

There are a variety of opinions about the meaning of this blessing.[74] One is that, until the age of thirteen, a father is responsible for the deeds of his son; thereafter, the son is responsible for his own deeds. Put in theological terms, the father is punished for the sins of his son until the age of thirteen; thereafter, the son is punished for his own sins.[75] A second maintains the opposite, that a son is punished for the sins of his father until the age of thirteen but not thereafter.[76] A third holds that both views are valid in that they are not mutually exclusive but are mutually inclusive. All three views share two common premises.

The first premise is the theological doctrine of vertical divine retribution: children are rewarded or punished for the deeds of their parents, and parents are rewarded and punished for the sins of their children. This doctrine assumes that individuals may be affected by the deeds of others on a vertical axis; namely, by those who chronologically precede or succeed them.[77] This premise relates to the status of parent and child to the age of bar mitzvah. The second premise, which relates to the post–bar mitzvah status, maintains the doctrine of individual responsibility. The parent is responsible for his deeds alone, and the child is responsible for his deeds alone. Conceptually, these two premises are in logical conflict. Historically, both premises are found in Jewish theological literature. The institution of this blessing seems to attempt to ease the tension between the conflicting premises by maintaining that both are valid although at different chronological points.[78] Vertical divine retribution applies to the pre–bar mitzvah situation, while individual divine retribution relates to the post–bar mitzvah situation. In this manner, an attempt is made to reconcile logically irreconcilable perspectives. The various conflicting opinions about the meaning of the blessing and the problematic nature of its theological claims represent only some of the complexities related to this blessing. Other problems exist.

First, the accuracy of the midrashic text upon which the practice is based is uncertain. Variant readings of the text claim that the proper reading is, "a man is responsible for his son until the age of *fifteen*."[79] A medieval text relates that it is not proper for a father to recite this blessing until the child reaches the age of twenty, when he becomes liable for punishment by the "Heavenly Court."[80]

Second, the custom of reciting the blessing is mentioned neither in Jacob ben Asher's code, *Arba'ah Turim*, nor in Joseph Karo's code, *Shulhan Arukh*. Its recitation seems to be of particular concern in Ashkenazic halakhic literature (e.g., in Moses Isserles's glosses to the codes) but not to the Sephardic halakhists. Even in Isserles's gloss to the *Shulhan Arukh* where he mentions this practice, his qualifying preamble, "there are those who" recite this blessing would seem to indicate doubt about whether recitation of the blessing is indeed required.[81]

For the preceding reasons, one may consider the practice of reciting this blessing to be both problematic and optional. There may be a modicum of wisdom in the practice of Reform Judaism and in most of Conservative Judaism in their elimination of the recitation of this blessing from their liturgies, despite its being the only unique characteristic of the ceremonies and practices traditionally associated with the celebration of bar mitzvah.

THE PARTY

The custom of having a party as part of the celebration of a child's becoming bar mitzvah seems to have been firmly established by the late sixteenth century, particularly among Polish Jews.[82] A precedent was sought to justify this practice. Such a "precedent" was located in the interpretations of the biblical verse, "And the child [Isaac] was weaned as he grew" (Gen. 21:8). A midrash comments, "[The verse indicates that] he [Isaac] was weaned from the inclination toward evil."[83] Commentaries to this midrash observe that Isaac was weaned from the inclination toward evil because the inclination toward good was infused within him at that time. Since, as we know from other sources, the inclination toward good is introduced into the child at the age of thirteen, it follows that Isaac was then thirteen years of age. The commentaries conclude, therefore, that Abraham made a party for Isaac upon Isaac's becoming thirteen years of age, that is, bar mitzvah.[84]

A more direct reference is found in the *Zohar Hadash*, where it is explicitly recorded that Rabbi Simeon bar Yohai made a party for his son, Eleazar, when the latter reached thirteen years of age.[85] This source seems to be the first explicit reference to a "bar mitzvah party." It is noteworthy that the *Zohar* and other texts compare the bar mitzvah banquet to the wedding banquet.[86] Indeed, it was a common practice in a number of Jewish communities to arrange a boy's marriage soon after the bar mitzvah, when the ability to procreate was presumed to have been attained.[87]

At a boy's circumcision, one beseeches God to permit the child's father to raise him "to [study of the] Torah, to the wedding canopy and to good deeds." Bar mitzvah is not mentioned. It seems that, for a number of texts, bar mitzvah was perceived as the initiation of the process of maturation that leads to marriage. However, seen from another perspective, the bar mitzvah completes the process begun at the *brit* (literally: "covenant," the rite of circumcision). Commenting on the bar mitzvah "party," Solomon Luria, the first author to discuss this manner of celebration in some detail, wrote, "The bar mitzvah feast that the Ashkenazic Jews presently observe is the most important *se'udat mitzvah*. . . . They are joyous and offer praise and thanks to God who permitted the child to merit becoming bar mitzvah. It is a great *mitzvah* that the father observes to merit raising his son to this [occasion] and to cause him completely to enter the covenant of the Torah."[88]

BAT MITZVAH

As discussed, a Talmudic source presumes that a male of thirteen years and one day has acquired the signs of physical maturity and is therefore considered to have attained the status of majority. This presumption became the basis for fixing the age of bar mitzvah at thirteen by subsequent halakhic authorities. Similarly, the same Talmudic text establishes the presumption that a female at the age of twelve years and one day has manifested the signs of physical maturity and has attained the status of majority.[89] While this presumption served to fix the age of female majority at twelve years and one day by subsequent halakhic authorities, it did not result in the development in the Middle Ages of particular ceremonies and practices similar to those for a male reaching majority. It was not until the late nineteenth century or early twentieth century that the idea and observance of bat mitzvah came into being.[90] Because this practice has no precedent in premodern Jewish literature, diverse views have been expressed about its validity and the nature of its celebration (by those who accept its validity).[91]

With regard to the female's "coming of age," a number of halakhists raise the question of whether the blessing discussed for bar mitzvah should be recited by the father when the female reaches the age of majority. According to these writers, the blessing was established to free the father from his responsibility for the subsequent religious education of his children or to free him from punishment for the transgressions of his children or both. Both would seem to apply equally to a son and to a daughter.

Those who reject this view maintain that if the sole purpose of the blessing is to free the father from the responsibility of educating his child, then the blessing could not be applicable to a daughter since a father has no obligation to provide for her religious education. However, the position that holds a father free from responsibility in the education of a daughter is not universally accepted in halakhic literature. A debate centering on the father's (and also the mother's) duty to provide a religious education for a daughter (and what the content of that education might be) continues throughout the centuries. To the argument that a father is responsible for his daughter's sins until the age of majority, the only response that could be given was that there is no precedent for reciting the blessing for a daughter. Indeed, the original textual reference specifically relates the blessing to the majority of a son. Unlike other features of coming of age in Judaism, the sources do not attempt to find a "precedent" for the recitation of this blessing on the occasion of the attainment of female majority.

The celebration of bat mitzvah seems to have been introduced in France and Italy during the late nineteenth century. In the United States, Mordecai M. Kaplan initiated this custom in 1921 with the bat mitzvah of his daughter.[92] Since then, various ways of celebrating the bat mitzvah have become popular throughout most of the world, with Conservative Judaism at the lead in encouraging its expansion. Most Reform and many Orthodox Jewish communities currently observe some form of a bat mitzvah celebration.

Objections to bat mitzvah have come from opposite ends of the Jewish religious spectrum. Some reform rabbis perceive the bat mitzvah as a challenge to the practice of confirmation which was introduced by Reform Judaism in nineteenth-century Germany. Since confirmation is held in the middle teens, some reform thinkers maintain that bat mitzvah offers an undesirable opportunity for the child to cease her religious education at the earlier age of bat mitzvah.[93] On the other side of the spectrum, orthodox halakhists, such as Moses Feinstein, consider any form of bat mitzvah celebration to be forbidden by Jewish law on the grounds that it copies "gentile practices."[94] Nevertheless, moderate orthodox authorities do approve of the celebration of bat mitzvah in a variety of forms.

In the mid-nineteenth century, the renowned German orthodox authority Jacob Ettlinger sanctioned a form of bat mitzvah to combat the inroads of Reform Judaism. While a number of halakhists specifically forbid a bat mitzvah celebration of any kind and disqualify a bat mitzvah banquet as a *se'udat mitzvah*, other orthodox halakhists not only permit but encourage it. For example, no less an authority than Sephardic Chief Rabbi of Israel Yitzhak Nissim encouraged the celebration of bat mitzvah and considered a bat mitzvah banquet to qualify as a *se'udat mitzvah*.[95] In a similar vein, Hanokh Zundel Grossberg wrote, "even though we have not heard that in previous generations a banquet was made for a girl as for a boy," he nevertheless encourages such an occasion.[96] Similarly, the noted orthodox halakhist Yehiel Yaakov Weinberg observed that, because of changes in modern Jewish life, where girls are subjected to the influences of secular culture and life, it has become "almost imperative to celebrate the attainment of the age of *mitzvot* for girls also. Moreover, the discrimination between boys and girls regarding the celebration of their reaching maturity would gravely offend the human feelings of the maturing girl."[97]

Among many orthodox halakhists, the view is that the bat mitzvah banquet should be celebrated as a "family affair" and that it should not be celebrated in the synagogue. Needless to say, Orthodox Judaism forbids women from ascending to the Torah. Some liberal orthodox communities allow the bat mitzvah to recite the *haftarah* after her father has been called to the Torah for the *aliyah* of *maftir*. In conservative synagogues that have accepted the egalitarian position and in reform synagogues that celebrate bat mitzvah, there is no impediment with regard to the young woman's being called to the Torah.

While the age of female majority is clearly established at twelve years and one day, it has become customary, particularly in many conservative and reform synagogues, to evoke the egalitarian principle as a justification for celebrating bat mitzvah at the age of thirteen. This practice is in clear opposition to Jewish legal precedent, which reflects the earlier maturation of females of that age than that of males. In this regard, Maimonides observed that women are required to fast on Yom Kippur at an earlier age than males because their physical stamina is established earlier than is that of males.[98] According to another source, not only are women intellectually superior to men but they are able to display their intellectual prowess earlier in life than men.[99]

Again, the age of majority was established at twelve for a girl and thirteen for a boy on the presumption that the child had reached puberty and the ability to procreate. Curiously, and relevant to the practice of bat mitzvah at thirteen, the most important Jewish biblical commentator, Rashi, observed the following in his commentary to Genesis (25:26). Referring to Rebecca's initial inability to conceive, Rashi noted, "until she became thirteen years old and able to conceive." By identifying female puberty with the age of thirteen, Rashi provides a precedent for bat mitzvah at that age.[100]

CONFIRMATION

The celebration of Jewish religious confirmation was first introduced in 1810 by the early German reformer Israel Jacobson. The first confirmation service in North America was held in 1843. Isaac Asher Francolm, a rabbi in nineteenth-century Königsberg, was probably the first to extend confirmation to females. Regarding the absence of a "coming of age ceremony" for girls, Francolm wrote, "Once again the female sex is treated here as less capable, as in Oriental custom."[101]

Unlike the bat mitzvah, which represented the extension of a Jewish ceremony—that is, bar mitzvah—to females, the notion of confirmation was clearly modeled after Christian practices, particularly those of the German Lutheran Church. Just as Luther had moved the age of religious confirmation to a later age than was the Catholic practice, so the participants in Jewish reformation moved the age of religious majority from twelve and thirteen to a later age, usually fifteen or sixteen. Furthermore, the conception of coming of age was also altered. The traditional Jewish claim is that, at the age of majority, the child becomes obliged to observe Jewish law. However, Reform Judaism minimized and even abolished the assumption that Jewish law is binding. It was therefore compelled to find another basis for coming of age. Following a Christian model, it based coming of age primarily upon intellectual rather than physiological grounds and upon confirmation of a specific religious creed rather than upon commitment to the observance of particular religious deeds (mitzvoth). It was assumed by many reform thinkers that at the age of twelve or thirteen the child was too intellectually immature to be capable of confirming the theological doctrines.[102]

Three attitudes developed within early Reform Judaism toward confirmation, specifically with reference to its relationship with bar mitzvah. One attitude was that confirmation represented a reformed version of bar mitzvah, that at the bar mitzvah ceremony, after he is called to the Torah, the child ought to demonstrate his affirmation and understanding of basic Jewish teachings, preferably by public examination. From this perspective, no new event was required. Confirmation simply represented an updated and expanded version of bar mitzvah.[103] A second attitude maintained that the celebration of bar mitzvah was dated and superfluous; it should therefore be abolished and replaced with confirmation. An early advocate of this position was the leading nineteenth-century American reform leader Kaufmann Kohler. He wrote, "Disregarding altogether the false claim of mental maturity of the thirteen-year-old boy for a true realization of life's sacred obligations, I maintain that the Bar Mitzvah rite ought not to be encouraged by any Reform rabbi, as it is a survival of orientalism . . . whereas the Confirmation . . . is a source for the regeneration of Judaism each year. . . . the whole Bar Mitzvah rite [has] lost all meaning, and the calling up of the same [to the Torah] is nothing less than a sham."[104] A third attitude encouraged the retention of bar mitzvah at the traditional age of majority and the addition of a confirmation ceremony at a later age, usually fifteen or sixteen. One of the stated purposes of this approach was the hope of thereby encouraging the child to extend the period of religious instruction beyond the age of thirteen.

Of these three attitudes, all are currently practiced within the Reform Jewish community, with the third apparently being the most popular. The confirmation is usually held as a class graduation on the Pentecost Festival (Shavuot) rather than as an individualized ceremony. In the Orthodox Jewish community, confirmation is virtually absent. In the Conservative Jewish community, confirmation (since 1930) has been at the discretion of each individual congregation.[105] Some do not accept its validity. Others use it as a manner of ˄ncouraging the extension of the child's religious education but do not consider it to have any particular theological meaning (such as the confirmation by the child of creedal presuppositions of Judaism).[106]

In an attempt to extend the religious education of Jewish children while dissociating themselves from the reform notion of confirmation, a number of Conservative Jewish leaders have on occasion called for the establishment of a ceremony at the age of sixteen or eighteen. "Ben Torah" is one of the most popular names proposed for this new ceremony. However, neither this notion nor this name has caught on, even within Conservative Jewish ranks.[107]

While the desire to extend the age of religious education beyond the traditional age of Jewish religious majority is praiseworthy, there seems to be no way of justifying the religious validity of confirmation or of other post–bar mitzvah and bat mitzvah Jewish religious occasions on even the most liberal of traditional Jewish grounds. Confirmation initially served a significant role as a vehicle for the inclusion of women into the celebration of coming of age in Judaism; but with the institution of bat mitzvah— which may be justified on traditional grounds—there seems to be no compelling reason to maintain confirmation—which is clearly a Christian import—within Jewish religious life.

Many proponents of the initiation and the perpetuation of confirmation maintain quite correctly that the child of twelve or thirteen cannot be assumed to be a fully mature adult, responsible for all his or her deeds. From this premise, however, they reach an indefensible conclusion; namely, that because the child is not an adult at twelve or thirteen, the age of religious majority should be postponed. However, as previously discussed, many classical sources unequivocally state that it is only at the age of twenty that complete majority is attained.

In various cases, the absence of a bar mitzvah or a bat mitzvah celebration is known to have caused psychological damage and to have influenced negatively the subsequent development of a child.[108] For this reason, as well as for the simple reason of wanting to experience as an adult what one had been denied as a child, the practice of adult bar mitzvah and bat mitzvah has gained increasing popularity. A number of observations about bar and bat mitzvah encourage the perpetuation of this practice of adult bar and bat mitzvah.

It should be reiterated that the bar mitzvah and bat mitzvah ceremony and celebration do not confer status of any kind upon the child. Rather, the ceremony and celebration merely attest to the fact that an individual has achieved the status of religious majority within the Jewish community. The ceremony and celebration represent public acknowledgment of a preexisting status, but they do not confer that status. Consequently, while desirable for spiritual, psychological, and social reasons, the ceremony and celebration are optional. As Moses Feinstein maintains, when the ceremony and celebration are antithetical to the event being acknowledged, they become superfluous and undesirable. However, with regard to the adult ceremony the desire of the individual to choose to take the effort and to make the commitment in this regard would indicate appropriate intention. What the adult bar mitzvah or bat mitzvah represents is the commitment to a status already attained but not yet publicly acknowledged or celebrated.

The eighteenth-century Hasidic master Menahem Nahum of Chernobyl suggested that there were two levels of majority. The first was granted automatically when the child reached the age of religious majority, which he called "primary majority." A second, higher level, which he called "secondary majority," could only be achieved through individual effort and explicit commitment.[109] Until the second level was attained, one was bar or bat mitzvah in name only. Thus, religious majority in Judaism may be viewed as occurring on three levels: the age of thirteen, the age of twenty, and the juncture in one's life at which an overt and specific religious commitment has both been made and affirmed. The acceptance of self-responsibility by an individual cannot automatically be conferred through a parent's recitation of a blessing. It can only be attained through an individual's unique act of will.

As noted, the *Zohar* describes the attainment of each of the various levels of majority as a spiritual metamorphosis, as a rebirth. For the Jewish mystics, one is "born anew" at each of these junctures.[110] Through conscious choice, one may acquire new and higher metaphysical attributes, new and higher "souls." One may attain spiritual maturity. The celebration of religious majority offers one an opportunity—if one grasps it—to become a new and improved person.

The Hasidic master Shalom of Belz once said, "When I became Bar Mitzvah, my grandfather, Eleazar of Amsterdam, of blessed memory, came to me one night in a vision and gave me another soul in exchange for mine. Ever since then, I have been a different person."[111]

❦ 10 ❦

The Sanctity of Life in an Age of Violence

They say, "Peace, peace," and there is no peace.
—JEREMIAH 6:14, 8:11

ACCORDING TO A RABBINIC LEGEND, the first staff meeting of the first religious organization took place in heaven on the sixth day of creation. God—the founder and executive director—called together His staff—the angels—to discuss initiating a new and controversial experimental program—the creation of human beings. There was but one item on the agenda of the meeting: "Shall we create man in our image and in our likeness?" (Gen. 1:26).

Timid bureaucrats, always in fear of losing their jobs, the angels did not know what to say. Being Jewish, they answered God's question with a question. "What will be his deeds? What will the human being do once he is created?"

After God described both the potentially violent nature of the human being and his potential sanctity, the angels submitted a unanimous response: "NO!"

Angered at the angels' dissent regarding what He thought to be a good idea—the creation of human beings—God extended a divine finger at the angels, whereupon they were immediately consumed by fire.

When a new staff of angels had been hired, God posed the same question. But when they offered the identical response to His question that the first set of angels had offered, He destroyed them too.

Finally, a third set of angels was hired, and again God posed His question. These angels, knowing what had happened to their predecessors

This chapter was delivered as part of a conference on "The Sanctity of Life in an Age of Violence," held at the University of Notre Dame in November 1982. The conference was cosponsored by the Synagogue Council of America, the Secretariat for Catholic-Jewish Relations of the National Conference of Catholic Bishops, and the University of Notre Dame.

and believing discretion to be the better part of valor, responded, "Sovereign of the Universe, what did it avail the former angels that they spoke to You as they did? The world is Yours and whatever You wish to do with it, You may do." And so the first human being was created.

After the sin of Adam and Eve, the fratricide of Abel by Cain, the sinful generations of the Flood, the rebellion against God at the Tower of Babel, the discreet angels sought an audience with God. "Lord of Worlds," they petitioned, "did not the first two groups of angels offer correct advice by warning you not to create human beings?"

At this point, we might expect God, like any good executive, to agree with the recommendations of His staff and to cancel the project—to terminate His experiment, to destroy humankind. After all, His research division had found this experiment to be bad for the institutional "image." The marketing division predicted that return on investment would be minimal. Nevertheless, God, being an optimist against His better judgment, decided to allow His experiment to continue. Perhaps one day, human realities and His divine hopes would meet. Perhaps, one day, the sacred nature of humankind would triumph over the violent nature of humankind.

After reviewing the reports of His staff regarding humankind, God dictated a memorandum to His staff and to Himself. The memo, a citation from Isaiah (46:4), read: "Even to old age I am the same, and even to hoary hairs I will bear." The memo was then conveyed to the division of hermeneutics where it was rendered as follows: "The Creator takes full responsibility for His creatures. Therefore, the Creator will allow human history to proceed. Furthermore, the Creator agrees to make certain adjustments in His initial blueprint to contend with the tension between His hopes and historical realities."[1]

In response to God's memorandum, the editorial page of the *Angelic Tribune* ran the following editorial:

> God's plan had a hopeful beginning
> But man spoiled his chances by sinning
> We know that the story will end with God's glory
> But, for now, the other side's winning.

According to this rabbinic legend, God recognized that His original plan for humankind must be modified to become attuned to the nature of the world and to the nature of the human creature He had created. If, as a midrash puts it, "in this world, war, suffering, the evil inclination, Satan and the angel of death hold sway," and if, as Job claims, "the earth is given into the hand of the wicked" (9:24), then God's revealed word must address the world as it is, and not as He might have hoped it would be.[2] In this view, God's initial blueprint for creation must be edited so that it may confront the proclivities of the human condition. The Torah—the incarnation of the divine will—must adopt a form pertinent to the exigencies of human history and to the realities of human imperfection.

According to a rabbinic tradition amplified by the medieval Jewish mystics, the Torah is essentially a celestial being, a perfect blueprint for a perfect world. The real Torah, the essential Torah, is thoroughly supernatural, exclusively spiritual. However, for the Torah to exist and operate in our world, it must adapt the accoutrements of our world. In the words of the *Zohar*, "The world could not endure the Torah if she had not garbed herself in the garments of this world."[3]

The Torah that we have in this world is a version of the essential Torah and not the Torah in its essential form. What we have is a Torah remolded and indeed corrupted to adjust to the features of our world. In this view, God had to compromise the Torah's initial, original perfection to allow it to deal with an imperfect world. The divine aspiration, the original blueprint for the world, the essential Torah, conceives only of a world at peace, a world devoid of violence, a world in which the presupposition that human life is intrinsically sacred is never challenged by the presence of violence and bloodshed. However, once violence becomes part of human experience, the initial plan, the essential Torah, must be reshaped to contend with the features of the world and with the nature of human experience in the world.

Once violence entered the arena of human history, with Cain murdering his brother Abel, God's script for the play that is human history— perfect though it was—needed to be rewritten to take into account the nature of the stage on which the play was to be performed and the nature of the actors who would improvise their parts.[4]

Just as God had to revise His initial plan so that humankind could continue to grope its way toward utopia, so did God have to compromise the moral and the religious truths of the Torah in its essential form so that the Torah in its manifested form could function in the world. Scripture therefore embraces a tension between the divine and the human, between divine hope and human experience. Confronting this tension, Scripture and subsequent Jewish tradition strive to navigate a course between faith and experience, between theological assumptions and historical realities. While it affirms the sanctity of human life, Scripture must also contend with the reality of war, murder, and violence. The Torah affirms the sanctity of human life, while it discusses laws of warfare and of capital punishment. The Torah was given to human beings and not to angels.[5] The Torah represents God's will for an imperfect world and for an imperfect human species.

The Hebrew term for violence, *hamas,* occurs for the first time in the Hebrew Bible in Genesis (6:11, 13) to describe the generation of the Flood. Once God recognized the existence of violence in the world, once God expressed His awareness of the evil aspect of human nature (Gen. 8:21), He articulated His willingness to compromise His original plan for mankind. Until this time, the ideal was assumed. For example, humans lived in harmony with other animals; humans were vegetarians. When violence arose, humans were permitted to eat meat as an expression of His compromise with human nature (Gen. 9:3–4).[6] Once violence entered the human arena, God revealed laws regarding the treatment of the murderer (Gen. 9:6).

A fundamental assumption of Jewish theology is that we live in historical times and not in messianic times. We live in an unredeemed world, a world in exile, a world alienated from its essence. We live in "messy" rather than messianic times. In the parlance of the Jewish mystics, God's presence in our world (*Shekhinah*) exists only in a state of exile, the Torah is in a state of exile from its essentially spiritual nature, and human nature is in a state of exile from its originally perfect state of being.[7] In this view, human experience is cyclical. The state of peace and perfection that prevailed in the Garden of Eden at the beginning will once again be realized at the end of history with the messianic advent, with the restoration of humankind to its original pristine perfection. The Garden of Eden marks both the beginning and the summation of the human adventure. In the meantime, however, throughout historical times, a clash ensues between God's dreams and human experience, between theological assumptions and historical events.

According to the biblical narrative, the first clash between the theological claim that human life is intrinsically sacred and an act of violence that poses a challenge to that assumption is the murder of Abel by Cain. The opening chapter of Genesis, as interpreted by Jewish tradition, claims that the human being was created in the divine image and likeness, that human life embodies sanctity.[8] However, by the fourth chapter of Genesis, the first murder, the first act of human violence, establishes the tension between the presumption that human life is of itself sacred and the awareness that acts of violence pervade human history and that they represent a compelling argument against the claim that human life is holy. The first place to look for the articulation of a position in Jewish theological literature about the sanctity of human life in an age of violence is in the reflections of the rabbis upon two already-mentioned biblical texts: the report of the creation of the first human being and the narrative description of Cain's murder of Abel. In examining the first text, the claim that human life is sacred is portrayed. In examining the second text, a rabbinic view of the moral and the theological implications of violence begins to emerge.

THE SANCTITY OF HUMAN LIFE

The theological claim that human life is intrinsically sacred rests upon three interlocking assumptions: (1) that human beings are created in the image of God, (2) that God is holy, and (3) that each human life is unique and irreplaceable.

To the biblical mind, there is no need to demonstrate God's holiness. God is presumed holy by His nature. Similarly, human life is considered holy as a matter of fact, not as an issue for debate. Created in the image of God, the human person is assumed to embody an innate holiness. According to the rabbis, the "likeness of God" refers to the attribute that we share with God—holiness. In each human being one finds an echo, an image, of divine sanctity. The Jewish mystics go one step further. They describe the human soul as a spark of God, as "a part of God from above." In their view, each human person is holy because within each person there is an element of divinity, a part of God, a spark of divine sanctity.[9]

The verse in Leviticus (19:2), "You shall be holy for I the Lord your God am holy," may be read "You are holy *because* I the Lord your God am holy."[10] Holiness, sanctity, is what human beings have in common with God. An essential attribute of the divine is an inherent quality of the human. Human life is sacred because God is holy. The "image of God" is an image of sanctity.[11]

The Ten Commandments forbid us to make an image of God. Yet God, in violation of His own law, made an image of Himself. Each person is an image of God. When one looks at another person, one is reminded of God. Rabbi Joshua ben Levi said, "A procession of angels pass before a human being wherever he goes, proclaiming: Make way for the image of God."[12]

The Talmudic rabbis remind us that the Ten Commandments were given on two tablets of five commandments each. They maintain that each commandment on each tablet supplements the corresponding commandment on the other tablet. The first commandment on the first tablet reads, "I am the Lord your God." The first commandment on the second tablet— the sixth commandment (according to the Jewish reading)—reads, "You shall not murder." Hence, the rabbis conclude,

> Scripture [thereby] tells us that whosoever spills blood, Scripture imputes it to him as if he has diminished the image of the King [God]. The matter is comparable to a king of flesh and blood who entered a city and erected icons and images and stamped coins [with his image upon them]. After a time, they pushed down the icons, smashed the images and destroyed the coins, and thereby diminished the image of the king. Therefore, whosoever spills blood, Scripture imputes it to him as if he had diminished the

image of the king, as it is written, "whosoever sheds human blood . . . for in the image of God He made man" [Gen. 9:6].[13]

According to the rabbis, acts of violence against the human person impact against the divine person. The God of pathos is affected by human violence. The sanctity of God, which is the origin and the guarantee of the sanctity of human life, is debased by each act of violence that impinges upon human life.[14]

In a Talmudic text, Rabbi Meir asks, How does God react when a criminal is executed for a capital crime? "Rabbi Meir said: 'What does God [Shekhinah] say? My head is too heavy for Me, my arm is too heavy for Me.' And if God is so grieved over the blood of the wicked that is shed, how much more so [is God grieved] over the blood of the righteous!'"[15]

Every insult to the sanctity and to the dignity of an individual is considered an affront to God. A midrash reads, "Rabbi Akiva said: 'You shall love your neighbor as Yourself, I am the Lord your God' [Lev. 19:18]. . . . Hence, one must not say, 'Since I have been put to shame let my neighbor be put to shame.' Rabbi Tanhuma said: 'If you do so know whom you shame [you shame God, for] in the likeness of God made He him.'"[16]

The Jewish mystics held that each human soul is a part of the soul of the primordial Adam. Ergo, each individual soul is a part of the same whole, of the same soul. An affront to any individual is an affront to all individuals. An act of violence against another is an act of masochism against one's self. From this perspective, one should love one's neighbor as oneself because one's neighbor is oneself. In the words of the sixteenth-century cabalist, Moses Cordevero, "One's neighbor's honor should be as dear to one as one's own honor; for he and his neighbor are one." Every human being is one's neighbor and what is done to another is done to one's own self. God is also one's neighbor. Any act of violence against another is construed as an act of violence both against ourselves and against God.[17] In Cordevero's words, "Just as the Holy One blessed be He desires neither our disgrace nor our suffering because we are His relatives, so, too, a person should not desire to witness evil befalling his neighbor nor see his neighbor suffer or disgraced. And these things should cause him [and Him] the same pain as if he were the victim."[18]

To this point, two of the three aforementioned assumptions upon which the claim that human life is intrinsically sacred have been discussed: first, that God is holy, and second, that human beings are created in the image of God. That image is an image of sanctity, and that sanctity represents what human beings and God have in common. For this reason, Jewish tradition maintains that an act of violence against another person is tantamount to an act of violence against all other persons and against God as well. The claim that human life is intrinsically sacred rests also upon a third assumption: the unique and irreplaceable nature of each human life. This assumption is linked to the other two. Created in the image of a God who is unique, each person can claim uniqueness. The holiness of God is linked to the unique nature of God. Therefore, the sanctity of each human life discloses the unique quality of each human life.

The Hebrew word that denotes the sacred, the holy, is the word "kadosh." The root of this word—"K-D-Sh"—means "set apart." In a sense, the holy is the unique. Holiness implies being distinct from all else, being sui generis, being one of a kind. Consequently, when Scripture claims that God is "one," it means that God is one of a kind, unique.[19] The term ehad—one—may be a synonym for the term kadosh. God's uniqueness is inherently linked to His sanctity. Uniqueness is a manifestation of sanctity. To affirm the sanctity of each human life is to affirm the unique nature of each human life.

The unique nature of each human life is a claim firmly stated in the Talmud. The Talmud raises the question of why God chose to create only one human being during the initial process of creation. Animals, birds, fish, plants, and other creatures were created en masse. Why then was but one human creature created?

> For this reason was man created alone: to teach that whosoever destroys a single soul, Scripture imputes [guilt] to him as though he destroyed a complete world, and whosoever preserves a single soul, Scripture ascribes [merit] to him as though he had preserved a complete world. . . . If a person strikes many coins from one mold they all resemble one another, but the Supreme King of Kings, the Holy One, blessed be He, fashioned every person in the stamp of the first human being, and yet not one of them is identical to another person. Therefore, every individual person is obliged to say: The world is created for my sake.[20]

This text articulates three claims of Jewish theology regarding human life: (1) each human life, each person, is unique; (2) because each person is unique, each human life is irreplaceable; and (3) because each individual human life is unique and therefore irreplaceable, each human life embodies intrinsic sanctity.

VIOLENCE: CAIN AND ABEL

The Talmudic text quoted in the previous section describes each person's being as unique and irreplaceable. However, this text is part of a larger text, which also discusses the murder of Abel. Describing the murder of

Abel, the biblical text uses the plural form of a collective noun. The Talmud is quick to sense the exegetical possibilities of this apparent lapse in grammatical accuracy. The verse reads, "the blood of your brother cries unto Me from the ground" (Gen. 4:10). The Hebrew word for blood is rendered in the plural form "*demei*" rather than in the singular form of the Hebrew noun for blood, "*dam*." One of the explanations the Talmud offers for this apparent grammatical error is as follows: "It is written, 'the bloods of your brother' and not 'the blood of your brother.' That is, his blood and the blood of his [potential] descendents."[21] This text articulates the claim that each individual person is a race unto himself or herself. Therefore, each murder is not only an act of fratricide but also an act of genocide. By murdering Abel, Cain killed one-quarter of the population of the world at that time. As already noted, the Jewish mystics, in their reflections on the verse, "You shall love your neighbor as yourself," claimed that you should love your neighbor as yourself because your neighbor is yourself. Thus, each murder is not only an act of fratricide and genocide; each murder is also a suicide.

For Jewish tradition, the challenge violence poses to the affirmation of the sanctity of human life is not simply a problem of theology, it also evokes the problem of theodicy. The persistence of violence is a problem for us and for God as well. In the words of the prophet Habakkuk's anguished cry:

> O Lord, how long shall I cry for help
> And You will not hear?
> Or cry to You of violence
> And You will not save? [Hab. 1:1–2]

If human beings are perpetrators of destruction and violence, then God is an accomplice for remaining a silent witness to that violence. After Cain kills Abel, God says to Cain, "The voice of your brother's blood cries to Me from the ground" (Gen. 4:10). Rabbi Simeon bar Yohai understood and translated the verse differently.

> It is difficult to say this thing and the mouth cannot utter it plainly. Think of two gladiators wrestling before the king; had the king wished, he could have separated them. But he did not so desire and one overcame the other and killed him. He [the victim] cried out [before he died]: Let my cause be pleaded before the king [I blame the king for not interceding to save my life]. Therefore, [understand the verse to read]: "The voice of your brother's blood cries out *against* Me from the ground."[22]

Although one strand in the complex weave that is Jewish theology describes God as a silent coconspirator in acts of human violence, another (already-mentioned) strand of Jewish theology describes God as a covictim in acts of violence, such as the execution of a criminal and the death of an enemy in time of war, and in acts of "justified" homicide, such as killing in self-defense. Thus, each act of violence that results in the death of a human individual is considered by the rabbis not only to be an act of fratricide, suicide, and genocide but also, in a sense, to be an act of deicide. When an individual is destroyed, the image of God within him or her is murdered. Killing a human being is like killing God.

In a Talmudic discussion regarding capital punishment of criminals executed for having committed capital crimes, the law insists that the body of an executed criminal must not be left hanging overnight (Deut. 21:23). Rabbi Meir offers this parable: "To what is the matter comparable? To two [identical] twin brothers [who lived] in the same city. One was appointed king and the other became a highway robber. At the king's command they hanged him [the robber]. But all who saw him exclaimed: The king is hanged. Whereupon the king issued a command and he was taken down."[23] Though God's holiness assures the sanctity of human life, God's holiness is affected by human deeds. Through the performance of sacred deeds we fortify God's sanctity; we "give strength to God" (Ps. 68:35). Through the performance of evil deeds, we weaken God's sanctity. In the words of a midrash, "Rabbi Azariah said in the name of Rabbi Judah ben Rabbi Simon: When Israel performs the will of the Omnipresent they add strength to God, as it is said, 'To God we render strength' [Ps. 60:14]. When Israel does not perform the will of the Omnipresent, they weaken, as it were, the great power of Him who is above."[24]

According to rabbinic theology, God is affected when human beings suffer, even if that suffering is necessitated by historical circumstances or by the stipulations of His own law. For example, the drowning of the Egyptians at the Red Sea was necessary to effect the liberation of Israel from bondage. According to the Talmud, when Israel passed through the walls of water at the Red Sea, leaving the Egyptians who pursued them to drown in the sea, God's ministering angels wished to sing praises to the God who saved His people from death and from bondage, but God reprimanded them. In the Talmudic account: "At that hour, the ministering angels wished to utter songs [of praise] before the Holy One, blessed be He, but He rebuked them saying: My handiwork [the Egyptians] is drowning in the sea; how can you utter song in my presence?"[25]

This Talmudic account of the defeat of the Egyptians at the Red Sea, along with a number of the texts that discuss capital punishment quoted above, reflects a further aspect of the attitude of Jewish tradition toward the clash between the premise that life is sacred and the presence of violence in the world.

VIOLENCE: A NECESSARY EVIL—SOMETIMES

According to the biblical narrative, it is God who causes the death of the Egyptians at the Red Sea. In the aforementioned parable of Rabbi Meir, which compares killing a person to killing God, the highway robber is killed at the command of the king, which is to say that capital punishment (according to this text) is established by divine dictate. Indeed, Scripture seeks to justify capital punishment for the crime of murder by appealing to the claim that the human being is created in the divine image: "Whoever sheds the blood of a man, by man shall his blood be shed; for in his image did God make man" (Gen. 9:6). In other words, because our world is an unredeemed world, because our world is an imperfect world, because the Torah and God's presence (*Shekhinah*) are in exile in our world, the observance of moral absolutes is rendered impossible. Not to recognize violence, not to defend oneself against violence, not to seek to destroy violence would be to permit violence a free hand in the world. Not to be aware of the existence of evil and not to take action to keep it in check would be to encourage violence, to provoke evil. While aspiring for peace, ethics must confront the reality of war. While affirming the sanctity of life, ethics must not be oblivious to the challenge posed by violence. While striving for the ideal, ethics must contend with the actual.

As victims of violence throughout history, the Jewish people were never unaware of the omnipresence of violence. However, what Jewish ethics feared even more than violence was the potential moral price attendant upon responding to violence with violence. In this regard, a midrash reflects upon the prelude to Jacob's meeting with his brother Esau.

When Jacob was returning home to Canaan, he learned that his brother Esau was coming to meet him. Upon hearing this news and upon remembering how he had betrayed his brother, Jacob feared that his brother was coming to kill him. The text in Genesis informs us that "Jacob was greatly afraid and he was distressed" (Gen. 32:8). A midrash comments, "Rabbi Judah ben Rabbi Ilai said: Are not fear and distress the same? The meaning [of the verse is] that 'he was afraid,' lest he be slain, 'and he was distressed,' lest he should slay. For he [Jacob] thought: if he [Esau] prevails against me he will slay me; while if I am stronger, I will slay him. This is the meaning of 'he was afraid'—lest he should be slain; 'and he was distressed'—lest he should slay."[26]

Another rabbinic commentary to this verse puts it this way: "Why did he [Jacob] fear him [Esau]? [Because Jacob was afraid] that he might shed blood. Jacob thought, 'No matter what, if I kill him I shall transgress [the commandment], "thou shall not murder"' [Exod. 20:13]."[27] This text is reminiscent of Golda Meir's oft-quoted statement: "We can forgive them for killing our children, but we cannot forgive them for forcing us to kill theirs."

For the rabbis, violence is repulsive. An act of violence—even in self-defense—is repugnant. Killing in self-defense is a last resort. Killing even for self-preservation is still considered homicide, albeit justified homicide. Though violence is sometimes *necessary*, it is always construed as a necessary *evil*.

Jewish law *requires* that one commit an act of violence in the defense of one's own life or even in the defense of the life of an imperiled party. With regard to self-defense, the Talmud asserts, "The Torah has decreed: If a person comes to kill you, arise and kill him first [Exod. 22:1]."[28] And with regard to saving the life of an imperiled party, the Talmud affirms that in the case of "a man who is pursuing his fellow to slay him . . . the Torah has said: 'Whoever sheds the blood of man, by man shall his own blood be shed' [Gen. 9:6], meaning, save the blood of the one pursued by shedding the blood of the pursuer."[29] In other words, killing a potential murderer is necessary to protect the sanctity of the life of the potential victim. According to Maimonides, "It is a commandment: Do not take pity on the life of the pursuer."[30] After further reflection upon this Talmudic law, the rabbis observed that the potential murderer must be stopped—even to the point of killing him—not just to preserve the life of his potential victim but also to save the potential murderer from committing the most heinous of violent crimes—premeditated murder.[31]

Despite the law requiring an act of violence in self-defense, Jewish law also demands that one may not kill another, even if failing to do so means the forfeiture of one's own life. If one is told: slay another or you will be slain, one is obliged to become a victim rather than to become a murderer. The Talmud reports, "A man came before Raba and said to him: The governor of my town has ordered me: Go and kill so and so; if not, I shall slay you. He [Raba] answered him: Let him slay you rather than you should commit murder. Who knows whether your blood is redder [than his]? Perhaps his blood is redder [i.e., you have no right to murder him to save yourself; his life is no less valuable than your own]."[32]

Acts of violence are matters of last resort, justifiable only in severely limited circumstances. If the quoted texts are any indication, Jewish tradition fears the moral implications attendant upon one's becoming a murderer, upon one's becoming violent, more than it fears the effects of violence itself, which seems to be why the Talmud urges, "[Rabbi Abbahu said:] A person should always strive to be rather of the persecuted than of the persecutors as there is none among the birds more persecuted than doves and pigeons, and yet Scripture made them [alone among the birds] eligible [for sacrifice] on the altar."[33]

By responding to violence with violence, the attacked person permits the provocateur to convert him or her into an accomplice in acts of violence; the potential victim becomes a potential victimizer. By meeting violence with violence, the attacked party in effect allows the provocateurs to impose their scenario, their values, upon himself or herself. By so acceding to the attacker, the potential victim becomes the attacker's comrade; the potential victim is manipulated into acts of violence by his or her attacker. For the potential victim of violence to respond with violence is to grant the perpetrator of violence a preemptive victory. However, when it is a matter of last resort, for an imperiled person not to respond to violence in self-defense is also to grant the provocateur a victory in the present as well as encouragement to commit other acts of violence in the future.

SUMMARY AND CONCLUSION

In summation and in conclusion, a Jewish view of the sanctity of life in an age of violence may be depicted by this tale:

During the First World War, the Czar's army needed troops to fight the army of the Kaiser. In order to help meet the draft quotas of the Russian army, Jewish students at many *yeshivot* were forced into service, and were sent for a brief but intensive basic training.

The students of one particular *yeshivah* surprisingly proved themselves to be expert sharpshooters. On the target range at the training camp, they surpassed all other recruits with their marksmanship. Because of their skill, they were sent to the front-line trenches. They crouched with their rifles in the trenches gazing into the mist that hovered over the field of battle. Without warning, the German troops began to charge, advancing toward their trenches. Seeing this, their Russian captain ordered them to fire. But the *yeshivah* students remained crouched in the trenches, their rifles cocked, but without pulling the triggers. Again, the Russian captain ordered them to fire, and once more they did not fire. The Russian captain began to scream at the students, commanding them to fire their rifles, cursing them with every anti-Semitic epithet he knew, and listing the punitive actions that would be taken against them for refusing to follow orders. Finally, one of the students turned to the captain and said, "We'd be happy to fire, captain. But there are people in the way. As soon as the men running toward us get out of the way, we shall fire."

❧ 11 ❧

Moral Implications of the Golem Legend

> The Golem? I've heard talk of it a lot. What do you know
> about the Golem . . . ? Always they treat it as a legend, till
> something happens and it turns into actuality once more.[1]
> —GUSTAV MEYRINK

THE GOLEM LEGEND

PRAGUE: City of mysteries, city of marvels, citadel of memories, birth-place of legends.

Prague: Its ghetto once teeming with Jews, now a mausoleum of Jewish memories. Once a capital of Jewish learning, now enveloped by the shadows of a lost Jewish Atlantis. A Jewish ghost town, its inhabitants murdered, Jewish Prague is now preserved only in legends. By telling their tales, the souls of people turned into smoke and cinders are granted a life after death. Their legends are their tombstones.

So many souls haunt the old ghetto of Prague. Their presence pervades the old synagogue in Prague. For there they go to commune with their master, the "Exalted" Judah Loew, called Maharal, rabbi of Prague. Though dead for centuries, he is still rabbi of Prague. Although there have been many rabbis *in* Prague, only he was and is rabbi *of* Prague. Revered by Jew and Gentile alike, Bohemians all consider him a symbol of providence over Prague.[2]

Of the many legends about Loew, the legend of the Golem has been the most durable. Ascribed to him more than a century after his death, the creation of the Golem, though not part of his biography, became a central feature of his hagiography.[3]

Legend and history blended to set the stage. The Jews, once so secure in Spain, had suffered the trauma of expulsion. The earthquake of

This chapter represents a substantial revision of my monograph *The Golem Legend: Origins and Implications*, published in 1985 by University Press of America.

exile that had devastated Spanish Jewry sent aftershocks of insecurity to all corners of the Jewish world. Were Jews secure anywhere?

After a period of calm and tranquillity, there were threats of expulsion against the Jews of Bohemia. Jewish books ignited bonfires in Austria. Martin Luther called for the expulsion of the Jews from Germany and for the confiscation of their property. Suspected of being in an alliance with the Ottoman enemy of the declining Holy Roman Empire, Jews were vilified as a fifth column in the European lands where they resided. The long-dormant "blood libel" once more burst to the surface.[4] The times required radical action. And so, the Jews of Europe turned to Judah Loew, the Maharal of Prague, cabalist and alchemist, mystical master and master magician, for a solution. What he did in life, he also accomplished in legend. Judah Loew responded with innovation and with courage to the challenge of the times.[5]

Knowing that, with the coming of the Passover for the year 5340 (i.e., 1580), the blood libel charge would escalate and persecutions would increase, Judah Loew decided to summon all of his magical and mystical power to create a being—immense in physical prowess, of awesome size and strength—to protect the Jews from the blood libel and from the inevitable pogroms that would ensue. This being—in many ways more than a man, and in some ways less than a man—was the Golem.

For a week, Judah Loew, his son-in-law Isaac Katz, and his disciple Sasson prepared themselves for the perilous undertaking. They fasted, and they purified their bodies by continual ritual immersions. They studied the relevant cabalistic texts about the creation of the Golem. They repented of their sins, and they prayed.

On the eve of the twentieth day of the Hebrew month of Adar, they met at the Altneuschul, the "old-new" synagogue, in final preparation for giving new life to a being that, until now, they had only encountered in old books and treatises. After making their last ritual ablutions, they studied for a final time the texts into which the mysteries of creation had been locked for so many centuries.

Before sunrise, Judah Loew led Isaac and Sasson to the Moldau River outside of Prague. Isaac lit a torch in the darkness. Three shadows stretched along the riverbank. Judah Loew took his staff and drew a human figure in the clay. Jewish law had forbidden drawing the human image and form. But, had God Himself not broken His own commandment when He created the very first human?

Loew silently drew with the skill of an accomplished artist until a facsimile of a human appeared in the clay. Then, he began to walk in a circle around the figure he had drawn, and he began to intone the secret names of God found in the cabalistic tracts he had studied for so many years. Isaac and Sasson accompanied him as he walked around the figure. Each proceeded in a separate orbit, repeating the names recited by Judah Loew.

As they circled the figure, it became progressively detached from the clay in which it had been drawn. Hair grew on its head. Nails sprouted on its fingers and toes. Its eyes opened—blank, dead eyes. Judah Loew stopped suddenly and so did Isaac and Sasson. Loew cautiously approached the creature, and under its tongue he placed a piece of parchment on which the words "The Lord is Truth" were written. Loew knew that only the power of God, not his own, could bestow life on inert matter.

Life came into the Golem's eyes. Breath entered its nose and chest. Firmly, Loew commanded, "Golem, stand." And the Golem rose from the clay, looking like anyone arising from a deep sleep. Now, four shadows, one towering above the others, stretched along the riverbank.[6] Isaac and Sasson dressed the Golem, who followed them back to the Altneuschul synagogue in Prague to begin its career as a protector of the Jews and to ensure Judah Loew's place in its legend.

According to some versions of the legend, the Golem thwarted plots that falsely accused Jews of using the blood of Christian children for various Jewish rituals, such as the making of *matzot* for Passover. Other versions of the legend portray the Golem as having physically defended the Jews against the onslaught of frenzied mobs trying to initiate a pogrom. Still other versions depict the Golem as a menial laborer in the home of Judah Loew.

According to all variations of the legend, the Golem was not completely human because it lacked one vital human trait. In some versions, it is intellect; in others, it is sexuality.[7] Yet, according to some accounts, the Golem had sexual designs on Judah Loew's granddaughter, Hava. Whatever the case, the time eventually came for Judah Loew to dismantle his creation. A number of explanations have been made about why this came to pass.

According to one view, with the cessation of the blood libel, the Golem had outlived its usefulness. Without a purpose, it had no *raison d'être*. Another view holds that Loew realized that it was not proper to employ a being, which had been created through such marvelous means, as a menial servant. A third view posits that the Golem had to be destroyed because its immense power ran amok. Indeed, some versions of the legend suggest that the Golem went mad when it realized that it could not marry Hava.

For some reason, or for no reason at all, the legend reports that one Friday afternoon, just before the Sabbath, the Golem began to destroy the Jewish ghetto of Prague. When Loew heard what the Golem was doing, he immediately went to search for it. Finding it, Loew ordered the Golem to go to the attic of the Altneuschul synagogue. No match for Loew, the Golem complied.

Loew commanded the Golem to lie down on a long table in the attic, to stretch its limbs, and to sleep. The Golem again complied. As the Golem's eyes fell into sleep, Loew reached under the Golem's tongue and removed the parchment with the name of God written on it, and the Golem fell into an eternal sleep. The Golem's body reverted back into clay, and Judah Loew, mourning his creature, wrapped the clay in prayer shawls and subsequently issued an order that no one—except his successors as chief rabbi of Prague—ever should ascend to the attic again.

For 150 years, no one tried, not even the subsequent chief rabbis of Prague. However, in the late eighteenth century, Judah Loew's successor, Ezekiel Landau, decided to go up. He fasted for many days in preparation for the ascent. He bathed in the ritual bath. He prayed and repented of his sins. Draped in a prayer shawl, wearing his tefillin, he began slowly up the stairs to the attic.

As he ascended, Landau was seized by a tremor. His entire body shook. His face turned pale. He turned around and stumbled back down the stairs. When he regained his composure, Landau decreed that all people would now be forbidden to go to the attic, even the chief rabbi of Prague.[8]

What did Landau fear? Why did he preclude future access to the Golem? Perhaps he was afraid that the Golem was not there, that the Golem was merely the subject of legend, and he wanted to preserve the legend. The opposite is also possible. Perhaps he knew that the Golem was indeed there and that by entering the attic he might disturb its rest. He might reawaken a creature too powerful to be controlled. Perhaps he saw in a flash of insight why Judah Loew had destroyed his creature. He may have felt the fear that Judah Loew felt when Loew realized that the being created to help and to protect its creator might eventually harm or even destroy its creator and those people and things its creator held dear.

As noted, the legend of the Golem was not identified with Judah Loew until more than a century after his death. Previously, various versions of the legend were identified with the sixteenth-century Polish rabbi Elijah of Chelm. According to one of these tales, after Elijah of Chelm had created a Golem, the creature spontaneously grew to a monumental size. Fearing that it might also grow beyond his control, afraid of its destructive potential, Elijah of Chelm reached up to the Golem's head to remove the parchment with God's name inscribed upon it, placed under the Golem's tongue. Upon the extraction of the parchment, the Golem immediately returned to clay, crushing Elijah of Chelm beneath its massive weight.[9]

Perhaps because he feared sharing the fate of Elijah of Chelm, Ezekiel Landau allowed the Golem to remain in eternal repose. Nevertheless, others have dared to resurrect the Golem and its legend. The moral issues engendered by the Golem legend are evermore pressing today than they were in the days of Loew, Landau, and Elijah of Chelm. The creation of "artificial life" is no longer mere legend; it is scientific fact. The process of the creation of artificial life is no longer the domain of cabalists but of scientists. However, while Jewish mystics and theologians—past and present—may not be able to create artificial life, they may be able to conjure insights from traditional sources of wisdom that can clarify and elucidate the moral implications related to the creation of artificial life. The discussions of the Golem legend in classical Jewish theological, ethical, and legal literature offer insights and guidelines for those persons who are concerned with creating resurrected Golems in a variety of forms. Before reviewing how classical Jewish literature dealt with its Golems, a glance at some of the problems brought up by today's Golems is in order.

TODAY'S GOLEMS

In 1972, Ananda Chakrabarty, a microbiologist, filed a patent application for a humanly engineered bacterium capable of breaking down multiple components of crude oil, a property found in no naturally occurring bacteria. This bacterium was believed to have particular value in the treatment of oil spills. While the U.S. Office of Patents and Trademarks granted a patent for the *process* of producing the bacterium, it denied Chakrabarty a patent for the bacterium itself on the grounds that microorganisms are "products of nature" and that as living entities they are not patentable.

Chakrabarty appealed the denial of a patent for the bacterium to the U.S. Court of Customs and Patent Appeals, which affirmed Chakrabarty's right to a patent. The court held that live organisms were not outside the scope of patentable inventions. On 17 March 1980, arguments on the case of U.S. Commissioner of Patents and Trademarks (Sidney Diamond) vs. Ananda Chakrabarty were presented before the U.S. Supreme Court. On 16 June 1980, in a five-to-four decision, the Supreme Court affirmed the decisions of the U.S. Court of Customs and Patent Appeals permitting Chakrabarty a patent on the bacterium. Speaking for the majority, Chief Justice Burger held that "a live, human-made, microorganism is patentable subject matter under statute providing for issuance of patent to a person who invents or discovers 'any' new or useful 'manufacture' or 'composition of matter.'"[10] Four hundred years later—almost to the day, 20 March

1580—when Judah Loew was described by legend as having created the Golem, the U.S. Supreme Court was hearing arguments related to the propriety of the creation of artificial life, the risks of the creation of artificial life-forms, the ownership of artificially created life-forms, and the legal status of such creations. Four days after the Supreme Court announced its decision, a letter was sent to President Jimmy Carter from the General Secretaries of the National Council of Churches, the U.S. Catholic Conference, and the Synagogue Council of America. The letter stated:

> With the Supreme Court decision allowing patents on new forms of life—a purpose that could not have been imagined when patent laws were written—it is obvious that these laws must be reexamined. The issue goes far beyond patents. New life-forms may have dramatic potential for improving human life. . . . They may also, however, have unforeseen ramifications, and at times the cure may be worse than the original problem. . . . Those who would play God will be tempted as never before. . . . Given all the responsibility to God and to our fellow human beings, do we have the right to let experimentation and ownership of new life-forms move ahead without public regulation? These issues must be explored, and they must be explored now.[11]

In response to this appeal, President Carter asked the President's Commission for the Study of Ethical Problems in Medicine and Biomedical and Behavioral Research to undertake a study of "the social and ethical issues of genetic engineering with human beings." In November 1982, the commission issued its findings in a work entitled *Splicing Life*. In this report, one finds the following observation:

> Like the tale of the Sorcerer's apprentice or the myth of the Golem created from lifeless dust by the 16th century rabbi, Loew of Prague, the story of Dr. Frankenstein's monster serves as a reminder of the difficulty of restoring order if a creation intended to be helpful proves harmful instead. Indeed, each of these tales conveys a painful irony: in seeking to extend their control over the world, people may lessen it. The artifices they create to do their bidding may rebound destructively against them—the slave may become the master.[12]

Apprehension that the Golem-slave will become the master of its creator was not simply a concern of the commission, nor is it merely a restatement of the master-slave dialectic developed by Hegel. That the Golem will enslave its master is a common theme in the literary spin-offs of the Golem legend. For example, in the Capek brothers' famous play, *R.U.R.*, where the term "robot" is first coined, we read, "Mankind will never cope with the Robots, and will never have control over them. Mankind will be overwhelmed in the deluge of these dreadful living machines, will be their slave, will live at their mercy."[13]

The report of the presidential commission notes a study done by the National Science Foundation (NSF) which found that most Americans opposed most restrictions on scientific research in all areas but one—creation of new life-forms and genetic engineering with human beings. While the commission concurred that there are valid reasons for this apprehension, it also asserted that much popular opposition to genetic engineering was based upon fear grounded in a lack of awareness of the nature of genetic engineering and of the potential benefits it holds forth. While the commission was sensitive to the possible moral abuses of genetic engineering, it also indicated that it might be unethical to stifle the potential benefits that genetic engineering may bring to many people. For example, drugs could be produced in large quantities at comparatively little cost that could help treat medical problems that otherwise either would not be treated or could be treated only at extraordinary cost. Already, gene-splicing techniques have produced several useful human growth hormones to treat dwarfism. Drugs to fight diabetes, hemophilia, and even cancer could be produced economically in great quantities through gene-splicing techniques. In addition, gene splicing could be utilized to correct genetic defects both before and after birth that otherwise would have tragic or even fatal consequences. Finally, because of natural or man-induced climatic or other changes in our environment, genetic engineering may forestall extensive catastrophe. For example, if a sudden shift of climate were to occur, the use of genetic engineering to alter quickly the genetic composition of agricultural plants might save whole populations from mass starvation.

As discussed later in this chapter, Judah Loew and others described the creation of artificial life as an action in consonance with the natural order of creation. In other words, such acts are essentially "natural" and do not represent a contravening of the natural order. Similarly, the commission observed that gene splicing occurs regularly within bacteria, and it concluded that "the basic processes underlying genetic engineering are thus *natural* and not revolutionary. Indeed, it was the discovery that these processes were [naturally] occurring that suggested to scientists the great possibilities and basic methods of gene splicing. What is new, however, is the ability of scientists to control the processes."[14]

That artificially created organisms might endanger human life was found by the commission to be a largely unfounded fear, grounded in the public's lack of knowledge about the controls under which such activities were conducted. It found both scientific and governmental controls upon such experimentation to be more than adequate. Seymour Siegel, a preeminent Jewish theologian who was a member of the commission, reported the following in an address to the Rabbinical Assembly:

The National Institute of Health has formulated guidelines to be followed by laboratories sponsoring DNA research. These guidelines have reduced the danger of these experiments to practically zero. . . . I can testify personally, as a member of the Biohazards Committee of the giant pharmaceutical firm, Hoffman-LaRoche, as to the exquisite care which is taken in the protection of the environment and the researchers involved in DNA experiments. . . . Thus it seems obvious to me that the potentially great benefits to mankind in carrying on these researches far outweigh any possible harm. [15]

Although the commission decided that genetic engineering is currently monitored adequately in the United States, it recommended that such careful monitoring continue. It also reinforced a popular apprehension regarding the dangers of genetic engineering in a nondemocratic political setting or for use in developing pathogenic microorganisims for biological warfare or for terrorism. Furthermore, the commission warned that the hubris of the scientist that might lead him or her to create artificial beings without regard to the potential physical and moral dangers of such action had to be controlled. It denounced as outrightly unethical certain possible uses of genetic engineering, such as the creation of a genetically engineered slave population of partly human and partly animal beings. In short, the commission, in general, and the theologians on the commission, in particular, felt that in itself genetic engineering is good, that it articulates the biblical view that human beings are cocreators with God. However, it also maintained that genetic engineering, like any human activity, can express itself as a misuse of human freedom with concomitant harmful results. [16] The commission concluded that the creation of artificial life should be permitted, even encouraged. However, such activities must be done with expert care and with a keen awareness of the potentially harmful consequences of such actions. [17] One of the issues raised but not elaborated upon by the commission was the development of new techniques in the treatment of barren couples, including "test-tube babies."

In Shakespeare's *Macbeth*, the witches predict that Macbeth could only be killed by one who was not of woman born. [18] Macduff, who was born by means of a cesarean section, fits into this category and slays Macbeth. Macduff's status as a human being—despite the conditions of his birth—is never questioned. However, in 1978, when the first test-tube baby was born in England, the news media compared the test-tube baby to the Golem. Conceived "artificially," outside of the womb, the test-tube baby might be comparable to a Golem.

The creation of test-tube babies by in vitro fertilization is only one of a number of techniques that may be used to bring about "artificial" conception. Nevertheless, all such methods of artificial conception have raised serious moral questions with which ethicists and theologians must deal. Among such techniques are artificial insemination, in vitro fertilization, artificial embryonization, parthenogenesis, and cloning. Some of these techniques are currently commonly practiced. Others may or may not have occurred. Others may be beyond the abilities of current scientific technology.

Artificial insemination is widely practiced today in the United States. It has been estimated that more than one-quarter of a million people have been conceived in this manner. As many as ten thousand to twenty-five thousand Americans each year may be conceived by artificial insemination. Because of the confidentiality surrounding this procedure, exact numbers cannot be known.

In in vitro fertilization, an ovum is removed from a woman who is unable to conceive children naturally because of some reproductive malfunction, usually in her Fallopian tubes. The ovum is then fertilized in a petri dish from the sperm of a man. If conception occurs and if gestation begins normally, the fetus is then placed into the uterus, where, it is hoped, it will become implanted and gestate until birth.

Artificial embryonization is a comparatively new procedure, which is somewhat like the opposite of donor insemination. Here, an ovum is taken from a female volunteer. It is then fertilized by a male, usually in vitro. The fertilized egg is then implanted within another woman who carries the pregnancy to term. For example, if a woman is barren because she is not ovulating, her husband would fertilize the egg of another woman. Fertilization could be done in vitro, as in the case of a test-tube baby, or the egg could be implanted in his wife's womb where it could be fertilized in vivo. The child would genetically be the father's but not the mother's. The woman giving birth to the child would be its natural mother but not its genetic mother.[19]

In parthenogenesis, an ovum would be stimulated to gestate either chemically or electrically. The child would always be female and would carry only the mother's chromosomes. No fertilization would occur. No sperm are involved. While parthenogenesis has been accomplished with animals, there is no evidence (though there is speculation) that it has been accomplished with humans.

In cloning, the nucleus of an ovum is replaced by the nucleus of a cell taken from the body of a person. The ovum is then planted in a womb. The resulting child would be genetically identical to the person from whose body the nucleus was taken. In this way, a person could reproduce himself or herself. Genetically speaking, one could become one's own parent-child. To date, there is no substantiated record of such a procedure having been done on humans, although cloning has been done on plants and animals. Cloning currently remains more a part of science fiction than of science.[20]

American law recognizes two categories of "persons": "natural" and "artificial." In American law, a person is a person not because he or she is human but because rights and duties are ascribed to him or her or it. A natural person is an individual human being. An example of an artificial person would be a corporation or a county or the estate of a deceased individual. Thus, American law readily allows for the creation of artificial legal persons.[21]

In many situations the wisdom of according artificial persons legal status may be questioned. For example, a corporation, by its very nature, would not be punishable in the same manner as would be a human being (such as imprisonment, capital punishment). A corporation that releases carcinogenic wastes or poisonous industrial substances into a lake from which people draw their drinking water might only be liable for a nominal statutory fine, while a person causing deliberate harm to other persons in an identical manner might also be liable to imprisonment. The acceptance of artificial persons as legal persons tends to encourage individual officials of corporations to seek personal legal immunity by hiding behind a "corporate shield." There may therefore be some wisdom to the position that refuses to grant legal personhood to artificial beings.

What status would an artificial person, a Golem, have according to law? Would a person conceived, gestated, or born through such methods as those just mentioned be a natural or an artificial person? Would killing an artificial person be murder? What would be the case if the victim had been part human and part machine, that is, a cyborg? This last question has been raised in science fiction literature. For example, in his story *Fires of Night*, Dennis Etchison asks whether killing a person with artificial limbs or organs would be murder. At what point would such an individual cross over the line from being a human to being a machine? When would such an individual stop being a human who is part machine and become merely a machine that is part human? Discussion of this issue is amplified by Martin Caidin in his novel *Cyborg*, which became the basis for the television program, "The Six-Million-Dollar Man." In this story, an American astronaut crash-lands. His destroyed limbs are replaced by bionic limbs. He is now literally half-human, half-machine. With the rapid pace of developments in bionics and the use of artificial organs, questions originally raised by science fiction writers currently fall under the domain of medical ethics.[22] While these issues have not yet been adequately treated by American courts, they have been addressed by classical Jewish literature regarding the Golem.

The problem of the "personhood" of an artificially created individual and the problem of responsibility for its actions are discussed in the literature on "artificial intelligence." If intelligence is a trait peculiar to human personhood, would an intelligent machine then be a person? A number of philosophers have maintained that we tend to confuse the data pro-grammed into a machine by a human being with intelligence. For example, as philosopher Michael Polanyi has observed, the thought that we detect in the working of a machine is properly speaking only the thought of the designer of the machine. In addition, philosopher William Barrett observes that "the computer only gives us back ourselves. It is a faithful mirror that reflects the human traits that are brought to it . . . there could be other human faces that the computer might give back to us—the face of arro-gance, of ruthlessness, of the lust for power."[23] A similar point to that made by Barrett is dramatized in Joseph and Karel Capek's famous play, R.U.R.

It is reasonable to assume that the Capek brothers, who were from Prague, were influenced by the Golem legend when they wrote R.U.R. It is in this work that the term "robot" was coined. "Robot" derives from a Slavic root meaning a "worker" in the sense of a slave laborer.

R.U.R. is the abbreviation for "Rossum's Universal Robots." The play takes place at an R.U.R. factory that manufactures robots. In the course of the play, the robots take over both the factory and the world. After the robots have all but annihilated the human race, Alquist, a clerk at the R.U.R. factory, asks the robots, "Why did you murder us?" Radius, one of the robots, replies, "Slaughter and domination are necessary if you want to be like man. Read history, read the human books. You must domineer and murder if you want to be like men."[24] Artificially created beings only reflect their creators. The evil a machine may do only reflects its creators. The artificial beings we create can tell us more about human nature than about the nature of technology or of machines. Their creation is not only an ex-pression of human achievement but an exercise—sometimes a horrifying one—in human self-understanding. Our fear of the results of technological achievement is simply a reflection of our fear of ourselves. This fear may not be unjustified. The threat of nuclear war indicates in a shockingly real way that the Golems we create to defend us may ultimately destroy us. The explosion of technology since the Industrial Revolution may indicate to us that, the more exposure to machines we experience, the more we may tend to define ourselves and to think of ourselves as machines. Machines may not only reflect human proclivities, they may cause us to alter the manner in which we think of human nature, of ourselves.

The tendency in modern Western thought to define the human being as a kind of machine and, conversely, to grant human status to certain kinds of machines is based upon a mechanistic and physicalist view of real-ity that is reductionistic in nature and in approach. This philosophy tends to obscure the spiritual dimension of the human creature and to treat the category of uniqueness as a superfluous bother. However, because this atti-tude has become so deeply ingrained in modern Western thought, it bears discussion.[25]

One of the traits unique to human beings is self-definition. Only human beings define themselves. How we define ourselves reflects what we think of ourselves, how we view ourselves. Beginning in the eighteenth-century, it became fashionable to define the human being as a kind of machine. Once internalized, this philosophical position becomes a determining factor in human behavior. Once accepted by the individual, this philosophical assumption becomes a psychological presupposition.

In the seventeenth-century, the eminent philosopher René Descartes introduced a distinction between "thinking beings" and "extended beings." He classified human beings as uniquely self-conscious thinking beings. For Descartes, animals were "extended beings." Descartes described animals as automata. In the eighteenth-century, the French philosopher Julien Offray de La Mettrie rejected Descartes's position out of hand. According to de La Mettrie, human beings are also machines. In his work, *Man, A Machine* (*L'Homme-machine*), de La Mettrie described the human body as "a machine that winds its own springs."[26]

De La Mettrie's view was expanded by mechanist and materialist philosophers and thinkers who came after him. For example, in the nineteenth century, the atheist philosopher Robert Ingersoll observed that "man is a machine into which we put what we call food and produce what we call thought." In other words, humans are thinking machines. The novelist Isak Dinesen went further by writing, "What is man when you come to think about him, but a minutely set, ingenious machine for turning, with infinite artfulness, the red wine of Shiraz into urine?" In the early twentieth century, an American philosopher defined the human being as "an ingenious array of portable plumbing."

It is all but inevitable that once internalized the conception of the human being as a variety of machine would influence our behavior toward others. Even our daily colloquial speech has been influenced. For example, we speak of ourselves as being "turned on" and "turned off." We "tune in" and "tune out." We provide "input" and "output." We go on vacations to "recharge our batteries." We "gear ourselves up" and "get our motors running" at the beginning of a day. By the end of a day, we are "wound up," so we must "unwind."

Even our sexual lives, our most intimate experiences, are influenced by technological thought, by the notion that the human being is a kind of machine. A basic concept of technological thought is that mastery of the proper technique will provide a solution to any given problem. One's only need is to find the right method and all problems in life will inevitably yield before it. The widespread acceptance of this notion accounts for the flood of how-to manuals. We tacitly assume that the right method will produce the desired results. The unavoidable consequence of this approach, when applied to sexuality, is that sex comes to be thought of mainly as problem of method and of technique. While Plato defined love as "madness," we tend to define love in terms of "method." Sex thereby becomes technique centered rather than person centered. Psychologist Rollo May has termed this view "salvation through technique."

According to May, the emphasis upon technique, when carried beyond a certain point, makes for a mechanistic attitude toward making love. One begins to think of oneself as a machine. One begins to use one's body as a machine. 'Performance" and "function" come to supersede feeling and emotion. Sex becomes "product" oriented. Achieving orgasm—the product of sexual technique—becomes the *primary* goal of sexual activity. The desire lies in being a great performer. The emphasis shifts from pleasure to performance. In May's words, "The Victorian person sought to have love without falling into sex; the modern person seeks to have sex without falling into love." The goal becomes "Making oneself feel less in order to perform better!"[27]

Gustav Meyrink's novel, *The Golem*, warns of the danger of "humans to dwindle to soulless entities as soon as was extinguished some slight spark of an idea."[28] Meyrink and others offer a warning while they pose a challenge. The warning is that if we conceive of ourselves as machines, then we become like machines—devoid of freedom, creativity, and spontaneity; we become soulless, mechanical entities. We regress from the status of human beings back to the golemic state; we choose thereby to evolve backwards. For these writers, and for others, the pressing problem is not whether Golems can be considered humans but how to prevent humans from becoming like Golems. The challenge they pose is the pressing need for human beings to intensify their quest to realize and to manifest those essentially human qualities that ultimately distinguish us from the Golems we have created. In this view, the omnipresence of Golems in our daily lives offers us a challenge to become more intensely human, to accentuate those characteristics that make us peculiarly human and that can promise to liberate us from the protohuman golemic state to which we have a tendency to regress.

YESTERDAY'S GOLEMS CONFRONT TODAY'S PROBLEMS

Many of the moral, psychological, and spiritual problems confronting us today seem to have been anticipated by the Golem legend. Daily newspapers and weekly magazines carry stories of modern Golems—the benefits they offer, the risks they represent. By reviewing the development of the nature and the implications of the Golem legend in classical Jewish religious literature, one may glean insights from the past that relate to the problems of the present. Understanding how previous ages dealt with their Golems may offer us some wisdom in dealing with the Golems of today. The place to begin this search is the Talmud.

> Raba said: If the righteous desired it, they could create worlds, for it is written: "But your iniquities have distinguished between you and your God" (Isa. 59:2). Rabbah created a man and sent him to Rabbi Zera. Rabbi Zera spoke to him [the artificially created man], but received no answer. Thereupon, he [Rabbi Zera] said to him [the artificially created man]: You are from the companions. Return to your dust. Rabbi Hanina and Rabbi Oshaia spent every Sabbath eve studying the *Sefer Yetzirah* (*The Book of Creation*), by means of which they created a third-grown calf which they ate.[29]

Raba's statement introduces two important concepts. First, human beings are capable of creating worlds.[30] Second, sin prevents humans from fully manifesting the creative abilities that they potentially share with God. Raba seems to be saying that the feature that we share with God is our creative ability. We strive for *imitatio Dei*. Therefore, when we are creators, we are most like God; we are most clearly in His image. Sin makes us un-Godlike. Sin separates us from that image. Sin stifles our potential to be creative.

It is noteworthy that Raba never questions the propriety of human beings striving to be Godlike, to be creators. Raba does not question the propriety of creating worlds or of creating artificial life. For Raba, and apparently for Rabbah, the creation of worlds and the creation of artificial life is not a usurpation of God's role as creator, it is instead a fulfillment of the human potential to become a creator. While other traditions and other religions considered the creation of artificial beings to be demonic, Jewish tradition embraced, and even encouraged, such creative activity.[31]

The term "Golem" is not found in our text; nevertheless, the text represents the first record of a creation of a Golem by a human being, and it was so understood by later commentaries. In fact, in many versions of the Golem legend, the term "Golem" is not used. In a number of post-Talmudic texts, the Golem is referred to as "a man created by means of the *Sefer Yetzirah*."[32] This description of the Golem, as we shall see, is rooted in the commentaries to the text under examination.

Perhaps because the text speaks of Rabbi Hanina and Rabbi Oshaia's ability to create a calf by means of the *Sefer Yetzirah*, or perhaps because he was in possession of early traditions regarding the creation of an artificial person, Rashi interprets "Rabbah created a man" to mean "Rabbah created a man by means of the *Sefer Yetzirah* in which he learned the letter-combinations of the Name."[33] Whether the *Sefer Yetzirah* that Rashi refers to is identical to the *Sefer Yetzirah* mentioned in the Talmudic text is open to some doubt. Nevertheless, Rashi and the later commentaries assumed that they were identical and that the *Sefer Yetzirah* mentioned by the Talmud is the *Sefer Yetzirah* required in the manufacture of a Golem.

The *Sefer Yetzirah* is traditionally ascribed to Abraham the Patriarch, although some cabalists claimed its author was Rabbi Akiba. A short work, fewer than two thousand words in length, the *Sefer Yetzirah* has inspired a plethora of commentary. Medieval Jewish philosophers (e.g., Saadia Gaon, and Judah ha-Levi) as well as mystics wrote commentaries to this work. The central subjects of the treatise—cosmology and cosmogony—were of great concern both to the medieval Jewish philosophers and to the medieval Jewish mystics. Although it was initially meant to be a speculative work, the *Sefer Yetzirah* was later considered by Jewish mystics to be a manual for use in the act of creation itself. From being a book *about* creation, the *Sefer Yetzirah* became a book *of* creation. Originally understood by the mystics as a work of *kabbalah iyyunit* (mystical speculation), it later came to be utilized as a work of *kabbalah ma'asit* (practical mysticism). Rashi's observation indicates that by his time (eleventh-century France), the *Sefer Yetzirah* was already understood to be a manual of magic. This tradition may predate Rashi, as one may assume that he reported a well-established tradition.

What is relevant to our discussion is that the *Sefer Yetzirah* describes the twenty-two letters of the Hebrew alphabet as being the foundation of creation. Through various combinations of the letters of the Hebrew alphabet, creation occurs. According to the *Sefer Yetzirah*, all twenty-two Hebrew letters derive from one name: tetragrammaton, the ineffable four-letter name of God. The *Sefer Yetzirah* states, "Twenty-two letter elements: He outlined them, hewed them out, weighed them, combined them, and exchanged them [i.e., He transformed them in accordance with certain laws], and through them [He] created the whole of all creation and everything else that would ever be created. . . . It comes about that all creation and all language issue from one name."[34]

The notion that God creates the world by means of language—through words—is biblical. The idea that human beings can share in God's creative power by mastering formulae that combine and permutate letters of the alphabet is rabbinic in origin but is considerably expanded by the medieval Jewish mystics.[35] For some medieval Jewish mystics, letter permutations were used in the process of attaining the mystical experience (e.g., Abraham Abulafia).[36] For other Jewish mystics, mastering the art of letter permutation and combination granted one the ability to create life itself. Rashi's comment regarding the ability of the Talmudic rabbis to create both a calf and a man by letter combinations of the name reflects this notion. By combining and permutating the letters of God's ineffable name, creation can take place. Since the letters of the alphabet were the building blocks of creation, knowing how to manipulate those letters gives one access to the same forces that brought the world into being.

Rashi's terse commentary to the Talmudic text under consideration introduces two elements that play an essential role in the development of the Golem legend: the use of the *Sefer Yetzirah* not simply as a work about cosmology but as a tool to be used in the creative enterprise; and the idea that language is pregnant with creative potency, that language has the power to create worlds as well as words.

To this point, we have discussed Rabbah's creation of the first humanly created Golem. The text continues by telling us that Rabbah sent this "man" to Rabbi Zera. When Rabbi Zera spoke to the "man," he received no reply, and from this he deduced that no ordinary person stood before him. Why did Rabbi Zera come to this conclusion? Furthermore, what Rabbi Zera said to the "man" is equally enigmatic, "You are from the companions. Return to your dust."

The commentaries (e.g., Rashi) point out that, when the "man" refused to respond, Rabbi Zera discerned that he was unable to speak. Since the ability to speak is unique to human beings who embody the human soul (as distinct form the animal soul), Rabbi Zera concluded that the person who stood before him was not human but was from the companions, that is, from those scholars who are involved with the *Sefer Yetzirah*.[37] In addition, the Aramaic word translated literally as "the companions" may also be translated as "the magical charmers" or simply as "magicians."

The term *ha-medaber* (the one who speaks) became a common designation for "human being" in medieval philosophical Hebrew. That the "man" who stood before Rabbi Zera failed to reply with words was taken by Rabbi Zera, as well as by medieval commentaries, as an indication that he was not truly human.[38]

Rabbi Zera's statement, "Return to your dust," was taken to mean that the "man" disintegrated at Rabbi Zera's command. As we shall see, the legal and moral implications of Rabbi Zera's act were discussed in an eighteenth-century responsum. At this point, however, one can identify two elements that are continuously found in subsequent versions of the Golem legend. First, the Golem is human in all respects except one. The Golem lacks one vital characteristic, which voids its claim to being human. In this text, that characteristic is the power of speech. As was mentioned, the commentaries interpreted the lack of speech as being indicative of the absence of a human soul. The Golem is a soulless, but not a lifeless, human being. Second, Rabbi Zera's command indicates that language has the power to destroy as well as to create.

The description of a Golem as a soulless human being is Talmudic in origin. In a Talmudic text in which the term "Golem" is used, the story of the creation of Adam is recounted. Unlike the previously discussed text, which describes the Golem as a human creation, here the Golem is described as a creation of God. By creating a Golem, the human being reflects not only God's general creative ability but His specific ability to create a Golem. Described in this text as a "primitive" form of human being, as a soulless human being, the Golem represents the human creature of an incompleted primordial state. In a sense, the human creator of the Golem confronts the human creature—himself—in his own primitive, underdeveloped form. The human creator of the Golem confronts the human being—himself—as he once was, as he might have remained, as pure matter devoid of form, as a soulless creature without life and purpose. This notion may be echoed in the use of the term "*Golem*" in medieval philosophical Hebrew to denote matter without form, substance without purpose. The Talmudic text reads, "Rabbi Johanan ben Hanina said: The [sixth day of creation] consisted of twelve hours. In the first hour his [Adam's] dust was gathered; in the second it [the dust] was made into a shapeless mass [Hebrew: *Golem*]; in the third his limbs were extended; in the fourth a soul was infused into him; in the fifth he arose and stood on his feet; in the sixth he gave [the animals] their names."[39]

In various midrashic variants of this text, the sequence is reported differently. In the first hour, God conceives of creating man; in the second, He takes counsel with the angels regarding whether He should create man; in the third, He assembles the dust; in the fourth, He kneads the dust; in the fifth, He shapes the form; in the sixth, He makes him into a Golem; in the seventh, He breathes a soul into him.[40] In this version, unlike the Talmudic version, the Golem already has a human form—Adam's form. In this text, the Golem is not a formless mass, but a manikin; human in shape but not in essence. Thus, this text describes the state of "Golem" as soulless, but *with* human form. Other midrashim reaffirm this description of Adam in his golemic stage, but they provide additional information about its activities in this state of suspended animation. For example, a midrash reads, "'And He breathed into his nostrils' [Gen. 2:7]. This teaches that He set him up as a Golem reaching from earth to heaven and then infused a soul into him."[41] From this text it is apparent that both the ensouled primordial Adam (i.e., Adam before he sinned), and Adam as Golem are described as a being of gigantic physical proportions. This motif surfaces in very late versions of the Golem legend, where the Golem is described as being capable of assuming huge physical dimensions.

The term "Golem" means an "unformed mass." A form of the word "Golem" appears only once in the Bible (Ps. 139:16): "Your eyes saw my unformed mass [*galmi*], it was all recorded in Your book." A midrash interprets the verse as Adam saying to God: Your eyes saw my Golem. Furthermore, the phrase, "it was all recorded in Your book," is related by the midrash to the creation of Adam because, according to tradition, Adam was created on the Jewish New Year (Rosh Hashanah), "when God assesses the record of human deeds written in His book."[42] The midrash reads:

Rabbi Tanhuma in Rabbi Banaya's name and Rabbi Berekiah in Rabbi Eliezer's name said: He created him a Golem and he lay stretching from one end of the world to the other, as it is written, Your eyes saw my Golem. Rabbi Judah ben Simon said: While Adam lay as a Golem before Him who spoke and the world came into being, He showed him every generation and its sages, every generation and its scribes, interpreters and leaders. Said He to him: Your eyes saw My Golem [i.e., the eyes of the Golem have seen My unformed world]; the unformed substance [i.e., the Golem's potential descendants] which your eyes have seen is already written in the book of Adam—[as it is written] "This is the book of the generations of Adam" [Gen. 5:1].[43]

It may be that this midrash is trying to tell us that we are not only the descendants of Adam but the descendants of a Golem as well. Perhaps, as the biblical verse indicates (Ps. 139:16), God saw Adam as Golem. In other words, God sees Adam—the human being—as essentially a Golem, who becomes human only when realizing his or her potential, which is symbolized in the text as the potential offspring of Adam-Golem.[44] Otherwise, why would God show Adam his potential while still in golemic form rather than in his completed form?

In the literature of the *Hasidei Ashkenaz*, one encounters a number of themes already noted as well as a number of supplementary notions regarding the Golem and its creation. *Hasidut* (piety) was the central concern among the *Hasidei Ashkenaz*. One clear indication of having achieved piety, they believed, was the ability, inherent in truly pious men, to create life. Therefore, among them, the creation of the Golem came to be viewed as a mystical rite of initiation. By creating a Golem, the initiate validated his status as one of the pious and demonstrated his mastery over the esoteric truths reserved for the pious. In this view, the creation of the Golem became an end in itself, a ritual of initiation into the mysteries of creation. For the *Hasidei Ashkenaz* a magical ritual served as an entrée to mystical communion with the divine. By penetrating the mystery of creation, by becoming himself a creator, one came to experience the mystical rapture of oneness with *the* creator. The creative experience thus became a conduit to mystical ecstasy.

Like Raba, the *Hasidei Ashkenaz* required piety and righteousness from the potential creator of a Golem. This prerequisite infused ethics into the endeavor of creating artificial life. The creator of the Golem had to demonstrate moral qualities as well as technical skills. Here one might find an anticipation of contemporary concerns about placing moral controls upon genetic engineering and upon those involved with the creation and the manipulation of life. For Raba and for the *Hasidei Ashkenaz*, something as precious as life itself was too delicate to be surrendered to the moral novice. For them, the use of technical skills assumed the prior mastery of ethical insight and behavior.[45]

The description of the ritual for the creation of a Golem by Eleazar Rokeah—one of the leading personalities of the *Hasidei Ashkenaz*—indicates that separate letter permutations are required for the creation of a female Golem from those required for the creation of a male Golem. The idea that a Golem may be female or male is found in a number of sources. Most noteworthy in this regard is a legend concerning Solomon ibn Gabirol.

Because he was afflicted by a severe skin disease, ibn Gabirol lived in isolation. He therefore created a woman to keep house for him. When what he did became known, ibn Gabirol was reported to the authorities. Because it was assumed that he had created her by magic, possibly for lewd activities, he was ordered to dismantle her. He did so, reducing her to the wood and hinges from which she was created.[46]

That a female Golem was created is not unique in the Jewish literature about the Golem. What is unique is that ibn Gabirol's Golem was not made of earth but of wood and hinges. Here one finds the roots of the portrayal of the Golem as a mechanical being, as an automaton, as a robot.

According to a text that Gershom Scholem dated to the early thirteenth century, the prophet Jeremiah and his son Sira created a Golem. After studying the *Sefer Yetzirah* for three years, they undertook the creation of a Golem through the use of letter permutations and combinations. On its forehead they wrote the phrase, "the Lord God is truth [*emet*]." But once the Golem became vital, it took the knife with which Jeremiah carved these words on its forehead, and it scratched out the letter *alef*. Now the phrase read, "the Lord God is dead." Jeremiah then asked the Golem why it did what it did. The Golem replied with a long parable. The message of the parable is that, once human beings become creators, they are in danger of forgetting *the* creator. Once the creature becomes a creator overwhelmed by his or her own achievements he or she may act as if God is dead and he or she is now God. "What solution is there?," Jeremiah asked of the Golem. The Golem advised Jeremiah to destroy it by reversing the letter combinations used to create it. Jeremiah did so, and the Golem returned to the elements.[47]

The Golem legends about Elijah of Chelm and Judah Loew of Prague remind us of the physical danger with which the Golem's creation may threaten us. This text, however, depicts the spiritual danger held forth by the Golem's creation. Jeremiah's wise and articulate Golem describes in its parable the danger of hubris when the human creature becomes a godlike creator.

While the human being is encouraged to develop his or her creative potentialities, he or she is also warned that there are dangers inherent in the creative endeavor; dangers to the physical, moral, and spiritual well-being of the human creature-creator. One such medieval warning tells that the biblical character Enosh learned that God had created Adam from the earth. Enosh then took some earth, kneaded it into a human form, and blew into its nostrils to animate it as God had done to give Adam life. Satan then slipped into the figure and gave it the appearance of life. Enosh and his generation worshipped the figure and, hence, idolatry began. The figure was worshipped instead of God. The product of human hubris and demonic ruse replaced God as an object of human adoration.[48]

Zevi Ashkenazi was a descendant of Elijah of Chelm. He also was related to Judah Loew of Prague. In a curious responsum, Ashkenazi raised the question of whether a Golem may be included in a quorum for prayer, a *minyan*. The complete text of the responsum follows in translation:

I became doubtful [concerning the resolution of the following question]: Is [the case of] a man, created by [means of magically employing] the *Sefer Yetzirah* identical [to the case] reported in the *Tractate Sanhedrin?* Namely, "Rabbah created a man [and sent him to Rabbi Zera. Rabbi Zera spoke to him but received no answer. Thereupon he said to him—You are a creature of magicians. Return to your dust."] So it has also been asserted concerning my ancestor, the Gaon, our Master and Teacher, Rabbi Elijah, chief rabbi of the Holy Community of Chelm. Who is allowed to be counted as one of ten [a quorum for prayer] in matters which require ten, i.e., [recitation of such prayers as] *Kaddish, Kedushah,* for it is written, "I [God] will be sanctified amidst Israel"? Do we include [such an individual as the artificially created man] or do we say that since it is taught in *Sanhedrin,* "He who raises an orphan in his home, Scripture ascribes it to him as though he had begotten him"? For it is written "Five sons of Michal, the daughter of Saul whom she bore to Adriel" [2 Sam. 21:8]. "Did not Merab bear them? Yes, but Michal raised them [and they are therefore called her sons]."[49] In the present case as well [the artificially created man is considered a child of the one who created him; therefore a regular human being; therefore he can be counted].

Since the workings of the hands of the righteous is involved, he is to be included, for the works of the hands of the righteous are their progeny. [So far, he is included.]

But it seems to me that as a result of meeting Rabbi Zera who said: "You are the work of magicians, return to your dust," he was killed. And do you not think that if there would have been a need to include him amongst a quorum that Rabbi Zera would have "cast him from the world"?

[It thus appears that] there is no prohibition of murder concerning him. [Otherwise Rabbi Zera would be guilty of murder.] For Scripture remarks—and I know there are other possible explanations: "Whosoever sheds a *man's* blood, by man shall his blood be shed [for in the image of God made He man," Gen. 9:5.] [That is to say,] only a *man* formed within a human being; that is, only [killing one who was] a fetus formed within his mother's womb [is counted as murder]. Nevertheless, since he [the artificially created man] has a purpose, he [Rabbi Zera] should not have cast him out of existence. But it is certain that he [the artificially created man] is not counted amongst the ten needed for holy deeds.[50]

This responsum is curious in that it is not a responsum at all. A responsum is a legal opinion offered by a rabbi in response to a question put to him. This "responsum" is a discussion of a problem the author put to himself. That Ashkenazi raised the question of whether a Golem may help form a *minyan* and that he and others treated it as a viable halakhic issue demonstrates the seriousness with which the Golem was taken.[51] Though Ashkenazi addressed the particular question of whether a Golem could be included in a *minyan*, he also implicitly raised a general question that becomes pertinent to a discussion of contemporary implications of the Golem legend.

Every legal system contains a notion of "persons in the law." A "person" is one with rights and duties, with privileges and obligations. In a sense, Ashkenazi raised the implicit question of whether "artificially" created entities can be "persons in the law," having privileges and duties under the law. As noted earlier in this chapter, Anglo-American law does admit the category of "artificial" persons, despite the moral problems such admission precipitates. By excluding the Golem from the *minyan*, Ashkenazi's responsum articulates the position that "artificial" individuals do not qualify as legal persons, that Jewish law is prudent in excluding the concept of "artificial" persons from its vocabulary.

Finally, Ashkenazi examined the question of whether Rabbi Zera was guilty of murder for destroying the "man" artificially created by Rabbah. He concluded that, since the "man" was not human, destroying him could not be murder. Nonetheless, Rabbi Zera's action may not be justifiable. The Golem may have been devoid of a human soul, but it was not without life. Killing it may not have been murder, but it was an act of killing. If the Golem is considered inert matter, however, then it cannot be considered alive. Therefore, destroying it might be classified as a tort, a destruction of property, but it is not a criminal act of murder. Nevertheless, Ashkenazi's approach, which frees Rabbi Zera from being culpable for murder, would deny a Golem any rights, and it would make a Golem vulnerable to many types of abuse.[52] This may not be desirable.

An interesting observation on this issue of "Golem abuse" was made by the sixteenth-century cabalist Isaiah Horowitz.[53] According to the biblical text, Joseph was a tattletale who reported his brothers' wrongdoings to his father, Jacob (Gen. 37:3). Some of the commentaries to this passage relate that one of the items Joseph reported was that his brothers were engaged in illicit sexual activities. Horowitz claims that such was the appearance but not the reality. According to Horowitz (who quotes the text from *Sanhedrin* regarding Rabbah's artificially created man), Joseph's brothers were not engaged sexually with a human woman but with a female Golem.

Horowitz reports that Abraham wrote the *Sefer Yetzirah* and passed it down to his son, Isaac, who then passed it down to his son, Jacob. Jacob, in turn, passed it down to his sons, Joseph's brothers. Jacob's sons used the *Sefer Yetzirah* to create a female Golem with which they enjoyed sexual relations. But, since it was not human, these actions could not be considered sinful. Joseph, therefore, rendered an inaccurate report. Unlike ibn Gabirol, the brothers were not required to destroy a female Golem created for sexual purposes. According to Horowitz, such activity is not prohibited because the female Golem cannot be considered human.

Zevi Hirsch Shapira commented on Horowitz's discussion. According to Shapira, the female Golem lacked the powers of speech and intelligence and, therefore, should be excluded from the category of being human.[54] But, what if the female Golem had intelligence? Would Jacob's sons have been guilty then for abusing her? What if Rabbah's male Golem had intelligence? Would Rabbi Zera have been guilty then of murder?

According to the *Sefer ha-Bahir,* Rabbah's Golem did not have the power of speech because it was not created by the completely righteous. However, if it were so created, it would have had the power of speech and would have been intelligent. Hence, the inability to create an intelligent Golem reflects a flaw in the creator of the Golem that is reflected in the Golem he created.[55]

The daring late Hasidic master Gershon Hanokh Leiner of Radzyn, in his controversial *Sidrei Taharot* went even further than the *Sefer ha-Bahir*. Gershon Hanokh agreed that Rabbi Zera was justified in killing Rabbah's Golem because it lacked intelligence and consequently was regarded "as an animal in human form and it is permissible to kill it." However, he added, if an intelligent Golem had been created, "he would have the legal status of a true man . . . even as regards being counted in a *minyan* . . . and he would be the same as if God had created him." Thus, Gershon Hanokh admitted the possibility of considering an artificially created being, who had all the normal human traits, including intelligence, as a human being. Gershon Hanokh would grant human personhood to such an "artificially" created human being.[56] Destroying such a Golem, it would follow, would be murder. If Joseph's brothers had sexually abused such a female Golem, Gershon Hanokh would hold them liable for rape.

In making his claim that a Golem might be considered human, Gershon Hanokh articulated his disagreement with the position of Judah Loew of Prague and others, who maintained that a Golem could never have all of the human characteristics, and, hence, could never be considered a human being. For Judah Loew, and for others previously noted, a human artifact could never be a human being. Gershon Hanokh's view is willing to eradicate any absolute distinction between humans and Golems. For Gershon Hanokh, a Golem that meets certain prerequisites can be considered human. Judah Loew, on the other hand, would insist upon a firm line of demarcation between humans and Golems. For Loew, a Golem by definition cannot be considered a human.[57]

THE PAST MEETS THE PRESENT

The creation of artificial life was generally sanctioned by Jewish religious tradition although with numerous caveats. A similar approach has been taken by various governmental agencies and by private industry. Ancient and medieval Jewish thinkers as well as contemporary ethicists, scientists, theologians, and philosophers have recognized that human creativity is a double-edged sword. The creative process is replete with dangers and risks. However, the consensus seems to be that, once certain controls and safeguards are applied, the potential benefits of the creation of artificial life outweigh the dangers. Furthermore, the president's commission echoed traditional Jewish teachings when it affirmed that the human being is most human as a creator, that through creativity the human being expresses his or her most Godlike qualities, that human creativity is *imitatio Dei*.

The versions of the Golem legend related to Elijah of Chelm and to Judah Loew of Prague underscore the possibility that what we create to help ensure our physical comfort and security might ultimately threaten that same physical comfort and security, indeed, our very existence. The nuclear age and the age of genetic engineering have witnessed the creation of Golems, created to defend us, which have the potential to destroy all life on our planet. The gigantic proportions of the power of these Golems transcend even the imagination of those who introduced and developed the legend of the Golem in Jewish literature. Nevertheless, while the Golem legend did not prevision the destructive possibilities inherent in today's Golems, it did anticipate a variety of problems related to the Golems that currently populate our world.

While both classical Jewish literature and contemporary popular literature confront the physical risks related to the creation of artificial life, it would seem that Jewish literature puts substantial and much-needed emphasis upon the psychological, spiritual, and moral risks attached to this undertaking. More than contemporary literature, classical Jewish literature stresses these features of the creative act. Jewish literature requires moral,

technical, and intellectual prerequisites of one who would deign to create
life. Furthermore, Jewish literature refuses to sever creature from creator.
Not only is the creator responsible for what the creature does but the creator is responsible for what the creature becomes. The creature reflects not
only the technical skill but also the moral nature of its creator. Conversely,
the nature of the creator is also affected by the nature of the creature and
by the psychological risks that characterize the act of creation itself. The
sources examined contend that creativity can provide psychological fulfillment, but it can also become psychologically self-destructive. Once the
human creature becomes a creator, he or she may think of himself or herself exclusively as a creator. One may develop delusions of grandeur and
omnipotence. Similarly, creativity can be an entrée to spiritual rapture, but
it also can be an invitation to idolatry. In other words, one may begin to
worship and to venerate what one creates, thereby becoming subservient
to one's own creation.

For the traditional religious mentality, the greatest spiritual danger is
heresy (the rejection and negation of God). The risk of "playing God" is
inextricably related to the possibility of rejecting God. Impressed by his or
her own creations, the individual may replace worship of God with self-
worship. Technological achievement, human-made miracles, may lead one
to the illusion of human self-sufficiency, to the conclusion that belief in
God is unnecessary. Technological advances—as Jeremiah was told by his
Golem—threaten to lead us to the conclusion that "God is dead."

As noted, ibn Gabirol's Golem was mechanical, a machine in human
form. The relationship between humans and machines is explored in a
work entitled *God and Golem, Inc.* by Norbert Wiener, the father of cy-
bernetics. Wiener identified the relationship between people and machines
as the central problem of our society. Wiener described the machine as
"the modern counterpart of the Golem" and depicted the problem of the
relationship between people and machines as having been anticipated by
the Golem legend.[58]

At a time when Golems populate our daily lives, at a time when we
must relate to machines on a daily basis, the challenge before us is not how
to build bigger and better Golems but how to prevent ourselves from becoming Golems and from having our lives controlled or even harmed by
the Golems we have created.

What the Golem legend can teach us is that the Golem, the machine,
while not human, is a reflection of the best and the worst of that which
makes us human. The potential harm and terror with which contemporary
Golems can afflict us is but the reflection of our own penchant for self-
harm and self-destruction. The potential of the Golem to wreak havoc and
destruction and the consequent need for the Golem's latent destructiveness
to be recognized and controlled offers us a serious warning: we must tem-

per our own destructiveness and that of the many powerful Golems we have created.

Though Judah Loew did not actually preoccupy himself with the creation of Golems, he did comment on the Talmudic reference to Rabbah's Golem. While Loew described mystical adhesion to God as a necessary prerequisite for the creation of a Golem, he also observed that the creation of a Golem with all human characteristics, for example, speech, is beyond the realm of possibility. Loew wrote, "For he [Rabbah] was a human being himself; and how would it then be possible for him to create a complete person like himself? Just as it is impossible to conceive that God, who is supreme over everything, would create one like Himself."[59] Furthermore, according to Loew, meditation on the divine names contained in the *Sefer Yetzirah* is like any other kind of prayer, "because [in prayer] one calls [upon God]. . . . Therefore, the *Sefer Yetzirah*, in which is recorded the divine names by which God created the world. . . . is not outside of nature . . . How can one claim that pronunciation of the names by which the world came into being is outside the natural order?"[60]

Loew's view that the use of various unusual techniques to bring about life is not outside the natural order was reaffirmed by the president's commission, which asserted that, in areas such as gene splicing, scientists were not creating new processes but had simply learned to control natural processes.[61] One may extend this argument to endorse technologies used in the treatment of infertile individuals, such as artificial insemination and in vitro fertilization.[62]

The more recent procedure of artificial embryonization is somewhat more complex. In this procedure, the egg of a donor is fertilized in vitro and is implanted into a second female who then births a child. If the sperm donor is the child's father and is married to the birthing mother, then who is the child's legal mother? Is it the genetic mother (the egg donor) or is it the birthing mother? An interesting responsum on this subject was published in Hungary in 1908. Despite the predilection of Jewish law to consider the genetic parents of a child as the child's actual parents, this responsum finds that in the case of a possible transplant of sexual organs from a fertile woman to a barren woman, a child subsequently born would be the child of the birthing mother and not of the organ donor. One may be justified in using this responsum to defend the view that, in a case of artificial embryonization, the birthing mother rather than the egg donor would be considered the child's mother.[63]

In a New York State case, a woman sued and collected damages when her egg, fertilized in vitro, was destroyed in the laboratory.[64] Assuming that life begins at conception, some theologians oppose processes such as in vitro fertilization because, in their view, ensouled fetuses are likely to be "killed."

Ashkenazi can provide a basis for an alternative position. Because his responsum identifies "artificial" conception but not "artificial" birth as the essential characteristic of a Golem, one may assume that he would consider a fetus *conceived* by artificial means to be a Golem, and therefore not human; while he would consider an artificially conceived child *delivered* vaginally or by cesarean section to be a normal human being. From such a perspective, a child conceived in vitro and delivered at birth would be considered a normal human person, but during the process of conception and gestation it would not necessarily fall under that category. Therefore, destroying such a fetus (as in the cases just mentioned above) would not be considered murder. Hence, a primary objection to the use of methods that might prove the only means by which barren couples could have children would be overcome.

Ashkenazi's denial of the status of human personhood to the Golem discussed in his responsum may be further interpreted as expressing the resistance of Jewish law to incorporate blatantly artificial entities into the category of legal "persons." Unlike Anglo-American law, Jewish law refuses to recognize the category of "artificial persons," such as corporations, treating such entities rather as partnerships, where each partner individually and collectively bears personal responsibility for the actions of the corporation. The wisdom of this approach is that it will not allow an individual to escape moral culpability behind a "corporate shield" for actions undertaken by a corporation. In Jewish law, moral and legal responsibility cannot be assigned to an agent, neither can it be diffused into a corporate personality. Personal individual responsibility in Jewish law remains that of individual natural persons.

Rabbah's Golem was considered flawed because Rabbah was himself flawed. The flaws of the creator reflect upon the creature. But what if Rabbah were not flawed, and what if his Golem were not flawed but possessed all the characteristics of a human being?

Judah Loew held that a Golem must be flawed by definition; an imperfect creator necessarily creates an imperfect creature. However, Gershon Hanokh disagreed, claiming that a Golem having all the traits of a human being could be created. In such a situation, this individual would have all the rights, duties, and status of any other human creature. Harming such an individual would be a crime. In Gershon Hanokh's view, had Rabbah's Golem possessed all human traits, Rabbi Zera would have been guilty of murder. Ashkenazi can only exonerate Rabbi Zera from murder because Rabbah's Golem did not possess the essential trait of human intelligence.

This collision of views between Judah Loew and Gershon Hanokh finds contemporary expression in the vast literature on the question of whether machines that appear to have human traits can be considered human in any sense. If, for example, one considers intelligence to be the cardinal characteristic in determining whether one is human, could an intelligent machine then be considered human? Gershon Hanokh might answer in the affirmative, while Judah Loew would answer in the negative. Like Judah Loew, some contemporary philosophers and scientists maintain that a machine, even an intelligent machine, could not be considered human because it always would lack some essential human trait. Some thinkers of this school would further maintain that human intelligence, like human nature, is sui generis and that, just as a machine must always be distinguished from a human being, so must mechanical intelligence or artificial intelligence be distinguished from human intelligence. Other thinkers of this school might argue that, while intelligence is an essential human trait, the possession of intelligence by a nonhuman being, for example, an extraterrestrial or a dolphin, would not ipso facto qualify such a being for human status. Nor would the absence of a normal degree of human intelligence (an imbecile) disqualify a human person from the status of being human.

Philosophers and theologians who refuse to grant human status or human intelligence or both to Golems and machines rest their argument upon a fundamental presupposition—the unique nature of the human being. Where these thinkers may disagree is on the question, what is it that makes human existence sui generis, what quality is it that makes human beings human? Some maintain that the very fact that each human being is different from every other human being is itself adequate evidence for affirming the unique nature not only of the human person but of each and every human person.[65] Machines and Golems can be duplicated; human beings cannot. Others hold that ensoulment is what makes the human being unique. The Golem, by definition, is a soulless, though not necessarily a lifeless, being. Thus, to speak of a "human Golem" in this view would be a contradiction in terms, a linguistically meaningless statement. Still others hold that such qualities as the ability to laugh, to create, to be embarrassed, to express emotion, to love, to carry on a telephone conversation, to be self-conscious, to act freely and spontaneously, to have hopes and dreams, to be inconsistent and unpredictable, are peculiarly human and cannot be found in machines. Furthermore, even if such paradigmatically "human" characteristics were apparently present in machines, such machines still would not qualify for human personhood because those traits would merely be a reflection of the characteristics of the designer of the machine. Following Judah Loew's thinking, just as the human person, though created in God's image, is not God, so a Golem or a machine into which certain human characteristics have been programmed would not be considered a human being.[66]

Finally, the legal status of Golems remains a problem. But the possibility of human beings devolving back to the golemic state is an urgent contemporary challenge. As a midrash quoted above reminds us, human beings emerged from the golemic state. The danger is that, as Golems become increasingly human, humans are threatened with becoming increasingly golemic. The Golem is created in our image. What must be resisted is allowing the converse to come to pass. Or, in the words of Israel of Rhyzen, "Judah Loew of Prague created a *Golem*, and this was a great wonder. But how much more wonderful it is to transform a man of flesh and blood into a *mentsh* [a morally developed human person]."

❦ 12 ❦

Reflections

IN VARIOUS CLASSICAL JEWISH TEXTS, Jewish tradition is compared to food, and its study to the consumption of food. Deprived of food, a person would perish. As a midrash observes, "Let a person think it over and realize that words of the Torah are like water and bread. What is the point of comparing Torah with bread and water? To teach you that just as it is impossible for a person to be without bread and water for even one day, so it is impossible for a person to be without words of Torah for even one hour."[1] Like food, learning not only sustains an individual but becomes incorporated as part of the individual. In the *Tanya*, the nineteenth-century Hasidic master Shneur Zalman of Liadi wrote,

> Seeing that through the knowledge of the Torah man's soul and mind encompass the Torah and are in turn encompassed by it, the Torah is called the food and sustenance of the soul. For just as material food sustains the body and enters it and is transformed in the body into flesh and blood, by virtue of which a man lives and endures, so it is with regard to knowledge of the Torah and its comprehension by he who studies with concentration until the Torah is grasped by the mind and becomes united with it.[2]

While the aim of early Western literature was entertainment, the perennial goal of Jewish literature has been the transmission of the constitutive values of the Jewish people. Since the uniting factor of the Jewish people is not blood or geography but a value system, the primary object of Jewish literature and its study has been to preserve the Jewish people and to ensure its continuity and that of its value system. While much of early classical Western literature represents a world viewed in the third person, classical Jewish literature projects a world to be viewed in the first person, as a participant, as a coauthor. The mutual relationship, the nexus, between the Jewish people and classical Jewish literature has been central to

the survival and continuous revival of Judaism, the Jewish people, and
their literature. The goal of Jewish learning is to transform the student's
perspective from the third person to the first person, to appropriate, to
consume, and to assimilate the text.[3] This goal is implicitly expressed in the
Talmudic adage, "At the beginning [the Torah] is called by the name of the
Lord, but at the end it will be called by his [the student's] name."[4] Or, as
the Jewish mystics would put it, "to be a thing is to know a thing, and to
know a thing is to be a thing."[5]

Objective, scientific, third-person scholarship is alien to Jewish thinking. By its very nature voyeuristic, it is like reading a menu with no intention of partaking of the food listed thereon. This approach results not in the
assimilation of Jewish learning into the scholar's own self, but the assimilation of the object of study, in this case—Judaism—into alien categories of
scholarship and thought. In 1907, Solomon Schechter observed, "there is a
difference between assimilating and being assimilated." Schechter analogized *assimilating* to a person's assimilation of a steak, the individual's becoming enriched and strengthened. He further analogized *being assimilated* to an individual who believes he or she can become a cow, to an
individual trying to become something he or she is not.[6]

Like all analogies, that of Jewish learning and scholarship to the consumption of food cannot be extended ad infinitum. For instance, while
there is a limit on the consumption of food, and while Jewish tradition itself
discourages gluttony, it places no limit on the consumption of learning.
Furthermore, while the menu offered is broad in scope and variety, it is
not without limit.

The wide range of ideas present in the enormous mass of texts that
comprise classical Jewish literature may be compared to a smorgasbord.
The assortment of dishes served is vast, though limited. As each individual
partaking of the repast takes an empty plate and proceeds along the table,
he or she creates a combination of foods particular to his or her taste and
appetite. Choices can only be made from those dishes that are on the table.
Similarly, the Jewish scholar constructs his or her collage of Judaism or of a
particular issue or problem of Jewish theology, ethics, or law from the
menu at hand. The menu derives from the smorgasbord of ideas and statements contained in classical Jewish literature.

Though "just as each blow of a hammer strikes forth many sparks, so a
single verse [of the Torah] unfolds into many meanings," however multi-
valent these interpretations are, they are not without limit.[7] The rabbinic
view that there are "seventy faces" of the Torah indicates that the interpretation and the exposition of Judaism embraces a wide but finite range.
The tradition itself defines the limits. The scholar who goes beyond them
forfeits his or her place within the ongoing development and growth of the

Jewish scholarly tradition. In this regard, the *Ethics of the Fathers* condemns even one who is "learned in the Torah and virtuous" when he or she
"reveals faces of the Torah that contradict tradition [halakhah]."[8] *Peshat* (the
literal or contextual meaning of a text) that cannot be legitimately assimilated into the corpus of tradition should not be incorporated into the corpus
of *Jewish* scholarship.[9]

The approach to Jewish scholarship discussed in this chapter and in
chapter 1 is the view presumed by the other chapters that comprise this
book. No attempt has been made at scientific scholarship. Rather, an effort
has been made at artistic scholarship. This volume has not been a quest for
the *peshat,* but for the applied meaning of classical Jewish texts to moral,
theological, and legal problems that confront and concern us today. In the
words of a midrash, "Let the Torah never be for you an antiquated decree
. . . but as a decree issued this very day."[10]

As the artist gathers his or her materials to create an objet d'art, so
does the scholar collect his or her texts to blend them into a portrait of the
subject at hand. Like the culinary artist, the scholar must be concerned
with what has been chosen to be placed on the serving platter and with the
manner of its presentation. The manner of presentation may be impres-
sionistic, but it must be clear. A primary goal of scholarship is transmission,
which requires clarity as well as authenticity.

Jewish scholarship must be faithful to the past while being pertinent
to the present. As a vital link between the past and the future, it must be
well forged to ensure it attains transmission. On occasion, the claims of
tradition will be demonstrated to be at odds with the agenda and with the
value system of the contemporary Jewish community. When such is the
case, Jewish scholarship discloses its "subversive" role, that is, its task to
make Jewish existence correlative with Jewish tradition, to put Jewish destiny in sync with Jewish history. In the final analysis, Jewish scholarship is
a séance. It provides a vehicle for the past to commune with the present.
In this regard, a Talmudic adage states that, when one quotes a tradition in
the name of a sage, one should at the same time be able to sense his
presence.[11] Jewish scholarship aims at making our ancestors our contempo-
raries so that they may share their problems with us and so that we may
share our problems with them.

In each of the preceding chapters, a particular idea or problem in
Jewish theology, law, or ethics has been presented. The approach has been
to fill a plate with that particular theme from the smorgasbord of classical
Jewish literature. To be sure, others seeking to fill such a plate might have
chosen to do so in a different manner. However, the choices of texts available to each participant in the feast of Jewish scholarship are identical in
the final analysis. Some are content to draw only from large, easily located

plates. Others search every nook and cranny of the table for obscure deli-
cacies. About those who seek sustenance at the smorgasbord of Jewish
learning, one may again turn to the Talmud.

> If someone tells you,
> "I have labored but not found,"
> do not believe him.
> If he says, "I have not
> labored, but I have found,"
> do not believe him.
> But, if he says, "I
> have labored and I have found,"
> then believe him.[12]

NOTES
BIBLIOGRAPHY
INDEX

NOTES

THE EXTENSIVE NOTES have been included to accomplish four goals. First, they extend the preceding discussion, either for reasons of further clarification or for reasons of further elucidation. Such material is placed in the notes, rather than in the text, to avoid interrupting the flow of the discussion. Second, the notes offer discussion of points that would only be of interest to specialists in various aspects of Jewish studies rather than being of interest to the general reader. Third, the notes offer references to sources quoted and referred to in the text. For the reader who wishes to consult references that are in Hebrew but who does not read Hebrew, available English translations of sources quoted are provided both in the notes and in the bibliography. Where an English translation of a source quoted or referred to is not given, it means either that an English translation is not available or that the translation offered is the author's. Fourth, sources are provided that point to further reading on the issues discussed.

A number of mechanical points require mention. Citations of the (Babylonian) Talmud, the Palestinian Talmud, the Mishnah and *Midrash Rabbah*, are given in the standard manner. The name of the tractate from the (Babylonian) Talmud and the folio page cited is noted (e.g., *Berakhot* 5a). The "Soncino" translation of the (Babylonian) Talmud is used when appropriate. Citations of the Palestinian Talmud are noted by tractate and section within the tractate and are preceded by the letter *P* (e.g., *P. Yoma* 3:2) and, where appropriate, by the folio page (e.g., *P. Yoma* 3a). Citations from the Mishnah are noted by tractate, chapter, and paragraph and are preceded by the letter *M* (e.g., *M. Yoma* 3:2). Citations from *Midrash Rabbah* are noted by book, chapter, and paragraph (e.g., *Midrash Exodus Rabbah* 6:2). The "Soncino" translation of *Midrash Rabbah* is used when appropriate.

Citations of other works in classical Jewish literature, especially legal works, are cited by the author, the name of the work, the book within the work, the section within the book (where appropriate), followed by the chapter and paragraph. Where an English translation is available, it too is cited (e.g., Moses Maimonides, *Mishneh Torah—Sefer ha-Mada*, "Hilkhot Teshuvah," 1:1. Eng. trans., p. 75). This method of utilizing standard citations of Hebrew classical sources provides the Hebrew reader with access to the quoted source in any edition of the Hebrew work cited, even if it differs from the edition used in this work. This method also makes the source available to the non-Hebrew reader.

Because sections of classical Hebrew texts are cited in this standard manner, page references are noted by *p*. and *pp*. to avoid confusion with citations of sections and paragraphs of works noted. Only in citations of journal articles, where such confusion is not likely to occur, are page references given without being preceded by *p*. and *pp*.

Full references for sources cited are given only the first time they appear in the notes. Subsequently, such sources are cited in abbreviated form, except where such abbreviated form might engender confusion (e.g., with other cited sources by the same author).

1. A PROGRAM FOR JEWISH SCHOLARSHIP

1. Abraham Joshua Heschel, *The Circle of the Ba'al Shem Tov*, ed. Samuel H. Dresner (Chicago: Univ. of Chicago Press, 1985), p. xxiv.

2. *Shabbat* 112b.

3. See, e.g., Louis Jacobs, *Theology in the Responsa* (London: Routledge and Kegan Paul, 1975), p. 131.

4. See, e.g., id., *A Jewish Theology* (New York: Behrman House, 1973), p. 202. This notion of "progressive revelation" (the most recent is the most true) was central to the supersessionist argument of Christianity with regard to Judaism. It was later used by Islam with regard to Christianity and Judaism. Subsequently, it was used by Bahaism to apply to Judaism, Christianity, and Islam. Apparently for this reason, the doctrine of "progressive revelation" was not a feature of classical Jewish theology. Early Reform Judaism, clearly influenced by Protestant Christianity, applied this concept in its attempt to justify theologically its reform of traditional Judaism.

5. See, e.g., id., *A Tree of Life* (New York: Oxford Univ. Press, 1984), pp. 255–56. In the nineteenth century, this view was expressed by Moses Schreiber as part of his attack on Reform Judaism.

6. On Bernard of Chartres, see, e.g., Fredrick Copelston, *A History of Philosophy: Medieval Philosophy, Part I* (New York: Image Books, 1962), pp. 190–203.

7. On the use in Jewish literature of the expression "a dwarf on the shoulders of a giant," see, e.g., Dov Zlotnick, "*Al Makor ha-Mashal ha-Nanas ve-ha-Anak ve-Gilgulav*," *Sinai* 77 (1975): 184–89; Hillel Levine, "Dwarfs on the Shoulders of Giants: A Case Study in the Impact of Modernization on the Social Epistemology of Judaism," *Jewish Social Studies* 40, no. 1 (Winter 1978): 63–72; Israel Ta-Shema, "*Halakhah ke-Batrei*," *Shenaton ha-Mishpat ha-Ivri* 6/7 (1979/1980): 418–22. The source for the statement in Isaiah di Trani is his collected responsa, *Teshuvot ha-Rid*, ed. Abraham Wertheimer (Jerusalem: Machon ha-Talmud ha-Yisraeli ha-Shalem, 1967), no. 62, p. 302.

8. Quoted and translated in Dov Zlotnick, "The Commentary of Rabbi Abraham Azulai to the Mishnah," *American Academy of Jewish Research Proceedings* 40 (1973): 163–64.

9. José Ortega y Gasset, *The Revolt of the Masses* (New York: Norton, 1957), pp. 110–12.

10. See, e.g., Lionel Kochan, *The Jew and His History* (Chico, Calif.: Scholars Press, 1985), p. 66.

11. Gershom Scholem, "The Science of Judaism—Then and Now," chapter in *The Messianic Idea in Judaism* (New York: Schocken, 1971), pp. 306–7. See also id., "*Mi-Tokh*

Hirhurim al Hokhmat Yisrael," in *Perakim ba-Yahadut,* ed. Ezra Spicehandler and Jakob Petuchowski (Jerusalem: Newman Publishing House, n.d.), pp. 312–27.

12. *Pesahim* 6b. For a discussion of the meaning of this term in rabbinic theology, see Abraham Joshua Heschel, *Torah min ha-Shamayim b'Ispaklariah shel ha-Dorot, vol. 1* (London: Soncino, 1962), pp. 199–202. For a discussion of this term and of its relevance to contemporary Jewish scholarship, see José Faur, *Golden Doves with Silver Dots* (Bloomington: Indiana Univ. Press, 1986), pp. xi–xv.

13. Quoted in Kochan, p. 81.

14. Ibid., p. 136, n. 41.

15. See, e.g., Yosef Hayim Yerushalmi, *Zakhor: Jewish History and Jewish Memory* (Philadelphia: Jewish Publication Society, 1982), p. 93.

16. Ibid., pp. 84–85; Max Wiener, "The Ideology of the Founders of Jewish Scientific Research," *YIVO Annual* 5 (1950): 195; Michael Meyer, *The Origins of the Modern Jew* (Detroit: Wayne State Press, 1967), p. 175; Ismar Schorsch, *Jewish Reactions to German Anti-Semitism* (New York: Columbia Univ. Press, 1972), p. 43.

17. See, e.g., Ismar Schorsch, *Thoughts from 3080* (New York: Jewish Theological Seminary, 1988), p. 28.

18. *Midrash Pesikta Rabbati,* ed. Meir Friedmann (Vienna: Herausgebers, 1880), chap. 21, p. 100b.

19. *Zohar* (Vilna: Romm, 1882), vol. 3, p. 152a.

20. See Faur, p. xv.

21. *Seder Eliyahu Rabbah ve-Seder Eliyahu Zuta,* ed. Meir Friedmann (Vienna: Ahiyasaf, 1904), "Zuta," chap. 2, p. 172.

22. See *Yebamot* 109b.

23. See Faur, p. xvi.

24. Immanuel Wolf, "On the Concept of a Science of Judaism," trans. Lionel Kochan, *Leo Baeck Institute Yearbook* 2 (1957): 201.

25. *Tzava'at Rivash* (Cracow, n.p., 1896), p. 86. See the English translation of this text in Harold I. Stern, "The Testament of the Baal Shem Tov" (Ph.D. diss., Northwestern Univ., 1976), pp. 97–98.

26. Judah Loew, *Netivot Olom,* 2 vols. (New York: Judaica Press, 1969), "Netiv ha-Torah," chap. 8, p. 34. See also, Byron L. Sherwin, *Mystical Theology and Social Dissent: The Life and Works of Judah Loew of Prague* (New York: Oxford Univ. Press, 1982), p. 140; Moshe Idel, *Kabbalah: New Perspectives* (New Haven: Yale Univ. Press, 1988), pp. 243–47.

27. Moses Hayyim Ephraim of Sudylkow, *Degel Mahaneh Ephraim* (Jerusalem: Hadar, 1963), "Aharei," p. 175.

28. Mordecai of Chernobyl, *Lekutei Torah* (New York: Noble Printing Co., 1954), "Le-Rosh ha-Shanah," p. 22b.

29. See Abraham Joshua Heschel, *God in Search of Man* (New York: Harper and Row, 1966), pp. 8–10.

30. See Alan Lazaroff, "Judaism As an Art," *Judaism* 30, no. 3 (Summer 1981): 355–63.

31. See, e.g., Harold Bloom, *Kabbalah and Criticism* (New York: Seabury, 1975); Faur, p. xxvii.

32. See *Soferim,* chap. 7. Eng. trans. Israel W. Slotki, in *The Minor Tractates of the Talmud,* ed. A. Cohen, 2 vols. (London: Soncino, 1965), vol. 1, pp. 242–46.

33. See Faur, pp. 122–23.

34. See the discussion and sources cited in Faur, pp. 11, 135–36.

35. *Sefer ha-Bahir*, ed. Reuven Margaliot (Jerusalem: Mosad ha-Rav Kook, 1951), no. 115, p. 51. See also Judah ha-Levi, *The Kuzari*, trans. Harry Slonimsky (New York: Schocken, 1964), 4:3, p. 202; *Zohar*, vol. 1, p. 15b.

36. David ibn Zimra, *Teshuvot ha-Radbaz, vol. 3* (Furth, 1781), no. 643, p. 43b. See also Menahem Zioni, *Commentary to the Torah* [Hebrew] (Lwow: Nissim Zis, 1882), p. 2b.

37. Moses Maimonides, *Moreh Nevukhim* (Jerusalem: n.p., 1960), Book 2, chap. 33, p. 71a.

38. Ibn Zimra, p. 43b. See also Idel, p. 214.

39. See Gershom Scholem, "The Meaning of the Torah in Jewish Mysticism," chapter in *On the Kabbalah and Its Symbolism*, trans. Ralph Manheim (New York: Schocken, 1965), pp. 81–82.

40. Judah Loew, *Tiferet Yisrael* (New York: Judaica Press, 1969), chap. 67, p. 205. Note Sherwin, p. 42. On the theological premises of this halakhic problem, see Abraham Joshua Heschel, *Torah min ha-Shamayim b'Ispaklariah shel ha-Dorot, vol. 2* (London: Soncino, 1965), pp. 364–67.

41. *Pesahim* 87b. There was a rabbinic tradition that the entire Torah was written on the tablets; see, e.g., Heschel, ibid., pp. 348–50.

42. See, e.g., *Baba Metzia* 59a–b.

43. See Faur, p. 14.

44. *Zohar*, vol. 2, p. 94b. See Idel, p. 228.

45. Idel, pp. 239, 388, n. 184.

46. *Ethics of the Fathers* 3:19.

47. Samuel of Uceda, *Midrash Shmuel* (Jerusalem: Brody-Katz, n.d.), pp. 61a–b.

48. Ibid., p. 60b.

49. Judah Loew, *Netivot Olom*, vol. 1, p. 32. These blessings derive from *Berakhot* 11a.

50. See *P. Berakhot* 1:2, *Midrash Leviticus Rabbah* 35:7, and Jonah Gerondi, *Sha'arey Teshuvah* (Jerusalem: Eshkol, 1978), 2:13, p. 42.

51. *Midrash Exodus Rabbah* 30:13.

52. *Berakhot* 55a.

53. On this expression, see Israel Davidson, *Otzar ha-Mashalim ve-ha-Pitgamim* (Jerusalem: Mosad ha-Rav Kook, 1969), no. 2851, p. 171, n. 39.

2. PHILOSOPHIES OF LAW

1. See Abraham Joshua Heschel, "God, Torah, and Israel," in *Theology and Church in Times of Change*, ed. E. L. Long and R. Handy (Philadelphia: Westminster, 1970), pp. 71–90. See also Idel, p. 390, n. 221. On the idea of covenant, see Delbert Hillers, *The Covenant: The History of a Biblical Idea* (Baltimore: Johns Hopkins Univ. Press, 1969).

2. See *Midrash Exodus Rabbah* 30:5, 33:7; *Midrash Song of Songs Rabbah* 8:11; *Pesikta de-Rav Kahana*, ed. Bernard Mandelbaum, 2 vols. (New York: Jewish Theological Seminary, 1962), 12:11, 19, vol. 1, pp. 210–11, 217. Eng. trans. William G. Braude and Israel J. Kapstein (Philadelphia: Jewish Publication Society, 1975), pp. 235, 241.

A second tradition describes God as the bridegroom who is married to Israel, His bride, at Mt. Sinai. See, e.g., *Midrash Numbers Rabbah* 12:8. See also *Ta'anit* 26b; *Midrash Song of Songs Rabbah* 3:11; *Midrash Exodus Rabbah* 33:7 and 52:51; *Midrash Tanhuma*, ed.

Solomon Buber (Vilna, 1885), *"Pekuday"* 8, p. 67a, and *"Ba-Midbar"* 5, p. 3a; *Pesikta de-Rav Kahana* 1:3, 22:5, vol. 1, pp. 7, 329. For scriptural roots of the portrayal of Israel as God's bride, see, e.g., Isa. 62:5, Jer. 2:1–3, Hos. 2:16–18, Ezek. 16, 23.

Some modern biblical scholars understand certain biblical festivals as having been observed originally as celebrations of a sacred marriage between God and Israel. See, e.g., Helmer Ringgren, *Israelite Religion* (Philadelphia: Fortress, 1966), pp. 190, 198–99. Note p. 197 on the Song of Songs as being rooted in the idea of a sacred marriage. The motif of the "sacred marriage" was utilized by the medieval Jewish mystics. On "sacred marriage" rituals practiced by the medieval Jewish mystics, see Scholem, *On the Kabbalah*, pp. 138–46.

A third tradition analogizes Mt. Sinai to a wedding between God and the Torah. See, e.g., *Zohar*, vol. 1, p. 8a. The mystic who studies the Torah the entire night of the first day of the Pentecost festival (*Shavuot*) is compared to the "best man" at the wedding. Note that in Scripture, Pentecost is considered only as a harvest festival and is not related to the theophany at Mt. Sinai; see, e.g., Exod. 23:16, 34:22, Num. 28:26. It seems that after the destruction of the Second Temple in the first century it became identified as the anniversary of the revelation at Mt. Sinai. On the Pharisaic identification of Pentecost with the time of the giving of the Torah, see, e.g., Louis Finkelstein, *The Pharisees* (Philadelphia: Jewish Publication Society, 1968), pp. 115–18. In Maimonides's succinct words, "The Pentecost is the day of the giving of the Torah." See Moses Maimonides, *The Guide of the Perplexed*, trans. Shlomo Pines (Chicago: Univ. of Chicago Press, 1963), Book 3, chap. 43, p. 571.

3. See, e.g., *Pirke de-Rabbi Eliezer* (New York: Ohm, 1946), chap. 41, p. 97b. Eng. trans. Gerald Friedlander (London: n.p., 1916), p. 32b, which compares God to the father of the Torah, the Torah to a bride, and Israel to the bridegroom, who is wed to his bride at Mt. Sinai.

4. *Midrash Exodus Rabbah* 33:1.

5. See, e.g., *Midrash Exodus Rabbah* 33:6.

6. See, e.g., *Midrash on Psalms*, ed. Solomon Buber (Vilna, 1891), 119:40, p. 249b. Eng. trans. William G. Braude (New Haven: Yale Univ. Press, 1959), 119:41, vol. 2, p. 273.

7. Levi Yitzhak of Berdichev, *Kedushat Levi* (Jerusalem: Mosad l'Hotza'at Sifrei Musar va- Hasidut, 1958), p. 33; quoted in Samuel H. Dresner, *Levi Yitzhak of Berditchev* (New York: Hartmore House, 1974), p. 111. Also see Eugene Kullman, *"Tikvah* and *Mitzvah,"* *Conservative Judaism* 10 (Summer 1956): 34–36.

8. See, e.g., the views of Judah Loew of Prague on the relationship of Torah to mitzvoth. Note the discussion and sources in Sherwin, *Mystical Theology*, pp. 75–78.

9. See Franz Rosenzweig, *On Jewish Learning* (New York: Schocken, 1955), p. 122, "Only in the commandment can the voice of him who commands be heard."

10. One may find some similarity between the approach taken in the following two sections of this chapter in identifying two views on the nature of Jewish law and that taken by Chaim Tchernowitz in *Toledot ha-Poskim*, vols. 2 and 3 (New York: n.p., 1947). Tchernowitz identified two trends: "the expansive trend" and "the restrictive trend." The former is roughly equivalent to the "dialogic view," which opposed codification, and the latter is roughly equivalent to the "monolithic view," which favored codification. While Tchernowitz's monumental work has been consulted in the preparation of the current discussion, it has not influenced the development of the ideas within this chapter. The present attempt is to relate theological views to philosophies of Jewish law, a point that is not central for Tchernowitz. His work has been consulted primarily for its historical data rather than for its ideological perspective.

11. *Shabbat* 88a.

12. The issue of the eternality of the covenant, of the enduring marriage between God and Israel, is a theological nonnegotiable in Jewish theology. This issue was a point of dispute between Jews and Christians in medieval theological polemics, Jewish theologians claiming

that the marriage is eternal, Christian theologians claiming that God had divorced Israel for faithlessness and had married another wife, the church, i.e., the "new" Israel. In an apparent response to this Christian theological challenge, Jewish theologians sought a scriptural precedent for a marriage that could not be ended with divorce. They found such an example in Deut. 21:10–14, with regard to a woman who had been raped and then married. Judah Loew of Prague and his brother, Hayyim ben Betsalel of Friedberg, utilized this motif both as a justification of the eternality of God's covenant with Israel and as an example of the coercion of Israel into the covenantal relation. See Byron L. Sherwin, "In the Shadows of Greatness: Rabbi Hayyim ben Betsalel of Friedberg," *Jewish Social Studies* 37, no. 1 (1975): 56–57, and id., *Mystical Theology*, p. 86, and sources noted there.

13. This citation is from the works of Uziel Meisels, a disciple of the Hasidic master Dov Baer, the Maggid of Mesritch. The translation is that of Louis Jacobs in his *Hasidic Prayer* (New York: Schocken, 1972), p. 122. On this theme in rabbinic and medieval literature, see Heschel, *Torah min ha-Shamayim, vol.* 2, pp. 215–17, 264–67, 335–37, 344–48.

14. *Midrash on Psalms* 90:4, p. 194.

15. The Targum translates *"navi"* (prophet) as *"meturgemanakh"* (interpreter). See *Targum Onkelos* and Rashi to Exod. 7:1, in standard editions of Hebrew Scripture with commentaries.

16. See Abraham Joshua Heschel, *The Prophets* (Philadelphia: Jewish Publication Society, 1962), pp. 335–37. Note Harry Wolfson, *Philo*, 2 vols. (Cambridge, Mass.: Harvard Univ. Press, 1947), vol. 2, pp. 22–43.

17. See *Baba Batra* 15a; *Midrash Sifre on Deuteronomy*, ed. Louis Finkelstein (Berlin: Judischer Kulterband in Deutschland, 1939), para. 357, p. 427. Eng. trans. Reuven Hammer (New Haven: Yale Univ. Press, 1986), p. 380.

18. See, e.g., discussion and sources in Louis Jacobs, *Principles of the Jewish Faith* (New York: Basic Books, 1964), pp. 302–7.

19. Maimonides, *Guide*, "Introduction to Book Three," pp. 415–16; id., *Mishneh Torah*, ed. Saul Lieberman (Jerusalem: Mosad ha-Rav Kook, 1964), "Introduction," pp. 13–14.

20. Joseph Karo, *Beit Yosef*, "Introduction," in Jacob ben Asher, *Arba'ah Turim— Orah Hayyim* (New York: Grossman, n.d.), unpaginated introduction.

21. See the extensive discussion by Isadore Twersky, "The *Shulhan Arukh:* Enduring Code of Jewish Law," *Judaism* 16 (1967): 141–59.

22. On this principle in Jewish law, see discussion and sources in Menahem Elon, *Ha-Mishpat ha-Ivri*, 3 vols. (Jerusalem: Magnes Press, 1973), vol. 1, pp. 232–36, and *Encyclopedia Talmudit* (Jerusalem: Talmudic Encyclopedia Publishing, 1984), vol. 9, pp. 141–45.

On Moses Isserles's use of this principle, see Elon, p. 235; Twersky, "The *Shulhan Arukh*," p. 147, and Asher Siev, *Rabbi Moses Isserles* [Hebrew] (New York: Yeshiva Univ. Press, 1972), pp. 158–59.

23. See Jacobs, *Tree of Life*, p. 77; Alan J. Yuter, "*Mehizah, Midrash* and Modernity," *Judaism* 28 (1979): 147–59. Note Ze'ev Falk, *Law and Religion* (Jerusalem: Mesharim Publishers, 1981), pp. 142–43, 148.

24. *Sabbath* 112b.

25. See, e.g., Moses Schreiber, *Sefer Hatam Sofer* (Vienna, 1892–95), *Orah Hayyim*, no. 28; *Yoreh Deah*, no. 19. Note Jacobs, *Tree of Life*, pp. 255–56.

26. See the discussion of Hirsch in Jacobs, *Principles*, pp. 291–315; id., *Jewish Theology*, pp. 215–18. On Hirsch's thought, see Noah Rosenbloom, *Tradition in an Age of Reform: The Religious Philosophy of Samson Raphael Hirsch* (Philadelphia: Jewish Publication Society,

1976); Isaac Heinemann, *Ta'amei ha-Mitzvot be-Sifrut Yisrael*, 2 vols. (Jerusalem: n.p., 1956), vol. 2, pp. 91–161.

27. Joseph B. Soloveitchik, *"Ish ha-Halakhah," Talpiot* 1 (1944): 651–734. See also his "The Lonely Man of Faith," *Tradition* 7 (Summer 1965): 5–67; id., *The Halakhic Mind* (New York: Macmillan, 1986). For a presentation and an analysis of Soloveitchik's views, see, e.g., Lawrence Kaplan, "The Religious Philosophy of Rabbi Joseph Soloveitchik," *Tradition* 14 (Fall 1973): 43–65. For a brutal critique of Soloveitchik's view, see Falk, *Law*, pp. 156–64, and Jacob B. Agus, *Guideposts in Modern Judaism* (New York: Bloch Publishing Co., 1954), pp. 37–44. It is noteworthy that the attempts of Soloveitchik's grandfather, Hayyim Soloveitchik of Brisk, to impose "method" on halakhah and the correlative attempt to analogize halakhic method with scientific method were condemned by early twentieth-century orthodox halakhists as "bringing a foreign spirit into the Oral Torah, and of causing more harm than good." See sources quoted by Jacobs, *Tree of Life*, pp. 59–60.

28. See Heschel, *God in Search of Man*, pp. 259–61. These two notions of revelation, monologic and dialogic, passive and participatory, are identified by Heschel as being characteristic of the schools of Rabbi Akiba and of Rabbi Ishmael, respectively. According to Heschel, Rabbi Akiba considered the prophet a passive recipient of revelation while Rabbi Ishmael considered the prophet an active partner in the revelatory event. See Heschel, *Torah min ha-Shamayim*, vol. 2, pp. 264–99.

29. *Berakhot* 35a.

30. *Mekhilta de Rabbi Yishmael*, ed. and trans. Jacob Lauterbach, 3 vols. (Philadelphia: Jewish Publication Society, 1933), *"Ba-hodesh,"* chap. 2, p. 207.

31. See the comprehensive essay by Scholem, "The Meaning of the Torah in Jewish Mysticism," chapter in *On the Kabbalah*, pp. 32–87.

32. *Zohar*, vol. 3, p. 152a.

33. See discussion and sources in Sherwin, *Mystical Theology*, pp. 70–82.

34. This notion is developed further by David Weiss Halivni, "Revelation and *Zimzum*," *Judaism* 21 (Spring 1972): 205–11.

35. See discussion and sources in Sherwin, *Mystical Theology*, pp. 121–22.

36. *Baba Metzia* 59b.

37. *Seder Eliyahu Rabba ve-Seder Eliyahu Zuta*, *"Zuta,"* chap. 2, p. 172.

38. See *Shabbat* 10a, and Jacob ben Asher, *Arba'ah Turim—Hoshen Mishpat*, beginning.

39. *Midrash Exodus Rabbah* 28:6; see also *Midrash Tanhuma [ha-Nidpas]* (Jerusalem: Levin-Epstein, 1964), *"Yitro,"* no. 11, p. 96.

40. Judah Loew, *Gur Aryeih*, 5 vols. (Jerusalem: Yahadut, 1972), vol. 5, p. 83.

41. See *Sifre on Deuteronomy*, ed. Meir Friedmann (Vienna, 1865), no. 345, n. 8.

42. See, e.g., Nahmanides, *Commentary to the Torah* [in Hebrew], ed. Charles B. Chavel, 2 vols. (Jerusalem: Mosad ha-Rav Kook, 1959), "Introduction," vol. 1, p. 3. Also in standard editions of Hebrew Scripture with commentaries.

43. *Hagigah* 3b.

44. *Erubin* 13b.

45. See, e.g., the twelfth-century commentary of Samuel ben Meir (Rashbam) to *Baba Batra* 130b, 131a, in standard editions of the Talmud.

46. Rashi to *Ketubot* 57a, in standard editions of the Talmud.

47. *Midrash on Psalms* 12:4 p. 54. Eng. trans., vol. 1, p. 173.

48. *Midrash on Psalms* 12:4 is a variant of *P. Sanhedrin* 4:2. This citation is derived from the commentaries to the latter text, i.e., Moses Margaliot's *P'nei Moshe* and Jacob David of Slutzk (Ridbaz), in standard editions of the Palestinian Talmud.

49. *P. Sandedrin* 4:2.

50. Moses Margaliot's eighteenth-century commentary, *P'nei Moshe* to *P. Sanhedrin* 4:2. Also see the fourteenth-century commentary of Yom Tov ibn Asevelli (Ritba), *Hiddushei ha-Ritva* to *Erubin* 13b, in standard editions of the Talmud.

51. Joseph Albo, *Sefer ha-Ikkarim—Book of Principles,* ed. and trans. Isaac Husik, 6 vols. (Philadelphia: Jewish Publication Society, 1930), 3:23, vol. 3, p. 203. See also Nahmanides, *Commentary to the Torah,* vol. 2, p. 376, on Deut. 6:18, and Vidal Yom Tov of Tolosa's fourteenth-century commentary *Maggid Mishnah* to Maimonides's *Mishneh Torah— Sefer Kinyan,* "Hilkhot Shekheinim" 14:5, in standard editions of the *Mishneh Torah.* There may be here some influence of Aristotle, who claimed that "law is always a general statement." See Aristotle, *Nicomachean Ethics* 5.10.4, 1137b, and *Politics* 3, chap. 15, para. 4, 1286a.

52. See responsum no. 97 of Abraham the son of Maimonides, quoted in Elon, p. 345.

53. Aryeh Leib Heller's eighteenth- century commentary, *Ketzot ha-Hoshen,* on Karo, *Shulhan Arukh—Hoshen Mishpat* (Lwow, 1888), "Introduction." See also Louis Jacobs, "Rabbi Aryeh Laib Heller's Theological Introduction to his *Shev Shema Tata,*" *Modern Judaism* 1 (Sept. 1981): 184–217, and Tchernowitz, vol. 3, pp. 246–52.

54. For literature on this problem, see, e.g., Elon, pp. 938–1213; *Tchernowitz,* vol. 3; Isaac Zev Cahana, *Mehkarim be-Sifrut ha-Teshuvot* (Jerusalem: Mosad ha-Rav Kook, 1973), pp. 8–96; Ziev, pp. 268–96; Sherwin, "In the Shadows of Greatness," pp. 43–47; id., *Mystical Theology,* pp. 178–80; Isadore Twersky, *Rabad of Posquieres* (Cambridge, Mass.: Harvard Univ. Press, 1962), pp. 128–98; Elliot Dorff and Arthur Rosett, *A Living Tree* (Albany: State Univ. of New York Press, 1988), pp. 366–402.

55. The idea that the codes were written as private compilations of their authors meant for their personal use only and not for widespread distribution was noted by Hayyim ben Betsalel of Friedberg and his brother Judah Loew of Prague. In a letter to Joseph ibn Aknin, Maimonides noted that his *original* intention in composing his code was to have a compilation of halakhic views only for his own private use. See Moses Maimonides, *Kovetz Iggerot ha-Rambam,* 2 vols. (1859; reprint, Jerusalem, 1967), vol. 2, p. 30c.

56. According to Judah Loew, it is better that one—even a novice in halakhah—make a faulty decision based upon a review of Talmudic and other sources than make a correct decision based only upon the codes. See Loew, *Netivot Olom,* "Netiv ha-Torah," chap. 15, p. 69. See also Asher ben Yehiel, *She'eilot u-Teshuvot ha-Rosh* (Jerusalem: n.p., 1965), 31:9, p. 31a. Judah Loew's view is in direct conflict with that of the early twelfth-century Spanish halakhist Joseph ibn Migash, who greatly influenced Maimonides. According to ibn Migash, it is preferable to make an incorrect decision based on the codes—especially if one is a novice in halakhah—than to try to make a decision based on complicated Talmudic sources. See Joseph ibn Migash, *Responsa* [Hebrew] (Jerusalem: Gitler, 1959), no. 114, p. 17.

57. See Solomon Luria, *Yam Shel Shelomo* (Stettin: Shrentzel, 1861), "*Baba Kamma*" 8:72, 2:5; id., *Responsa* [Hebrew] (Lublin, 1774), no. 16. Note Simon Horwitz, *The Responsa of Solomon Luria* (New York: Bloch Publishing Co., 1968), p. 14. See also Moses Isserles, *Responsa* [Hebrew], ed. Asher Siev (Jerusalem: n.p., 1970), no. 6.

58. Nahmanides, *Commentary to Maimonides's Sefer ha-Mitzvot* [Hebrew], printed in Moses Maimonides, *Sefer ha-Mitzvot* (Jerusalem: Levin-Epstein, 1965), "Introduction," p. 3. This translation is from Twersky, *Rabad,* pp. 217–18.

59. For contemporary attempts to articulate philosophies of Jewish law that approximate what is termed here "the dialogic view," see, e.g., Eliezer Berkovits, *Not in Heaven*

(New York: Ktav, 1983), especially chap. 2; Jacobs, *Tree of Life*. Note Berkovits, *Ha-Halakhah: Koha ve-Tafkedah* (Jerusalem: Mosad ha-Rav Kook, 1981).

60. On custom (*minhag*), see Elon, pp. 713–67; id., s.v. *"Minhag,"* *Encyclopedia Judaica*, ed. Cecil Roth (Jerusalem: Keter, 1971); Cahana, pp. 108–17; Burton Leiser, "Custom and Law in Talmudic Jurisprudence," *Judaism* 20 (1971): 396–403; Joseph Kalir, "The *Minhag*," *Tradition* 7 (1965), pp. 89–95; Chaim Tchernowitz, *Toledoth ha-Halakhah* (New York: n.p., 1945), vol. 1, pp. 144–51; Alexander Guttmann, "*L'She'elat ha-Yahas Minhag-Halakhah bi-Tekufat ha-Talmud*," *Bitzaron* (1946): 192–99; Dorff and Rosett, pp. 421–35; Joel Roth, *The Halakhic Process* (New York: Jewish Theological Seminary, 1986), pp. 205–31.

61. Joshua Boaz, *Shaltei ha-Gibborim* to the Mordecai, in standard editions of the Talmud, "*Gittin*," para. 444, where a responsum of Jacob Tam to Joseph of Orleans is recorded.

62. See Moses Maimonides, *Hakdamah le-Peirush ha-Mishnah*, ed. Mordecai Rabinowitz, (Jerusalem: Mosad ha-Rav Kook, 1961), section 5, p. 41; see also id., *Mishneh Torah—Sefer Shofetim*, "*Hilkhot Mamrim*," 1:2–3, 2:2–5. *The Book of Judges*, Eng. trans. A. M. Hershman (New Haven: Yale Univ. Press, 1949), pp. 138–41. In his discussion of custom in the *Mishneh Torah*, Twersky notes, "Inasmuch as he [Maimonides] envisaged his code as fulfilling a universal role, his standards had to transcend localism or nativism." See Isadore Twersky, *Introduction to the Code of Maimonides* (New Haven: Yale Univ. Press, 1980), p. 127; also see pp. 124–34 on Maimonides's treatment of custom in the *Mishneh Torah*. In considering custom as a variety of law, and not as an extralegal entity, Maimonides may have been influenced by the Greeks. See Boaz Cohen, *Law and Tradition* (New York: Ktav, 1969), p. 47, n. 27. Blackstone, in his classification of British law, also considered custom a variety of law. See also Benjamin Cardozo, *The Nature of the Judicial Process* (New Haven: Yale Univ. Press, 1921), pp. 58–60, and Elon, p. 718. It is perhaps ironic that had Isserles's glosses containing Ashkenazic custom not been incorporated into the printed text of the *Shulhan Arukh*, Karo's code would not have gained universal Jewish acceptance. In a sense, this consideration for custom furthered the aims of codification.

63. See, e.g., Moses Isserles in the name of the late thirteenth-century halakhist Jacob Moelln (Maharil) in his gloss to Karo, *Shulhan Arukh—Yoreh De'ah*, para. 376:4, in standard editions of the *Shulhan Arukh;* Judah Loew, *Netivot Olam*, "*Netiv ha-Avodah*," chap. 7, p. 97; Jacob ben Asher, *Arba'ah Turim—Orah Hayyim*, para. 619 (end); see para. 551 (end), "It is forbidden to alter the custom of our forefathers." S.v. *Tosafot* on *Menahot* 20b, in standard editions of the Talmud. See Isserles, *Responsa*, no. 20, p. 130; no. 51, p. 250; no. 132, p. 512.

64. Asher ben Yehiel, *She'eilot u-Teshuvot ha-Rosh*, no. 101:1, p. 94, with regard to giving "stripes" for defamation of character. See *Kiddushin* 28a.

65. See the responsum of the thirteenth-century German halakhist Samson ben Zadok Duran, *Responsa Tashbeitz* [Hebrew] (Lwow, 1891), 2:63. See also Isserles, *Responsa*, no. 19, p. 127, "Even in times of persecution, custom should not be altered." Isserles, in this responsum, referred to the fifteenth-century halakhist Joseph Colon, *Responsa Maharik* [Hebrew] (Venice, 1519), "*Shoresh*" 9, "*Anaf*" 3, who says, "We follow custom even if it means going against the law, for custom is established according to the sages of the place."

66. Quoted in Twersky, *Rabad of Posquieres*, p. 241.

67. *Midrash Mishlei*, ed. Solomon Buber (Lwow, 1893), 22:38, p. 47a.

68. *Pesahim* 50a; see also Asher ben Yehiel, *Arba'ah Turim—Orah Hayyim*, para. 551.

69. See Tchernowitz, *Toledot ha-Halakhah*, vol. 1, p. 145.

70. *P. Baba Metzia* 7:1; *P. Yebamot* 12:1. See also *Soferim* 14:8: "People have adopted the following procedure, i.e., that no ruling is authoritatively laid down unless a custom has

been definitely established. As regards the saying of the rabbis that a custom abrogates a law, it applies to a custom that has no support from the Torah is only like an error in judgment."

71. See Elon, pp. 724, 738, 739. On the influence of custom over law in the area of communal taxation, see Karo, *Shulhan Arukh—Hoshen Mishpat*, para. 163, and the long discussion there in Abraham Zevi Eisenstadt's nineteenth-century commentary *Pithei Teshuvah*, nos. 1, 16; see also Elon, pp. 746–49. On other commercial areas, see Steven M. Passamaneck, *Insurance in Rabbinic Law* (Chicago: Aldine Publishing Co., 1974), pp. 170–71. For examples, see Isserles, *Responsa*, no. 20, p. 130; no. 51, p. 250.

72. See Ze'ev W. Falk, *Jewish Matrimonial Law* (New York: Oxford Univ. Press, 1966), especially pp. 1–86; H. J. Zimmels, *Ashkenazim and Sephardim* (London: Oxford Univ. Press, 1958), pp. 6, 166–81.

73. Asher ben Yehiel, *She'eilot u-Teshuvot ha-Rosh*, no. 101:1, p. 94.

74. Maimonides, *Mishneh Torah—Sefer Zemanim*, "Hilkhot Shevitat Assor," 3:3. Also see id., *Teshuvot ha-Rambam*, (Tel Aviv: Mekitzei Nirdamim, 1934), nos. 25, 33, pp. 22, 30.

75. Solomon ben Simeon Duran, *Responsa Rasbash*, nos. 419, 562, quoted in Cahana, p. 115.

76. See the gloss of Abraham ben David of Posquieres (Rabad) to Maimonides, *Mishneh Torah—Sefer Zera'im*, "Hilkhot Ma'aser Sheni," 1:3, in standard editions of the *Mishneh Torah*.

77. *P. Pe'ah* 7:5 end, *P. Ma'aser Sheni* 5:2 end, *P. Yebamot* 7:3. See also *Berakhot* 45a; *Erubin* 14b, *Menahot* 35b; *Pesahim* 54b. Note that in the Palestinian Talmud the citation ends with the injunction, "and do likewise," unlike the Babylonian Talmud, which just recommends surveying popular practice. Thus, for the Palestinian Talmud, custom is more a lawmaking force than it is for the Babylonian Talmud.

On the role of custom in arbitrating legal decisions, see Asher ben Yehiel, *She'eilot u-Teshuvot ha-Rosh*, no. 55:10, p. 53, "As the Palestinian Talmud teaches—when the *halakhah* is uncertain, follow custom. This means that if there is an uncertainty, and it is unclear according to whom the *halakhah* is to be decided, observe the common practice, i.e., follow custom. One may rely on the fact that if notable [halakhists] practice this custom, it must be in accordance with *halakhah*."

78. See, e.g., Elon, p. 738; Zimmels, *Ashkenazim and Sephardim*, pp. 109–15; Herman Pollack, *Jewish Folklore in Germanic Lands* (London: MIT Press, 1971), especially pp. 125–26, 167–68. Cabalistically inspired liturgical changes were introduced, especially in the late Middle Ages and by the Hasidim; see, e.g., Jacobs, *Tree of Life*, pp. 82–91; id., *Theology in the Responsa*, pp. 123, 183, 334–37.

79. See, e.g., Solomon B. Freehof, "Ceremonial Creativity Among the Ashkenazim," *Jewish Quarterly Review*, 75th Anniversary Volume (1967): 210–24. On bar mitzvah, see chap. 9 below.

80. The Talmud describes the many laws derived from scant scriptural reference as "mountains hanging by a hair." See *Hagigah* 10a–11a.

81. Quoted in Pollack, p. 161. For a similar view, see Moses Schreiber, *She'eilot u-Teshuvot Hatam Sofer* [Hebrew] (Vienna: n.p., 1883), *Yoreh De'ah*, no. 191, p. 74a, and *Orah Hayyim* (Vienna, 1895), no. 51, p. 186. See also H. J. Zimmels, "The Significance of the Statement 'We Are Not Acquainted Any More,'" in *Leo Jung Jubilee Volume* (New York: n.p., 1962), pp. 223–35.

82. Karo, *Shulhan Arukh—Orah Hayyim*, para. 690:17; see commentary there Judah Ashkenazi, *Be'er Heiteiv*, no. 15.

83. See, e.g., Jacob ben Asher, *Arba'ah Turim—Orah Hayyim*, para. 551 end.

84. See discussion and sources in Jacobs, *Tree of Life*, p. 228.

85. See Jacobs, *Principles*, pp. 297–98, and Heinemann, vol. 2, pp. 91–182.

86. The influence of German romantic philosophy upon protoconservative nineteenth-century German Jewish thought is clearly evident. See, e.g., Mordecai M. Kaplan, *Greater Judaism in the Making* (New York: Reconstructionist Press, 1960), pp. 354–57. See also David Rudavsky, "The Historical School of Zecharia Frankel," *Jewish Social Studies* 5 (1963): 224–44.

87. Schechter often used the term "Catholic Israel." The term itself seems to have been coined by Isaac Leeser.

88. See Jacobs, *Principles*, pp. 297–98.

89. See Robert Gordis's views in "Authority in Jewish Law," *Proceedings of the Rabbinical Assembly* 8 (1941–44), pp. 78–81.

90. Louis Ginzberg was perhaps the first modern Jewish scholar to examine the role of economics in Jewish law. His investigations, however, were largely limited to the Talmudic period. See Louis Ginzberg, "The Significance of the Halacha for Jewish History," in *On Jewish Law and Lore* (New York: Atheneum, 1970), pp. 77–127. He was followed in this approach by Louis Finkelstein and others. See Finkelstein's *Pharisees*. Note Jacob Neusner, "The Rabbinic Traditions About the Pharisees in Modern Historiography," *CCAR Journal* 19 (Apr. 1972):106. On the role of economic conditions in halakhic decision making in the medieval period, see, e.g., Jacob Katz, *Exclusiveness and Tolerance* (New York: Schocken, 1962), pp. 3–67; id., *Tradition and Crisis* (New York: Schocken, 1971), pp. 3–79.

The first important precedent regarding economic considerations and halakhic change was probably the *prosbul;* see *M. Shevi'it* 10:3–4, *Gittin* 36a-b.

The institution of a legal fiction providing for the sale of *hametz* to a non-Jew during Passover seems to have originated as a result of economic conditions in late medieval Poland, where Jews in the business of manufacturing liquor from grains could not economically survive divestment of their stock of grain during Passover. This practice, apparently introduced for a specific commercial group, at a specific historical time, led to a popular and common practice in subsequent periods. See, e.g., Joel Sirkes's seventeenth-century commentary *Bayyit Hadash* to Jacob ben Asher, *Arba'ah Turim—Orah Hayyim*, para. 448:1, in standard editions of the *Arba'ah Turim*.

On the clash between Judah Loew of Prague and Moses Isserles on the question of whether economic factors can play a role in halakhic decision making, particularly on the issue of Jewish use of gentile wine, see Sherwin, *Mystical Theology*, pp. 94–102. Loew opposed the intrusion of economic considerations into halakhah. Isserles was a leading advocate of considering economic conditions in halakhic decision making. For example, on Isserles's use of the principle of *hefseid merubeh*, see his glosses to Karo, *Shulhan Arukh—Yoreh Deah*, paras. 31:1, 32:5, 35:5. Isserles even permitted Jewish peddlers to sell Christian religious items. On *bateil b'shishim*, see Isserles, *Responsa*, no. 53, p. 263.

For other discussions of economic considerations in legal decision, see, e.g., Zimmels, *Ashkenazim and Sephardim*, pp. 54, 199–200, 207–17, and Solomon Zucrow, *Adjustment of Law to Life in Rabbinic Literature* (Boston: Stratford, 1928), pp. 54–74, 75–100.

91. Menahem Meiri, *Beit ha-Behirah—Hullin* (Jerusalem: n.p., 1970), p. 164.

92. The idea that changed conditions lead to changed laws crystallizes in the notion of "*ha-iddana*," (nowadays). See especially *Tosafot* to *Beitzah* 6a. Also see discussion and sources noted in Immanuel Low, "*Ha-Iddana*," *Hebrew Union College Annual* 11 (1936): 193–206.

There was a belief that even human nature and anatomy changed. For example, it was believed that in ancient times children matured more quickly than in medieval times, and were able to propagate at the age of eight. See, e.g., *Tosafot* to *Sanhedrin* 69a, Meir Schiff to *Sanhedrin* 69a, in standard editions of the Talmud; and Solomon Luria, *Yam Shel Shelomo*, "*Baba Kamma*" 7:37.

93. *M. Sukkah* 2:1; Isserles's gloss to Karo, *Shulhan Arukh—Orah Hayyim*, para. 639:2.

94. See *M. Shabbat* 16:1; *Shabbat* 116a, and Mordecai ben Hillel to *Shabbat*, no. 393.

95. On *Takkanot ha-Kahal*, see Isaac Levitas in *Encyclopedia Judaica*, s.v. *takkanot*.

96. On *gezerot* and *takkanot*, see Elon, pp. 367–713; Dorff and Rosett, pp. 402–21.

97. *Rosh ha-Shanah* 29b.

98. Asher ben Yehiel, *Tosafot ha-Rosh* (in standard editions of the Talmud), to *Shabbat* 164a writes, "Behold, I am also amazed at how the ge'onim could innovate a *gezerah* after Rav Ashi completed the Talmud." See *Encyclopedia Talmudit*, vol. 5, pp. 530–40, especially p. 540.

99. See, e.g., Katz, *Exclusiveness and Tolerance*, pp. 24–36, discussion and sources noted.

100. See, e.g., the custom of *kapparot*. Though many authorities opposed it and even condemned it as a pagan custom, it was nevertheless retained. See Karo's *Beit Yosef* to Joseph ben Asher, *Arba'ah Turim—Orah Hayyim*, para. 605.

101. See Mordecai Friedman, "The Monogamy Clause in Jewish Marriage Contracts," in *Perspectives in Jewish Learning, Volume Four*, ed. Nathaniel Stampfer (Chicago: Spertus College of Judaica Press, 1972), pp. 20–40.

102. Compare Cardozo, p. 178, "What is erroneous is pretty sure to perish. The good remains the foundation on which new structures will be built. The bad will be rejected and cast off in the laboratory of the years."

103. See Maimonides, *Mishneh Torah—Sefer Shofetim*, "Hilkhot Mamrim," 2:6–7.

104. The idea that aspects of the "oral law" might have preceded the "written law" is presented by Yehezkel Kaufmann in *Toledot ha-Emunah ha-Yisraelit*, 8 vols. (Tel Aviv: Mosad Bialik, 1966), especially vol. 8, p. 346. What Kaufmann claims about the development of Jewish law in its earliest epoch is at least equally true of later eras. See also Faur, p. 117.

105. See nn. 23 and 27 for this chapter.

106. On the whole question of plural modes in halakhah, see Jakob Petuchowski, "Plural Modes Within the *Halakhah*," *Judaism* 19 (Winter 1970): 77–90; the rejoinder by Walter Wurzburger, "Plural Models and the Authority of *Halakhah*," *Judaism* 20 (Fall 1971): 390–96; Eugene Borowitz, "Subjectivity and the Halachic Process," *Judaism* 13 (Spring 1964): 211–20, and Jacob B. Agus, *Dialogue and Tradition* (New York: Abelard Schuman, 1971), pp. 555–61.

The clear divergence between the monolithic and the dialogic views as expressed respectively by advocates of Orthodox and Conservative Judaism is apparent in the following excerpt from an evaluation of the Conservative *Beth Din's* decision concerning the role of women by a leading spokesman for American Orthodox Judaism. He begins by quoting the statement of the chairman of the Rabbinical Assembly's Committee on Jewish Law, which accompanied the decision on women. The statement is "The approach to Jewish law in Conservative Judaism has always been to change existing norms where they do not further ethical or spiritual values. When an existing norm reflects a world-view or social situation which no longer exists, then the *halakhah* is modified." The spokesman for Orthodox Judaism responds as follows: "These sentiments belie a lack of recognition of the fact that *Halakhah* possesses an enduring validity which, while applicable to changing circumstances, is not subject to change by lobbying or by the exertion of pressure in any guise or form. . . . Normative Judaism teaches that *Halakhah* is not derived from any temporal 'world view' or 'social situation' but expresses the transcendental view of the Divine Lawgiver." See J. David Bleich, "Women in a Minyan?" *Tradition* 14 (1973): 117.

For example, orthodoxy would be unable, from the perspective of the monolithic view, to justify such recent innovations as proclaiming Israel Independence Day a religious holiday, which sets aside certain observances of *sefirah* and introduces new liturgical elements.

107. See, e.g., *Eleh Divrei ha-Brit* (Altona, 1819).

108. See Jacobs, *Tree of Life*, p. 243.

109. On the institution of a professional, salaried rabbinate, see ibid., pp. 148–50 and sources noted there, and Zucrow, pp. 54–67.

110. See Isserles's gloss to Karo, *Shulhan Arukh—Yoreh Deah*, para. 242:14. Note Zimmels, *Ashkenazim and Sephardim*, p. 273. Compare Sherwin, *Mystical Theology*, pp. 167–68. Note R. J. Zwi Werblowsky, *Joseph Karo* (Philadelphia: Jewish Publication Society, 1977), pp. 122-27. See also J. Newman, *Semikah [Ordination]* (Manchester: n.p., 1950).

111. Judah Loew, *Netivot Olom* vol. 1, "*Netiv ha-Torah*," chap. 15; id., *Tiferet Yisrael*, chap. 56.

112. *Baba Kamma* 79b, *Horayot* 3b. See also *P. Shabbat* 1:4, "Every decree which is decreed on the community, but which is not accepted by the majority of the community, is no decree."

113. Asher ben Yehiel, *She'eilot u-Teshuvot ha-Rosh*, no. 55:10, p. 53. See also *Pesahim* 56a and *Tosafot* to *Baba Batra* 2a. Compare Maimonides, *Responsa*, no. 25, p. 22.

114. In recent years the liberal wing of Conservative Judaism has also taken the position that halakhah is not binding but is only a guide to observance. Those who have adopted this view have thereby rejected the ideology of the founders of Conservative Judaism and have embraced the ideological position of those on the right wing of Reform Judaism. The left wing of Reform Judaism, which embraces Classical Reform Judaism, considers halakhah to be neither binding nor a guide to observance. Classical Reform Judaism invoked such notions as rationality, conscience, aesthetics, and modernity as criteria upon which to reject halakhic norms and to institute new practices and beliefs.

115. As far as I know, the first person to call himself a "Conservative Jew" was a rabbi from Vienna named Simon Szanto. He attended the 1871 Augsburg Synod at which the question of whether the composition of a new *Shulhan Arukh* was desirable was discussed. The orthodox position clearly was that the *Shulhan Arukh* is binding and authoritative and need not be replaced. The reform position was that halakhah is not binding; therefore, any code is altogether unnecessary. Szanto, however, identified himself as a "Conservative Jew," which he defined as one who holds halakhah to be binding and the codes not to be authoritatively binding. He, therefore, spoke against the composition of a new code. See David Philipson, *The Reform Movement in Judaism* (New York: Macmillan, 1907), pp. 452–53. This position was also endorsed by Boaz Cohen in "The *Shulhan Arukh* as a Guide for Religious Practice Today," in his *Law and Tradition*, pp. 62–100. This writing represents a rejection by Cohen of his earlier view (1935) that the codes are binding; see p. 59. The position of the codes as guides was affirmed by the Rabbinical Assembly in 1949. In the 1880s, the conservative camp was divided between those who accepted halakhah and the codes as binding and those who accepted halakhah as binding but not the codes. The former group, represented by people such as Sabato Morais, eventually joined the orthodox camp, while the latter group, represented by such people as Alexander Kohut, stayed in the conservative camp and helped it develop during its critical period of reorganization. See Moshe Davis, *The Emergence of Conservative Judaism* (Philadelphia: Jewish Publication Society, 1963), pp. 231–39. Before the conservative- reform split, why orthodoxy opposed the position that considered the codes no longer binding is understandable. It was often tied together with a rejection of Talmudic authority.

116. Note Cardozo, p. 106. The quote from Holmes is cited from his *The Common Law* by Cardozo, p. 33.

117. See *Baba Metzia* 85b-86a.

118. See Louis Jacobs, "Rabbi Joseph Hayyim of Baghdad," in *Perspectives on Jews and Judaism*, ed. Arthur Chiel (New York: The Rabbinical Assembly, 1978), p. 191.

3. THE NATURE OF ETHICS

1. On Jewish ethical literature see *Encyclopedia Judaica*, s.v. "Ethical Literature" by Joseph Dan, vol. 6, pp. 922–32; id., *Sifrut ha-Musar ve-ha-Derush* (Jerusalem: Keter, 1975). See also Zevi Zahavy, ed., *Mivhar ha-Mahshavah ve-ha-Musar ba-Yahadut* (Tel Aviv: Zioni, 1954).

2. *Niddah* 16b. See also Maimonides, *Teshuvot ha-Rambam*, ed. A. Frieman, no. 345, pp. 309–10.

3. Moses Maimonides, *The Eight Chapters of Maimonides on Ethics*, ed. and trans. Joseph I. Gorfinkle, (New York: Columbia Univ. Press, 1912), p. 42 (Heb. sec.), p. 84 (Eng. sec.).

4. Moses Maimonides, *Commentary to the Mishnah—Abot* (Jerusalem: Mosad ha-Rav Kook, 1961), 1:14, p. 24. *Moses Maimonides — The Commentary to Mishnah Abot*, Eng. trans. Arthur David (New York: Bloch Publishing Co., 1968), p. 14.

5. Noted by Louis Ginzberg, "Rabbi Israel Salanter," chapter in *Students, Scholars and Saints* (Philadelphia: Jewish Publication Society, 1928), p. 174.

6. See, e.g., Abraham Joshua Heschel, *The Earth Is the Lord's* (New York: Schuman, 1950), p. 9. The Yiddish term *"a shainer yid"* conveys a particularly Jewish notion of aesthetics. Beauty is defined by action and life-style rather than by sheer being. In this regard, note Jakob Petuchowski, "The Beauty of God," in *The Life of Covenant*, ed. Joseph Edelheit (Chicago: Spertus College of Judaica Press, 1986), pp. 125–31.

7. In a letter from Solomon Schechter to Solomon Solis-Cohen, dated 11 July 1904. Quoted in Norman Bentwich, *Solomon Schechter: A Biography* (New York: Burning Bush Press, 1964), p. 238.

8. See, e.g., the views of the Hasidic master Mendel of Kotsk on "working with the self" discussed in Abraham Joshua Heschel, *Kotsk*, 2 vols. [Yiddish] (Tel Aviv: Menorah, 1973), vol. 1, pp. 131–36.

9. This statement is attributed to Mendel of Kotsk. See *Emet me-Kotsk Tizmah* (Bnei Brak: Nezah, 1961), pp. 51–52; Abraham Joshua Heschel, *A Passion for Truth* (New York: Farrar, Straus, and Giroux, 1973), p. 38; id., *Kotsk*, vol. 2, p. 33. A similar statement is attributed to Israel of Rhyzen, *Knesset Yisrael* (Warsaw: n.p., 1906), pp. 16–17.

10. These are but some of the issues treated in Jewish ethical literature that are addressed in this chapter. One issue not treated is the relationship between Jewish law and ethics, particularly whether Jewish ethics is a distinct entity with regard to its relationship to Jewish law. For other discussions of the nature and application of Jewish ethics, see, e.g., Jacob B. Agus, *The Vision and the Way* (New York: Ungar, 1966); Marvin Fox, ed., *Modern Jewish Ethics* (Columbus: Ohio State Univ. Press, 1975); Louis Jacobs, *Jewish Values* (London: Vallentine, Mitchell, 1960); Menachem Marc Kellner, ed., *Contemporary Jewish Ethics* (New York: Hebrew Publishing Co., 1978); Shubert Spero, *Morality, Halakha and the Jewish Tradition* (New York: Ktav, 1983).

11. Aryeh Leib Heller's commentary to Karo, *Shulhan Arukh*, entitled *Ketzot ha-Hoshen*, "Introduction." See also Jacobs, "Rabbi Aryeh Leib Heller's Theological Introduction," pp. 184– 217. Compare Margaliot, *Pnei Moshe* to *P. Sanhedrin* 4:12, in standard editions of the Palestinian Talmud, and ibn Asevelli, *Hiddushei ha-Ritva* to *Erubin* 13b, in standard editions of the (Babylonian) Talmud.

12. For a succinct statement of a variety of positions in modern secular ethics, see, e.g., Andrew C. Varga, *The Main Issues in Bioethics* (New York: Paulist Press, 1980), pp. 3– 15. Note William Frankena's succinct presentation, *Ethics* (New York: Prentice-Hall, 1963). Compare various studies on Christian ethics as a variety of theological ethics, e.g., Paul

Ramsey, *Basic Christian Ethics* (New York: Scribner's, 1970); Bernard Haring, *The Law of Christ* (Westminster, Md.: Newman Press, 1963), and the works of James M. Gustafson, noted in the bibliography. Also, compare studies that relate Jewish ethics to modern secular ethics, e.g., articles by Fackenheim and Samuelson in Kellner, ed.

13. See, e.g., Kurt Baier, *The Moral Point of View: A Rational Basis of Ethics* (New York: Random House, 1967). On various notions of "rationality," see, e.g., Bryan R. Wilson, ed., *Rationality* (New York: Harper and Row, 1971).

14. On the intuitive view, see, e.g., G. E. Moore, *Principia Ethica* (Cambridge: Cambridge Univ. Press, 1903). Compare G. J. Warnock, *Contemporary Moral Philosophy* (New York: Macmillan, 1967), pp. 4–18.

15. See, e.g., Charles L. Stevenson, *Ethics and Language* (New Haven: Yale Univ. Press, 1944). Compare Warnock, pp. 18–30. Ernest Hemingway's view that immoral behavior is that after which a person feels badly is a crude version of the emotive approach. In Clint Eastwood's film "Dirty Harry," a habitual killer is described as murdering simply because it makes him feel good.

16. See, e.g., G. E. Moore, 1:7, p. 7. A variety of this approach is found among some religious thinkers who maintain that moral intuition is a human faculty implanted by God.

17. *Mekhilta d' Rabbi Yishmael*, ed. H. Horovitz and I. Rabin (Jerusalem: Wahrmann, 1960), "Yitro," on Exod. 20:16, chap. 8, p. 233. Eng. trans., vol. 2, p. 262.

18. See, e.g., Sherwin, *Mystical Theology*, p. 138, and Louis Jacobs, "The Doctrine of the Divine Spark in Man in Jewish Sources," in *Studies in Rationalism, Judaism and Universalism*, ed. R. Loew (London: n.p., 1966), pp. 87–115. See also, Yitzhak of Radvil, "The Holiness of Man," trans. Samuel Dresner, *Judaism* 37 (Spring 1988): 156–59.

19. See Moses Cordevero, *Tomer Devorah* (Tel Aviv: Friedman, 1965), pp. 12–13. *The Palm Tree of Deborah*, Eng. trans. Louis Jacobs (London: Vallentine, Mitchell, 1960), pp. 52–53.

20. *Abot d'Rabbi Natan*, ed. Solomon Schechter (Vienna, 1887), A, chap. 16 end, p. 326. *The Fathers According to Rabbi Nathan*, Eng. trans. Judah Goldin (New Haven: Yale Univ. Press, 1955), p. 86.

21. *Baba Kamma* 30a.

22. Samuel Edels's commentary to the Talmud, *Hiddushei Halakhot ve-Aggadot*, is found in standard editions of the Babylonian Talmud while that of Judah Loew is not. For Judah Loew, see his *Hiddushei Aggadot*, 4 vols. (New York: Judaica Press, 1969), vol. 3, p. 40. This tripartite division of Jewish ethics was also espoused by Elijah, the Gaon of Vilna, in his commentary on Proverbs 2:9; see *Sefer Mishlei im Biur ha-Gera* (Petah Tikvah: n.p., 1985), p. 39.

23. Judah Loew, *Derekh ha-Hayyim* (New York: Judaica Press, 1969), 1:2, p. 24, "Introduction," p. 9.

24. This view is already found in Plato (*Charmides* 156–57) and Aristotle (*Nicomachean Ethics* 1:13). In Jewish sources, see, e.g., Maimonides, *Eight Chapters*, chap. 1, p. 38; id., *Mishneh Torah—Sefer ha-Mada*, "Hilkhot Deot," 2:11; Abraham ibn Daud, *Emunah Ramah* (Frankfurt, 1852), vol. 3, p. 98; Joseph ibn Aknin, *Hygiene of the Soul*, trans. Abraham Halkin, *Proceedings of the American Academy for Jewish Research*, 4 (1933); 25–147; also the ethical will of Joseph ibn Kaspi in *Hebrew Ethical Wills*, ed. and trans. Israel Abrahams (Philadelphia: Jewish Publication Society, 1926), p. 136.

25. *Sefer ha-Yashar*, ed. and trans. Seymour J. Cohen (New York: Ktav, 1973), chap. 7, pp. 156–59.

26. Solomon ibn Gabirol, *The Improvement of the Moral Qualities*, trans. Stephen S. Wise (New York: Columbia Univ. Press, 1901), "Introduction" and 4:1, esp. pp. 84–85.

27. On these and other related views in Jewish mysticism, see, e.g., Gershom Scholem, *Major Trends in Jewish Mysticism* (New York: Schocken, 1961), pp. 205–86; Abraham Joshua Heschel, "The Mystical Element in Judaism," chapter in *The Jews*, ed. Louis Finkelstein, 2 vols. (Philadelphia: Jewish Publication Society, 1949), vol. 2, pp. 932–54; Isaiah Tishbi, *Torat ha-Ra v'ha-Kelipot b'Kabbalat ha-Ari* (Jerusalem: Hebrew Univ. Press, 1963); Joseph Dan, *Jewish Mysticism and Jewish Ethics* (Seattle: Univ. of Washington Press, 1986).

28. Jacob Joseph of Polnoye, *Toledot Ya'akov Yosef* (Jerusalem: n.p., 1967), "*Ekev*" end, pp. 633–34. See also Mordecai of Chernobyl, "*Hadrakhah*" 2, p. 4.

29. Moses Hayyim Luzzatto, *Mesillat Yesharim—The Path of the Upright*, trans. and ed. Mordecai M. Kaplan (Philadelphia: Jewish Publication Society, 1966), pp. 24, 37.

30. Ibid., p. 28.

31. Quoted and translated in Ivan Marcus, *Piety and Society* (Leiden: E. J. Brill, 1981), p. 34.

32. Scholem, *Major Trends*, p. 118.

33. *Sefer Hasidim*, ed. J. Wistinetzki and J. Freimann (Frankfurt: Wahrmann Verlag, 1924), para. 115, p. 58.

34. Quoted in Marcus, p. 84.

35. Maimonides, *Guide*, Book 3, chap. 54. Eng. trans., pp. 634–35. See Alexander Altmann, "Maimonides' Four Perfections," *Essays in Jewish Intellectual History* (Hanover, N.H.: Univ. Press of New England, 1981), pp. 65–77.

36. Maimonides, *Eight Chapters*, chap. 5, p. 70.

37. Ibid. See also Byron L. Sherwin, "*Moses Maimonides on Perfection of the Body*," *Listening* 9, nos. 1, 2 (1974): 28–37 and sources noted there.

38. Maimonides, *Guide*, Book 3, chap. 8. Eng. trans., pp. 432–34.

39. Maimonides, *Eight Chapters*, chap. 4, p. 62.

40. Moses Maimonides, *Mishneh Torah—Sefer ha-Mada*, "Hilkhot Deot," 4:15. See also id., *Treatise on Asthma*, trans. S. Muntner (Philadelphia: Lippincott, 1963), p. 24; id., *The Medical Aphorisms of Moses Maimonides*, trans. Fred Rosner and S. Muntner, (New York: Yeshivah Univ. Press, 1971), chap. 20. Also note Joseph ben Meir Zabara, *The Book of Delight*, trans. Moses Hadas (New York: Columbia Univ. Press, 1982), pp. 116–18, and Abraham ibn Ezra on Exod. 23:25, in standard editions of the Hebrew Scripture with commentaries.

41. Maimonides, *Guide*, Book 3, chap. 33., p. 533.

42. Maimonides, *Eight Chapters*, chap. 5, p. 71.

43. Maimonides, *Mishneh Torah—Sefer ha-Mada*, "Hilkhot Deot," 3:3.

44. Maimonides, ibid., 2:1.

45. See, e.g., Maimonides, *Guide*, Book 1, chap. 33, Book 3, chap. 12. Eng. trans., pp. 81, 445.

46. Luzzatto, chap. 9, p. 122.

47. Maimonides, *Mishneh Torah—Sefer ha-Mada*, "Hilkhot Deot," 1:7.

48. Maimonides, *Guide*, Book 3, chap. 54. Eng. trans., p. 635.

49. Maimonides, *Eight Chapters*, chap. 5.

50. Yehiel ben Yekutiel of Rome, *Sefer Ma'alot ha-Middot* (Jerusalem: Eshkol, 1968), p. 242.

4. HEALTH, HEALING, AND TRADITION

1. Maimonides, *Eight Chapters*, chap. 5, p. 70.

2. Attributed to Solomon ibn Gabirol, *Choice of Pearls*, trans. A. Cohen (New York: Bloch Publishing Co., 1925), n. 457, p. 98.

3. Samuel Noah Kramer, *The Sumerians* (Chicago: Univ. of Chicago Press, 1963), p. 99.

4. Based on *Sanhedrin* 38a, and *"Midrash Konen"* in *Beth ha-Midrash*, ed. Adolph Jellinek, 6 vols. (1855; reprint, Jerusalem: n.p., 1967), vol. 2, pp. 26– 27.

5. *"Sefer Noah,"* in *Beth ha-Midrash*, ed. Jellinek, vol. 3, pp. 155–60. See also Nahmanides, *"Torat ha-Adam"* in *Kitve Rabenu Moshe ben Nahman*, ed. Charles B. Chavel, 2 vols. (Jerusalem: Mosad ha-Rav Kook, 1964), vol. 2, p. 295, and Solomon Muntner, *Introduction to the Book of Asaph the Physician* [Hebrew] (Jerusalem: Geniza Press, 1957), pp. 147– 54.

6. On Hezekiah's suppression of the "Book of Remedies," see *Berakhot* 10b, *Pesahim* 56a. On the legend of Shem's ascent, see Samson ben Zadok Duran, *Sefer Tashbeitz*, no. 445, p. 38b. On Shem's ascent and Hezekiah's censorship, see Hayyim Joseph David Azulai's commentary *Kiseih Rahamim* to *Avot d'Rabbi Nathan* (Livorno, 1803), chap. 2, end. Compare Moses Maimonides, *Peirush la-Mishnah*, ed. Joseph Kapah (Jerusalem: Mosad ha-Rav Kook, 1963), *"Pesahim"* 4:10, pp. 112–13.

7. Paul Ramsey, *Fabricated Man* (New Haven: Yale Univ. Press, 1970), p. 138.

8. Ibid., p. 38.

9. Id., *The Patient as Person* (New Haven: Yale Univ. Press, 1970), p. xiii.

10. This view concurs with that of H. J. Zimmels, *Magicians, Theologians and Doctors* (London: Goldston, 1952), p. 170, n. 45, but is rejected by Immanuel Jakobovits, *Jewish Medical Ethics* (New York: Bloch Publishing Co., 1959), p. 5.

11. See Arthur Green, *Tormented Master: A Life of Rabbi Nahman of Bratslav* (University: Univ. of Alabama Press, 1979), p. 243. Similarly, the thirteenth-century writer Jedaiah ben Abraham Bedersi observes, "Most physicians you meet reach a ripe old age, because the Angel of Death wishes to give him a chance to increase his victims," quoted by Harry Friedenwald in *The Jews and Medicine*, 2 vols. (Baltimore: Johns Hopkins Univ. Press, 1944), vol. 1, p. 72.

Zabara tells the story of a philosopher who was so sick that his physician gave up treating him. Nevertheless, the patient recovered. The convalescent was walking along the street when he met his physician.

"You come from the other world?" asked the doctor.

"Yes," said the patient. "And there I saw the terrible punishments that fall upon doctors, for they kill their patients. But, don't you feel alarmed, for I swore to them there that you were no doctor." Quoted in Israel Abrahams, *The Book of Delight and Other Papers* (Philadelphia: Jewish Publication Society, 1912), p. 12.

12. See, e.g., Shem Tov ben Joseph ibn Falaquera, *The Book of the Seeker*, trans. M. H. Levine (New York: Yeshivah Univ. Press, 1976), p. 49, and Zabara, chap. 10, p. 142.

The Karaites, the Jewish sect that flourished in the Middle Ages, rejected both medical and pharmacological practice. According to the Karaites, Scripture relegates healing to God alone. See Leon Nemoy, "Al-Qirqisani's Criticism of Anan's Prohibition of the Practice of Medicine" [Hebrew], *Ha-Rofeh ha-Ivri* (1938), Part 2, pp. 73–83, 205–7.

13. See, e.g., Num. 12:8–11, Deut. 28:58, 2 Kings 5:26–27, 2 Chron. 26:16–21; note Lev. 14:30–31. In rabbinic and medieval literature, note, e.g., *Shabbat* 31b, 32a; *Midrash*

Leviticus Rabbah 16:8; Nahmanides, *Commentary to the Torah,* vol. 2, pp. 185–86 on Lev. 26:11.

14. See, e.g., Deut. 32:39, Ps. 41:5, Job 5:18. See the discussion by Julius Preuss, *Biblical and Talmudic Medicine,* trans. Fred Rosner (New York: Sanhedrin Press, 1978), pp. 18–27.

15. *M. Kiddushin* 4:14, *Kiddushin* 82a. See also *Soferim* 15:10; see the discussion by Samuel Kutak in *Sefer Assia,* ed. A. Steinberg [Hebrew] (Jerusalem: Schlesinger Institute, 1976), vol. 2, pp. 21–28.

16. See Judah Loew, *Nezah Yisrael* (New York: Judaica Press, 1969), chap. 30, p. 142; id., *Hiddushei Aggadot,* vol. 2, p. 153 on *Kiddushin* 82a.

17. Moses Matt, *Mateh Moshe* (Warsaw: n.p., 1976), *"Bikkur Holim,"* chap. 3, p. 110b.

18. H. Brody, ed., and trans. N. Salaman, *Selected Poems of Jehudah ha-Levi,* (Philadelphia: Jewish Publication Society, 1924), p. 113; see also Ben Sirach 38:1– 2a.

19. Quoted in Friedenwald, vol. 1, p. 274. Moses Maimonides's celebrated "Physician's Prayer," it should be noted, was not written by Maimonides. It was most probably authored by Marcus Herz, a modern Jewish physician.

20. Abraham Joshua Heschel, *The Insecurity of Freedom* (New York: Schocken, 1966), pp. 31, 33.

21. Quoted in Salo Baron, *A Social and Religious History of the Jews,* 17 vols. (New York: Columbia Univ. Press, 1958), vol. 8, p. 260; see also Moses Maimonides, *Hanhagat ha-Beri'ut (Regimen Sanitas),* ed. Solomon Muntner and trans. Moses ibn Tibbon, (Jerusalem: Mosad ha-Rav Kook, 1957), pp. 44, 70; ibn Falaquera, p. 44.

22. *Sabbath* 10a.

23. *Baba Kamma* 85a.

24. *Baba Kamma* 81b.

25. Maimonides, *Peirush la-Mishnah,* "Nedarim" 4:4.

26. Nahmanides, *"Torat ha- Adam,"* p. 42.

27. On coming to the aid of the imperiled, see *Sanhedrin* 73a, Maimonides, *Mishneh Torah—Sefer Nezikin,* "Laws of Murder and The Preservation of Life," 1:14, 16; Jacob ben Asher, *Arba'ah Turim—Hoshen Mishpat,* para. 426. Note the exhaustive discussions of B. Wein, "Aspects of the Prohibition of Standing Idly by the Blood of Thy Neighbor" [Hebrew], *Ha-Darom* 33 (1971):61–80; Aaron Kirshenbaum, *The 'Good Samaritan' and Jewish Law* (Tel Aviv: Tel Aviv Univ. Press, 1976).

28. See Rashi to *Baba Kamma* 85a.

29. See Abraham ibn Ezra and Bahya ben Asher on Exod. 21:19.

30. See, e.g., Matt, p. 110b.

31. Nahmanides, *Commentary to the Torah,* vol. 2, pp. 185–86 on Lev. 26:11. See so, e.g., the fifteenth-century thinker Isaac Arama's *Akedat Yitzhak* (Salonika, 1522), on "Va-hlah"; compare David ben Samuel ha-Levi's seventh-century commentary, *Turei Zahav* on o, *Shulhan Arukh—Yoreh Deah,* para. 336:1, in standard editions of the *Shulhan Arukh.*

32. Hayyim Joseph David Azulai, *Birkhei Yoseph,* (Vienna, 1843), *"Yoreh Deah,"* para. 85b.

33. Maimonides, *Mishneh Torah—Sefer Hafla'ah,* "Hilkhot Nedarim," 6:8; also see the th-century commentary by Zevi Hirsch Hayyot, *Maharitz Hayyot* to *Baba Kamma* ndard editions of the Talmud. Maimonides seems here to be following Isaac Alfasi lduces no scriptural proof text in his code.

cob Zahalon, *Otzar ha-Hayyim* (Venice, 1683), "Introduction"; see Friedenwald,

35. *Midrash Samuel*, ed. Solomon Buber (Cracow, 1893), p. 54, and *Midrash Temurah*, chap. 2 in *Otzar Midrashim*, ed. Judah D. Eisenstein, 2 vols. (New York: n.p., 1915), vol. 2, pp. 580–81.

36. David ben Samuel, *Turei Zahav* on Karo *Shulhan Arukh—Yoreh Deah*, para. 336:1, in standard editions of the *Shulhan Arukh*; see also Bahya ibn Pakuda, *The Book of Direction to the Duties of the Heart*, trans. Menahem Mansoor (London: Routledge and Kegan Paul, 1973), "On Reliance on God Alone," chap. 4, p. 247, "A man must put his trust in God but at the same time he must try to preserve his health with the proper means, and drive away sickness in the usual ways."

37. That Jewish law required one to live in a town in which a physician resides (*Sanhedrin* 17b) and that honor was demanded to be shown to the physician (*Midrash Exodus Rabbah* 21:7, Ben Sirach 38:1) seems to fortify the position that medical care was deemed desirable and obligatory. That a commentary on the verse in Exodus describing God as the proper healer (15:26) is interpreted to mean that God heals in the world to come, would imply that healing in this world is the proper province of human beings; see *Yalkut Shimoni* (New York: Pardes, 1944) "Exodus," para. 257, p. 78a. That a blessing is to be recited, according to some authorities, after receiving medical treatment would indicate its propriety; see Karo, *Shulhan Arukh—Orah Hayyim*, para. 230:4, and Judah Ashkenazi's commentary *Be'er Heiteiv* there, based on *Berakhot* 60a.

38. *Midrash Deuteronomy Rabbah* 6:13.

39. See, e.g., *Tosafot* to *Baba Kamma* 85a.

40. Jacob ben Asher, *Arba'ah Turim—Yoreh Deah*, para. 336:1. In his commentary *Be'ur ha-Gra* to Karo, *Shulhan Arukh—Yoreh Deah*, para. 336:1, Elijah, the Gaon of Vilna, expressed his view that healing is an unequivocal obligation. Nahmanides's view that healing is an obligation is often quoted by subsequent sources. See Nahmanides, *Torat ha-Adam*, p. 41; note Karo's commentary *Beth Yosef* on Jacob ben Asher, *Arba'ah Turim—Yoreh Deah*, para. 336:1.

41. See *Yoma* 85b; note *Yoma* 83a, *Gittin* 9b; Karo, *Shulhan Arukh—Orah Hayyim*, para. 329:1–3.

42. Karo, *Shulhan Arukh—Yoreh Deah*, para. 328:1–4.

43. Jacob ben Asher, *Arba'ah Turim*, and Karo, *Shulhan Arukh—Yoreh Deah*, para. 336:1.

44. Solomon ibn Verga, *Shevet Yehudah* (Jerusalem: n.p., 1955), chap. 41, p. 113.

45. See *Tosefta*, ed. Moses Zuckermandel (Vienna, 1877), *Gittin* 4:6, p. 328; Jacob ben Asher, *Arba'ah Turim*, and Karo, *Shulhan Arukh—Yoreh Deah*, para. 336:1; also Nahmanides, "*Torat ha-Adam*," p. 41. Nahmanides's view is often quoted in the commentaries to the late medieval codes, e.g., Karo's *Beth Yosef* on Jacob ben Asher, *Arba'ah Turim—Yoreh Deah*, para. 336:1, and Shabbatai ben Meir's seventeenth-century commentary *Siftei Kohen* on Karo, *Shulhan Arukh—Yoreh Deah*, para. 336:1.

46. See, e.g., Karo *Shulhan Arukh—Yoreh Deah*, para. 336:2; note Immanuel Jakobovits, "Medicine and Judaism" [Hebrew], *Ha-Rofeh ha-Ivri* (1956) Part 2, pp. 87–99, 156–59.

47. *Baba Kamma* 85a.

48. See, e.g., Rashi to *Kiddushin* 82a; ibn Falaquera, p. 49. Compare Plato, *Republic* 1:342. A blessing recorded in the Talmud refers to God as He who heals for free, as compared to the physician who heals for a fee; see *Berakhot* 60a.

49. *Ta'anit* 21b.

50. *Sefer Hasidim,* ed. Reuven Margaliot (Jerusalem: Mosad ha-Rav Kook, 1960), para. 592, p. 385.

51. "A Father's Admonition by Judah ibn Tibbon," in *Hebrew Ethical Wills,* p. 76. Plato also had stressed the pedagogic role of the physician; see *Laws* 9, para. 857.

52. Joseph ibn Kaspi, "Guide to Knowledge," in *Hebrew Ethical Wills,* p. 136; Maimonides, *Treatise on Asthma,* p. 84; ibn Falaquera, p. 43.

53. Maimonides, *Hanhagat ha-Beri'ut,* p. 43; see also Friedenwald, vol. 1, p. 25.

54. Maimonides, *Treatise on Asthma,* p. 83.

55. See Friedenwald, vol. 2, p. 273.

56. Maimonides, *Hanhagat ha-Beri'ut,* p. 44.

57. Maimonides, *Treatise on Asthma,* p. 99.

58. Hayyim ibn Attar, *Or ha-Hayyim* to Exod. 21:19, in standard editions of Hebrew Scripture with commentaries. See also Joel Sirkes's commentary *Bayit Hadash* to Jacob ben Asher, *Arba'ah Turim—Yoreh Deah,* para. 336:1.

59. See Yehudah Ayash, *Shevet Yehudah* (Livorno, 1683) on Karo, *Shulhan Arukh—Yoreh Deah,* para. 336:1.

60. *Midrash Leviticus Rabbah* 16:8.

61. See Karo, *Shulhan Arukh—Yoreh Deah,* para. 116:5 particularly Isserles's gloss there.

62. *Baba Kamma* 91b; Maimonides, *Mishneh Torah—Sefer Nezikin,* "Laws of Murder and the Preservation of Life," 11:4–5.

63. *Abodah Zarah* 18a.

64. Quoted in Israel Chodos, "A Critical Edition of Shem Tov Ben Joseph Falaquera's *Bate Hanhagat Guf Habari,*" *Ha-Rofeh ha- Ivri* (1938) Part 1, p. 193.

65. *Midrash Leviticus Rabbah* 34:3; see *Shabbat* 50b and *Berakhot* 53b.

66. Maimonides, *Treatise on Asthma,* p. 6.

67. Ibid., p. 36, see also pp. 73–74; id., *Hanhagat ha-Beri'ut,* pp. 67– 68. On smoking, see Fred Rosner, *Modern Medicine and Jewish Law* (New York: Yeshivah Univ. Press, 1972), and A. Aberbach, "Smoking and Halakhah," *Tradition* 10, no. 3 (1969): 49–60.

68. Maimonides, *Mishneh Torah—Sefer ha-Mada,* "Hilkhot Deot," 4:15.

69. Id., *Treatise on Asthma,* p. 24.

70. Id., *Hanhagat ha-Bri'ut,* p. 31; see also pp. 31–43 on diet. In addition to the citations given above, Maimonides also discussed diet in his medical aphorisms; see Maimonides, *The Medical Aphorisms of Moses Maimonides,* trans. Fred Rosner and S. Muntner (New York: Yeshivah Univ. Press, 1971), chap. 20.

71. Zabara, pp. 116–18.

72. Ibid., pp. 120, 123.

73. On proper diet, also see Abraham ibn Ezra's observation in his commentary to Exod. 23:25 that all illnesses come from food. Also, Judah ibn Tibbon's "ethical will" in Abrahams, *Hebrew Ethical Wills,* p. 76, and Chodos, Part 1, pp. 113–25, 189–95, Part 2, pp. 150–70.

74. See, e.g., Maimonides, *Mishneh Torah—Sefer ha-Mada,* "Hilkhot Deot" 1:2–2:4; id., *Eight Chapters,* chap. 4, pp. 54–55.

75. See Abraham Halkin, "Classical and Arabic Material in ibn Aknin's 'Hygiene of the Soul,'" *Proceedings of the American Academy for Jewish Research,* vol. 4, p. 111, and S. Muntner, "A Medieval Treatise on Melancholy," *Ha-Rofeh ha-Ivri* (1953), Part 1, pp. 62–80, 163–65.

76. Maimonides, *Medical Aphorisms*, chap. 18, p. 51.

77. Maimonides, *Mishneh Torah—Sefer ha-Mada, "Hilkhot Deot,"* 4:14.

78. See Chodos, Part 1, pp. 114, 191.

79. Ibid., 4:14, 20.

80. *Berakhot* 60b.

81. Ibid., 55a.

82. Maimonides, *Mishneh Torah—Sefer ha-Mada, "Hilkhot Deot,"* 4:1, 13.

83. Ibid., 4:14, 20.

84. See, e.g., Maimonides, *Guide*, Book 3, chap. 12. Eng. trans., p. 445.

85. Luzzatto, chap. 9, p. 122.

86. For a general discussion on the nature of health, see, e.g., *International Encyclopedia of the Social Sciences*, ed. David L. Sills (New York: Macmillan, 1968–74), s.v. "Health," 5:330–36; *Encyclopedia of Bioethics*, ed. Warren T. Reich (New York: Free Press, 1978), 2: 599–606; *Contemporary Issues in Bioethics*, eds. Tom L. Beauchamp and Leroy Walters (Belmont, Calif.: Wadsworth, 1982), chap. 2; and Leon R. Kass, "Regarding the End of Medicine and the Pursuit of Health," chapter in *Ethical Issues in Modern Medicine*, ed. Hunt and Arras (Palo Alto, Calif.: Mayfield, 1977), pp. 483–515.

87. Plato, *Charmides* 156–57.

88. Maimonides, *Eight Chapters*, chap. 1, p. 38; see also Maimonides, *Mishneh Torah—Sefer ha-Mada, "Hilkhot Deot,"* 2:1. Compare Aristotle, *Nicomachean Ethics* 1:13.

89. See Abraham Halkin, "Classical and Arabic Material in ibn Aknin's 'Hygiene of the Soul,'" *Proceedings of the American Academy for Jewish Research* 4, pp. 25–147.

90. Abraham ibn Daud, *Emunah Ramah*, vol. 3, p. 98, Maimonides's use of the term "the improvement of the moral qualities" seems to be an allusion to Solomon ibn Gabirol's moral treatise by that name. To be sure, ibn Gabirol conceived of ethics to be—figuratively speaking—like the attempt of the physician to rearrange the bodily elements with a view toward restoring harmony, which is health. See ibn Gabirol, *The Improvement of Moral Qualities*, p. 16, n. 3.

91. See Maimonides, *Mishneh Torah—Sefer ha-Mada, "Hilkhot Deot,"* 2:1.

92. Maimonides, *Medical Aphorisms* 25:9, p. 203.

93. On the analogy of medicine and morality, see also Joseph ibn Kaspi, in *Hebrew Ethical Wills*, ed. Abrahams, p. 136, "It is a familiar truth that sickness of the soul and its cure are analogous to the disease and the healing of the body." Also *Sefer ha-Yashar*, chap. 7, pp. 156–59.

94. Ephraim Lunshitz, *Klei Yakar* on Deut. 4:9, in standard editions of Hebrew Scripture with commentaries.

95. ibn Falaquera, p. 31.

96. Maimonides, *Eight Chapters*, chap. 5, p. 71.

97. Green, p. 234.

98. Maimonides, *Treatise on Asthma*, p. 89.

99. *Yoma* 82a.

100. Mordecai Winkler, *Levushei Mordecai, "Hoshen Mishpat,"* no. 39, quoted in David M. Feldman, *Health and Medicine in the Jewish Tradition* (New York: Crossroad, 1986), p. 46.

101. Zabara, p. 103.

5. A VIEW OF EUTHANASIA

1. *Pesahim* 75a.

2. On definitions of death and "brain death" in Jewish law, see Fred Rosner and J. David Bleich, eds., *Jewish Bioethics* (New York: Hebrew Publishing Co., 1969), pp. 277–317, and Gedaliah Rabinowitz's and Mordecai Konigsberg's Hebrew essay "The Definition of Death and the Time of Death According to Jewish Law" in *Ha-Darom* 32 (1970): 59–76. In a resolution, the (Conservative) Rabbinical Assembly has opted for a definition of death related to the "cessation of spontaneous brain function." It should be noted that death is increasingly being understood as a process rather than as an event, thus making the exact moment of death difficult to determine precisely.

3. On the requirement to sacrifice one's own life rather than transgress, see, e.g., *Sanhedrin* 74a, *Yoma* 82a; Karo, *Shulhan Arukh—Yoreh Deah*, para. 357. Because martyrdom represented the ultimate expression of self-sacrifice for God (*Kiddush ha-Shem*), it has been considered the highest virtue—transcending the obligation to preserve life—by many prominent rabbinic figures and Jewish religious movements throughout history. In early post-biblical Jewish literature, see, e.g., 2 Macc. 14:37–46; *Berakhot* 61b (the martyrdom of Rabbi Akiba); *Sanhedrin* 110b; *Sifra* (Vienna: Shlossberg, 1862), "*Emor*" no. 9, p. 9; *Mekhilta de-Rabbi Ishmael*, ed. Lauterbach, "*Ba-Hodesh*," chap. 6 end, p. 247; *Midrash Song of Songs* 2:7. Emulating Rabbi Akiba, the medieval German Hasidim extolled and followed his example. For example, commenting on the verse, "For He is our God, and we are the people in His care" (Ps. 95:7), the *Sefer Hasidim*, ed. J. Wistinetzki and J. Freimann (Frankfurt: Wahrmann Verlag, 1924), no. 256, p. 84, comments, "When do we acknowledge that He is our God? When we are slaughtered like sheep for the sanctification of His Name, He is our God." Also, see the discussion and sources collected in Shalom Spiegel, *The Last Trial* (New York: Pantheon, 1967). On Hasidic attitudes to martyrdom during the Holocaust, see Pesach Shindler, "The Holocaust and Kiddush Ha-Shem in Hasidic Thought," *Tradition* 13/14 (1973): 88–105, where the idea of martyrdom as a privilege is discussed. See also Charles W. Reines, "The Jewish Attitude Toward Suicide," *Judaism* 10 (1961): 161–70.

4. Jewish tradition recognizes certain categories of "justifiable homicide." One such category is killing in self-defense; see, e.g., Exod. 22:1, *Sanhedrin* 72a–b. Another such category relates to killing a potential murderer to ensure the safety of his or her intended victim; see, e.g., *Sanhedrin* 73a; Maimonides, *Mishneh Torah—Sefer Nezikin*, "Laws of Murderers," 1:9. *The Book of Torts*, Eng. trans. Hyman Klein (New Haven: Yale Univ. Press, 1954), pp. 196–97. Other examples include killing in certain types of "just wars" and capital punishment.

5. *Encyclopedia Judaica*, s.v. "Homicide" by Haim H. Cohen. See also the discussion within this chapter on this issue. Note, e.g., Rashi on Exodus 21:4; *Mekhilta d'Rabbi Ishmael*, ed. Horovitz and Rabin, "*Mishpatim*," no. 4, p. 263.

6. *Abodah Zarah* 18a.

7. *Sefer Hasidim*, ed. Wistinetzki, no. 315, p. 100.

8. *Semahot* 1:1, 1:4. *The Tractate Mourning*, Eng. trans. Dov Zlotnick (New Haven: Yale Univ. Press, 1966), p. 30. For definitions and discussion of *goses*, see *Encyclopedia Talmudit*, vol. 5, 393–403. See especially Isserles on Karo, *Shulhan Arukh—Even ha-Ezer*, para. 121:7, and *Shulhan Arukh—Hoshen Mishpat*, para. 211:2; Yom Tov Lipmann Heller's sixteenth-century commentary *Tosfot Yom Tov* on *M. Arakhin* 1:3, in standard editions of the Mishnah.

9. For additional sources that prohibit active euthanasia, note the following: *Shabbat* 151b and Rashi there. The mishnaic text there reads, "He who closes the eyes [of a dying person] at the point of death [thereby accelerating death] is a murderer." In his commentary to *Baba Kamma* 85a, Solomon Luria observed that it is not permissible to accelerate death to

relieve suffering; the patient is forced to "choose life." See Luria, *Yam Shel Shelomo*, "*Perek ha-Hovel*," no. 59. Similarly, Moses Schreiber maintained that even a suffering individual who actively ends his or her life "is a murderer and dies in guilt." See his *Responsa Hatam Sofer—Yoreh Deah*, no. 326. "To do anything that causes death to be accelerated is forbidden," wrote Moses Isserles, *Darkhei Moshe* to Jacob ben Asher, *Arba'ah Turim—Yoreh Deah*, para. 339:1, in standard editions of *Arba'ah Turim*.

10. Maimonides, *Mishneh Torah—Sefer Shofetim*, "Laws of Mourning," 4:5. Eng. trans., p. 174.

11. Jacob ben Asher, *Arba'ah Turim—Yoreh Deah*, para. 339.

12. Karo, *Shulhan Arukh—Yoreh Deah*, para. 339:1.

13. Solomon Ganzfried, *Kitzur Shulhan Arukh* (Lwow, 1860), *Yoreh Deah*, para. 194:1.

14. *Abodah Zarah* 18a. Also see Ezek. 18:4; Maimonides, *Mishneh Torah—Sefer Nezikim*, "Laws of Murder," 1:4. Eng. trans., p. 195. David ibn Zimra's commentary to Maimonides, *Mishneh Torah—Sefer Shofetim*, "Laws of the Sanhedrin," 18:6; Shneur Zalman of Liady, *Shulhan Arukh ha-Rav* (Zhitomir, 1856), *Yoreh Deah*, "Laws of Injuring the Body," para. 4.

15. See *Yoma* 84–85; Karo, *Shulhan Arukh—Orah Hayyim*, para. 329:4.

16. *Baba Kamma* 91b; *Abodah Zarah* 18a; *Midrash Genesis Rabbah* 34:13; Maimonides, *Mishneh Torah—Sefer Nezikin*, "Laws of Murderers," 2:3. Eng. trans., p. 199. Note *Midrash Pesikta Rabbati*, ed. Friedmann, 24:1, p. 134b. See also *Sefer Hasidim*, ed. Margaliot, nos. 675–76, pp. 428–29, where neglecting one's own physical and spiritual health is considered a form of self-injury, and even of suicide. On self-injury, see also *Tosefta*, ed. Zuckermandel, *Baba Kamma*, chap. 9, p. 366, and *Yalkut Shimoni* on Gen. 9:5 "Noah," no. 60. In the medieval codes, see Maimonides, *Mishneh Torah—Sefer Nezikin*, "Laws of Wounding and Damaging," 5:1. Eng. trans., pp. 176–77; and Karo, *Shulhan Arukh—Hoshen Mishpat*, para. 420:31. Also Solomon Luria, *Yam Shel Shelomo* on *Baba Kamma* 91a, no. 59.

17. *Kiddushin* 42b; *Midrash Genesis Rabbah* 34:14. Note Peretz Segal, "No Agency for an Illegal Act," *Annual of the Institute for Research in Jewish Law* 9/10(1982–83): 73–95.

18. See the gloss of Shabbatai ben Meir, *Siftei Kohein* on Karo, *Shulhan Arukh—Yoreh Deah*, para. 336:1, in standard editions of the *Shulhan Arukh*.

19. On the specific issue of withdrawal of insulin treatment from a diabetic, see Nissan Telushkin's Hebrew essay, "*Ha-Nimuk ha-Musari she-ba-Mitzvot ha-Teluyot ba-Aretz*," *Orha-Mizrah* 2 (1961): 20–24, and Abraham Steinberg's Hebrew essay, "Mercy Killing" in *Assia* 5, no. 3 (Jan. 1978): 30–31. See also Fred Rosner, "Rabbi Moses Feinstein on the Treatment of the Terminally Ill," *Judaism* 37 (Spring 1988): 188–99.

20. *Sefer Hasidim*, ed. Wistinetzki, no. 315, p. 100.

21. See Isserles's gloss on Karo, *Shulhan Arukh—Yoreh Deah*, para. 339:1.

22. *Sefer Hasidim*, ed. Wistinetzki, no. 316, p. 100; Karo, *Shulhan Arukh—Yoreh Deah*, para. 339:1.

23. Isserles's commentary *Darkhei Moshe* to Jacob ben Asher, *Arba'ah Turim—Yoreh Deah*, para. 339:1.

24. *Sefer Hasidim*, ed. Wistinetzki, no. 316, p. 100; ed. Margaliot, no. 723, p. 443; see Joshua Boaz on Isaac Alfasi's commentary to *Mo'ed Katan* 16b, in standard editions of the Talmud.

While most of the sources agree that the removal of external impediments to the process of dying is permitted, there is disagreement regarding the removal of treatment that has already begun. The classic reference in the *Sefer Hasidim* refers to the removal of things like the sound of wood being chopped, which would disturb a patient in a death swoon. This precedent, however, would not justify the removal of already-employed heroic measures.

Consequently, many contemporary orthodox authorities sanction a decision not to introduce artificial life-support systems but prohibit the removal of such once introduced.

The *Sefer Hasidim*, in the same text, i.e., ed. Wistinetzki, no. 315, p. 100, prohibits "placing salt in the mouth of a dying person to prevent death from overtaking him or her." In a case in which salt already has been placed, most authorities prohibit its removal. Such action is proscribed as an act of active euthanasia, which would cause the patient to be touched or moved, i.e., an action that would actively accelerate death. See, e.g., Karo, *Shulhan Arukh*— *Yoreh Deah*, para. 339:1, commentaries of Isserles, Shabbatai ben Meir, and David ben Samuel. However, in his note on this text, Zevi ben Azriel of Vilna, *Beit Lehem Yehudah* (Zulka, 1733), maintained that removal of the salt is an example of passive euthanasia in keeping with the principle that the removal of any impediment to the process of dying is not an action at all and hence permissible. In so doing, he cautioned, the patient must not be moved. He, therefore, interpreted the prohibition of the earlier authorities as being related to the apprehension of moving the patient and not to an absolute prohibition against the removal of the salt. According to this view, if translated to contemporary parlance, the introduction of heroic measures to a terminal patient is not encouraged and may be prohibited. However, if heroic measures have been introduced, they may be removed. See also C. D. Halevi, "Disconnecting a Terminal Patient From an Artificial Respirator," in *Crossroads* (Jerusalem: Zomet, 1987), pp. 147–55.

25. Jacob ben Samuel, *Beit Ya'akov* (Dyrenfurerth, 1696), no. 59. In this responsum, the author also maintained that one may not violate the Sabbath to save a dying patient. These views are rebutted by the eighteenth-century halakhist Jacob Reischer in *Shevut Ya'akov* (Lwow, 1860), 3:13. For a review of these arguments, see Solomon Eiger, *Gilyonei Maharshah* to Karo, *Shulhan Arukh—Yoreh Deah*, para. 339:1, in standard editions of the *Shulhan Arukh*.

26. *Sefer Hasidim*, ed. Margoliot, no. 234, p. 208.

27. See, e.g., *Sanhedrin* 77a; Maimonides, *Mishneh Torah—Sefer Nezikin*, "Laws of Murderers," 3:10. Eng. trans. p. 204. Leopold Greenwald, *Kol Bo al-Aveilut* (New York: Moriah Printing Co., 1947), 1:10, p. 21.

28. *Sefer Hasidim*, ed. Margaliot, no. 234, p. 208.

29. See, e.g., Moses Feinstein, *Iggrot Moshe—Yoreh Deah*, 2 vols. (New York: Balshon, 1963), vol. 2, p. 174, where the view is that it is forbidden to prolong the agony of a *goses* unnecessarily.

30. Jakobovits, pp. 123–24. See also Simon Federbush, "The Problems of Euthanasia in Jewish Tradition," *Judaism* 1 (1952): 64–68; G. B. Haliburd, "Euthanasia," *Jewish Law Annual* 1 (1978): 196–99; Fred Rosner and J. David Bleich, eds., *Jewish Bioethics*, pp. 33, 253–331; Steven Saltzman, "The Sanctity of Life in Jewish Law" (D.H.L. diss., Jewish Theological Seminary, 1982), pp. 227–312. Note Immanuel Jakobovits's Hebrew essay on euthanasia in *Ha-Pardes* 31:1, 3 (1956): 16–19, 28–31.

31. *Beitzah* 32b.

32. Israel Lipschutz, *Tiferet Israel* (Hanover, 1830) on *M. Yoma* 8:3; *Semahot* 1:1.

33. *M. Arakhin* 1:3; *Arakhin* 6b. However, on suffering as being preferable to death, see, e.g., Ps. 118:18; Yom Tov Lippmann Heller, *Tosafot Yom Tov* on *M. Sota* 1:9; Solomon Luria, *Yam Shel Shelomo* on *Baba Kamma* 91a, no. 59. Note Eliezer Waldenberg, *Tzitz Eliezer*, 10 vols. (Jerusalem: n.p., 1954—), vol. 9, 47, 5.

34. The case of King Saul's death provoked considerable discussion in classical Jewish literature that concerned itself with suicide. Wounded in battle, Saul asked to be killed rather than to be handed over to his enemies. According to one version, Saul killed himself by falling on his sword (1 Sam. 31:1–6). According to a second version, he asked a youth to kill him: "Stand over me and finish me off, for I am in agony and barely alive" (2 Sam. 1:9), and the

Amalekite youth complied. David consequently had this youth executed for killing God's "anointed" (2 Sam. 1:13–17). Commentators debate whether the youth was justified in killing Saul, whether David was justified in killing the youth, and if so, on what grounds? The text suggests that David had the youth executed not because he put Saul out of agony but because he presumed to slay God's anointed king. In any case, Saul was found justified in his action by some rabbinic authorities because he chose death, martyrdom, rather than to be abused by the enemies of Israel, a precedent followed throughout Jewish history. What is particularly relevant to euthanasia is the comment of the twelfth-century biblical commentator David Kimhi (Radak) on this episode. Kimhi commented (to 2 Sam. 1:9) that Saul's statement means: "I suffer so severely from my wound, and my soul is yet in me; therefore, I want you to accelerate my death." Thus, according to Kimhi, Saul's motive was to choose death rather than to continue to suffer, rather than to choose death to escape being abused by his enemies. If both Saul's action and his motive (according to Kimhi) are considered justifiable, then this text would serve as a precedent for active euthanasia. Kimhi's commentary is found in standard editions of Hebrew Scripture with commentaries. On Saul's action see the lengthy discussion of Joel Sirkes's *Bayit Hadash* and Karo's *Beit Yosef* on Jacob ben Asher, *Arba'ah Turim—Yoreh Deah*, para. 157, and Israel Lipschutz's *Tiferet Yisrael* on *M. Yoma* chap. 8, where he proscribes Saul's action. Sirkes's commentary is found in standard editions of *Arba'ah Turim*.

35. *Tosafot* on *Gittin* 57b and *Abodah Zarah* 18a. Some primary texts and some commentaries stress the notion that one can take one's own life to avoid sufferings certain to result in death while others stress the idea that death is only preferable when that suffering will lead to such sins as sexual sins (as in the case of the children) or to apostasy (see, e.g., *Ketubot* 33b). Others claim that these instances are not applicable to euthanasia since here the affliction is the result of human oppression whereas in cases of euthanasia, the affliction is from illness which may be the will of God; see, e.g., Jakobovits in *Ha-Pardes*, 31, no. 1:29. Nevertheless, it is noteworthy that the language of the deathbed confessional of a dying person is remarkably reminiscent of that of a martyr. In one version of the confessional, the patient says, "I surrender my life, my body and my soul for the unification of the Divine Name." Here there is a clear parallel between the martyr and the dying person.

36. One finds the view in the Talmud, e.g., *Abodah Zarah* 27b; and in the medieval codes, e.g., Karo, *Shulhan Arukh—Yoreh Deah*, para. 155: 5–7 and Abraham Zevi Eisenstadt's commentary *Pithei Teshuvah* there that it is sometimes preferable, particularly in the case of a terminal patient, to choose death rather than to be treated by a gentile physician who may try to entice the Jewish patient to apostasy or who may use "idolatrous" practices to effect a cure. In such instances extending "momentary life is not considered." This clearly indicates that the preservation of life in itself was not always of paramount importance or consideration.

37. Saul Berlin, *Responsa Besomim Rosh* [Hebrew] (Berlin, 1793). In some subsequent editions, this responsum has been eliminated by the printer. No doubt the reason is because Berlin's view, which, in effect, redefines "suicide," is without precedent in halakhic literature.
Berlin was a protoreformer and a distinguished talmudist who associated with the "enlightened" circle of Moses Mendelssohn. Interestingly, Berlin's collection of responsa, *Besomim Rosh*, is a pseudepigraphal work. Berlin claimed that this collection of responsa was written, not by himself, but by the famous fourteenth-century halakhic authority, Asher ben Yehiel, known by the acronym Rosh. Actually, these responsa were written by Berlin himself. The book was attacked as a forgery soon after its first publication. On this whole matter, see discussion and sources noted in Jacobs, *Theology in the Responsa*, Appendix 1, pp. 347–52; M. Siemet, "The *Besamim Rosh* of Rabbi Saul Berliner," *Kiryat Sefer* 48 (1972/1973): 509–23. On the initial question of whether mourning for a suicide is prohibited, see the uncharacteristically "liberal" view of Moses Schreiber, *Responsa Hatam Sofer*, no. 326. Schreiber holds

that relatives of a suicide should indeed observe mourning rites. Also, see the lengthy discussion in Eisenstadt's *Pithei Teshuvah* to Karo, *Shulhan Arukh—Yoreh Deah*, para. 345:2, where suicide is virtually defined out of existence; note the reference there to the *Besomim Rosh*. See also in this regard the lengthy discussion and sources noted in Greenwald, pp. 319–20.

38. *Yalkut Shimoni*, "Proverbs," No. 943.

39. Contemporary halakhists are divided on the question of whether "pulling the plug" is a form of withholding treatment (i.e., passive euthanasia), and therefore permitted, or an overt act of intervention designed to shorten life (i.e., active euthanasia), and therefore prohibited. See discussion and sources in J. D. Bleich, "The Quinlan Case: A Jewish Perspective," in *Jewish Bioethics*, ed. Rosner and Bleich, p. 275, n. 2.

40. For praying or not praying for the recovery of a sick individual actually *causing* life or death, see the statement of Rav Dimi and the commentaries on that statement in *Nedarim* 40a.

41. *Ketubot* 104a. On praying for one's own death, see, e.g., 1 Kings 19:4, Jon. 4:3, *Ta'anit* 23a. On praying for the death of another person, see *Baba Metzia* 84a. However, see an opposite view in Waldenberg, 9:47, 5. Steinberg, p. 36, refers to a specific prayer for another to die to free him or her from pain. Without noting a specific source, Steinberg refers to such a prayer in Isaac Lampronti's *Pahad Yitzhak*.

42. Nissim (Rabbenu Nissim) on *Nedarim* 40a, in standard editions of the Talmud. In his nineteenth-century commentary on *M. Yoma* chap. 8, Israel Lipschutz maintained that the case of the handmaiden's praying for the death of Rabbi Judah (*Ketubot* 104a) relates not only to the case of Rabbi Judah but to any individual case because "great suffering is worse than death." Lipschutz did, however, claim that taking any action other than prayer that accelerates death is forbidden.

43. Hayyim Palaggi's responsum is found in vol. 1 of his collected responsa, *Hikkeke Lev* (Salonika, 1840), no. 50, pp. 90a–91a. I am grateful to the Klau Library of Hebrew Union College for lending me this volume for use. A translation and extended analysis of this responsum is found in Peter J. Haas, "Toward a Semiotic Study of Jewish Moral Discourse: The Case of Responsa," *Semeia* 34 (1985): 59–85. Also note Greenwald, 1:9, p. 20, no. 14, where Pelaggi's responsum is briefly summarized. See also the reference to Palaggi in Solomon B. Freehof, *Reform Responsa* (Cincinnati: Hebrew Union College Press, 1960), p. 120–21.

44. *Niddah* 19b.

45. *Sanhedrin* 45a, 52a; *Baba Kamma* 51a; *Pesahim* 75a. In his eighteenth-century commentary to the Talmud, *Glosses of Ya'avetz*, in standard editions of the Talmud, Jacob Emden observed that the practice of giving a painkilling drug to a criminal about to be executed was practiced so that the pain of execution would not hamper the exit of the soul and extend the person's pain and anguish. See gloss to *Sanhedrin* 43a.

46. *Arakhin* 6b.

47. See, e.g., *Midrash Song of Songs Rabbah* 2:7. For a diametrically opposite view, see Solomon Luria, *Yam Shel Shelomo* on *Baba Kamma*, "Perek ha-Hovel" no. 59.

48. If one person kills another by performing a surgical procedure aimed at alleviating pain where the condition is not life threatening, there may be no legal culpability. See, e.g., Menahem Meiri, *Beit ha-Behirah—Sanhedrin* (Jerusalem: n.p., 1965), p. 85a. See also Nahmanides, *Torat ha-Adam*, vol. 2, pp. 42–43. Also note the discussion and sources quoted by Greenwald, p. 21, no. 16. On endangering the individual with possible death regarding treatment for an ailment or a potential ailment that may or may not be life threatening, see Lipschutz, *M. Yoma*, chap. 8. See the extensive discussion and sources noted in *Jewish Bioethics*, ed. Rosner and Bleich, pp. 32–34.

49. Rashi on Exod. 21:14. Also see *Mekhilta de-Rabbi Yishmael,* ed. Horovitz and Rabin, *"Mishpatim,"* 4, p. 263.

50. *Sanhedrin* 78a; Maimonides, *Mishneh Torah—Sefer Nezikin,* "Laws of Murderers," 2:8. Eng. trans., p. 200. On the definition of a *tereifah:* Rashi on *Sanhedrin* 78a maintains that the definition of a human *tereifah* is the same as that of an animal *tereifah* while Maimonides disagrees and defines a human *tereifah* as one with internal injuries. See Steinberg, pp. 12–13. Note the important responsum by Schreiber, *Hatam Sofer—Yoreh Deah,* no. 52. See also Moses Feinstein, "Medical Responsa," in *Crossroads,* pp. 129–34. Note the significant study by Daniel B. Sinclair, *Tradition and the Biological Revolution* (Edinburgh: Edinburgh Univ. Press, 1989), pp. 19–70.

See also the intriguing argument by Werner in *Torah she-be-al Peh* 18 (1976), no. 40, which states that active euthanasia is not prohibited to Gentiles. This argument is based upon the Amalekite's killing of Saul to end his agony (2 Sam. 1:5–10), and the torturer's actions in the death of Hanina ben Teradion, *Abodah Zarah* 18a.

51. See David M. Shohet, "Mercy Death in Jewish Law," *Conservative Judaism* 8, no. 3 (1952): 1–15.

6. THE ETHICS OF GIVING AND RECEIVING

1. On Jewish philanthropy in the United States, see, e.g., Marc Lee Raphael, ed., *Understanding American Jewish Philanthropy* (New York: Ktav, 1979); Harry L. Lurie, *A Heritage Affirmed* (Philadelphia: Jewish Publication Society, 1961); Philip Bernstein, *To Dwell in Unity* (Philadelphia: Jewish Publication Society, 1983).

2. For a historical survey of *zedakah,* see Ephraim Frisch, *An Historical Survey of Jewish Philanthropy* (New York: Cooper Square Publishers, 1924); Yehudah Bergman, *Ha-Zedakah be-Yisrael* (Jerusalem: Tarshish, 1944); Kaufmann Kohler, "The Historical Development of Jewish Charity," chapter in *Hebrew Union College and Other Addresses* (Cincinnati: Ark Publishing Co., 1916), pp. 229–53; Israel Chipkin, "Judaism and Social Welfare," in *The Jews,* ed. Finkelstein, vol. 2, pp. 1043–75. For discussion of *zedakah* in the rabbinic period, see Roger Brooks, *Support for the Poor in the Mishnaic Law of Agriculture: Tractate Pe'ah* (Chico, Calif.: Scholars Press, 1983); G. F. Moore, vol. 2, pp. 162–79; Ephraim E. Urbach, *"Magamot Datiot ve-Hevratiot be-Torat ha-Zedakah shel Hazal,"* *Zion* 16 (1951): 1–27. On the medieval period, see, e.g., Israel Abrahams, *Jewish Life in the Middle Ages* (New York: Meridian, 1958), pp. 307–39; Salo Baron, *The Jewish Community,* 3 vols. (Philadelphia: Jewish Publication Society, 1942), vol. 2, pp. 319–33. Also note, Jacob Neusner, *Tzedakah: Can Jewish Philanthropy Buy Jewish Survival?* (Chappaqua, N.Y.: Rossel Books, 1982); Isadore Twersky, "Some Aspects of the Jewish Attitude Toward the Welfare State," *Tradition* 5, no. 2 (Spring 1963): 137–58; David Hartman and Tzvi Marx, "Charity," chapter in *Contemporary Jewish Religious Thought,* ed. Arthur A. Cohen and Paul Mendes-Flohr (New York: Scribner's, 1987), pp. 47–55; Meir Tamari, *With All Your Possessions* (New York: Macmillan, 1987), pp. 25–61, 248–69.

3. *Baba Batra* 9a.

4. Maimonides, *Mishneh Torah—Sefer Zera'im,* "Laws Regarding Gifts to the Poor," 9:3, *The Book of Agriculture,* Eng. trans. Isaac Klein (New Haven: Yale Univ. Press, 1979), p. 77. Unless otherwise noted, citations from Maimonides in this chapter come from this source.

5. Nahmanides, *Kitve Rabbenu Moshe ben Nahman,* vol. 1, pp. 207–8. This citation comes from Nahmanides's "Sermon on Ecclesiastes" in which he offers a lengthy discussion of *zedakah* in biblical and rabbinic literature, pp. 204–10.

6. Solomon Schechter, "Notes of Lectures in Jewish Philanthropy," *Studies in Judaism, Third Series* (Philadelphia: Jewish Publication Society, 1924), p. 240. A lengthy but diffuse

work, *Me'il Zedakah* was published only twice, i.e., 1731 (Smyrna) and 1859 (Lemberg, i.e., Lwow). An abridged edition, *Zedakah l'Hayyim* was published by Hayyim Palaggi in 1873. An extensive study of the *Me'il Zedakah* was written by the late Abraham Cronbach, "The *Me'il Zedakah,*" *Hebrew Union College Annual* 11 (1936): 503–69, 12/13 (1938): 635–97, 14 (1939): 479–559.

Elijah ha-Kohen of Smyrna, the author of *Me'il Zedakah* was a prolific author, a popular preacher, an erudite scholar and cabalist, and an important Jewish communal leader in eighteenth-century Turkey. Some of his works were published, while others survive only in manuscript form or were altogether lost. There is evidence that he was a Sabbatean, a follower of the seventeenth-century Jewish pseudomessiah, Shabbatai Zevi. Either his Sabbatean leanings or the thoroughly diffuse and disorganized nature of the *Me'il Zedakah* have prevented it from achieving the wide circulation and popularity one might otherwise expect of the only exhaustive study of *zedakah* in Jewish literature.

7. Schechter, pp. 241–45.

8. *Ethics of the Fathers* 3:8.

9. Yehiel ben Yekutiel, p. 94.

10. *Midrash Pesikta Rabbati*, ed. Friedmann, chap. 25, p. 126b. Eng. trans. William G. Braude (New Haven: Yale Univ. Press, 1968), p. 514.

11. *Sefer Hasidim*, ed. Margaliot, para. 415, p. 297; ed. Wistinetzki, para. 1345, p. 331. On *zedakah* in the *Sefer Hasidim*, see Abraham Cronbach, "Social Thinking in the *Sefer Hasidim,*" *Hebrew Union College Annual* 22 (1949): 1–149.

12. Moses Alsheikh, *Torat Moshe*, 2 vols. (Warsaw: Munk, 1879), vol. 1, p. 80b. On *epitropos*, see Marcus Jastrow, *A Dictionary of the Targumim, the Talmud Babli and Yerushalmi*, 2d ed. (New York: Pardes, 1950), p. 102.

13. The idea that giving *zedakah* is the administration of funds "deposited" (Hebrew: *pikadon*) in our trust by God is pervasive in the literature. See, e.g., Bahya ibn Pakuda, pp. 222, 227, Matt, p. 100a; Abraham ha-Levi Horowitz, *Sefer Yesh Nohalin* (Jerusalem: Edison, 1960), no pagination. Also see Hayyim Hillel Ben-Sasson, *Hagut ve-Hanhagah* (Jerusalem: Mosad Bialik, 1959), pp. 73–74.

14. Cronbach, "The *Me'il Zedakah,*" p. 637.

15. *Tanna Debe Eliyahu Zutta*, in *Seder Eliyahu Rabbah ve-Seder Eliyahu Zutta*, ed. Meir Friedmann, 2d ed. (Jerusalem: Wahrmann, 1960), chap. 5, p. 181. Eng. trans. William G. Braude and Israel J. Kapstein (Philadelphia: Jewish Publication Society, 1981), p. 417. See also *Midrash Exodus Rabbah* 31:5.

16. See Yitzhak Baer, *A History of the Jews in Christian Spain*, 2 vols. (Philadelphia: Jewish Publication Society, 1966), vol. 1, p. 265, and sources noted there. According to the *Zohar*, *zedakah* brings about the union between the "male" and "female" potencies within the divine. See Isaiah Tishbi, *Mishnat ha-Zohar*, 2 vols. (Jerusalem: Mosad Bialik, 1961), vol. 2, p. 441, and sources noted there. On attitudes toward the poor and the wealthy in sixteenth-century central and eastern European Jewish literature, see Ben-Sasson, *Hagut ve-Hanhagah*, pp. 73–110; id., "*Osher ve-Oni be-Mishnato shel ha-Mokhiah Rabbi Ephraim Ish Lunschitz,*" *Zion* 19 (1954): 142–66.

17. See, e.g., *Baba Batra* 10a.

18. *Erubin* 41b, *Nedarim* 64b, *Baba Batra* 116a.

19. *Midrash Exodus Rabbah* 31:12, 14.

20. *Midrash Leviticus Rabbah* 34:6.

21. *Ketubot* 67b.

22. Maimonides, 7:3. See *P. Pe'ah* 8:8, 21a.

23. *Midrash Exodus Rabbah* 31:3. See also *Shabbat* 151b.

24. *Sifre on Deuteronomy*, ed. Finkelstein, "Re'eh," para. 118, p. 177. Eng. trans., pp. 163–64.

25. In the medieval codes, see Maimonides, 7:3; Jacob ben Asher, *Arba'ah Turim— Yoreh Deah*, para. 250.

26. *Tosefta Shekalim* 2:16.

27. *Ketubot* 67b.

28. *Baba Batra* 9b.

29. *P. Shekalim* 5:4; see also *Midrash on Psalms*, 41:3, p. 130b. Note Tzvi Marx, "Priorities in Zedakah and Their Implications," *Judaism* 28 (1969): 87. On this Talmudic text, the eighteenth-century commentator David Frankel of Berlin in his commentary, *Korban ha-Edah*, reiterated the goal of assuring the dignity of the recipient by utilizing means that will not lead to his embarrassment. *Korban ha-Edah* is found in standard editions of the Palestinian Talmud.

30. *Shabbat* 63a.

31. *Abot d'Rabbi Natan*, ed. Schechter, A, chap. 41, p. 66a. Eng. trans., p. 171.

32. Rashi on Lev. 25:35.

33. Maimonides, 7:6.

34. *M. Pe'ah* 8:9; cf. *Ketubot* 68a and *Abot d'Rabbi Natan*, chap. 3.

35. Maimonides, 7:9; *Ketubot* 67b.

36. Maimonides, 10:18.

37. Maimonides, 7:13.

38. Isaac Aboab, *Menorat ha-Ma'or* (Jerusalem: Mosad ha-Rav Kook, 1961), p. 411. Cf. Judah ben Asher *Arba'ah Turim—Yoreh Deah*, para. 251. See also Isaac Lampronti, *Pahad Yitzhak* (Lyck: Mekitzei Nirdamim, 1874), s.v. "zedakah," p. 8.

39. *Ketubot* 50a.

40. Maimonides, 6:12.

41. See, e.g., *Baba Batra* 8b, Maimonides, 8:10–12. Note Baron, pp. 333–43.

42. For an erudite and penetrating comparison of early rabbinic and early Christian views, see Urbach, pp. 18–27.

43. *Orhot Zaddikim*, trans. Seymour J. Cohen (New York: Feldheim Publishers, 1960), "On Generosity," p. 303.

44. *Sanhedrin* 39a.

45. Rashi on Exod. 22:24.

46. Maimonides, 7:1–2.

47. Ibid., 10:1.

48. Rashi on *Sukkah* 49b.

49. Judah Loew, *Netivot Olom*, "Netiv Gemilut Hasadim," vol. 1, chap. 2, p. 154.

50. *Sukkah* 49b.

51. Yehiel ben Yekutiel, p. 84.

52. Maimonides, *Guide*, Book 3, chap. 53, pp. 630–32.

53. *M. Pe'ah* 1:1.

54. Rashi on Genesis 47:29.

55. Aboab, p. 420; see also *Tosafot to Abodah Zarah* 17b.

56. Maimonides, 10:7–14. Though Maimonides's "eight levels" are the best known, other authors also depicted acts of benevolence in a series of gradations. While Maimonides's stages are presented in descending order, others arrange their gradations in ascending order

as if to describe the upward ascent on the rungs of a ladder of benevolent action. Legal codes, such as the *Arba'ah Turim* and the *Shulhan Arukh*, "*Yoreh Deah*," para. 249, follow Maimonides's approach. However, such works as Moses of Coucy's *Sefer Mitzvot Gadol* and Israel ibn Al-Nakawa's *Menorat ha-Ma'or* present the levels in an ascending order. See Abraham Cronbach, "The Gradations of Benevolence," *Hebrew Union College Annual* 16 (1941): 163–87. See also the eleven levels of *zedakah* of Matt, pp. 101–2.

57. Aboab, p. 417.

58. Rashi on *Hagigah* 5a. Cf. *Abot d'Rabbi Natan*, A, chap. 7, on the diverse attitudes of Abraham and Job to *zedakah*. On the question of whether *zedakah* is enforceable by a rabbinic court, see Twersky, p. 156 n. 29.

59. *Midrash Pesikta Rabbati*, ed. Friedmann, 11:2, Eng. trans., pp. 200–201.

60. *Baba Batra* 9bff.

61. *Pirke de Rabbi Eliezer*, Eng. trans., chap. 33, pp. 239–51.

62. *Nedarim* 64b.

63. *Midrash on Psalms*, ed. Buber, 41:2, 130a. Eng. trans., p. 436. Cf. *Midrash Eliyahu Zutta*, chap. 1.

64. For the *Me'il Zedakah*, see Cronbach, "The Me'il Zedakah," p. 671. In *Orhot Zaddikim*, p. 305. The rabbinic text is *Abot d'Rabbi Natan*, A, chap. 3 end. For an intensive discussion of *zedakah* practiced for self-serving motives as treated by Jewish legal tradition, see Eliakum Devorkes, *Ispaklarit ha-Zedakah* (Jerusalem: n.p., 1974), pp. 49–54.

65. *Gittin* 7a.

66. *Ketubot* 50a. In the codes, see Maimonides, 7:5; Karo, *Shulhan Arukh—Yoreh Deah*, para. 249:1–2.

67. *Ketubot* 67a.

68. There are many versions of this Hasidic story, see, e.g., Elie Wiesel, *Four Hasidic Masters* (London: Univ. of Notre Dame Press, 1978), pp. 97–98.

7. REPENTANCE IN JUDAISM

1. See *Shabbat* 89a.

2. Judah Loew, *Derekh ha-Hayyim* to *Abot* 3:15, pp. 147–48.

3. Maimonides, *Mishneh Torah—Sefer ha-Mada*, "Laws of Repentance," 5:1, 3, *The Book of Knowledge*, Eng. trans. Moses Hyamson (Jerusalem: Boys Town Publishers, 1965), pp. 86b–87a. Unless otherwise noted, citations in this chapter from Maimonides refer to this text.

4. Ibid., 5:4, p. 87a.

5. *Midrash Leviticus Rabbah* 10:5.

6. Maimonides, *Guide*, Book 3, chap. 36, p. 540.

7. A valuable anthology of references in classical Jewish religious literature on *teshuvah* is Hayyim Abramowitz, *Heikhal ha-Teshuvah* (B'nei Brak: Nezah, 1961). On sin and repentance in rabbinic theology, see, e.g., Jakob J. Petuchowski, "The Concept of *Teshuvah* in the Bible and the Talmud," *Judaism* 17 (1968): 175–86; G. F. Moore, vol. 1, pp. 460–545; Solomon Schechter, *Some Aspects of Rabbinic Theology* (New York: Macmillan, 1909), pp. 219–41, 293–343; Ephraim E. Urbach, *The Sages*, trans. Israel Abrahams (Cambridge, Mass.: Harvard Univ. Press, 1987), pp. 462–71; Adolf Buchler, *Studies in Sin and Atonement* (1928, reprint, New York: Ktav, 1967). Most of the significant medieval sources regarding repentance

are referred to within this chapter. On sin and repentance in modern Jewish theology, see, e.g., Kaufmann Kohler, *Jewish Theology* (1918, reprint, New York: Ktav, 1968), pp. 238–56; Samuel S. Cohon, *Judaism* (New York: Schocken, 1962), pp. 273–314; Alter B. Z. Metzger, *Rabbi Kook's Philosophy of Repentance* (New York: Yeshivah Univ. Press, 1968); Pinhas Peli, ed., *Soloveitchik on Repentance* (Ramsey, N.J.: Paulist Press, 1984).

8. Alexander Pope, "An Essay on Criticism," in *Alexander Pope: Selected Works*, ed. L. Kronenberger (New York: Modern Library, 1948), p. 47.

9. Although the idea of "original sin" is generally rejected by Judaism, the concept is present in a number of forms. See, e.g., Samuel S. Cohon, "Original Sin," *Hebrew Union College Annual* 21 (1948): 275–331, and, more recently, Deborah Schechterman's Hebrew study, "Maimonides's View of Original Sin as Reflected in Jewish Thought in the Thirteenth Century and in the Fourteenth Century," *Da'at* 20 (Winter 1988): 65–135. To be sure, many sources, particularly medieval Jewish texts, polemicized against the notion of original sin. For example, the *Zohar*, vol. 1, p. 57bf, states that "Adam comes before every person at the moment of death in order to declare that the individual is dying not because of Adam's sin, but on account of his own sins." In this regard, one specific Talmudic text not discussed by Cohon requires discussion.

According to a rabbinic legend, the serpent in the Garden of Eden had sexual intercourse with Eve and injected a substance into her that infected all newborn children. This taint was removed from the people of Israel when they stood at Mt. Sinai, but it remains among non-Jews. See *Shabbat* 146a, *Yebamot* 103b, *Abodah Zarah* 22b. Note Louis Ginzberg, *The Legends of the Jews*, 7 vols. (Philadelphia: Jewish Publication Society, 1955), vol. 5, p. 133. Abraham ben David of Posquieres utilizes this text to explain the otherwise enigmatic statement in the "*Dayyenu*" prayer of the Passover seder, "If we had stood at Mt. Sinai and had not received the Torah, it would have been sufficient."

One might suggest that since the entire purpose of standing at Mt. Sinai was to receive the Torah, how could it be sufficient if the Israelites stood at Mt. Sinai, and did not receive the Torah? Abraham ben David explains that, since the original taint injected into Eve was removed when the Israelites stood at Mt. Sinai, the accomplishment would have sufficed in and of itself. See Abraham ben David, *Teshuvot u-Fesakim* (Jerusalem: Mosad ha-Rav Kook, 1964), no. 11, p. 55.

The Talmudic text and its interpretation may be taken in one of two ways, first, that an idea of original sin was accepted by the rabbis and the congregation of the Israelites at Mt. Sinai was considered the vehicle by which it was removed or, second, that these texts are a polemic against the Christian conception of original sin. If interpreted as a polemic, these texts may be taken to claim that it is not the Jews who retain the taint of original sin for not having accepted Christ, it is the non-Jews who retain the taint of original sin for not having received the Torah.

10. Before the destruction of the Temple, the sacrificial cult served as the primary vehicle for repentance. In this regard, it is significant that the Hebrew word for "sacrifice"— "*korban*"—derives from the root meaning "to bring near," i.e., the sacrifices reduce the alienation between God and the penitent. After the destruction of the Temple, the rabbis assigned to the process of repentance many of the spiritual goals of the individual previously accomplished by means of the sacrificial cult. As Maimonides, 1:3, p. 82a, succinctly put it, "At the present time, when the Temple no longer exists, and we have no altar for atonement, nothing is left but repentance." Consequently, various parts of the process of repentance were compared to a sacrifice. For example, Eliezer Azkiri, in his mystical treatise *Sefer Hareidim* (Jerusalem: n.p., 1987), chap. 63, p. 243–44, described the words of confession and that which is denied the self in ascetic practices related to repentance as a sacrifice. Similarly, the cabalist Elijah di Vidas, *Reshit Hokhmah* (Tel Aviv: Esther Press, n.d.), "*Shaar Teshuvah*," chap. 3, p. 109a, described the contrition of a broken heart as a penetential sacrifice. Indeed, the Talmud

compares the fat and blood lost through a penitential fast as a substitute for sacrifice of atonement; see *Berakhot* 17a.

11. Bahya ben Asher, *Kad ha-Kemah* (Lwow, 1892), p. 66a. *Encyclopedia of Torah Thoughts,* Eng. trans. Charles B. Chavel (New York: Shilo Publishing House, 1980), pp. 587–88. See also Bahya ibn Pakuda, pp. 330, 333; *Orhot Zaddikim,* pp. 460–61; Isaac Aboab, p. 593; Azkiri, chap. 62, p. 240.

12. Albo, vol. 4, chap. 25, p. 224.

13. Ibid., p. 237. See also Jonah Gerondi, *Shaarey Teshuvah,* trans. S. Silverstein (New York: Feldheim Publishers, 1971), 2:8, pp. 80–81.

14. Bahya ibn Pakuda, p. 333.

15. In most of the medieval literature on *teshuvah,* twenty-four obstacles to repentance are listed. See, e.g., Maimonides, 4:1–6, pp. 856–66; Gerondi, pp. 69–71; Menachem Meiri, *Hibbur ha-Teshuvah,* ed. A. Schreiber (New York: Schulzinger, 1950), pp. 72–112; *Orhot Zaddikim,* pp. 480–89; Israel ibn Al-Nakawa, *Menorat ha-Ma'or,* ed. H. G. Enelow (New York: Bloch Publishing Co., 1931), pp. 48–51. The eleventh-century codifier Isaac Alfasi is the first scholar to list these twenty-four obstacles to *teshuvah* in his commentary to the end of the Talmudic tractate *Yoma.* He appears to be quoting an earlier source, but this source was unknown to later commentators. For example, (Rabbenu) Nissim, in his super-commentary to Alfasi on the Talmud, observed, "I do not know where this has been [previously] taught." Similarly, in a responsum, Maimonides stated that an earlier source than Alfasi is also unknown to him; see Maimonides, *Teshuvot ha-Rambam,* ed. J. Blau, no. 121, vol. 1, pp. 216–17.

16. Bahya ibn Pakuda, p. 34b.

17. Luzzatto, p. 122. See also, Bahya ibn Pakuda, p. 346.

18. Albo, p. 235.

19. Isaiah Horowitz, *Shnei Luhot ha-Brit,* 3 vols. (Jerusalem: Edison, 1960), "Hilkhot Teshuvah," vol. 3, p. 173b. In "Shaar Teshuvah," chap. 2, p. 108a, Elijah di Vidas relates action, speech, and deeds to the three levels of the human soul, i.e., *nefesh, ruah, neshamah.*

20. Moses di Trani, *Beth Elohim* (Warsaw: Goldman, 1852), p. 29b. Moses di Trani may have been anticipated by the twelfth-century Jewish philosopher Joseph ibn Zaddik in his *Olam ha-Katan,* ed. S. Horovitz, (Breslau: Schatzky, 1903), 4:1, p. 71.

21. Bahya ibn Pakuda, p. 334.

22. Albo, vol. 4, pp. 237–38.

23. *Ethics of the Fathers* 3:1; see also 2:1.

24. *Shabbat* 153a. See also *Ethics of the Fathers* 2:15.

25. *Midrash Ecclesiastes Rabbah* 1:1.

26. Jonah Gerondi, pp. 70–71.

27. *Ethics of the Fathers* 1:14; Horowitz, vol. 3, p. 177a; Samuel of Uceda, p. 16b.

28. Jonah Gerondi, vol. 2, pp. 26, 30–31, pp. 115, 119. On contemplation of death as a spur to repentance, see also Maimonides, 7:2, p. 89; *Orhot Zaddikim,* pp. 508–11; di Vidas, chap. 1, p. 102b; Bahya ibn Pakuda, p. 338; Isaiah Horowitz, p. 177a.

29. See, e.g., *Midrash Pekikta Rabbati,* ed. Friedmann, 44:8, p. 184a. Eng. trans., p. 777.

30. Bahya ibn Pakuda, pp. 351, 335, 337–38.

31. See, e.g., *Yoma* 86b.

32. Isaiah Horowitz, p. 175b. See also Albo, 4:25, vol. 4, pp. 225–26. Albo did not consider repentance motivated by fear of punishment or by fear of death to be repentance at

all. On attitudes of fear, love, and reverence for God, see Byron L. Sherwin, "Fear of God," chapter in Cohen and Mendes-Flohr, eds., pp. 255–61.

33. Di Vidas, *"Shaar ha-Teshuvah,"* chap. 3, p. 113a.

34. Maimonides, 7:6, 7, p. 89b.

35. Albo, vol. 4, pp. 232, 464.

36. *Midrash Pesikta Rabbati* 44:9, pp. 184b–185a. Eng. trans. p. 779.

37. *Zohar*, vol. 3, p. 122a.

38. See, e.g., Isaiah Horowitz, vol. 3, p. 180a.

39. *Zohar*, vol. 3, p. 122a.

40. On repentance in the *Zohar*, see Tishbi, *Mishnat ha-Zohar*, vol. 2, pp. 735–44.

41. Maimonides, 2:2, p. 82. Note Jacob ben Asher, *Arba'ah Turim—Orah Hayyim,* para. 607; Meiri, *Hibbur*, pp. 194–201.

42. For further sources regarding confession, see Abramowitz, pp. 65–94.

43. Maimonides, 1:1, p. 81.

44. A form of private confession not usually identified with Judaism is confession to another person. While not pervasive in Judaism, this form of confession was practiced by the medieval *Hasidei Ashkenaz* as well as by adherents to various schools of nineteenth-century eastern European Hasidism, especially the Brazlaver Hasidim. In both these movements, confession was made to a spiritual mentor who would then assign the penitent tasks to perform (i.e., penances) to affect the realization of repentance. For this practice among the *Hasidei Ashkenaz*, see Marcus, pp. 77–78, 131, 141–65. In later Hasidism, see Aaron Wertheim, *Halakhot ve-Halikhot ba-Hasidut* (Jerusalem: Mosad ha-Rav Kook, 1960), pp. 22–23. Note Jacobs, *Jewish Theology*, pp. 257–58. On confession to a friend in Hasidism, see Joseph Weiss, *Studies in Eastern European Jewish Mysticism*, ed. David Goldstein (New York: Oxford Univ. Press, 1985), pp. 160–67. On Brazlaver Hasidism, see, e.g., Green, pp. 45–46, and Ada Rappoport Albert, "Confession in the Circle of Rabbi Nahman of Bratslav," *Bulletin of the Institute of Jewish Studies* 1 (1973): 65–75.

45. Isaiah Horowitz, p. 171b.

46. *Yoma* 36b. See also *Tosefta Yoma* 2:1, and *Sifra* (Vienna: Shlossberg, 1862), *"Aharei"* 2:9, p. 80b–81a.

47. See Schechter, *Some Aspects*, pp. 219–63, 293–343.

48. Maimonides, 2:1, pp. 81–82. In the Talmud, see *M. Yoma* 6:2, 8:9, *Yoma* 86b, *Ta'anit* 16b.

49. Jonah Gerondi, vol. 1, pp. 50–51.

50. Various harsh ascetic practices related to *teshuvah* were observed by Jews. For historical reasons, these bear mention. Such practices included self-mortification, self-flagellation, voluntary "exile," long fasts, sleep deprivation, and more. Specific mention may be made of *teshuvat mishkal* where the penitent inflicted pain upon himself at least equal to the pleasure experienced during the committing of a particular sin. These were practiced by the *Hasidei Ashkenaz*, and were incorporated into later treatises of Jewish ethics. The observance of these practices demonstrates that the popular notion that asceticism and Judaism are incompatible is a fiction that cannot be substantiated on the basis of historical fact or textual evidence.

On the *Hasidei Ashkenaz*, see, e.g., Marcus. For the discussion of these practices in later works, see, e.g., *Orhot Zaddikim*, pp. 510–53. Compare the rejection of self-affliction as a desirable means of repentance in ibn Al-Nakawa, *Menorat ha-Ma'or*, pp. 82–83.

51. *Midrash Leviticus Rabbah* 21:5; *Orhot Zaddikim*, p. 473.

52. Abraham bar Hiyya, *The Meditation of the Sad Soul*, trans. Geoffrey Wigoder (London: Routledge and Kegan Paul, 1969), pp. 87–88.

53. See, e.g., Jonah Gerondi, vol. 1, p. 62–63, and *Orhot Zaddikim*, pp. 478–79.

54. See, e.g., *Rosh ha-Shanah* 17b; Maimonides, 2:9, pp. 83a–83b.

55. See, e.g., *Yoma* 85b, 87a; *Baba Kamma* 110a.

56. *Midrash Leviticus Rabbah* 5:8.

57. See, e.g, *Berakhot* 34b; *Zohar*, vol. 1, p. 106b. See the discussion of this text in Bahya ibn Pakuda, p. 345.

8. PARENT-CHILD RELATIONS IN JEWISH TRADITION

1. *Midrash on Psalms*, ed. Buber, 92:13, p. 412; Eng. trans., vol. 2, p. 122. See also *Yalkut Shimoni*, "Psalms," no. 846.

2. Plato, *Phaedrus* 265.

3. Abrahams, *Jewish Life in the Middle Ages*, p. 122.

4. *Mekhilta de-Rabbi Yishmael*, ed. Horovitz and Rabin, "Yitro," chap. 5 on Exod. 20:12, p. 232. Eng. trans., vol. 2, p. 259.

5. See, e.g., Nahmanides, *Commentary to the Torah* to Exod. 20:12, vol. 1, p. 403. See also Bahya ben Asher, *Kad ha-Kemah* (Lwow, 1892), "Kibbud Av," p. 107a. *Encyclopedia of Torah Thoughts*, Eng. trans. Charles B. Chavel, p. 314; ibn Al-Nakawa, vol. 4, p. 24.

6. See, e.g., Judah Loew, *Gur Aryeih*, vol. 5, p. 36, on Deut. 5:16.

7. See, e.g., *Kiddushin* 31a and *Midrash Pesikta Rabbati*, chap. 23/24, p. 122. Eng. trans., vol. 2, pp. 496–97.

8. This citation is from a responsum of the sixteenth-century halakhist Benjamin Ze'ev ben Mattitayhu *Binyamin Ze'ev* (Venice, 1539), no. 169. The collection of his responsa was unavailable to me. I rely instead on Abramowitz's invaluable anthology regarding parent-child relations, where it is quoted. See Hayyim Abramowitz, *Ha-Dibrah ha-Hamishit* (Jerusalem: Reuven Mass, 1971), p. 116.

9. Abraham ibn Ezra on Exod. 20:12. See also Yosef Bekhor Shor, *Commentary to the Torah*, 3 vols. [Hebrew] (Jerusalem: Tehiyah, 1956), vol. 1, p. 92, on Exod. 20:12. On the "ethos of gratitude," see Gerald Blidstein, *Honor Thy Father and Mother* (New York: Ktav, 1975), pp. 8–19.

10. *Sefer ha-Hinukh*, ed. and trans. Charles Wengrov (Jerusalem: Feldheim Publishers, 1978), no. 33, pp. 180–83.

11. Don Isaac Abravanel, *Commentary to the Torah* [Hebrew] 3 vols. (Jerusalem: Bnei Abarbanel, 1964), vol. 2, pp. 109–11, on Lev. 19:3.

12. *Kiddushin* 31a.

13. See, e.g., Moses Hafetz, *Malekhet Mahshevet* (Warsaw: Cahana, 1914), p. 148b, on Deut. 5:16.

14. ibn Al-Nakawa, vol. 4, p. 18.

15. Bahya ibn Pakuda, p. 177.

16. See, e.g., Nahmanides's commentary to Exod. 20:12, 13.

17. *Niddah* 31a; see also *Kiddushin* 30b. See, e.g., *Zohar*, vol. 1, p. 49; vol. 3, p. 219b ("Raya Mehemna"); see also "Midrash Pesikta Haddeta" in *Beth Ha-Midrash*, ed. Jellinek, vol. 6, p. 44.

18. *Zohar*, vol. 3, p. 83a ("Raya Mehemna").

19. Plato, *Laws*, para. 790. Maimonides, *Guide*, Book 3, chap. 41. Eng. trans., p. 562.

20. Gersonides, *Commentary to the Torah*, 2 vols. [Hebrew] (Venice: Bomberg, 1547), pp. 50b–81a, on Exod. 20:12.

21. Abravanel, vol. 2, pp. 190–91, on Exod. 20:12; Albo, vol. 3, pp. 251–52.

22. See Blidstein, pp. 37–60.

23. *P. Pe'ah* 1:1, *Midrash Deuteronomy Rabbah* 6:2. See also *Pesikta Rabbati* 23/24: 2; *Midrash Tanhuma*, "*Ekev*," no. 3, p. 9a; Eliezer of Metz, *Sefer Yere'im* (Livorno: Rokeah, 1837), no. 56, p. 49b.

24. *Kiddushin* 31b.

25. *P. Pe'ah* 1:1.

26. Maimonides, *Peirush la-Mishnah*, "*Kiddushin*" 1:7, p. 197. See also Maimonides, *Sefer ha-Mitzvot*, ed. Joseph Kapah (Jerusalem: Mosad ha-Rav Kook, 1971), nos. 210, 211, p. 166.

27. Maimonides, *Mishneh Torah—Sefer Shofetim*, "Laws of Rebels," 5:16:14. Eng. trans., pp. 150–61.

28. *Kiddushin* 31b. See also *Tosefta*, ed. Zuckermandel, "*Kiddushin*" 1:1; *Midrash Pesikta Rabbati* 23/24: 2; *Sifra* (New York: Ohm, 1947), p. 87a, "*Kedoshim*" beginning.

29. Kiddushin 30b; *Mekhilta de-Rabbi Ishmael*, "*Yitro*," ed. Horovitz and Rabin, chap. 8, p. 233.

30. *P. Kiddushin* 1:7, also see Rashi's commentary to *Kiddushin* 31a–b.

31. Rashi on *Kiddushin* 32a; Azkiri, chap. 9, nos. 36–38, pp. 68–69; *Zohar*, vol. 3, pp. 281a–b.

32. *Kiddushin* 31b; Karo, *Shulhan Arukh—Yoreh Deah*, para. 240:9.

33. *Semahot* 9:19.

34. See Blidstein, pp. 60–75.

35. See, e.g., *P. Kiddushin* 1:7.

36. See, e.g., *Kiddushin* 32a; Karo, *Shulhan Arukh—Yoreh Deah*, para. 240.

37. See Moses Isserles's commentary to Karo, *Shulhan Arukh—Yoreh Deah*, para. 240:5, and Ahai Gaon, *She'iltot*, ed. S. K. Mirsky, 6 vols. (Jerusalem: Mosad ha-Rav Kook, 1964), no. 56, vol. 3, pp. 164–65.

38. See, e.g., *Sanhedrin* 77a, 84b–85b; Karo, *Shulhan Arukh—Yoreh Deah*, para. 241. Also see Nahmanides's commentary to Exod. 21:15, Lev. 20:9, Deut. 21:18–21.

39. See, e.g., Moses Hafetz on Lev. 20:9, p. 103a. See also Abravanel's commentary on Deut. 5:16.

40. Maimonides, *Mishneh Torah—Sefer Shofetim*, "Laws of Rebels," 6:10. Eng. trans., p. 156; Karo, *Shulhan Arukh—Yoreh Deah*, para. 240:10.

41. Maimonides, *Mishneh Torah—Sefer Shofetim*, "Laws of Rebels," 6:8, Eng. trans., p. 156; see also *Kiddushin* 32a.

42. *Sefer Hasidim*, ed. Margaliot, nos. 152, 565, pp. 153, 372.

43. See Blidstein, pp. 126–27, 155–56.

44. *Sotah* 49a.

45. Nahmanides on Gen. 2:24.

46. *Pirke de-Rabbi Eliezer* (Warsaw, 1852), p. 73a. Eng. trans., chap. 32, p. 234.

47. *Kiddushin* 30b; Maimonides, *Mishneh Torah—Sefer Nashim*, "Hilkhot Kiddushin," 13:12–14. *The Book of Women*, Eng. trans. Isaac Klein (New Haven: Yale Univ. Press, 1972), pp. 83–84.

48. Solomon ibn Adret, *Responsa, Part Four* [Hebrew] (Pietrikov: Belkhatavsky, 1883), no. 168, p. 25b. See also Blidstein, pp. 83–98, 100–109.

49. *Mekhilta de Rabbi Ishmael,* ed. Horovitz and Rabin, "*Yitro,*" chap. 1, p. 190; *Yalkut Shimoni,* "1 Samuel," no. 133; *Midrash on Psalms* 7:4, p. 33a; Karo, *Shulhan Arukh—Yoreh Deah,* para. 240:24.

50. Azkiri, chap. 12, p. 76.

51. *Ketubot* 103a.

52. Karo, *Shulhan Arukh—Yoreh Deah,* para. 240:22, 23.

53. *Yebamot* 62b; *Kiddushin* 4a; *Baba Batra* 143b; *Pirke de-Rabbi Eliezer.* Eng. trans., chap. 36, p. 270; *Zohar,* vol. 2, p. 233a.

54. See, e.g., *Sotah* 49a.

55. See, e.g., *Midrash Genesis Rabbah* 94:5; Rashi and Nahmanides on Gen. 46:1; Moses Isserles's gloss on Karo, *Shulhan Arukh—Yoreh Deah,* para. 240:24; Azkiri, chap. 12, pp. 75–76. Azkiri also included aunts and uncles. Note the responsum by Yom Tov ibn Asevelli, *Responsa* [Hebrew] ed. J. Kapah (Jerusalem: n.p., 1959), no. 134, where he maintained that, while emotionally grandchildren may be equal to children, legally they are not so considered. See his responsum no. 134, translated and explained in Louis Jacobs, *Jewish Law* (New York: Behrman House, 1968), pp. 187–91.

56. *Kiddushin* 29a; see also variant readings in *P. Kiddushin* 1:7; *Midrash Numbers Rabbah* 17:1; *Midrash Ecclesiastes Rabbah* 9:8. See also Blidstein, pp. 122–36.

57. *Mekhilta de-Rabbi Ishmael,* ed. Horovitz and Rabin, "*Bo,*" chap. 18, p. 73.

58. *Kiddushin* 30b.

59. See, e.g., Judah Ashkenazi, *Be'er Heiteiv* on Karo, *Shulhan Arukh—Even ha-Ezer,* para. 73:1.

60. *Ketubot* 49–50.

61. Karo, *Shulhan Arukh—Even ha-Ezer,* para. 71:1; see also Maimonides, *Mishneh Torah—Sefer Nashim,* "Hilkhot Ishut" 12:16, Eng. trans., pp. 76–77.

62. Karo, *Shulhan Arukh—Yoreh Deah,* para. 245:4.

63. Maimonides, *Mishneh Torah—Sefer ha-Mada,* "Hilkhot Talmud Torah," 1:1. Eng. trans., p. 57a. See *Kiddushin* 29a, and Karo, *Shulhan Arukh—Yoreh Deah,* para. 245:1. See Blidstein, pp. 137– 57.

64. *Yebamot* 62b.

65. *Sukkah* 46b.

66. *Shabbat* 127a.

67. See, e.g., *Kiddushin* 32a; Maimonides, *Mishneh Torah—Sefer Shofetim,* "Laws of Rebels" 6:7. Eng. trans., p. 155.

68. Maimonides, "Laws of Rebels," 6:7. Eng. trans., p. 156; see also Karo, *Shulhan Arukh—Yoreh Deah,* paras. 240:18, 241:4.

69. See, e.g., Isserles's glosses to Karo, *Shulhan Arukh—Yoreh Deah,* para. 240:18.

70. Eliezer of Metz, no. 56, p. 49b.

71. Ibn Al-Nawaka, vol. 4, p. 18.

72. *Sifra* on Lev. 19:3; see also *Yebamot* 5b.

73. *Kiddushin* 32a; Maimonides, "Laws of Rebels," 6:13.

74. *Megillah* 16b; Karo, *Shulhan Arukh—Yoreh Deah,* paras. 240:13, 242:1.

75. See, e.g., Rashi and *Yalkut Shimoni,* "Proverbs," no. 950 on Prov. 13:25.

76. See Blidstein, pp. 126–27, 155–56.

77. See Joseph Yuspa Hahn, *Yosif Ometz* (Frankfurt: Hermon, 1928), p. 279.

9. BAR MITZVAH, BAT MITZVAH

1. Moses Feinstein, *Iggerot Moshe—Orah Hayyim* (New York: Gross and Weiss, 1959), no. 104.

2. See, e.g., Isaac Levitas, "Communal Regulation of Bar Mitzvah," *Journal of Jewish Social Studies* 11, no. 2 (Apr. 1949): 153–62.

3. Quoted in Isaac Rivkind, *Le-Ot u'le-Zikaron* (New York: n.p., 1942), p. 62.

4. Quoted in Hayyim Lieberman, *A House on Fire* (New York: n.p., n.d.), p. 62.

5. See, e.g., Sheldon S. Brown, *Guidance and Counselling for Jewish Education* (New York: Bloch Publishing Co., 1964).

6. See Mordecai Richler, *The Apprenticeship of Duddy Kravitz* (New York: Ballantine Books, 1974), pp. 127–47.

7. *Niddah* 30b; cf. Plato, *Meno* 80d–86a.

8. Gerson Rosensweig, *Massekhet America* (New York, 1891).

9. Quoted in W. Gunther Plaut, *The Rise of Reform Judaism* (New York: World Union for Progressive Judaism, 1963), p. 172.

10. Franz Rosenzweig, p. 37.

11. Solomon Luria, *Yam Shel Shelomo*, "*Baba Kamma*," 7:37.

12. See, e.g., Rivkind; Byron L. Sherwin, "Bar Mitzvah," *Judaism* 22 (Winter 1973): 53–65; Benjamin Adler, *Halakhot ve-Halikhot Bar-Mitzvah* (Jerusalem: Or Torah, 1964). See also *Encyclopedia Talmudit*, s.v. "Bar Mitzvah," vol. 4, pp. 165–67; Israel Lebinger, "The Minor in Jewish Law," *Jewish Quarterly Review*, n.s. 6 (1915/1916): 459–93, 497, n.s. 7 (1916/1917): 145–74; Boaz Cohen, "The Minor in Jewish and Roman Law," chapter in *Studies in Jewish and Roman Law*, 2 vols. (New York: Jewish Theological Seminary, 1966), vol. 2, pp. 1–9; Shlomo Goren, "The Age of Maturity for Individual and Social Majority" [Hebrew], *Mahanayim* 23: 7–13; Judah David Eisenstein, *Otzar Dinim u-Minhagim* (New York: Hebrew Publishing Co., 1917), pp. 50–51.

13. See Jacob Arlow, "A Psychoanalytic Study of a Religious Rite: Bar Mitzvah," *Psychoanalytic Study of the Child* 6 (20 Dec. 1953): 353–74.

14. *Baba Metzia* 96a.

15. *Sanhedrin* 84b.

16. See, e.g., H. Pereira Mendes, *Bar Mitzvah* (New York: Union of Orthodox Jewish Congregations, 1945), p. 94: "To be Bar Mitzvah means one who is bound to observe the commandments."

17. The origin of this idea in modern studies of the issue appears to be Leopold Low, *Die Liebensalter in der Judischen Literatur* (Szegedin: Druck von Sigmund Berger, 1875), pp. 210, 410, no. 62. Cf. Rivkind, pp. 13–15. Low's view clearly influenced the following: Solomon Schechter, "The Child in Jewish Literature," chapter in *Studies in Judaism* (Philadelphia: Jewish Publication Society, 1896), vol. 1, pp. 307, 312; Kaufmann Kohler, "Bar Mitzvah," *Jewish Encyclopedia* (New York: Funk and Wagnalls, 1902), vol. 2, pp. 509–10; Zvi Kaplan, "Bar Mitzvah," *Encyclopedia Judaica*, vol. 4, pp. 243–47. *Encyclopedia Judaica* claims that the term is first used to denote the occasion of assuming religious and legal obligations in Menahem Zioni's fifteenth-century work *Sefer Zioni*. I could not locate the term there. Rather, the term *onshin* denoting responsibility for sin is used there to refer to a thirteen-year-old. However, this text rejects the view that a child of thirteen is responsible for his deeds and maintains that only at age twenty does one become responsible. See Zioni, pp. 6a–6b.

18. *Midrash Tanhuma [Ha-Nidpas]*, "*Bo*," para. 14, p. 84a.

19. See Louis Ginzberg, *Peirushim ve-Hiddushim be-Yerushalmi*, 3 vols. (New York: Jewish Theological Seminary, 1941), vol. 2, p. 145, no. 19.

20. See Rivkind, p. 14.

21. On the issue of age and status, see, e.g., A. H. Shaki, "Is Age a Matter of Status?," *Israel Law Review* 4 (1969): 371–91.

22. Asher ben Yehiel, *She'eilot u-Teshuvot ha-Rosh*, "Klal" 13:13, p. 15a; see also 16:1, p. 19b. In his commentary to Lev. 20:9, ibn Ezra discussed the biblical law that a "man" who curses his parents is liable to the death penalty. Regarding the definition of "man," he wrote, "we require a tradition from our forefathers. . . . it [the text] does not define how old one must be to be 'bar mitzvah'." Abraham ibn Ezra, *Commentary to the Torah*, 5 vols. [Hebrew] (Tel Aviv: Moreib, 1961), vol. 3, pp. 193–94.

23. Aaron ha-Kohen mei-Lunel, *Orhot Hayyim* (Jerusalem: n.p., 1956), "Hilkhot Berakhot," no. 58, and Rivkind, p. 16. The meaning of this blessing is discussed later in this chapter. It is significant that this text does not state the age of his son.

24. *Soferim* 18:5.

25. See, e.g., *Niddah* 45b–46a; *Gittin* 68b; *Tosefta*, ed. Zuckermandel, "Niddah," chap. 6, p. 647; Rashi to *Nazir* 29b; Maimonides, *Peirush la-Mishnah*, "Yoma," 8:2, p. 172, "Sanhedrin," 7:4, p. 121, "Niddah," 5:6, p. 374; id., *Mishneh Torah—Sefer Nashim*, "Laws of Marriage," 2:9. Eng. trans., p. 10; *Sefer Shofetim*, "Laws of Evidence," 9:8. Eng. trans., p. 101.

26. See, e.g., Solomon B. Freehof, "Ceremonial Creativity Among the Ashkenazim," pp. 217–24.

27. See, e.g., *Hullin* 24b; *Tosefta*, ed. Zuckermandel, "Hagigah," 1:3, p. 232; "Zevahim," 11:6, p. 496.

28. The criteria that the emergence of "two hairs" alone establishes majority is found, in the following representative sources: *Hullin* 24b; *Nazir* 29b; *Sanhedrin* 68b–69a; *Niddah* 45b and Rashi there; *Tosefta*, "Hagigah," 1:3, p. 232.

29. See, e.g., *Sanhedrin* 69a and *Tosafot* there, s.v. "Ba-Yaduah." According to some views, one who cannot procreate is not granted majority until the age of twenty. See, e.g., *M. Niddah* 7:2; *Tosefta*, "Niddah," chap. 6, p. 647. Note *Niddah* 47b. See also Karo, *Shulhan Arukh—Orah Hayyim*, para. 55:5; id., *Even ha-Ezer*, para. 155:13. Maimonides claimed that, since one who is sterile will never be able to procreate, majority should be granted at thirteen years and one day for a male. See Maimonides, *Mishneh Torah—Sefer Nashim*, "Laws of Marriage," 2:13–14. Eng. trans., p. 11. Other authorities claim that majority for such an individual should not be granted until after he or she has lived the "majority" of his or her years, i.e., after the age of thirty-five. See, e.g., Karo, *Shulhan Arukh*—sources noted above in this note. See also Adler, p. 200.

30. See, e.g., *Niddah* 46a; Maimonides, *Peirush la-Mishnah*, "Yoma," 8:2, p. 172; "Sanhedrin," 7:4, p. 121; id., *Mishneh Torah—Sefer Nashim*, "Laws of Marriage," chap. 2. Eng. trans., pp. 1–14; id., *Mishneh Torah—Sefer Shofetim*, "Laws of Evidence," 9:8. Eng. trans., p. 101; Karo, *Shulhan Arukh—Orah Hayyim*, paras. 55:9, 616:2; Ovadiah Bertinoro to *M. Niddah* 5:6, in standard editions of the Mishnah; Jacob Moelln, *She'eilot u-Teshuvot Maharil* (Cracow: Fisher ve-Deitcher, 1881), no. 51, pp. 16b–17a. See also the discussion and sources in Saul Lieberman, *Tosefta Kifshuta* (New York: Jewish Theological Seminary, 1962), "Hagigah," 1:3, pp. 376, 1272–76.

31. Sources that accept the criterion of age alone include, e.g., *Niddah* 46a; *Yoma* 82a; Isserles's glosses on Karo, *Shulhan Arukh—Orah Hayyim*, paras. 37:3, 55:5, 199:10. See especially Hayyim Mordecai Margaliot's nineteenth-century commentary, *Sha'arei Teshuvah* in standard editions of the *Shulhan Arukh* (to 37:3): "One who reached the age of thirteen years and one day, even if it is not known if he brought forth two hairs, is obliged by law to don *tefillin* because of Rava's presumption that anyone who fulfills the age requirement of

majority is presumed to have manifested the signs." Note Maimonides, *Peirush la-Mishnah*, *"Niddah"*; id., *Mishneh Torah—Sefer Hafla'ah*, "Laws of Vows," 11:3. *The Book of Assevera-tions*, Eng. trans. B. D. Klein (New Haven: Yale Univ. Press, 1962), p. 101; Karo, *Shulhan Arukh—Yoreh Deah*, para. 233:3. See also sources noted in Meir Greenwald, *Zoheir ha-Brit* (Israel: Gellis, 1931), pp. 192–93.

32. Luria, *Yam shel Shelomo*.

33. Meir Schiff, and *Tosafot*, s.v., *ba-Yaduah* on *Sanhedrin* 69a, both in standard edition of the Talmud.

34. See, e.g., *M. Yoma* 3:1; *Hagigah* 2b; *Menahot* 93a; *Hullin* 13a; *Gittin* 23a; *Yebamot* 99b. See also Schreiber, *Responsa—Yoreh Deah*, no. 317, pp. 125–27. On various views of why and in what sense minors are exempt from legal obligations, see, e.g., Adler, pp. 3–5. In its discussion of the age of majority for non-Jews, the literature expresses two views. One is that the age criterion is crucial. The second view is that the intellectual criterion is crucial. See Adler, pp. 59, 157.

35. *Mekhilta d'Rabbi Yishmael*, ed. Horovitz and Rabin, *"Mishpatim,"* chap. 4, p. 263; *Pesikta d'Rav Kahana*, ed. Mandelbaum, vol. 1, chap. 11, p. 180.

36. See, e.g., *Berakhot* 48a; Maimonides, *Mishneh Torah—Sefer Ahavah*, "Laws of Blessings," 5:6. *The Book of Adoration*, Eng. trans., Moses Hyamson (Jerusalem: Boys Town Publishers, 1965), p. 150a.

37. See, e.g., Karo, *Shulhan Arukh—Orah Hayyim*, para. 37:3.

38. *M. Megillah* 4:6; *Megillah* 23a. See José Faur, *"Din Aliyat ha-Katan Likro ba-Torah,"* chapter in *Sefer Zikaron le-Kavod Yitzhak Nissim* (Jerusalem: n.p., 1984), pp. 113–33; Lieberman, pp. 356, 1176–78.

39. Rashi to *Niddah* 45b.

40. *Niddah* 45b; *Nazir* 29b; In this case Maimonides deviated from his usual criteria of signs and age and followed the Talmudic precedent. See Maimonides, *Peirush la-Mishnah*, *"Niddah,"* 5:6, pp. 374–75; id., *Mishneh Torah—Sefer Hafla'ah*, "Laws of Vows," 11:3. Eng. trans., p. 101; Karo, *Shulhan Arukh—Yoreh Deah*, para. 233:2. Cf. Rashi to *Nazir* 29b. It is important to note that the acceptance of the age requirement alone as the necessary and sufficient criterion for majority only relates to laws of rabbinic decree and not to laws of biblical origin. See Isserles's gloss to Karo, *Shulhan Arukh—Orah Hayyim*, para. 55. This may be why an effort was made to root bar mitzvah in biblical precedent.

41. See Isserles's gloss on Karo, *Shulhan Arukh—Orah Hayyim*, paras. 37:3; 119:10; note para. 55:5. Rava's presumption relates to males (thirteen years and one day) as well as to females (twelve years and one day).

42. *Niddah* 45b.

43. See, e.g., Solomon Schechter, *Some Aspects*, pp. 242–93.

44. See, e.g., *Sanhedrin* 91b; *Midrash on Psalms*, ed. Buber, 9:5, p. 41b. Eng. trans., vol. 1, p. 135; *Abot d'Rabbi Natan*, A, chap. 16, p. 31b. Eng. trans., p. 83; *Midrash Ecclesiastes Rabbah*, 4:9, para. 1; *Midrash Genesis Rabbah* 53:10; *Zohar*, vol. 1, pp. 78b, 165b; vol. 2, p. 98a. See also Samuel Edels to *Mo'ed Katan* 9b and to *Sukkah* 52a.

45. *Pirke de-Rabbi Eliezer* (1946), chap. 26, p. 60b. Eng. trans., p. 187.

46. *Sanhedrin* 69b.

47. *Midrash Genesis Rabbah* 80:10; *Yalkut Shimoni*, "Genesis," no. 135.

48. Simeon ben Zemah Duran, *Magen Abot* (Livorno, 1785), on *Abot* 5:21; Aaron Ha-Kohen, no. 73; Rashi to *Nazir* 29b and *Abot* 5:21.

49. *Midrash Genesis Rabbah* 63:10.

50. See, e.g., Maimonides, *Peirush la-Mishnah*, "*Sanhedrin*," 7:4, pp. 120–24; id., *Mishneh Torah—Sefer Nashim*, "Laws of Marriage," 2:9. Eng. trans., p. 10; Karo, *Shulhan Arukh—Orah Hayyim*, para. 616:2.

51. Simeon ben Zemah Duran to *Abot* 5:21; Jacob Moelln, no. 51, p. 16b; Aaron Ha-Kohen mei-Lunel, no. 73; Hayyim ben Betsalel of Friedberg, *Sefer ha-Hayyim* (Jerusalem: Weinfeld, 1965), "*Hayyim Tovim*," chap. 2, p. 27a.

52. *Sukkah* 5b; *Erubin* 4a. See also Asher ben Yehiel, *She'eilot u-Teshuvot*, "*Klal*," 16:1.

53. Asher ben Yehiel, *She'eilot u-Teshuvot*, "*Klal*," 16:1, p. 19b; Jacob Moellen, no. 51, pp. 16b–17a; Simeon ben Zemah Duran and Rashi to *Abot* 5:21.

54. See Maimonides, *Hakdama le-Peirush ha-Mishnah*, "Introduction," para. 4, p. 31.

55. See Rashi and Ovadiah Bertinoro on *Abot* 5:21. See also Simeon ben Zemah Duran on *Abot* 5:21.

56. *Zohar*, "*Mishpatim*," vol. 2, p. 89a, and "*Sitre Torah*"—"*Lekh L'kha*," vol. 1, p. 78b.

57. *Midrash Numbers Rabbah* 18:4. Cf. Zevi Ashkenazi, *She'eilot u-Teshuvot Hakham Zvi* (Jerusalem: n.p., 1970), no. 49, p. 31b. See also the sources collected in Viktor Aptowitzer, *Kain und Abel in der Agada* (Vienna: Lowit Verlag, 1922), pp. 97–100, and Adler, p. 195.

58. Rashi to *Shabbat* 89b, in standard editions of the Talmud. See also the nineteenth-century commentary of Ze'ev Einhorn (Maharzu) to *Midrash Rabbah*, i.e., to *Midrash Numbers Rabbah* 18:4, in standard editions of *Midrash Rabbah*; cf. *Midrash Numbers Rabbah* 16:23.

59. *Zohar*, vol. 2, p. 101a.

60. *Zohar*, vol. 2, p. 98a.

61. See, e.g., *Baba Batra* 115a, 156a; Karo, *Shulhan Arukh—Hoshen Mishpat*, para. 235:8, 9. See also Isaac Herzog, *Main Institutions of Jewish Law*, 2 vols. (London: Soncino, 1936), vol. 1, pp. 42, 51, 275, vol. 2, p. 151. Note Adler, p. 198.

62. See, e.g., *Soferim* 14:17.

63. See *Hullin* 24b; *Tosefta*, "*Zebahim*," 11:6, p. 496; "*Hagigah*," 1:13, p. 232. See also Saul Lieberman, *Tosefta Kifshuta*, "*Hagigah*," pp. 1274–76.

64. See *Midrash Numbers Rabbah* 16:23, 18:4, and Einhorn's commentary there; cf. Rashi to *Shabbat* 89b.

65. Goren, pp. 12–13.

66. Ibid., p. 12, finds a major difficulty in his suggestion. A basic source for his distinction between the two levels of maturity was the text from the *Zohar* quoted earlier in this chapter. According to his view one should become a *ben-Knesseth Yisrael* ("a son of the community of Israel") at twenty, the time of social obligation, of obligation to the community of Israel, rather than at thirteen as the text of the *Zohar* insists. Goren's difficulty, however, may be easily eliminated when it is remembered that in the *Zohar* these two terms, "Community of Israel" and "Holy One blessed be He," are apprehended as symbols for two aspects of the Godhead (*Sefiroth*). The "Community of Israel" refers to the lowest manifestation of the divine while "The Holy One blessed be He" or "Father" refers to "Wisdom" (*Hokhmah*), a very high manifestation of the divine. The passage, therefore, from being "a son of the Community of Israel" to being "a son of the Holy One blessed be He" need not be understood in the literal sense; it may be understood to indicate a spiritual development marked by a progression of attachment to a higher (Holy One) rather than a lower (Community of Israel) manifestation of divine spirituality.

67. See *Midrash Genesis Rabbah* 14:7; *Midrash Numbers Rabbah* 12:8; *Midrash Song of Songs Rabbah* 3:11. Note *Hullin* 60a. See also Robert Gordis, "The Knowledge of Good and Evil in the Old Testament and the Qumran Scrolls," *Journal of Biblical Literature* 76, no. 2 (June 1957): 124, 137–38.

68. *Midrash Genesis Rabbah* 63:10. The requirement to recite this blessing on the occasion of the bar mitzvah is not stated in the text either of Jacob ben Asher's code, *Arba'ah Turim*, or in Karo's code, *Shulhan Arukh*. The requirement is noted, however, in Isserles's commentary, *Darkhei Moshe* to *Arba'ah Turim—Orah Hayyim*, para. 225, and, in his gloss to *Shulhan Arukh—Orah Hayyim*, para. 225:2. Isserles noted this tradition in the name of Mordecai ben Hillel, who is quoted by Jacob Moelln. Isserles raised the question, debated among the other commentaries to the *Shulhan Arukh* and in responsa literature, about whether the blessing should be recited in a complete form (i.e., with *shem* and *malkhut*) or in the shortened form given in the midrashic text. On this issue see, e.g., Adler, pp. 77–78, and Isaac Nissim, "Al Birkhat Barukh she-Petarani," *No'am* 7 (1964): 1–2. The fifteenth-century German halakhist Israel Isserlin is cited as having favored an Aramaic translation of the blessing. See Joseph Moses of Munster, *Leket ha-Yosher* (Berlin: Mekitzei Nirdamim, 1903), pp. 40–41. The blessing is usually recited when at the Torah; and according to some authorities, it is also recited at the bar mitzvah banquet.

69. See the discussion and sources noted in Adler, pp. 90–94.

70. See Rivkind, pp. 19–20.

71. *M. Megillah* 4:6; *Megillah* 23a.

72. See the discussion and sources noted by Adler, pp. 86–88, 92–94.

73. Solomon Luria claims that if a learned address (*derasha*) is delivered, then it qualifies as a *se'udat mitzvah*. See the seventeenth-century commentary *Magen Avraham* by Abraham Gombiner on Karo, *Shulhan Arukh—Orah Hayyim*, para. 225:2.

74. See Nissim, pp. 1–5.

75. See, e.g., commentaries *Be'er Heiteiv, Magen Avraham* to Karo, *Shulhan Arukh— Orah Hayyim*, para. 225:2. Some sources argue that since this blessing is not recited for a daughter, it cannot denote that parents are punished for the sins of children and are freed from that punishment at the child's coming into majority. See, e.g., David Luria's commentary *Hiddushei ha-Radal* to *Midrash Genesis Rabbah* 63:10, in standard editions of *Midrash Rabbah*. Furthermore, that the bar mitzvah is encouraged to do repentance for sins committed while a minor would seem to be in opposition to the view that parents are punished for the sins of their children when they are minors. See, e.g., Adler, p. 120; Jacobs, *Theology in the Responsa*, pp. 265–66.

76. That the son is punished for the sins of the father and its relationship to this blessing is found, e.g., in Judah Ashkenazi's commentary *Be'er Heiteiv* on Karo, *Shulhan Arukh—Orah Hayyim*, para. 225:2, and the commentary of Einhorn on *Midrash Genesis Rabbah* 83:10. Note discussion and sources in Adler, p. 77, and Menahem Kasher, *Torah Sheleimah* (Jerusalem: Encyclopedia Humash Torah Sheleimah, 1934), vol. 4, p. 1024, no. 152. On children being punished for the sins of their parents, see, e.g., *Yalkut Shimoni*, "Ruth," no. 600, which states that until the age of thirteen, a son is afflicted for the sins of his father. Note *Shabbat* 33b; *Midrash Ecclesiastes Rabbah* 4:1. See also Kalmen Eliezer Frankel, *Encyclopedia l'Var Mitzvah* (Tel Aviv: Ha-Kerem, 1973), pp. 32–33. Some sources quote the blessing as, "Blessed be He who has freed me from the responsibility of my father." See Rivkind, p. 38, n. 53, and Adler, p. 78, n. 10.

A number of sources observe that since Scripture (e.g., Exod. 34:7) establishes that children are punished for the sins of their forebears, children cannot be freed from punishment for the sins of their parents and that even those who have entered majority are indeed liable to punishment for the sins of their forebears. Others maintain that since complete majority is granted not at thirteen but at twenty, when one becomes liable to punishment from the "Heavenly Court," one cannot become liable for punishment for one's parent's sins until then. See, e.g., Joshua ibn Shoeib and others quoted by Kasher, vol. 6, p. 1438, no. 202, p. 1450, no. 37.

77. See, e.g., Solomon Schechter, "The Doctrine of Divine Retribution in Rabbinic Literature," chapter in *Studies in Judaism* (New York: Meridian, 1958), pp. 105–23; Byron L. Sherwin, "Theodicy," in Cohen and Mendes-Flohr, eds., pp. 959–71; Robert Gordis, *The Book of God and Man* (Chicago: Univ. of Chicago Press, 1965), pp. 94, 141, 269.

78. In this regard, see, e.g., Shelomo Kluger, op. cit.

79. See *Midrash Tanhuma*, ed. Buber, "Toledot," para. 2, no. 5, vol. 1, p. 63a. Rashi on Gen. 25:27 quoted the "thirteen" reading. As Buber noted, Elijah Mizrahi, in his commentary there, attempted to reconcile the two conflicting readings of "thirteen" and "fifteen" by suggesting that Esau began to commit evil acts in private at thirteen and in public at fifteen.

80. Noted by Adler, p. 77, n. 5. See also Kasher, vol. 6, p. 1438, n. 202, p. 1450, n. 37.

81. See Isserles's gloss on Karo, *Shulhan Arukh—Orah Hayyim*, para. 225:2. Note Freehof, pp. 217–21. See also Isserles's commentary *Darkhei Moshe* to Jacob ben Asher, *Arba'ah Turim—Orah Hayyim*, para. 225: "I have not found this blessing in the Talmud, and I am troubled about reciting a blessing noted neither in the Talmud or in other legal sources [*posekim*]."

82. See Freehof, p. 220.

83. *Midrash Genesis Rabbah* 53:10.

84. See, e.g., the sixteenth-century commentary *Matnat Kehunah* by Issachar Baer Bremen Ashkenazi to *Midrash Genesis Rabbah* in standard editions of *Midrash Rabbah*. See his note to *Midrash Genesis Rabbah*, 53:10.

85. See the "*Midrash ha-Ne'elam*" in *Zohar Hadash*, ed. Judah ha-Levi Ashlag (Switzerland: n.p., n.d.), vol. 9, p. 151, para. 416, and Tishbi, *Mishnat ha-Zohar*, vol. 2, pp. 45–46.

86. See the various commentaries on Joseph Karo, *Shulhan Arukh—Orah Hayyim*, para. 225:2. See also Adler, pp. 67, 73, 226, and Rivkind, p. 47.

87. See, e.g., *Sanhedrin* 76b; *Yebamot* 62; Jacob ben Asher, *Arba'ah Turim—Even ha-Ezer*, para. 1. Note Adler, p. 192.

88. Luria, *Yam shel Shelomo*. Note Rivkind, p. 47.

89. See, e.g., *M. Niddah* 5:2; *Niddah* 45b–46a; Maimonides, *Mishneh Torah—Sefer Nashim*, "Laws of Marriage," 2:1. Eng. trans., p. 8; Karo, *Shulhan Arukh—Orah Hayyim*, paras. 343:1, 617:2, *Even ha-Ezer*, para. 155:12. On the development of the theme of female majority, see Bernard Bamberger, "*Qetana, Na'arah, Bogereth*," *Hebrew Union College Annual* 32 (1961): 281–94. Note Adler, pp. 185–86.

90. See, e.g., *Encyclopedia Judaica*, "Bar Mitzvah, Bat Mitzvah," vol. 4, p. 246; J. David Bleich, "Survey of Recent Halakhic Periodical Literature," *Tradition* 14, no. 2 (Fall 1973): 126.

91. See, e.g., Bleich, ibid.; Immanuel Jakobovits, "Review of Recent Halakhic Literature," *Tradition* 6, no. 2 (Fall 1963): 90–91; Adler, p. 76.

92. This information was conveyed to me by Mordecai Kaplan's daughter, Judith Kaplan Eisenstein, in a conversation held in New York on 31 Dec. 1968.

93. See, e.g., Solomon B. Freehof, *Reform Responsa for Our Time* (Cincinnati: Hebrew Union College Press, 1977), pp. 23–24.

94. See Feinstein, *Iggerot Moshe—Orah Hayyim*, and sources noted by Adler, p. 76.

95. Nissim, p. 8.

96. Hanokh Zundel Grossberg, "*Se'udat Bat Mitzvah*," *Ha-Ma'ayan* (Fall 1977): 41–42.

97. Quoted in Jakobovits, p. 90.

98. Maimonides, *Peirush la-Mishnah*, "*Yoma*," 8:2, p. 172.

99. Asher ben Yehiel, *Tosefot ha-Rosh* to *Niddah* 45b. See also Adler, p. 54.

100. Rashi to Gen. 25:26.

101. Plaut, p. 174.

102. See, e.g., David Philipson, quoted in W. Gunther Plaut, *The Growth of Reform Judaism* (New York: World Union for Progressive Judaism, 1965), p. 312.

103. See, e.g., W. Gunther Plaut, *The Rise of Reform Judaism*, pp. 171–78.

104. Kaufmann Kohler, quoted in Plaut, *The Growth of Reform Judaism*, p. 312.

105. Morris Silverman, "Report of Survey on Ritual," *Proceedings of the Rabbinical Assembly* 4 (1930–1932): 335–37.

106. On Confirmation, see Low, pp. 218–23. See also Mordecai M. Kaplan, *Questions Jews Ask* (New York: Reconstructionist Press, 1956), pp. 249–50.

107. See, e.g., Elias Charry, "*Ben Torah*," *Conservative Judaism* 16 (Fall 1961): 52–55; Stuart Rosenberg, "The Right Age for Bar Mitzvah," *Religious Education* 60, no. 4 (July 1965): 298–300; Albert Pappenheim, "Will 13 + 3 Equal Bar Mitzvah?," *Your Child* 3, no. 2 (Mar. 1970): 22–26; Phillip Arian, "Bar Mitzvah at 15," *Conservative Judaism* 15 (Summer 1961): 37–38.

108. See, e.g., Richard L. Rubenstein, *Power Struggle* (New York: Scribner's, 1974), pp. 36–40.

109. Menahem Nahum of Chernobyl, *Me'or Einayyim* (Jerusalem: Me'or Einayyim, 1966), "*Terumah*" end, p. 116.

110. *Zohar*, vol. 2, pp. 97b–98a, 101a. See especially the commentary *Shvivi Nogah* quoting Moses Cordevero on *Zohar*, vol. 2, p. 98a. Note Adler, pp. 114–15.

111. Quoted in Martin Buber, *Tales of the Hasidim*, trans. Olga Marx, 2 vols. (New York: Schocken, 1948), vol. 2, p. 206.

10. THE SANCTITY OF LIFE IN AN AGE OF VIOLENCE

1. Based on *Sanhedrin* 38b. Compare *Erubin* 13b, where the rabbis conclude that it might have been better had human beings not been created.

2. "*Midrash Va-Yoshah*," in *Beth ha-Midrash*, ed. Jellinek, vol. 1, p. 55.

3. *Zohar*, vol. 3, p. 152a.

4. According to the *Zohar*, the first set of tablets given to Moses at Mt. Sinai represented the perfect revelation. But when it became apparent that utopia had not been realized, a second set of tablets—written by man not by God—was required. Thus, the original perfect Torah was rewritten and recast for humankind in its imperfect state. See Scholem, *On the Kabbalah*, pp. 69–70.

5. *Shabbat* 88b.

6. On the permission to eat animal flesh, denied to Adam but permitted to Noah, see *Midrash Genesis Rabbah* 34:13.

7. See Heschel, *God in Search of Man*, pp. 263–76.

8. The notion that human life is intrinsically sacred is nowhere stated explicitly in Scripture. It is implicitly stated and understood as such by rabbinic commentaries on Scripture.

9. Sherwin, *Mystical Theology*, p. 237, and Jacobs, "The Doctrine of the Divine Spark."

10. Compare *Abot d'Rabbi Natan*, ed. Schechter, p. 32b, A, chap. 16 end, "'You shall love your neighbor as yourself, I am the Lord' (Lev. 19:18). Why? Because I [God] have created him."

11. See *Midrash Tanhuma*, ed. Buber, "Leviticus," p. 37a, on Lev. 19:2. Note Schechter, *Some Aspects*, chap. 13. According to the *Ethics of the Fathers* (3:18), God's grace is evident not only in His creating human beings in His image but in His communicating this fact to His creatures, "Beloved is man for he was created in the image of God. Still greater was the love in that it was made known to him that he was created in the image of God, as it is written, 'For in the image of God made He man' [Gen. 9:8]." It should be noted that all rabbinic references to *imitatio Dei* refer only to God's mercy and grace and not to His "harsher" attributes, such as justice.

12. *Midrash Deuteronomy Rabbah* 4:4, *Midrash on Psalms (Midrash Tehillim)* 17:8.

13. *Mekhilta d'Rabbi Yishmael*, ed. Horovitz and Rabin, p. 233, on Exod. 20:16.

14. On the God of pathos in biblical and rabbinic thought, see Heschel, *The Prophets*, pp. 221–32, 247–68; id., *Torah min ha-Shamayim*, vol. 1, pp. 65–93.

15. *Sanhedrin* 46a.

16. *Midrash Genesis Rabbah* 24:8, see *Abot d'Rabbi Natan*, p. 32b, A chap. 16 end.

17. Moses Cordevero, *Palm Tree of Deborah*, p. 53 (Eng. trans.). In his commentary to Hillel's restatement of "You shall love your neighbor as yourself," Rashi stated that the neighbor referred to here is God. See Rashi on *Shabbat* 31a.

18. Ibid.

19. See Jacobs, *Principles*, p. 96.

20. *Sanhedrin* 37a; see *Abot d'Rabbi Natan*, A chap. 31 beginning.

21. *Sanhedrin* 37a.

22. *Midrash Genesis Rabbah* 22:9.

23. *Sanhedrin* 46b.

24. *Midrash Lamentations Rabbah* 1:6. See Avraham Holtz, "*Kiddush* and *Hillul ha-Shem*," *Judaism* 10 (Fall 1961): 360–67. Holtz claims that in biblical Judaism only God can sanctify His Name, but human beings may be held responsible for defaming it. Rabbinic thought, however, introduced the idea that human beings may sanctify God, that human beings need not await God's actions, but through their daily acts, they may sanctify the divine. Note also *Yalkut Shimoni*, "Isaiah," no. 455, "You are My witnesses, says God—when you are my witnesses, I am God, but when you are not my witnesses, it is as if I am not God."

25. *Sanhedrin* 39b.

26. *Midrash Genesis Rabbah* 76:2.

27. Quoted in Reuven Kimmelman, "Non-Violence in the Talmud," *Judaism* 17 (Summer 1968): 324.

28. *Sanhedrin* 72a, *Berakhot* 58a; compare *M. Ohalot* 7:6. On the application of this law to therapeutic abortion, see David Feldman, *Birth Control in Jewish Law* (New York: New York Univ. Press, 1968), pp. 275–84.

29. *Sanhedrin* 72b.

30. Maimonides, *Mishneh Torah—Sefer Nezikin*, "Laws of Murderers," 1:9.

31. *Sanhedrin* 73a.

32. *Sanhedrin* 74a; compare *Tosefta*, ed. Zuckermandel, *"Terumot,"* 7:20, p. 39. Note David Daube, *Collaboration with Tyranny in Rabbinic Law* (Oxford: Oxford Univ. Press, 1965).

33. *Baba Kamma* 93a. Compare Matt. 5:10.

11. MORAL IMPLICATIONS OF THE GOLEM LEGEND

1. Gustav Meyrink, *The Golem*, trans. Madge Pemberton (New York: Ungar, 1964), p. 41.

2. See Sherwin, *Mystical Theology*, pp. 13–19.

3. See Scholem, "The Idea of the Golem," chapter in *On the Kabbalah and Its Symbolism*, p. 203. See also Sherwin, *Mystical Theology*, pp. 194–95, n. 14; J. Lion and J. Lukas, *Das Prage Ghetto* (Prague: Artia, 1959).

4. Threats of expulsion, book burnings, accusations of a secret alliance with the Ottoman Empire, and Luther's anti-Jewish views are historically verifiable. See, e.g., Sherwin, *Mystical Theology*, pp. 28–30. However, the blood libel, which plays such a crucial part in eighteenth-century and subsequent versions of the Golem legend, was not a significant issue in sixteenth-century Bohemia.

5. Much of the retelling of the Golem legend that follows is based upon Rosenberg's work, *Nifla'ot Maharal*, and works that derived from it. Rosenberg's claim that his work is a Yiddish translation of a manuscript found in the library of Metz, containing an eye-witness account of the creation of the Golem by Loew's son-in-law, Isaac Katz, was taken at face value by a number of subsequent writers, such as Chayyim Bloch and Gershon Winkler. However, as Scholem and others have shown, the manuscript is a forgery, written by a Hasidic Jew in about 1910. See Scholem, *On the Kabbalah*, p. 189; Sherwin, *Mystical Theology*, p. 195, no. 15. Judah Rosenberg, *Nifla'ot Maharal* (Pyotrkow: n.p., 1909); Hayyim Bloch, *The Golem*, Harry trans. Schneiderman (Vienna: Vernay, 1925); Gershon Winkler, *The Golem of Prague* (New York: Judaica Press, 1980).

6. For a discussion of various procedures in making a Golem, see Scholem, *On the Kabbalah*, pp. 184–96. Also, see the definitive study by Moshe Idel, *Golem* (Albany: SUNY Press, 1990), published after the writing of this chapter and thus not available for reference.

7. The theme of the Golem's sexuality is explored in the classic Yiddish play by Halper Leivick, *Der Golem* (Vilna: Kletzkin, 1927). *The Great Jewish Plays*, Eng. trans. Joseph C. Landis (New York: Avon, 1972), pp. 217–356. See also the novel by Abraham Rothberg, *The Sword of the Golem* (New York: McCall Publishing, 1970).

8. This episode regarding Landau is found in a footnote in Meir Perles, *Megillat Yuhasin* (Prague, 1864), no pagination. Perles was a great-grandnephew of Judah Loew. His work was written in 1727. The original version of Perles's work makes no mention of the Golem legend. Had the legend been associated with Loew at the time (1727), Perles surely would have mentioned it. As was noted above, it would seem that the legend of the Golem became associated the Loew sometime in the eighteenth century, but after 1727.

9. Jacob Emden, the son of Zevi Ashkenazi, and a descendant of Elijah of Chelm, recorded this story in his various works. See, e.g., Jacob Emden's autobiography, *Megillat Sefer* (Warsaw, 1896), p. 4.

10. *Diamond vs. Chakrabarty*, 447 U.S. 303 (1980); 100 *Supreme Court Reporter* 2204–14. Of more recent relevance is the issue of whether patents should be granted on new

forms of animals such as the "geep," which is a hybrid of a goat and a sheep. See, e.g., David Wheeler, "Grant Patents on Animals?" *Chronicle of Higher Education* 33, no. 28 (25 March 1987): 1, 8; Terence Monmaney, "Should Man Make Beast?" *Newsweek,* 4 May 1987, p. 64; David Wheeler, "Harvard University Receives First U.S. Patent Issued on Animals," *Chronicle of Higher Education* 34, no. 32 (20 Apr. 1988): 1, 8.

11. President's Commission for the Study of Ethical Problems in Medicine and Biomedical and Behavioral Research, *Splicing Life* (Washington: U.S. Government Printing Office, 1982), pp. 95–96.

12. Ibid., p. 58.

13. Joseph Capek and Karel Capek, *R.U.R.,* trans. P. Selver (London: Oxford Univ. Press, 1961), p. 28. For literary spin-offs of the Golem legend, see Byron L. Sherwin, *The Golem Legend: Origins and Implications* (Lanham, Md.: Univ. Press of America, 1985), and Arnold L. Goldsmith, *The Golem Remembered* (Detroit: Wayne State Univ. Press, 1981). While the relationship of the Golem legend to the Frankenstein legend has received extensive discussion, the relationship of the Golem legend to the story of Pinocchio requires additional discussion. As noted later in this chapter, the issue of whether "artificial" beings can attain human status, explored by C. Collodi's story of Pinocchio, is discussed in classical Jewish literature related to the Golem and in contemporary literature related to "artificial" life.

14. *Splicing Life,* pp. 31–32.

15. Seymour Siegel, "Genetic Engineering," *Proceedings of the Rabbinical Assembly* 40 (1978): 165.

16. On the ethical implications of various forms of genetic engineering and "artificial" procedures used to overcome infertility, e.g., "test-tube babies," see, e.g., Paul Ramsey, *Fabricated Man;* Hans Jonas, *Philosophical Essays* (Englewood Cliffs, N.J.: Prentice-Hall, 1974), pp. 141–67; Leon R. Kass, *Toward a More Natural Science* (New York: Free Press, 1985), pp. 43–157; Varga, pp. 52–95; Thomas Shannon, ed., *Bioethics* (New York: Paulist Press, 1976), pp. 295–373; June Goodfield, *Playing God* (New York: Random House, 1977).

17. See, e.g., the novels by John Saul, *The God Project* (New York: Bantam, 1982), and Michael Crichton, *The Andromeda Strain* (New York: Knopf, 1969). See also Charles Piller and Keith Yamamoto, *Gene Wars: Military Control over the New Genetic Technologies* (New York: Morrow, 1988).

18. William Shakespeare, *Macbeth* (New York: Washington Square Press, 1959), Act 4, Scene 1; Act 5, Scene 8.

19. See, e.g., Harris Brotman, "Human Embryo Transplants," *New York Times Magazine,* 8 Jan. 1984, pp. 42–51.

20. See, e.g., Willard Gaylin, "We Have the Awful Knowledge to Make Exact Copies of Human Beings," *New York Times Magazine,* 6 Mar. 1972, pp. 12–14, 41–44, 48; David Rorvik, *In His Image: The Cloning of a Man* (Philadelphia: Lippincott, 1978). Note the novel by Ira Levin, *The Boys from Brazil* (New York: Dell, 1976).

21. See, e.g., Henry C. Black, *Black's Law Dictionary,* Revised 4th Edition (St. Paul, Minn.: West Publishing Co., 1968), s.v. "Person," pp. 1294–1300. Note William Blackstone, *Commentaries on the Laws of England, of the Rights of Persons* (Oxford: Clarendon Press, 1765), pp. 455–73.

22. Martin Caidin, *Cyborg* (New York: Warner, 1972).

23. William Barrett, *The Illusion of Technique* (New York: Doubleday, 1978), p. 103.

24. Capek and Capek, p. 94.

25. See, e.g., William Barrett, *Death of a Soul* (New York: Doubleday, 1986).

26. Julien Offray de La Mettrie, *Man, A Machine* (LaSalle, Ill.: Open Court, 1912), p. 21 (French section), p. 93 (English section). See also Harry Geduld and Ronald Gottesman, *Robots* (Boston: Little, Brown, 1978), p. 31.

27. Rollo May, *Love and Will* (New York: Norton, 1969), pp. 46, 55.

28. Meyrink, p. 26.

29. *Sanhedrin* 65b.

30. Compare *Midrash Genesis Rabbah* 39:14. Note the following statement in *Sifre Deuteronomy*, ed. Finkelstein, p. 54, no. 32. Eng. trans., p. 59: "Is it not true that if all the creatures in the world were to convene in order to create just one gnat and endow it with a soul, they would not be able to do so?"

31. According to the legend of Faust, Faust created an artificial person through powers granted by the devil. According to a Christian legend, Albertus Magnus made an automaton that was destroyed by St. Thomas Aquinas on the grounds that it was the work of the devil. See, e.g., Geduld and Gottesman, *Robots*, p. 18.

32. As Scholem notes, pp. 194–95, the term "Golem" to refer to an artificially created person is used most often by Polish and German Jewish literature. Sephardic literature and earlier Jewish literature use the term, "a man created by the *Sefer Yetzirah*."

33. See Rashi on *Sanhedrin* 67b.

34. *Sefer Yetzirah* 2:2, 5.

35. See, e.g., *Berakhot* 55a.

36. See, e.g., Moshe Idel, *The Mystical Experience in Abraham Abulafia* (Albany: SUNY Press, 1988), pp. 13–55, 73–179. It should be noted that Abulafia opposed the creation of artificial life through the use of letter permutations. As he bluntly put it, those who desire to create cows, are cows. See Scholem, *Major Trends*, p. 145.

37. See, e.g., the commentary of Samuel Edels to this passage, in standard editions of the Talmud.

38. See, e.g., Nahmanides, *Commentary to the Torah*, vol. 1, p. 33, on Genesis 2:7; Moses Cordevero, *Pardes Rimonim*, 2 vols. (Jerusalem: n.p., 1962), vol. 2, p. 63a, sec. 24, chap. 10.

39. *Sanhedrin* 38b.

40. *Midrash Leviticus Rabbah* 29:1. Compare variants of this text: *Midrash on Psalms*, ed. Buber, 92:3, p. 202, Eng. trans., vol. 2, pp. 111–12; *Midrash Pesikta Rabbati*, ed. Friedmann, chap. 46, p. 187b. Eng. trans., p. 791; *Pirke de-Rabbi Eliezer*. Eng. trans., chap. 11, pp. 77–78; *Abot d'Rabbi Natan*, ed. Schechter, p. 3a. Eng. trans., p. 11. Note Ginzberg, *The Legends of the Jews*, vol. 5, p. 79.

41. *Midrash Genesis Rabbah* 14:8.

42. See *Midrash Leviticus Rabbah* 29:1, where it is stated that God decided and began to create Adam on New Year's Day.

43. *Midrash Genesis Rabbah* 24:2. Compare *Midrash Exodus Rabbah* 40:3; *Midrash on Psalms* 139:6, p. 265b; *Yalkut Shimoni* "Psalms," para. 887; *Yalkut ha-Makiri*, ed. Solomon Buber, (Berditchev: Sheftal, 1900), 139:32, pp. 135a–b.

44. See also *Yalkut Shimoni*, "Genesis," para. 34; *Sanhedrin* 22b.

45. See, e.g., Scholem, "The Idea of the Golem," pp. 178–80.

46. Ibid., p. 199. See Emmanuel Bin Gorion, ed., *Mimekor Yisrael: Classical Jewish Folktales*, trans. I. M. Lask, (Philadelphia: Jewish Publication Society, 1976), p. 752. For a female Golem in contemporary literature, note Cynthia Ozick, *Levitation* (New York: Knopf, 1982).

47. Scholem, "The Idea of the Golem," p. 180.

48. Ibid., p. 181.

49. *Sanhedrin* 19a.

50. Zevi Ashkenazi, *She'eilot u-Teshuvot*, no. 93. See no. 76 for a direct reference to Judah Loew. Later authorities upheld the views stated in this responsum. See, e.g., the responsa of Ashkenazi's son, Jacob Emden, *She'eilat Yavetz* (Altona, 1739), Part 2, no. 82.

51. For example, Jewish legal literature discusses the propriety of eating meat when the animal was ritually slaughtered by a Golem. See discussion and sources noted in Zvi Hirsch Shapira, *Darkhei Teshuvah* (Jerusalem: n.p., 1967) vol. 1/2, pp. 38–39, no. 11 on Karo, *Shulhan Arukh—Yoreh Deah*, para. 7:1.

52. See also Cordevero, *Pardes Rimonim*, vol. 2, p. 63a, sec. 24, chap. 10.

53. Isaiah Horowitz, "*Torah she-Bikhtav*"—"*va-yeishev*," vol. 3, p. 65a.

54. Shapira, pp. 38–39, no. 11.

55. *Sefer ha-Bahir*, no. 196, p. 89.

56. Gershon Hanokh Lainer of Radzyn, *Sidrei Taharot—Ohalot* (Pyotrkow: n.p., 1903), p. 5a.

57. Judah Loew, *Hiddushei Aggadot*, vol. 3, pp. 166–67.

58. Norbert Wiener, *God and Golem, Inc*. (Cambridge, Mass.: MIT Press, 1964), pp. 71, 95.

59. Judah Loew, *Hiddushei Aggadot*, vol. 3, pp. 166–67.

60. Id., *Be'er ha-Golah* (New York: Judaica Press, 1969), chap. 2, pp. 27–28.

61. *Splicing Life*, pp. 31–32.

62. For a review of Jewish teachings on artificial insemination, see Fred Rosner, "Artificial Insemination in Jewish Law," *Judaism* 19 (Fall 1970): 452–65. For a discussion of test-tube babies in Jewish Law, and in particular its relation to Ashkenazi's responsum, see, e.g., Judah Gershuni, "The First Test-tube Baby in the Light of Jewish Law," *Or ha-Mizrah* 27, no. 1 (Oct. 1978): 15–21.

63. For a translation and discussion of this responsum by Joseph Schwartz, see Azriel Rosenfield, "Judaism and Gene Design," *Tradition* 13, no. 2 (1972): 71–81. See also Z. N. Goldberg and E. Bick, "Maternity in Fetal Implant," *Crossroads*, pp. 71–87.

64. *Del Zio vs. Presbyterian Hospital*, 74 Civ. 3588, New York City. On the more recent Tennessee case, Davis vs. Davis vs. King, see, e.g., George Annas, "A French Homunculus in a Tennessee Court," *Hastings Center Report* 19:6 (Dec. 1989): 20–22.

65. See, e.g., *Sanhedrin* 37a.

66. See, e.g., Gershom Scholem, "The Golem of Prague and the Golem of Rehovot," chapter in *The Messianic Idea in Judaism*, pp. 335–41; Azriel Rosenfield, "Human Identity: Halakhic Issues," *Tradition* 16, no. 3 (Spring 1977): 58–75; Rosenfield, "Religion and the Robot," *Tradition* 8, no. 3 (Fall 1966): 15–28.

12. REFLECTIONS

1. *Seder Eliyahu Rabbah ve-Seder Eliyahu Zuta*, ed. Friedmann, "*Zuta*," chap. 13, p. 195. Eng. trans., p. 456.

2. Shneur Zalman of Liadi, *Likutei Amarim [Tanya]* (Brooklyn: Otzar ha-Hasidim, 1965), chap. 5, pp. 18–19.

3. See José Faur, "Some General Observations on the Character of Classical Jewish Literature," *Journal of Jewish Studies* 38, no. 1 (Spring 1977): 31–36. See also Erich Auerbach, *Mimesis*, trans. Willard Trask, (Princeton, N.J.: Princeton Univ. Press, 1968), pp. 11–23.

4. *Abodah Zarah* 19a. See also *Kiddushin* 32a. "Indeed the Torah is his [the scholar's]."

5. See Solomon Schechter, *Seminary Addresses and Other Papers* (New York: Burning Bush Press, 1959), p. 111.

6. From a letter from Solomon Schechter to Max Heller dated 1 Feb. 1907. Quoted in Sefton Tempkin, "Solomon Schechter and Max Heller," *Conservative Judaism* 16 (Winter 1962): 55.

7. *Sanhedrin* 34a.

8. *Ethics of the Fathers* 3:15.

9. Compare David Weiss Halivni, *Midrash, Mishnah and Gemara* (Cambridge, Mass.: Harvard Univ. Press, 1986), pp. 103–12. Weiss notes the attempt of Samuel ben Meir (Rashbam) and others to discover the *peshat* of biblical verses. However, as Weiss also admits (pp. 112–15), the approach of Samuel ben Meir and other early medievals who sought the *peshat* independent from its halakhic application or from rabbinic exegetical interpretation was discontinued in subsequent Jewish tradition. Furthermore, as Weiss also notes, Samuel ben Meir did not apply the quest for the *peshat* in his Talmudic commentaries. Weiss further notes (p. 108) that Talmudic literature continuously warned against scholarship unrelated to action. As Louis Jacobs notes in his review of Weiss's book, the sages did not seek the "plain" meaning of the text, but the "true" meaning as defined by the parameters of tradition. See Louis Jacobs, "Jews and Law," *Judaism* 37 (Spring 1988): 246– 47. See also Faur, *Golden Doves*, pp. xv-xvi, 123–24.

10. *Pesikta de-Rav Kahana*, ed. S. Buber, 12:12, p. 102a.

11. *P. Kiddushin* 1:7.

12. *Megillah* 6b.

BIBLIOGRAPHY

THE BIBLIOGRAPHY is divided into two sections: Classical Jewish Sources and Other Sources. The first section primarily lists Hebrew works from the ancient and medieval periods. The editions of these works used in the preparation of this book are included in the entries. Citations of these works in the Notes are given in such a manner as to allow scholars to locate sources quoted or referred to in other editions. Where available, English translations of these works are listed as well.

Because commentary is such a dominant form of classical Jewish literature, and because commentaries are often printed together with the earlier text on which they comment, commentaries are cited, where appropriate, by noting the earlier work in which they usually appear. For example, Judah Ashkenazi's commentary *Be'er Heiteiv* on Joseph Karo's legal code *Shulhan Arukh*, which appears printed in standard editions of the *Shulhan Arukh* alongside the text of the *Shulhan Arukh* on many pages of that text, is listed under "Ashkenazi, Judah." There, it is noted that this work may be found in editions of the *Shulhan Arukh* cited under "Karo, Joseph. *Shulhan Arukh*." Thus, this commentary is cited as follows: Ashkenazi, Judah. *Be'er Heiteiv*. In Joseph Karo. *Shulhan Arukh* [with commentaries].

CLASSICAL JEWISH SOURCES

Aaron ha-Kohen mei-Lunel. *Orhot Hayyim*. Jerusalem: n.p., 1956.

Aboab, Isaac. *Menorat ha-Ma'or*. Jerusalem: Mosad ha-Rav Kook, 1961.

Abot d'Rabbi Natan. Edited by Solomon Schechter. Vienna, 1887. 2d ed. New York: Feldheim Publishers, 1967. *The Fathers According to Rabbi Nathan*. Translated by Judah Goldin. New Haven: Yale Univ. Press, 1955.

Abrahams, Israel, ed., *Hebrew Ethics Wills*. Philadelphia: Jewish Publication Society, 1926.

Abravanel, Don Isaac. *Commentary to the Torah* [in Hebrew]. 3 vols. Jerusalem: Bnei Abarbanel, 1964.

Ahai Gaon. *She'iltot*. Edited by S. K. Mirsky. 6 vols. Jerusalem: Mosad ha-Rav Kook, 1964.

Albo, Joseph. *Sefer ha-Ikkarim (The Book of Principles)*. Translated by Isaac Husik. 6 vols. Philadelphia: Jewish Publication Society, 1930.

Alsheikh, Moses. *Torat Moshe*. 2 vols. Warsaw: Munk, 1879.

Arama, Isaac. *Akedat Yitzhak*. Salonika, 1522.

Ashkenazi, Judah. *Be'er Heiteiv*. In Joseph Karo. *Shulhan Arukh* [with commentaries].

Ashkenazi, Zevi. *She'eilot u-Teshuvot*. Amsterdam, 1812.

———. *She'eilot u-Teshuvot Hakham Zvi*. Jerusalem: n.p., 1970.

Ayash, Judah. *Shevet Yehudah*. Livorno, 1683.

Azkiri, Eliezer. *Sefer Hareidim*. Jerusalem: n.p., 1987.

Azulai, Hayyim Joseph David. *Birkhei Yoseph*. Vienna: 1843.

———. *Kiseih Rahamim*. Livorno, 1803.

Bar Hiyya, Abraham. *The Meditation of the Sad Soul*. Translated by Geoffrey Wigoder. London: Routledge and Kegan Paul, 1969.

Bekhor Shor, Joseph. *Commentary to the Torah* [in Hebrew]. 3 vols. Jerusalem: Tehiya, 1956.

Ben Asher, Bahya. *Commentary to the Torah* [in Hebrew]. Edited by Charles B. Chavel. 3 vols. Jerusalem: Mosad ha-Rav Kook, 1971.

———. *Kad ha-Kemah*. Lwow, 1892. *Encyclopedia of Torah Thoughts*. Translated by Charles B. Chavel. New York: Shilo Publishing House, 1980.

Ben Asher, Jacob. *Arba'ah Turim* [Sections are: *Orah Hayyim, Yoreh Deah, Even ha-Ezer, Hoshen Mishpat*]. 1550. Reprint. New York: Grossman, n.d. [with commentaries].

Ben David, Abraham. *Hassagot of Ravad*. In Moses Maimonides. *Mishneh Torah* [with commentaries].

———. *Teshuvot u-Fesakim*. Jerusalem: Mosad ha-Rav Kook, 1964.

Ben Mattitayhu, Benjamin Ze'ev. *Binyamin Ze'ev*. Venice: 1539.

Ben Meir, Samuel (Rashbam). *Commentary to the Talmud*. In *Talmud* [with commentaries].

———. *Commentary to the Torah* [in Hebrew]. In standard editions of *Mikraot Gedolot*.

Ben Samuel, Jacob. *Beit Ya'akov*. Dyrenfuerth, 1696.

Ben Yehiel, Asher. *She'eilot u-Teshuvot ha-Rosh*. Jerusalem: n.p., 1965.

———. *Tosfot ha-Rosh*. In *Talmud* [with commentaries].

Berlin, Saul. *Responsa Besomim Rosh* [in Hebrew]. Berlin, 1793.

Beth ha-Midrash Edited by Adolph Jellinek. 6 vols. 1855. Reprint. Jerusalem: Wahrmann, 1967.

Boaz, Joshua. *Shiltei ha-Gibborim*. In *Talmud* [with commentaries].

Colon, Joseph. *Responsa Maharik* [in Hebrew]. Venice, 1519.

Cordevero, Moses. *Pardes Rimonim*. 2 vols. Jerusalem: n.p., 1962.

———. *Tomer Devorah*. Tel Aviv: Friedman, 1965. *The Palm Tree of Deborah*. Translated by Louis Jacobs. London: Vallentine, Mitchell, 1960.

David ben Samuel. *Turei Zahav*. In Joseph Karo. *Shulhan Arukh* [with commentaries].

Di Trani, Isaiah. *Teshuvot ha-Rid*. Edited by Abraham Wertheimer. Jerusalem: Machon ha-Talmud ha-Yisraeli ha-Shalem, 1967.

Di Trani, Moses. *Beit Elohim*. Warsaw: Goldman, 1852.
Di Vidas, Elijah. *Reshit Hokhmah*. Tel Aviv: Esther Press, n.d.
Duran, Samson ben Zadok. *Responsa Tashbeitz* [in Hebrew]. Lwow, 1891.
————. *Sefer Tashbeitz*. Warsaw: n.p., 1902.
Duran, Simeon ben Zemah. *Magen Abot*. Livorno, 1785.

Edels, Samuel. *Hiddushei Halakhot ve- Aggadot*. In *Talmud* [with commentaries].
Eiger, Solomon. *Gilyonei Maharshah*. In Joseph Karo. *Shulhan Arukh* [with commentaries].
Einhorn, Ze'ev. *Maharzu*. In *Midrash Rabbah* [with commentaries].
Eisenstadt, Abraham Zevi. *Pithei Teshuvah*. In Joseph Karo. *Shulhan Arukh* [with commentaries].
Eleh Divrei ha-Brit. Altona, 1819.
Eliezer of Metz. *Sefer Yere'im*. Livorno: Rokeah, 1837.
Elijah ha-Kohen. *Me'il Zedakah*. Izmir, 1731.
Elijah of Vilna. *Be'ur ha-Gra*. In Joseph Karo. *Shulhan Arukh* [with commentaries].
————. *Sefer Mishlei im Biur ha-Gera*. Petah Tikvah: n.p., 1985.
Emden, Jacob. *Glosses of Ya'avetz*. In *Talmud* [with commentaries].
————. *Megillat Sefer*. Warsaw, 1896.
————. *She'eilat Yavetz*. Altona, 1739.
Emet me-Kotsk Tizmah. Bnei Brak: Nezah, 1961.

Feinstein, Moses. *Iggerot Moshe—Orah Hayyim*. New York: Gross and Weiss, 1959.
————. *Iggerot Moshe—Yoreh Deah*. 2 vols. New York: Balshon, 1963.
Frankel, David. *Korban ha-Edah*. In *Palestinian Talmud* [with commentaries].

Ganzfried, Solomon. *Kitzur Shulhan Arukh*. Lwow, 1860.
Gerondi, Jonah. *Shaarey Teshuvah*. Jerusalem: Eshkol, 1978. Translated by S. Silverstein. 2 vols. New York: Feldheim Publishers, 1971.
Gershon Hanokh Lainer of Radzyn. *Sidrei Taharot—Ohalot*. Pyotrkow: n.p., 1903.
Gersonides (Levi ben Gershon). *Commentary to the Torah* [in Hebrew]. Venice: Bomberg, 1547.
Gombiner, Abraham. *Magen Avraham*. In Joseph Karo. *Shulhan Arukh* [with commentaries].
Greenwald, Meir. *Zoheir ha-Brit*. Israel: Gellis, 1931.

Hafetz, Moses. *Malekhet Mahshevet*. Warsaw: Cahana, 1914.
Ha-Levi, Judah. *The Kuzari*. Translated by H. Slonimsky. New York: Schocken, 1964.
————. *Selected Poems of Jehudah ha-Levi*. edited by H. Brody and translated by N. Salaman. Philadelphia: Jewish Publication Society, 1924.
Hahn, Joseph Yuspa. *Yosif Ometz*. Frankfurt: Hermon, 1928.
Hayyim ben Betsalel. *Sefer ha-Hayyim*. Jerusalem: Weinfeld, 1965.
Hayyot, Zvi Hirsch. *Maharitz Hayyot*. In *Talmud* [with commentaries].
Heller, Aryeh Leib. *Ketzot ha-Hoshen*. Lwow, 1888.
Heller, Yom Tov Lipmann. *Tosfot Yom Tov*. In *Mishnah* [with commentaries].

Horowitz, Abraham ha-Levi. *Sefer Yesh Nohalin*. Jerusalem: Edison, 1960.
Horowitz, Isaiah. *Shnei Luhot ha-Brit*. 3 vols. Jerusalem: Edison, 1960.

Ibn Adret, Solomon. *Responsa, Part Four* [in Hebrew]. Pietrikov: Belkhatavsky,
    1883.
Ibn Aknin, Joseph. *The Hygiene of the Soul*. Translated by A. Halkin. In *Proceed-
    ings of the American Academy for Jewish Research* 4 (1933).
Ibn Al-Nakawa, Israel. *Menorat ha-Ma'or*. Edited by H. G. Enelow. New York:
    Bloch Publishing Co., 1931.
Ibn Asevelli, Yom Tov. *Hiddushei ha-Ritba*. In *Talmud* [with commentaries].
————. *Responsa* [in Hebrew]. Edited by J. Kapah. Jerusalem: n.p., 1959.
Ibn Attar, Hayyim. *Or ha-Hayyim*. In *Mikraot Gedolot*.
Ibn Daud, Abraham. *Emunah Ramah*. Frankfurt, 1852.
Ibn Ezra, Abraham. *Commentary to the Torah* [Hebrew]. 5 vols. Tel Aviv: Moreib,
    1961. Also in *Mikraot Gedolot*.
Ibn Falaquera, Shem Tov ben Joseph. *The Book of the Seeker*. Translated by M. H.
    Levine. New York: Yeshiva Univ. Press, 1976.
Ibn Gabirol, Solomon. *Choice of Pearls*. Translated by A. Cohen. New York: Bloch
    Publishing Co., 1925.
————. *The Improvement of the Moral Qualities*. Translated by Stephen S. Wise.
    New York: Columbia Univ. Press, 1901.
Ibn Migash, Joseph. *Responsa* [in Hebrew]. Jerusalem: Gitler, 1959.
Ibn Pakuda, Bahya. *The Book of Direction to the Duties of the Heart*. Translated by
    Menahem Mansoor. London: Routledge and Kegan Paul, 1973.
Ibn Verga, Solomon. *Shevet Yehudah*. Jerusalem: n.p., 1955.
Ibn Zaddik, Joseph. *Olam ha-Katan*. Edited by S. Horowitz. Breslau: Schatzky,
    1903.
Ibn Zimra, David. *Ha-Radbaz*. In Maimonides. *Mishneh Torah* [with commen-
    taries].
————. *Teshuvot ha-Radbaz*. Furth, 1781.
Israel of Rhyzen. *Knesset Yisrael*. Warsaw: n.p., 1906.
Issachar Baer Bremen Ashkenazi. *Matnat Kehunah*. In *Midrash Rabbah* [with com-
    mentaries].
————. *Glosses* [in Hebrew]. In Joseph Karo. *Shulhan Arukh* [with commen-
    taries].
————. *Responsa* [in Hebrew]. Edited by Asher Siev. Jerusalem: n.p., 1970.

Jacob David of Slutzk. *Ridbaz*. In *Palestinian Talmud* [with commentaries].
Jacob Joseph of Polnoye. *Toledot Ya'akov Yosef*. Jerusalem: n.p., 1967.
Joseph Moses of Munster. *Leket ha-Yosher*. Berlin: Mekitzei Nirdamim, 1903.

Karo, Joseph. *Beit Yosef*. In Jacob ben Asher. *Arba'ah Turim* [with commentaries].
————. *Keseph Mishnah*. In Maimonides. *Mishneh Torah* [with commentaries].
————. *Shulhan Arukh* [Sections are: *Orah Hayyim, Yoreh De'ah, Even ha-Ezer,
    Hoshen Mishpat*]. Reprint. Vilna: Romm, 1911 [with commentaries].

Kimhi, David. *Commentary to the Bible* [in Hebrew]. In *Mikraot Gedolot*.

Lampronti, Isaac. *Pahad Yitzhak*. Lyck: Mekitzei Nirdamim, 1874.

Levi Yitzhak of Berdichev. *Kedushat Levi*. Jerusalem: Mosad l'Hotza'at Sifrei Musar va'Hasidut, 1958.

Lipschutz, Israel. *Tiferet Israel*. Hanover, 1830.

Loew, Judah. *Be'er ha-Golah*. New York: Judaica Press, 1969.

———. *Derekh ha-Hayyim*. New York: Judaica Press, 1969.

———. *Gur Aryeih*. Jerusalem: Yahadut, 1972.

———. *Hiddushei Aggadot Maharal mi-Prag*. 4 vols. New York: Judaica Press, 1969.

———. *Netivot Olom*. New York: Judaica Press, 1969.

———. *Nezah Yisrael*. New York: Judaica Press, 1969.

———. *Tiferet Yisrael*. New York: Judaica Press, 1969.

Lunshitz, Ephraim. *Keli Yakar*. In *Mikraot Gedolot*.

Luria, David. *Hiddushei ha-Radal*. In *Midrash Rabbah* [with commentaries].

Luria, Solomon. *Responsa* [in Hebrew]. Lublin, 1774.

———. *Yam shel Shelomo*. Stettin: Shrentzel, 1861.

Luzzatto, Moses Hayyim. *Mesillat Yesharim—The Path of the Upright*. Translated by Mordecai M. Kaplan. Philadelphia: Jewish Publication Society, 1966.

Maimonides, Moses. *The Book of Adoration (Mishneh Toreh—Sefer Ahavah)*. Translated by Moses Hyamson. Jerusalem: Boys Town Publishers, 1965.

———. *The Book of Agriculture (Mishneh Torah—Sefer Zera'im)*. Translated by Isaac Klein. New Haven: Yale Univ. Press, 1979.

———. *The Book of Asseverations (Mishneh Torah—Sefer Hafla'ah)*. Translated by B. D. Klein. New Haven: Yale Univ. Press, 1962.

———. *The Book of Judges (Mishneh Torah—Sefer Shofetim)*. Translated by A. M. Hershman. New Haven: Yale Univ. Press, 1949.

———. *The Book of Knowledge (Mishneh Torah—Sefer ha-Mada)*. Translated by Moses Hyamson. Jerusalem: Boys Town Publishers, 1965.

———. *The Book of Torts (Mishneh Torah—Sefer Nezikin)*. Translated by Hyman Klein. New Haven: Yale Univ. Press, 1954.

———. *The Book of Women (Mishneh Torah—Sefer Nashim)*. Translated by Isaac Klein. New Haven: Yale Univ. Press, 1972.

———. *Commentary to the Mishnah—Abot*. Jerusalem: Mosad ha-Rav Kook, 1961. *The Commentary to Mishnah Abot*. Translated by Arthur David. New York: Bloch Publishing Co., 1968.

———. *The Eight Chapters of Maimonides on Ethics*. Translated by Joseph I. Gorfinkle. New York: Columbia Univ. Press, 1912.

———. *Hakdamah le-Peirush ha-Mishnah*. Edited by Mordecai Rabinowitz. Jerusalem: Mosad ha-Rav Kook, 1961.

———. *Hanhagat ha-Beri'ut (Regimen Sanitas)*. Edited by S. Munter and translated by Moses ibn Tibbon. Jerusalem: Mosad ha-Rav Kook, 1957.

———. *Kovetz Iggerot ha-Rambam*. 2d ed. Jerusalem: n.p., 1967.

————. *The Medical Aphorisms of Moses Maimonides*. Translated by Fred Rosner and S. Muntner. New York: Yeshiva Univ. Press, 1971.

————. *Mishneh Torah* [with commentaries]. 6 vols. 1509. Reprint. New York: Friedman, 1963.

————. *Mishneh Torah—Sefer ha-Mada*. Edited by Saul Lieberman. Jerusalem: Mosad ha-Rav Kook, 1964.

————. *Moreh Nevukhim*. Jerusalem: n.p., 1960. *The Guide of the Perplexed*. Translated by Shlomo Pines. Chicago: Univ. of Chicago Press, 1963.

————. *Peirush la-Mishnah*. Edited by Joseph Kapah. Jerusalem: Mosad ha-Rav Kook, 1963.

————. *Sefer ha-Mitzvot*. Edited by Joseph Kapah. Jerusalem: Mosad ha-Rav Kook, 1971.

————. *Teshuvot ha-Rambam*. Edited by A. Frieman. Tel Aviv: Mekitzei Nirdamim, 1934. *Teshuvot ha-Rambam*. Edited by J. Blau. 3 vols. Jerusalem: Mekitzei Nirdamim, 1948.

————. *Treatise on Asthma*. Translated by S. Muntner. Philadelphia: Lippincott, 1963.

Margaliot, Hayyim Mordecai. *Sha'arei Teshuvah*. In Joseph Karo. *Shulhan Arukh* [with commentaries].

Margaliot, Moses. *P'nei Moshe*. In *Palestinian Talmud* [with commentaries].

Matt, Moses. *Mateh Moshe*. Warsaw, 1876.

Meiri, Menahem. *Beit ha'Behirah—Hullin*. Jerusalem: n.p., 1970.

————. *Beit ha-Behirah—Sanhedrin*. Jerusalem: n.p., 1965.

————. *Hibbur ha-Teshuvah*. Edited by A. Schreiber. New York: Schulzinger, 1950.

Mekhilta d'Rabbi Yishmael. Edited by Hayyim Horovitz and Israel Rabin. Jerusalem: Wahrmann, 1960. *Mechilta de Rabbi Ishmael*. Edited and translated by Jacob Lauterbach. 3 vols. Philadelphia: Jewish Publication Society, 1933.

Menahem Nahum of Chernobyl. *Me'or Einayyim*. Jerusalem: Me'or Einayyim, 1966.

Midrash Mishlei. Edited by Solomon Buber. Lwow, 1893.

Midrash Pesikta Rabbati. Edited by Meir Friedmann. Vienna: Herausgebers, 1880. Reprint. Tel Aviv: n.p., 1968. *Pesikta Rabbati*. Translated by William G. Braude. New Haven: Yale Univ. Press, 1968.

Midrash Rabbah. Vilna: Romm, 1921 [with commentaries]. Translated under the editorship of H. Freedman and Maurice Simon. 10 vols. London: Soncino, 1939.

Midrash Samuel. Edited by Solomon Buber. Cracow, 1893.

Midrash Tanhuma.Edited by Solomon Buber. Vilna, 1885.

Midrash Tanhuma—ha-Nidpas. Jerusalem: Levin-Epstein, 1964.

Midrash Tehillim. Edited by Solomon Buber. Vilna: Romm, 1891. *Midrash on Psalms*. Translated by William G. Braude. New Haven: Yale Univ. Press, 1959.

Mikraot Gedolot [Hebrew Scripture with commentaries]. 5 vols. New York: Tanach, 1959.

Mishnah [with commentaries]. Jerusalem: Horeb, 1952.

Moelln, Jacob. *She'eilot u-Teshuvot Maharil*. Cracow: Fisher ve-Deitcher, 1881.

Mordecai of Chernobyl. *Lekutei Torah*. New York: n.p., 1954.
Moses Hayyim Ephraim of Sudylkow. *Degel Mahaneh Ephraim*. Jerusalem: Hadar, 1963.
Moses of Coucy. *Sefer Mitzvot Gadol*. Venice, 1522.

Nahmanides, Moses. *Commentary to Maimonides's Sefer ha-Mitzvot*. In Maimonides. *Sefer ha-Mitzvot*. Jerusalem: Levin-Epstein, 1965.
———. *Kitve Rabenu Moshe ben Nahman*. Edited by Charles B. Chavel. 2 vols. Jerusalem: Mosad ha-Rav Kook, 1964.
———. *Commentary to the Torah* [Hebrew]. Edited by Charles B. Chavel. Jerusalem: Mosad ha-Rav Kook, 1959. Also in *Mikraot Gedolot*.
Nissim (Rabbenu Nissim). *Ran*. In *Talmud* [with commentaries].

Orhot Zaddikim. Translated by Seymour J. Cohen. New York: Feldheim Publishers, 1960.

Palaggi, Hayyim. *Hikkeke Lev*. Salonika, 1840.
Palestinian Talmud [with commentaries]. Krotoschin, 1886.
Perles, Meir. *Megillat Yuhasin*. Prague, 1864.
Pesikta de-Rav Kahana. Edited by Solomon Buber. Lyck: Mekitzei Nirdamim, 1868. Edited by Bernard Mandelbaum. 2 vols. New York: Jewish Theological Seminary, 1962. Translated by William G. Braude and Israel J. Kapstein. Philadelphia: Jewish Publication Society, 1975.
Pirke de-Rabbi Eliezer. Warsaw, 1852. Reprint. New York: Ohm, 1946. Translated by Gerald Friedlander. London: n.p., 1916.

Rashi (Solomon Yitzhaki). *Commentary to the Talmud*. In *Talmud* [with commentaries].
———. *Commentary to the Torah* [Hebrew]. In *Mikraot Gedolot*.
Reischer, Jacob. *Shevut Ya'akov*. Lwow, 1860.
Rosenberg, Judah. *Nifla'ot Maharal*. Pyrotrkow: n.p., 1909.
Rosensweig, Gerson. *Massekhet America*. New York, 1891.

Samuel of Uceda. *Midrash Shmuel*. Jerusalem: Brody-Katz, n.d.
Schiff, Meir. *Maharam Schiff*. In *Talmud* [with commentaries].
Schreiber, Moses. *She'eilot u-Teshuvot Hatam Sofer—Yoreh Deah*. Pressburg, 1841. Reprint. Vienna, 1883. *Orah Hayyim*. Vienna, 1895.
———. *Sefer Hatam Sofer*. Vienna, 1892–1895.
Seder Eliyahu Rabbah ve-Seder Eliyahu Zutta. Edited by Meir Friedmann. Vienna: Ahiyasaf, 1904. *Tanna Debe Eliyahu*. Eng. trans. William G. Braude and Israel J. Kapstein. Philadelphia: Jewish Publication Society, 1981.
Sefer ha-Bahir. Edited by Reuven Margaliot. Jerusalem: Mosad ha-Rav Kook, 1951.
Sefer Hasidim. Edited by Jehuda Wistinetzki and J. Freimann. Frankfurt: Wahrmann Verlag, 1924. Edited by Reuven Margaliot. Jerusalem: Mosad ha-Rav Kook, 1960.

Sefer ha-Hinukh. Eduted and translated by Charles Wengrov. Jerusalem: Feldheim Publishers, 1978.

Sefer ha-Yashar—The Book of Righteousness. Translated by Seymour J. Cohen. New York: Ktav, 1973.

Sefer Yitzirah. 1562. Reprint. Jerusalem: Levin-Epstein, 1965.

Semahot. The Tractate Mourning. Translated by Dov Zlotnick. New Haven: Yale Univ. Press, 1966.

Shabbatai ben Meir. *Siftei Kohen*. In Joseph Karo. *Shulhan Arukh* [with commentaries].

Shapira, Zevi Hirsch. *Darkhei Teshuvah*. Jerusalem: n.p., 1967.

Shneur Zalman of Liadi. *Likutei Amarim [Tanya]*. Brooklyn: Otzar ha-Hasidim, 1965.

————. *Shulhan Arukh ha-Rav*. 4 vols. Zhitomir, 1856.

Sifra. Vienna: Schlossberg, 1862. Reprint. New York: Ohm, 1947.

Sifrei. Edited by Meir Friedmann. Vienna, 1865. Edited by Louis Finkelstein. Berlin: Judischer Kulturband in Deutschland/Abteilung Verlag, 1939. *Midrash Sifre on Deuteronomy*. Translated by Reuven Hammer. New Haven: Yale Univ. Press, 1986.

Sirkes, Joel. *Bayyit Hadash*. In Jacob ben Asher. *Arba'ah Turim* [with commentaries].

Soferim. In *Talmud* [with commentaries]. Translated by Israel W. Slotki. In *The Minor Tractates of the Talmud*. Edited by A. Cohen. 2 vols. London: Soncino, 1965.

Talmud [with commentaries]. Vilna: Romm, 1895. Reprint. 20 vols. New York: Otzar ha-Sefarim, 1958. Eng. translation edited by Isadore Epstein. *The Talmud*. 18 vols. London: Soncino, 1948–52.

Targum Onkelos. In *Mikraot Gedolot*.

Tosafot. In *Talmud* [with commentaries].

Tosefta. In *Talmud* [with commentaries]. Edited by Moses Zuckermandel. Vienna, 1877. Reprint. Berlin: Calvary, 1899.

Tzava'at Rivash. Cracow, 1896.

Vidal Yom Tov of Tolosa. *Maggid Mishnah*. In Maimonides. *Mishneh Toreh* [with commentaries].

Yalkut ha-Makiri. Edited by Solomon Buber. Berdichev: Sheftal, 1900.

Yalkut Shimoni. New York: Pardes, 1944.

Yehiel ben Yekutiel of Rome. *Sefer Ma'alot ha-Middot*. Jerusalem: Eshkol, 1968.

Yitzhak of Radvil. "The Holiness of Man." Translated by Samuel Dresner. In *Judaism* 37 (Spring 1988).

Waldenberg, Eliezer. *Tzitz Eliezer* 10 vols. Jerusalem: n.p., 1954— .

Zabara, Joseph ben Meir. *The Book of Delight*. Translated by Moses Hadas. New York: Columbia Univ. Press, 1932.

Zahalon, Jacob. *Otzar ha-Hayyim*. Venice, 1683.

Zedakah l'Hayyim. Abridged ed. of *Me'il Zedakah*. Edited by Hayyim Pelaggi. 1873.

Zevi Hirsch ben Azriel of Vilna. *Beit Lehem Yehudah*. Zulka, 1733.

Zioni, Menahem. *Sefer Zioni*. Lwow: Nissim Zis, 1882.

Zohar. 3 vols. Vilna: Romm, 1882.

OTHER SOURCES

Aberbach, A. "Smoking and Halakhah." *Tradition* 10, no. 3 (1969).

Abrahams, Israel. *The Book of Delight and Other Papers*. Philadelphia: Jewish Publication Society, 1912.

––––––. *Jewish Life in the Middle Ages*. New York: Meridian, 1958.

Abramowitz, Hayyim. *Ha-Dibrah ha-Hamishit*. Jerusalem: Reuven Mass, 1971.

––––––. *Heikhal ha-Teshuvah*. B'nei Brak: Nezah, 1961.

Adler, Benjamin. *Halakhot ve-Halikhot Bar-Mitzvah*. Jerusalem: Or Torah, 1964.

Agus, Jacob B. *Dialogue and Tradition*. New York: Abelard Schuman, 1971.

––––––. *Guideposts in Modern Judaism*. New York: Bloch Publishing Co., 1954.

––––––. *The Vision and the Way*. New York: Ungar, 1966.

Albert, Ada Rappoport. "Confession in the Circle of Rabbi Nahman of Bratslav." *Bulletin of the Institute of Jewish Studies* 1 (1973).

Altmann, Alexander. "Maimonides' Four Perfections." In *Essays in Jewish Intellectual History*. Hanover, N.H.: Univ. Press of New England, 1981.

Annas, George. "A French Homunculus in a Tennessee Court." *Hastings Center Report* 19:6 (Dec. 1989).

Aptowitzer, Viktor. *Kain und Abel in der Agada*. Vienna: Lowit Verlag, 1922.

Arian, Phillip. "Bar Mitzvah at 15." *Conservative Judaism* 15 (Summer 1961).

Aristotle. *Nicomachean Ethics*. Translated by Martin Ostwald. New York: Bobbs-Merrill Co., 1962.

––––––. *Politics*. In *The Politics of Aristotle*. Translated by Ernest Barker. New York: Oxford Univ. Press, 1962.

Arlow, Jacob. "A Psychoanalytic Study of a Religious Rite: Bar Mitzvah." *Psychoanalytic Study of the Child* 6 (20 Dec. 1953).

Auerbach, Erich. *Mimesis*. Translated by Willard Trask. Princeton, N.J.: Princeton Univ. Press, 1968.

Baer, Yitzhak. *A History of the Jews in Christian Spain*. 2 vols. Philadelphia: Jewish Publication Society, 1966.

Baier, Kurt. *The Moral Point of View: A Rational Basis of Ethics*. New York: Random House, 1967.

Bamberger, Bernard. "Qetana, Na'arah, Bogereth." *Hebrew Union College Annual* 32 (1961).

Baron, Salo. *The Jewish Community*. 3 vols. Philadelphia: Jewish Publication Society, 1942.

––––––. *A Social and Religious History of the Jews*. 17 vols. New York: Columbia Univ. Press, 1958.

Barrett, William. *Death of a Soul*. New York: Doubleday, 1986.
————. *The Illusion of Technique*. New York: Doubleday, 1978.
Beauchamp, Tom L., and Leroy Walters. *Contemporary Issues in Bioethics*. Belmont, Calif.: Wadsworth, 1982.
Ben-Sasson, Hayyim Hillel. *Hagut ve-Hanhagah*. Jerusalem: Mosad Bialik, 1959.
————. "Osher ve-Oni be-Mishnato shel ha-Mokhiah Rabbi Ephraim Ish Lunschitz." *Zion* 19 (1954).
Bentwich, Norman. *Solomon Schechter: A Biography*. New York: Burning Bush Press, 1964.
Bergman, Yehudah. *Ha-Zedakah be-Yisrael*. Jerusalem: Tarshish, 1944.
Berkovits, Eliezer. *Ha-Halakhah: Koha ve-Tafkedah*. Jerusalem: Mosad ha-Rav Kook, 1981.
————. *Not in Heaven*. New York: Ktav, 1983.
Bernstein, Philip. *To Dwell in Unity*. Philadelphia: Jewish Publication Society, 1983.
Bin Gorion, Emmanuel, ed., *Mimekor Yisrael: Classical Jewish Folktales*. Translated by I. M. Lask. Philadelphia: Jewish Publication Society, 1976.
Black, Henry C. *Black's Law Dictionary*. 1891. Reprint. St. Paul, Minn.: West Publishing Co., 1968.
Blackstone, William. *Commentaries on the Laws of England, of the Rights of Persons*. Oxford: Clarendon Press, 1765.
Bleich, J. David. "Survey of Recent Halakhic Periodical Literature." *Tradition* 14, no. 2 (Fall 1973).
————. "Women in a Minyan?" *Tradition* 14, no. 2 (1973).
Blidstein, Gerald. *Honor Thy Father and Mother*. New York: Ktav, 1975.
Bloch, Hayyim. *The Golem*. Translated by Harry Schneiderman. Vienna: Vernay, 1925.
Bloom, Harold. *Kabbalah and Criticism*. New York: Seabury, 1975.
Borowitz, Eugene. "Subjectivity and the Halachic Process." *Judaism* 13 (Spring 1964).
Brooks, Roger. *Support for the Poor in the Mishnaic Law of Agriculture: Tractate Pe'ah*. Chico, Calif.: Scholars Press, 1983.
Brotman, Harris. "Human Embryo Transplants." *New York Times Magazine*, 8 Jan. 1984.
Brown, Sheldon S. *Guidance and Counselling for Jewish Education*. New York: Bloch Publishing Co., 1964.
Buber, Martin. *Tales of the Hasidim* Translated by Olga Marx. 2 vols. New York: Schocken, 1948.
Buchler, Adolf. *Studies in Sin and Atonement*. 1928. Reprint. New York: Ktav, 1967.

Cahana, Isaac Zev. *Mehkarim be-Sifrut ha-Teshuvot*. Jerusalem: Mosad ha-Rav Kook, 1973.
Caidin, Martin. *Cyborg*. New York: Warner, 1972.
Capek, Joseph, and Karel Capek. *R.U.R.* Translated by P. Selver. London: Oxford Univ. Press, 1961.

Cardozo, Benjamin. *The Nature of the Judicial Process*. New Haven: Yale Univ. Press, 1921.

Charry, Elias. "Ben Torah." *Conservative Judaism* 16 (Fall 1961).

Chipkin, Israel. "Judaism and Social Welfare." In *The Jews*, edited by L. Finkelstein.

Chodos, Israel. "A Critical Edition of Shem Tov Ben Joseph Falaquera's *Bate Hanhagat Guf Habari*." *Ha-Rofeh ha-Ivri* (1938).

Cohen, Arthur A., and Paul Mendes-Flohr, eds., *Contemporary Jewish Religious Thought*. New York: Scribner's, 1987.

Cohen, Boaz. *Law and Tradition*. New York: Ktav, 1969.

————. *Studies in Jewish and Roman Law*. 2 vols. New York: Jewish Theological Seminary, 1966.

Cohon, Samuel S. *Judaism*. New York: Schocken, 1962.

————. "Original Sin." *Hebrew Union College Annual* 21 (1948).

Copelston, Fredrick. *A History of Philosophy: Medieval Philosophy, Part I*. New York: Image Books, 1962.

Crichton, Michael. *The Andromeda Strain*. New York: Knopf, 1969.

Cronbach, Abraham. "The Gradations of Benevolence." *Hebrew Union College Annual* 16 (1941).

————. "The *Me'il Zedakah*." *Hebrew Union College Annual* 11 (1936).

————. "Social Thinking in the *Sefer Hasidim*." *Hebrew Union College Annual* 22 (1949).

Crossroads. Jerusalem: Zomet, 1987.

Dan, Joseph. "Ethical Literature." In *Encyclopedia Judaica*.

————. *Jewish Mysticism and Jewish Ethics*. Seattle: Univ. of Washington Press, 1986.

————. *Sifrut ha-Musar ve-ha-Derush*. Jerusalem: Keter, 1975.

Daube, David. *Collaboration with Tyranny in Rabbinic Law*. Oxford: Oxford Univ. Press, 1965.

Davidson, Israel. *Otzar ha-Mashalim ve-ha-Pitgamim*. Jerusalem: Mosad ha-Rav Kook, 1969.

Davis, Moshe. *The Emergence of Conservative Judaism*. Philadelphia: Jewish Publication Society, 1963.

de La Mettrie, Julien Offray. *Man, A Machine*. LaSalle, Ill.: Open Court, 1912.

Del Zio vs. Presbyterian Hospital. New York City. 74 Civ. 3588.

Devorkes, Eliakum. *Ispaklarit ha-Zedakah*. Jerusalem: n.p., 1974.

Diamond vs. Chakrabarty. 44 U.S. 303 (1980).

Dorff, Elliot, and Arthur Rosett. *A Living Tree*. Albany: SUNY Press, 1988.

Dresner, Samuel H. *Levi Yitzhak of Berditchev*. New York: Hartmore House, 1974.

Eisenstein, Judah D., ed., *Otzar Dinim u-Minhagim*. New York: Hebrew Publishing Co., 1917.

————. *Otzar Midrashim*. 2 vols. New York: n.p., 1915.

Elon, Menahem. *Ha-Mishpat ha-Ivri*. Jerusalem: Magnes Press, 1973.

Encyclopedia Judaica. Edited by Cecil Roth. Jerusalem: Keter, 1971.

Encyclopedia of Bioethics Edited by Warren T. Reich. 4 vols. New York: Free
    Press, 1978— .
Encyclopedia Talmudit. Jerusalem: Makhon ha-Encyclopedia ha-Talmudit, 1947— .

Falk, Ze'ev. *Jewish Matrimonial Law*. New York: Oxford Univ. Press, 1966.
———. *Law and Religion*. Jerusalem: Mesharim Publishers, 1981.
Faur, José. "Din Aliyat ha-Katan Likro ba-Torah." In *Sefer Zikaron le-Kavod
    Yitzhak Nissim*. Jerusalem: n.p., 1984.
———. *Golden Doves with Silver Dots*. Bloomington: Indiana Univ. Press, 1986.
———. "Some General Observations on the Character of Classical Jewish Litera-
    ture." *Journal of Jewish Studies* 38, no. 1 (Spring 1977).
Federbush, Simon. "The Problem of Euthanasia in Jewish Tradition." *Judaism* 1
    (1952).
Feinstein, Moses. "Medical Responsa." In *Crossroads*.
Feldman, David M. *Birth Control in Jewish Law*. New York: New York Univ.
    Press, 1968.
———. *Health and Medicine in the Jewish Tradition*. New York: Crossroad, 1986.
Finkelstein, Louis, ed., *The Jews: Their History, Culture and Religion*. 2 vols.
    Philadelphia: Jewish Publication Society, 1949.
———. *The Pharisees*. Philadelphia: Jewish Publication Society of America, 1968.
Fox, Marvin, ed., *Modern Jewish Ethics*. Columbus: Ohio State Univ. Press, 1975.
Frankel, Kalmen Eliezer. *Encyclopedia l'Var Mitzvah*. Tel Aviv: Ha-Kerem, 1973.
Frankena, William. *Ethics*. New York: Prentice-Hall, 1963.
Freehof, Solomon B. "Ceremonial Creativity Among the Ashkenazim." *Jewish
    Quarterly Review*, 75th Anniversary Volume (1967).
———. *Reform Responsa*. Cincinnati: Hebrew Union College Press, 1960.
———. *Reform Responsa for Our Time*. Cincinnati: Hebrew Union College Press,
    1977.
Friedenwald, Harry. *The Jews and Medicine*. 2 vols. Baltimore: Johns Hopkins
    Univ. Press, 1944.
Friedman, Mordecai. "The Monogamy Clause in Jewish Marriage Contracts." In
    Perspectives in Jewish Learning, edited by Nathaniel Stampfer, vol. 4. Chi-
    cago: Spertus College of Judaica Press, 1972.
Frisch, Ephraim. *An Historical Survey of Jewish Philanthropy*. New York: Cooper
    Square Publishers, 1924.

Gaylin, Willard. "We Have the Awful Knowledge to Make Exact Copies of Human
    Beings." *New York Times Magazine*, 6 Mar., 1972.
Geduld, Harry, and Ronald Gottesman. *Robots*. Boston: Little, Brown, 1978.
Gershuni, Judah. "The First Test-tube Baby in the Light of Jewish Law." *Or ha-
    Mizrah* 27, no. 1 (Oct. 1978).
Ginzberg, Louis. *The Legends of the Jews*. 7 vols. Philadelphia: Jewish Publication
    Society, 1955.
———. *Peirushim ve-Hiddushim be-Yerushalmi*. 3 vols. New York: Jewish Theo-
    logical Seminary, 1941.
———. "The Significance of the Halacha for Jewish History." In *On Jewish Law
    and Lore*. New York: Atheneum, 1970.

————. *Students, Scholars and Saints*. Philadelphia: Jewish Publication Society, 1928.

Goldberg, Z. N. and E. Bick. "Maternity in Fetal Implant." In *Crossroads*.

Goldsmith, Arnold L. *The Golem Remembered*. Detroit: Wayne State Univ. Press, 1981.

Goodfield, June. *Playing God*. New York: Random House, 1977.

Gordis, Robert. "Authority in Jewish Law." In *Proceedings of the Rabbinical Assembly* (1941–44).

————. *The Book of God and Man*. Chicago: Univ. of Chicago Press, 1965.

————. "The Knowledge of Good and Evil in the Old Testament and the Qumran Scrolls." *Journal of Biblical Literature* 76, no. 2 (June 1957).

Goren, Shlomo. "The Age of Maturity for Individual and Social Majority" [in Hebrew]. *Mahanayim* 23.

Green, Arthur. *Tormented Master: A Life of Rabbi Nahman of Bratslav*. University: Univ. of Alabama Press, 1979.

Greenwald, Leopold. *Kol Bo al-Aveilut*. New York: Moriah Printing Co., 1947.

Grossberg, Hanokh Zundel. "Se'udat Bat Mitzvah." *Ha-Ma'ayan* (Fall 1977).

Gustafson, James M. *Can Ethics be Christian?* Chicago: Univ. of Chicago Press, 1975.

————. *Christian Ethics and the Community*. New York: Pilgrim Press, 1975.

————. *Contributions of Theology to Medical Ethics*. Milwaukee: Marquette Univ. Press, 1975.

————. *Ethics From a Theocentric Perspective*. 2 vols. Chicago: Univ. of Chicago Press, 1981.

————. *Protestant and Roman Catholic Ethics: Prospects for Rapprochement*. Chicago: Univ. of Chicago Press, 1978.

————. *Theology and Christian Ethics*. Philadelphia: United Church Press, 1974.

Guttmann, Alexander. "L'She'elat ha-Yahas Minhag-Halakhah b'Tekufat ha-Talmud." *Bitzaron* (1946).

Haas, Peter J. "Toward a Semiotic Study of Jewish Moral Discourse: The Case of Responsa." *Semeia* 34 (1985).

Halevi, C. D. "Disconnecting a Terminal Patient From an Artificial Respirator." In *Crossroads*.

Haliburd, G. B. "Euthanasia." *Jewish Law Annual* 1 (1978).

Halivni, David Weiss. *Midrash, Mishnah and Gemara*. Cambridge: Mass.: Harvard Univ. Press, 1986.

————. "Revelation and *Zimzum*." *Judaism* 21 (Spring 1972).

Halkin, Abraham. "Classical and Arabic Material in ibn Aknin's 'Hygiene of the Soul.'" *Proceedings of the American Academy for Jewish Research* 4.

Hartman, David and Marx, Tzvi. "Charity." In *Contemporary Jewish Religious Thought*, edited by Cohen and Mendes-Flohr.

Haring, Bernard. *The Law of Christ*. Westminster, Md.: Newman Press, 1963.

Herzog, Isaac. *Main Institutions of Jewish Law*. 2 vols. London: Soncino, 1936.

Heschel, Abraham Joshua. *The Circle of the Baal Shem Tov*. Edited by Samuel H. Dresner. Chicago: Univ. of Chicago Press, 1985.

————. *The Earth Is the Lord's*. New York: Schuman, 1950.

————. *Existence and Celebration*. New York: Council of Jewish Federations and Welfare Funds, 1965.

————. *God in Search of Man*. New York: Harper and Row, 1966.

————. "God, Torah, and Israel." In *Theology and Church in Times of Change*, edited by E. L. Long and R. Handy. Philadelphia: Westminster, 1970.

————. *The Insecurity of Freedom*. New York: Farrar, Straus, and Giroux, 1966.

————. *Kotsk* [in Yiddish]. 2 vols. Tel Aviv: Menorah, 1973.

————. "The Mystical Element in Judaism." In *The Jews*, edited by Louis Finkelstein.

————. *A Passion for Truth*. New York: Farrar, Straus, and Giroux, 1973.

————. *The Prophets*. Philadelphia: Jewish Publication Society, 1962.

————. *Torah min ha-Shamayim b'Ispaklariah shel ha-Dorot*. 2 vols. London: Soncino, 1962, 1965.

Heinemann, Isaac. *Ta'amei ha-Mitzvot b'Sifrut Yisrael*. 2 vols. Jerusalem: n.p., 1956.

Hillers, Delbert. *The Covenant: The History of a Biblical Idea*. Baltimore: Johns Hopkins Univ. Press, 1969.

Holtz, Avraham. "Kiddush and Hillul ha-Shem." *Judaism* 10 (Fall 1961).

Horwitz, Simon. *The Responsa of Solomon Luria*. New York: Bloch Publishing Co., 1968.

Idel, Moshe. *Golem*. Albany: SUNY Press, 1990.

————. *Kabbalah: New Perspectives*. New Haven: Yale Univ. Press, 1988.

————. *The Mystical Experience in Abraham Abulafia*. Albany: SUNY Press, 1988.

International Encyclopedia of the Social Sciences. Edited by David L. Sills. 18 vols. New York: Macmillan, 1968–79.

Jacobs, Louis. "The Doctrine of the Divine Spark in Man in Jewish Sources." In *Studies in Rationalism, Judaism and Universalism*, edited by R. Loew. London: n.p., 1966.

————. *Hasidic Prayer*. New York: Schocken, 1972.

————. *Jewish Law*. New York: Behrman House, 1968.

————. *A Jewish Theology*. New York: Behrman House, 1973.

————. *Jewish Values*. London: Vallentine, Mitchell, 1960.

————. "Jews and Law." *Judaism* 37 (Spring 1988).

————. *Principles of the Jewish Faith*. New York: Basic Books, 1964.

————. "Rabbi Aryeh Laib Heller's Theological Introduction to his *Shev Shema Tata*." *Modern Judaism* 1 (Sept. 1981).

————. "Rabbi Joseph Hayyim of Baghdad." In *Perspectives on Jews and Judaism*, edited by Arthur Chiel. New York: Rabbinical Assembly, 1978.

————. *Theology in the Responsa*. London: Routledge and Kegan Paul, 1975.

————. *A Tree of Life*. New York: Oxford Univ. Press, 1984.

Jakobovitz, Immanuel. "Euthanasia" in [Hebrew]. *Ha-Parades* 31, nos. 1, 3 (1956).

————. *Jewish Medical Ethics*. New York: Bloch Publishing Co., 1959.

————. "Medicine and Judaism" [in Hebrew]. *Ha-Rofeh ha-Ivri* (1956).

————. "Review of Recent Halakhic Literature." *Tradition* 6, no. 1 (Fall 1963).

Jastrow, Marcus. *A Dictionary of the Targumim, the Talmud Babli and Yerushalmi.* 2d ed. New York: Pardes, 1950.

Jewish Encyclopedia. New York: Funk and Wagnalls, 1902.

Jonas, Hans. *Philosophical Essays.* Englewood Cliffs, N.J.: Prentice-Hall, 1974.

Kalir, Joseph, "The Minhag." *Tradition* 7 (1965).

Kaplan, Lawrence. "The Religious Philosophy of Rabbi Joseph Soloveitchik." *Tradition* 14 (Fall 1973).

Kaplan, Mordecai M. *Greater Judaism in the Making.* New York: Reconstructionist Press, 1960.

———. *Questions Jews Ask.* New York: Reconstructionist Press, 1956.

Kaplan, Zvi. "Bar Mitzvah." In *Encyclopedia Judaica.*

Kasher, Menahem. *Torah Sheleimah.* Jerusalem: Encyclopedia Humash Torah Sheleimah, 1934.

Kass, Leon R. "Regarding the End of the Medicine and the Pursuit of Health." In *Ethical Issues in Modern Medicine,* edited by Hunt and Arras. Palo Alto, Calif.: Mayfield, 1977.

———. *Toward a More Natural Science.* New York: The Free Press, 1985.

Katz, Jacob. *Exclusiveness and Tolerance.* New York: Schocken, 1962.

———. *Tradition and Crisis.* New York: Schocken, 1971.

Kaufmann, Yehezkel. *Toledot ha-Emunah ha-Yisraelit.* 8 vols. Tel Aviv: Mosad Bialik, 1966.

Kellner, Menachem Marc, ed., *Contemporary Jewish Ethics.* New York: Hebrew Publishing Co., 1978.

Kimmelman, Reuven. "Non-Violence in the Talmud." *Judaism* 17 (Summer 1968).

Kirshenbaum, Aaron. *The 'Good Samaritan' and Jewish Law.* Tel Aviv: Tel Aviv Univ. Press, 1976.

Kochan, Lionel. *The Jew and His History.* Chico, Calif.: Scholars Press, 1985.

Kohler, Kaufmann. "Bar Mitzvah." In *Jewish Encyclopedia.*

———. *Hebrew Union College and Other Addresses.* Cincinnati: Ark Publishing Co., 1916.

———. *Jewish Theology.* 1918. Reprint. New York: Ktav, 1968.

Kramer, Samuel Noah. *The Sumerians.* Chicago: Univ. of Chicago Press, 1963.

Kullman, Eugene. "Tikvah and Mitzvah." *Conservative Judaism* 10 (Summer 1956).

Lazaroff, Alan. "Judaism as an Art." *Judaism* 30 (Summer 1981).

Lebinger, Israel. "The Minor in Jewish Law." *Jewish Quarterly Review,* new series, 6–7 (1915/1916, 1916/1917).

Leiser, Burton. "Custom and Law in Talmudic Jurisprudence." *Judaism* 20 (1971).

Leivick, Halper. *Der Golem.* Vilna: Kletzkin, 1927. *The Golem.* Translated by Joseph C. Landis. In *The Great Jewish Plays.* New York: Avon Books, 1972.

Levin, Ira. *The Boys from Brazil.* New York: Dell, 1976.

Levine, Hillel. "Dwarfs on the Shoulders of Giants: A Case Study of the Impact of Modernization on the Social Epistemology of Judaism." *Jewish Social Studies* 40, no. 2 (Winter 1978).

Levitas, Isaac. "Communal Regulation of Bar Mitzvah." *Journal of Jewish Social Studies* 11, no. 2 (Apr. 1949).

Lieberman, Hayyim. *A House on Fire*. New York: n.p., n.d.

Lieberman, Saul. *Tosefta Kifshuta*. New York: Jewish Theological Seminary, 1962.

Lion, J., and J. Lukas. *Das Prage Ghetto*. Prague: Artia, 1959.

Low, Immanuel. "Ha-Iddana." *Hebrew Union College Annual* 11 (1936).

Low, Leopold. *Die Liebensalter in der Judishen Literatur*. Szegedin: Druck von Sigmund Berger, 1875.

Lurie, Harry L. *A Heritage Affirmed*. Philadelphia: Jewish Publication Society, 1961.

Marcus, Ivan. *Piety and Society*. Leiden: E. J. Brill, 1981.

Marx, Tzvi. "Priorities in Zedakah and Their Implications." *Judaism* 28 (1969).

May, Rollo. *Love and Will*. New York: Norton, 1969.

Metzger, Alter B. Z. *Rabbi Kook's Philosophy of Repentance*. New York: Yeshiva Univ. Press, 1968.

Meyer, Michael. *The Origins of the Modern Jew*. Detroit: Wayne State Press, 1967.

Meyrink, Gustav. *The Golem*. Translated by Madge Pemberton. New York: Ungar, 1964.

Monmany, Terence. "Should Man Make Beast?" *Newsweek*, 4 May 1987.

Moore, G. E. *Principia Ethica*. Cambridge: Cambridge Univ. Press, 1903.

Moore, George Foot. *Judaism in the First Centuries of the Christian Era*. 3 vols. Cambridge, Mass.: Harvard Univ. Press, 1966.

Muntner, S. *Introduction to the Book of Asaph the Physician* [in Hebrew]. Jerusalem: Geniza Press, 1957.

———. "A Medieval Treatise on Melancholy." *Ha-Rofeh ha-Ivri* (1953).

Nemoy, Leon. "Al-Qirqisani's Criticism of Anan's Prohibition of the Practice of Medicine" [Hebrew]. *Ha-Rofeh ha-Ivri* (1938).

Neusner, Jacob. "The Rabbinic Traditions About the Pharisees in Modern Historiography." *CCAR Journal* 19 (Apr. 1972).

———. *Tzedakah: Can Jewish Philanthropy Buy Jewish Survival?* Chappaqua, N.Y.: Rossel Books, 1982.

Newman, J. *Semikah [Ordination]*. Manchester: n.p., 1950.

Nissim, Isaac. "Al Birkhat Barukh she-Petarani." *No'am* 7 (1964).

Ortega y Gasset, José. *The Revolt of the Masses*. New York: Norton, 1957.

Ozick, Cynthia. *Levitation*. New York: Knopf, 1982.

Pappenheim, Albert. "Will 13 + 3 Equal Bar Mitzvah?" *Your Child* 3, no. 2 (Mar. 1970).

Passamaneck, Steven M. *Insurance in Rabbinic Law*. Chicago: Aldine Publishing Co., 1974.

Peli, Pinchas, ed., *Soloveitchik on Repentance*. Ramsey, N.J.: Paulist Press, 1984.

Pereira Mendes, H. *Bar Mitzvah*. New York: Union of Orthodox Jewish Congregations, 1945.

Petuchowski, Jacob. "The Beauty of God." In Joseph Edelheit, ed. *The Life of Covenant*. Chicago: Spertus College of Judaica Press, 1986.

――――. "The Concept of *Teshuvah* in the Bible and the Talmud." *Judaism* 17 (1968).

――――. "Plural Modes Within the Halakhah." *Judaism* 19 (Winter 1970).

Philipson, David. *The Reform Movement in Judaism*. New York: Macmillan, 1907.

Piller, Charles, and Keith Yamamoto. *Gene Wars: Military Control Over the New Genetic Technologies*. New York: Morrow, 1988.

Plato. *The Dialogues of Plato*. Translated by B. Jowett, 1920. Reprint. 2 vols. New York: Random House, 1937.

Plaut, W. Gunther. *The Growth of Reform Judaism*. New York: World Union for Progressive Judaism, 1965.

――――. *The Rise of Reform Judaism*. New York: World Union for Progressive Judaism, 1963.

Pollack, Herman. *Jewish Folkways in Germanic Lands*. London: MIT Press, 1971.

Pope, Alexander. "An Essay on Criticism." In *Alexander Pope: Selected Works*, edited by L. Kronenberger. New York: Modern Library, 1948.

President's Commission for the Study of Ethical Problems in Medicine and Biomedical and Behavioral Research. *Splicing Life*. Washington: U.S. Government Printing Office, 1982.

Preuss, Julius. *Biblical and Talmudic Medicine*. Translated by Fred Rosner. New York: Sanhedrin Press, 1978.

Rabinowitz, Gedaliah, and Mordecai Konigsberg [Hebrew]. "The Definition of Death and Time of Death According to Jewish Law." *Ha-Darom* 32 (1970).

Ramsey, Paul. *Basic Christian Ethics*. New York: Scribner's, 1970.

――――. *Fabricated Man*. New Haven: Yale Univ. Press, 1970.

――――. *The Patient as Person*. New Haven: Yale Univ. Press, 1970.

Raphael, Marc Lee, ed., *Understanding American Jewish Philanthropy*. New York: Ktav, 1979.

Reines, Charles W. "The Jewish Attitude Toward Suicide." *Judaism* 10 (1961).

Richler, Mordecai. *The Apprenticeship of Duddy Kravitz*. New York: Ballantine Books, 1974.

Ringgren, Helmer. *Israelite Religion*. Philadelphia: Fortress Press, 1966.

Rivkind, Isaac. *Le-Ot u-le-Zikaron*. New York: n.p., 1942.

Rorvik, David. *In His Image: The Cloning of Man*. Philadelphia: Lippincott, 1978.

Rosenberg, Stuart. "The Right Age for Bar Mitzvah." *Religious Education* 60, no. 4 (July 1965).

Rosenbloom, Noah. *Tradition in an Age of Reform: The Religious Philosophy of Samson Raphael Hirsch*. Philadelphia: Jewish Publication Society, 1976.

Rosenfield, Azriel. "Human Identity: Halakhic Issues." *Tradition* 16, no. 3 (Spring 1977).

――――. "Judaism and Gene Design." *Tradition* 13, no. 2 (1972).

――――. "Religion and the Robot." *Tradition* 8, no. 3 (Fall 1966).

Rosenzweig, Franz. *On Jewish Learning*. New York: Schocken, 1955.

Rosner, Fred. "Artificial Insemination in Jewish Law." *Judaism* 19 (Fall 1970).

――――. *Modern Medicine and Jewish Law*. New York: Yeshiva Univ. Press, 1972.

Rosner, Fred, and J. David Bleich, eds., *Jewish Bioethics*. New York: Hebrew
    Publishing Co., 1969.
Rosner, Fred, and Moses Feinstein. "Treatment of the Terminally Ill." *Judaism* 37
    (Spring 1988).
Roth, Joel. *The Halakhic Process*. New York: Jewish Theological Seminary, 1986.
Rothberg, Abraham. *The Sword of the Golem*. New York: McCall Publishing, 1970.
Rubenstein, Richard L. *Power Struggle*. New York: Scribner's, 1974.
Rudavsky, David. "The Historical School of Zecharia Frankel." *Jewish Social
    Studies* 5 (1963).

Saul, John. *The God Project*. New York: Bantam, 1982.
Saltzman, Steven. "The Sanctity of Life in Jewish Law." D.H.L. diss., Jewish Theo-
    logical Seminary, 1982.
Schechter, Solomon. *Seminary Addresses and Other Papers*. New York: Burning
    Bush Press, 1959.
———. *Some Aspects of Rabbinic Theology*. New York: Macmillan, 1909.
———. *Studies in Judaism*. 3 vols. Philadelphia: Jewish Publication Society, 1896.
———. *Studies in Judaism: A Selection*. New York: Meridian, 1958.
———. *Studies in Judaism, Third Series*. Philadelphia: Jewish Publication Society,
    1924.
Schechterman, Deborah. "Maimonides's View of Original Sin as Reflected in Jewish
    Thought in the Thirteenth Century and in the Fourteenth Century [Hebrew]."
    Da'at 20 (1988).
Scholem, Gershom. *Major Trends in Jewish Mysticism*. New York: Schocken, 1961.
———. *The Messianic Idea in Judaism*. New York: Schocken, 1971.
———. "Mi-Tokh Hirhurim al Hokhmat Yisrael." In *Perakim ba-Yahadut*, edited
    by Ezra Spicehandler and Jakob Petuchowski. Jerusalem: Newman Publish-
    ing House, n.d.
———. *On the Kabbalah and Its Symbolism*. Translated by Ralph Manheim. New
    York: Schocken, 1965.
Schorsch, Ismar. *Jewish Reactions to German Anti-Semitism*. New York: Columbia
    Univ. Press, 1972.
———. *Thoughts from 3080*. New York: Jewish Theological Seminary, 1988.
Segal, Peretz. "No Agency for an Illegal Act." *Annual of the Institute for Research
    in Jewish Law* 9/10 (1982–83).
Shaki, A. H. "Is Age a Matter of Status?" *Israel Law Review* 4 (1969).
Shakespeare, William. *Macbeth*. New York: Washington Square Press, 1959.
Shannon, Thomas, ed., *Bioethics*. New York: Paulist Press, 1976.
Sherwin, Byron L. "Bar Mitzvah." *Judaism* 22 (Winter 1973).
———. "Fear of God." In *Contemporary Jewish Religious Thought*, edited by Co-
    hen and Mendes-Flohr.
———. *The Golem Legend: Origins and Implications*. Lanham, Md.: University
    Press of America, 1985.
———. "Moses Maimonides on Perfection of the Body." *Listening* 9:1/2 (1974).
———. "In the Shadows of Greatness: Rabbi Hayyim ben Betsalel of Friedberg."
    Jewish Social Studies 37, no. 1 (1975).

————. *Mystical Theology and Social Dissent: The Life and Works of Judah Loew of Prague*. New York: Oxford Univ. Press, 1982.

————. "Theodicy." In *Contemporary Jewish Religious Thought*, edited by Cohen and Mendes-Flohr.

Shindler, Pesach. "The Holocaust and Kiddush ha-Shem in Hasidic Thought." *Tradition* 13/14 (1973).

Shohet, David M. "Mercy Death in Jewish Law." *Conservative Judaism* 8, no. 3 (1952).

Siegel, Seymour. "Genetic Engineering." *Proceedings of the Rabbinical Assembly* 40 (1978).

Siemet, M. "The Besomim Rosh of Rabbi Saul Berliner." *Kiryat Sefer* 48 (1972/1973).

Siev, Asher. *Rabbi Moses Isserles*. New York: Yeshiva Univ. Press, 1972.

Silverman, Morris. "Report of Survey on Ritual." *Proceedings of the Rabbinical Assembly* 4 (1930–32).

Sinclair, Daniel B. *Tradition and the Biological Revolution*. Edinburgh: Edinburgh Univ. Press, 1989.

Soloveitchik, Joseph B. *The Halakhic Mind*. New York: Macmillan, 1986.

————. "Ish ha-Halakhah." *Talpiot* 1 (1944).

————. "The Lonely Man of Faith." *Tradition* 7 (Summer 1965).

Spero, Shubert. *Morality, Halaka and the Jewish Tradition*. New York: Ktav, 1983.

Spiegel, Shalom. *The Last Trial*. New York: Pantheon, 1967.

Steinberg, Abraham, ed., *Sefer Assia*. Jerusalem: Schlesinger Institute, 1976.

————. "Mercy Killing" [Hebrew]. *Assia* 5, no. 3 (Jan. 1978).

Stern, Harold I. "The Testament of the Ba'al Shem Tov." Ph.D. diss., Northwestern Univ., 1976.

Stevenson, Charles L. *Ethics and Language*. New Haven: Yale Univ. Press, 1944.

Tamari, Meir. *With All Your Possessions*. New York: Macmillan, 1987.

Ta-Shema, Israel. "Halakhah ke-Batrei." *Shenaton ha-Mishpat ha-Ivri* 6/7 (1979/1980).

Tchernowitz, Chaim. *Toledot ha-Halakhah*. 3 vols. New York: n.p., 1945.

————. *Toledot ha-Poskim*. 4 vols. New York: n.p., 1947.

Telushkin, Nissan. "Ha-Nimuk ha-Musari she-ba-Mitzvot ha-Teluyot ba-Aretz." *Or-ha-Mizrah* 2 (1961).

Tempkin, Sefton. "Solomon Schechter and Max Heller." *Conservative Judaism* 16 (Spring 1962).

Tishbi, Isaiah. *Mishnat ha-Zohar*. 2 vols. Jerusalem: Mosad Bialik, 1961.

————. *Torat ha-Ra v'ha-Kelipot b'Kabbalat ha-Ari*. Jerusalem: Hebrew Univ. Press, 1963.

Twersky, Isadore. *Introduction to the Code of Maimonides*. New Haven: Yale Univ. Press, 1980.

————. *Rabad of Posquieres*. Cambridge, Mass.: Harvard Univ. Press, 1962.

————. "The *Shulhan Arukh:* Enduring Code of Jewish Law." *Judaism* 16 (1967).

————. "Some Aspects of the Jewish Attitude Toward the Welfare State." *Tradition* 5, no. 2 (Spring 1963).

Urbach, Ephraim E. "Magamot Datiot ve-Hevratiot be-Torat ha-Zedakah shel Hazal." *Zion* 16 (1951).
————. *The Sages*. Translated by Israel Abrahams. Cambridge, Mass.: Harvard Univ. Press, 1987.

Varga, Andrew C. *The Main Issues in Bioethics*. New York: Paulist Press, 1980.
Warnock, G. J. *Contemporary Moral Philosophy*. New York: Macmillan, 1967.
Wein, B. "Aspects of the Prohibition of Standing Idly by the Blood of Thy Neighbor" [Hebrew]. *Ha-Darom* 33 (1971).
Weiss, Joseph. *Studies in Eastern European Jewish Mysticism*. Edited by David Goldstein. New York: Oxford Univ. Press, 1985.
Werblowsky, R. J. Zwi. *Joseph Karo*. Philadelphia: Jewish Publication Society, 1977.
Werner, Z. "Euthanasia" [Hebrew]. *Torah she-be'al Peh* 18 (1976).
Wertheim, Aaron. *Halakhot ve-Halikhot ba-Hasidut*. Jerusalem: Modad ha-Rav Kook, 1960.
Wheeler, David K. "Grant Patents on Animals?" *Chronicle of Higher Education* 33, no. 28 (25 Mar. 1987).
————. "Harvard University Receives First U.S. Patent Issued on Animals." *Chronicle of Higher Education* 34, no. 32 (20 Apr. 1988).
Wiener, Max. "The Ideology of the Founders of Jewish Scientific Research." *YIVO Annual* 5 (1950).
Wiener, Norbert. *God and Golem, Inc*. Cambridge, Mass: MIT Press, 1964.
Wiesel, Elie. *Four Hasidic Masters*. London: Univ. of Notre Dame Press, 1978.
Wilson, Bryan R., ed., *Rationality*. New York: Harper and Row, 1971.
Winkler, Gershon. *The Golem of Prague*. New York: Judaica Press, 1980.
Wolf, Immanuel. "On the Concept of a Science of Judaism." Translated by L. Kochan. *Leo Baeck Institute Yearbook* 21 (1957).
Wolfson, Harry. *Philo*. 2 vols. Cambridge, Mass.: Harvard Univ. Press, 1947.
Wurzberger, Walter. "Plural Models and the Authority of Halakhah." *Judaism* 20 (Fall 1971).

Yerushalmi, Yosef Hayim. *Zakhor: Jewish History and Jewish Memory*. Philadelphia: Jewish Publication Society, 1982.
Yuter, Alan J. "Mehizah, Midrash and Modernity." *Judaism* 28 (1979).

Zahavy, Zevi, ed. *Mivhar ha-Mahshavah ve-ha-Musar ba-Yahadut*. Tel Aviv: Zioni, 1954.
Zimmels, H. J. *Ashkenazim and Sephardim*. London: Oxford Univ. Press, 1958.
————. *Magicians, Theologians and Doctors*. London: Goldston, 1952.
————. "The Significance of the Statement 'We Are Not Acquainted Any More.'" In *Leo Jung Jubilee Volume*. New York: n.p., 1962.
Zlotnick, Dov. "Al Makor ha-Mashal ha-Nanas ve-ha-Anak ve-Gilgulav." *Sinai* 77 (1975).
————. "The Commentary of Rabbi Abraham Azulai to the Mishnah." *American Academy of Jewish Research Proceedings* 40 (1973).
Zucrow, Solomon. *Adjustment of Law to Life in Rabbinic Literature*. Boston: Stratford, 1928.

INDEX

283

IN PARTNERSHIP WITH GOD

was composed in 10 on 12 Caledonia on a Mergenthaler Linotron 202
with display type in Deepdene Italic,
by Eastern Graphics;
printed by sheet-fed offset on 50-pound, acid-free Glatfelter Natural Hi Bulk,
and Smyth-sewn and bound over binder's boards in Holliston Roxite B
by Braun-Brumfield, Inc.;
designed by Sara L. Eddy;
and published by

SYRACUSE UNIVERSITY PRESS
SYRACUSE, NEW YORK 13244-5160